CLASS AND STATE IN *ANCIEN RÉGIME* FRANCE

Class and State in Ancien Régime *France* explores the economic, social, ideological and political foundations of French absolutism. David Parker's challenging interpretation presents French absolutism as a remarkably successful attempt to preserve the political and ideological structures of the traditional order.

This argument rejects the widespread tendency to treat French absolutism as an instrument of either capitalism or political modernisation. Parker compares the situation in England where it was precisely the decay of monarchical authority which facilitated the development of capitalism and the emergence of a genuinely modern state. In France, the cost of French absolutism was the impoverishment of the state, which ultimately left the *ancien régime* unable to compete with England.

David Parker's reassessment runs contrary to much revisionist historiography whilst also diverging sharply from previous Marxist interpretations. It discusses a number of contentious issues such as the agrarian foundations of capitalism, the relationship between class and status, as well as the structure and ideology of the absolute state itself. It will be of interest to early modern historians of France, Britain and Europe.

David Parker is Senior Lecturer in Modern History at the University of Leeds. He is the author of *The Making of French Absolutism*, 1983.

CLASS AND STATE IN *ANCIEN RÉGIME* FRANCE

The road to modernity?

David Parker

London and New York

First published 1996
by Routledge
11 New Fetter Lane, London EC4P 4EE

Simultaneously published in the USA and Canada
by Routledge
29 West 35th Street, New York, NY 10001

Typeset in Palatino by Florencetype Ltd, Stoodleigh, Devon
Printed and bound in Great Britain by TJ Press (Padstow) Ltd,
Padstow, Cornwall

British Library Cataloguing in Publication Data
A catalogue record for this book is available from the British Library

Library of Congress Cataloguing in Publication Data
A catalogue record for this book has been requested

ISBN 0–415–13647–4

To
Dave Priscott (1918–1995)

CONTENTS

ILLUSTRATIONS

FIGURES

TABLES

PREFACE

Fifteen years have passed since my perception of the limitations of existing Marxist treatments of French absolutism first gave me the idea of writing this book. At the time, Marxist debate was alive and well and looked as though it had a bright future. Marxist history had a ready and sympathetic audience. In the years that have elapsed, a generation of young people has grown up in the shadow of Thatcherite ideology for whom Marxism has little or no resonance. The sudden collapse of Communism in 1989 means that for them it definitely belongs to a bygone era. But not only for them; *marxisant* intellectuals and political activists everywhere have been thrown into disarray. Some concluded, almost overnight, that their entire outlook stood condemned by history; others have forsaken the jargon of the Stalinist era for that of discourse theory or even the simplicities of political correctness. Questions of class, economic structures and political power have been eclipsed by identity politics and a preoccupation with the subjective.

At the same time – and surely not coincidentally – the historical landscape has been remoulded by an enthusiasm to revise everything. In its more extreme manifestations revisionism would eliminate the English revolutions of the seventeenth century and the industrial revolution of the next, and reduce the French Revolution to a catastrophic series of accidents; eighteenth-century England, it is now suggested, was not merely an aristocratic polity but an *ancien régime*, performing little better than France; all monarchies, it is claimed, were absolute in theory but equally limited in practice.

Not surprisingly, the emphasis of this book has shifted during its preparation to reflect the challenges of this new historical agenda. Yet the need for a Marxism which can survive in the post-1989 world is even greater than it was. This means abandoning the expectation that it will provide universal solutions to the human condition which has led to so much disillusionment. It also means steering a course between a structureless relativism on the one hand and economic reductionism on the other. In fact, an approach which meets these exigencies has long been present in the empirical tradition of Marxist history writing characteristic of post-war Britain. It is true that changing times make it necessary to be more explicit about analytical concepts which were merely implicit in the works of some of the most celebrated British Marxist historians; but their approach still offers the best prospect for a Marxism which makes it possible to come to grips with realities past, present and future. If this study makes a modest contribution to this endeavour it will do something to repay an immense intellectual debt.

A debt is owed equally to all those historians of many persuasions whose works and ideas I have plundered to produce a synthesis with which many of them will disagree. In the midst of disagreement, historians thankfully remain dependent on each other. This book, although shaped by my own predilections, would not have been possible without the flowering of French history in the United States and Britain during the last thirty years. It is simply not possible to mention all those from whose encouragement and/or scepticism I have benefited. The vigorous and stimulating exchange of views with colleagues and students at the University of Sheffield remains particularly vivid. I am immensely grateful to those who have read and commented on parts of the book in draft form or who have responded to my queries. To Bill Beik in Atlanta, Al Hamscher in Kansas, Marvin Rosen in Northern Illinois, Bill Speck, John Chartres, Jeffrey Dryhurst and Gordon Forster in Leeds, particular thanks are due. Marvin was both generous and immensely helpful in allowing me to consult the draft of his *Structure of English Capitalism 1689–1722*. Robin Briggs read the whole text and saved me from a variety of sins. Those that remain are due either to my own misunderstandings or to my convictions.

I should also like to acknowledge my debt to the British Academy over a number of years; though this work is not an archival monograph it owes much to ideas developed in the course of earlier research. Publication at a tolerable price was made possible by the generous financial assistance of the University of Leeds which I also warmly acknowledge.

This book has been completed – where it was first conceived – at Vanderbilt University. Were it not for the opportunity provided by the Leeds–Vanderbilt exchange it would not be finished yet. My time in Nashville has provided a salutary reminder of the benefits of a rational and manageable relationship between the demands of teaching and scholarship, so threatened by current government policies in Britain. Much has also been made possible by the high quality of the libraries and their staff at both Leeds and Vanderbilt, as well as the facilities put at my disposal by the Department of History at Vanderbilt. To Margaret, who has endured the multifarious consequences of my wish to write this book, I offer my deepest appreciation and the prospect of a holiday without the word processor.

This work is dedicated to the memory of Dave Priscott who embodied so much that was good about the 'short twentieth century'.

ACKNOWLEDGEMENTS

The author and publisher gratefully acknowledge the University of Leeds for its financial contribution towards this book.

David Parker
Nashville
18 March 1995

GLOSSARY OF FRENCH TERMS

aides	indirect taxes, largely on drinks
anoblis	newly ennobled/first-generation nobility
arpenteur	land surveyor
arpent	100 perches of land; either 74, 91 or 111 per cent of an acre depending on the region. A linear perch might contain 18, 20, or 22 feet
avocat-général	major legal officer representing the king in a sovereign court
bailliage	intermediate royal court and/or its jurisdiction
banalités	seigneurial monopolies most commonly of mills and presses
ban et arrière-ban	feudal levy, call to arms
banlieu	extent of municipal jurisdiction beyond the town walls
baux mixtes	leases combining different forms of payment
boisseaux	a variable measure of grain or other solids
brassier	agricultural worker, probably paid by the year partly in kind
burats	a strong but supple wool cloth
bureaux des finances	the bureaux of the treasurers of France established in each *généralité* (see p. 175)
capitouls	the municipal councillors of Toulouse
cassations	annulment of legal decisions by the royal council
cens	honorific due payable by holder of a *censive*
censive	'commoner' or holding property dependent on a seigneur
chambre des comptes	'sovereign' courts of accounting with particular responsibility for the business of the royal *domaine*
chambre des requêtes	chamber of a *parlement* with particular competence in litigation involving those with legal privileges
chambre tournelle	chamber of a *parlement* dealing with criminal cases

champarts	seigneurial due paid in kind as a proportion of the harvest
charretiers	carters
charrue à versoir	heavy plough with moulding board
cinq grosses fermes	twelve northern provinces embraced by a single customs boundary and comprising an area of internal free trade
closier	cultivator of enclosed garden or of a vineyard
commissaire	royal agent whose authority depended on a specific or revocable commission
contrôleur-général	director of finances from Louis XIV's reign onwards
corps de ville	municipal council
cour des aides	'sovereign' financial court with responsibility for litigation relating to the *taille* and other taxes
droguets	drugget; heavy cloth, half serge and half linen
droit d'aînesse	privileged position of eldest child in matters of inheritance
droits d'amortissement	taxes payable on land acquired by corporate institutions, usually the ecclesiastical bodies, and therefore withdrawn from circulation
droit écrit	term used to distinguish Roman law from customary law despite the fact that customary law was also written down by the seventeenth century
droit de franc-fief	tax payable by commoners in order to hold a fief
droit de tabellionage	tax payable on notarial transactions
échevinage	municipality or town council (in the north)
écuyer	esquire – the lowest rank of nobility
élection	A sub-division of a *généralité* and also a court with competence relating to the *taille*, *aides* and other taxes
élus	principal officeholders in the *éléctions*
étapes	military staging or supply posts
évocation	removal of a law case from its natural or ordinary jurisdiction
fermage	leasehold farming (see p. 61ff.)
fermiers	leaseholding tenant farmers whose leases might also embrace seigneurial dues
fief de dignité	fiefs which carried a title of honour: *duchés*, baronies, marquisates, *comtés*, etc.
franc-aleu	allodial holding (see p. 153)
fumiers	manure, dung

gabeleurs	literally, a salt tax farmer but an epithet popularly used to describe tax collectors in general
gabelle	general term for a variety of impositions on salt consumption and trade
gages	small emolument attached to an office
généralité	major administrative sub-division
gens sans aveu	narrowly, people with no seigneur or master, used to denote those without domicile, pejoratively vagabonds
grand conseil	offshoot of the royal council with sovereign jurisdiction of specified matters notably in ecclesiastical affairs
grande entrée	court privilege which gave access to the *petit lever du roi*
grands jours	special assizes established from time to time by the sovereign courts in distant and troublesome localities
grenier du sel	government salt store
hectare	a metric measure of land equalling 2.47 acres
jardinier	market gardener
journalier	day labourer, journeyman
laboureur	better-off peasant usually possessor of a plough
libertin	freethinker
lits de justice	procedure enabling the Crown to compel registration of its edicts by the courts
lods et ventes	due payable on the succession or alienation of dependent land
maîtres des requêtes	officeholders who serviced the royal council and from whom most intendants were drawn
manouvrier	cottager dependent on by-employments
menu peuple	lower orders, the crowd, the populace
métairie	farm holding usually with buildings, requiring a plough and held by someone other than the proprietor
métayage	sharecropping (see p. 61ff.)
muids	a measure of liquids or grains
négociants	wholesale or overseas merchants
noblesse de robe	nobility of the Robe, acquired by office
officiers	venal officeholders
parlement	'sovereign' law court (see p. 175)
partisans	financiers
paulette	tax payable every nine years by officeholders enabling them to dispose of their offices freely

pays d'états	provinces with surviving Estates, representative institutions
petit lever	court ceremony which began the king's day on the drawing back of the curtains on the royal bed
présidial	intermediate royal court (see p. 175)
prête-noms	straw men
procureur du roi	attorney in a law court
rente foncière	land rent
rentes	either a state bond on which interest was payable or a private loan approximating to a mortgage
requêtes de l'hôtel	the court/jurisdiction of the *maîtres des requêtes*
retrait féodale	procedure for the recovery of improperly alienated dependent land on payment of compensation to the current holder
retrait lignager	analogous to the *retrait féodale* but for alienated family property (see p. 128)
roman à clef	novel introducing real characters under fictitious names
semestre	the division of a court and its sessions into two, accompanied by the necessary creation of offices
sénéchaussées	the southern equivalent of a *bailliage*
subdélégués	subordinates of the intendants
terroir	land encompassed by a rural community
trésoriers de France (*trésoriers-généraux*)	the principal treasurers who staffed the *bureaux des finances*
vaine pâture	uncultivated land on which grazing was permitted by custom or agreement

INTRODUCTION

A central purpose of this book is to modify recent Marxist interpretations of the genesis, function and nature of absolute monarchy through a study of the French variant which reached its apogee under Louis XIV. The general thrust of my argument is that the various attempts to relate absolutism to the rise of capitalism have failed to show any significant or necessary connection. This view also involves a challenge to liberal treatments which stress the modernity of the absolute state. Both Marxist and liberal approaches have contributed to a widespread tendency to minimise or reduce the differences between the social and institutional evolution of France and England. The Soviet historian Lublinskaya firmly bracketed them together with the United Provinces as the three countries which had embarked on the capitalist road.[1] If this view has never received outright endorsement, it has, ironically enough, received support from revisionist historians of the eighteenth century who have pointed in the same general direction. By minimising the speed of English industrialisation and stressing the rapidity of French economic growth, the disparities in performance have become very blurred. More cautiously, but persistently, some French social and economic historians have also drawn parallels between the agrarian structures of northern France and those of England.[2] Meanwhile, revisionist historians have been busy nibbling away at the institutional differences between the two countries. The legitimate desire to deconstruct the vulgar conception of French absolutism as unlimited personal rule has overflowed into suggestions that, at heart, it was little different from the constitutional monarchy which emerged across the Channel. Such notions have been reinforced, rather indirectly and innocently, by revisionist attempts to eradicate every vestige of the Whiggish emphasis on the power and peculiarity of the English Parliament.[3] Much less innocently, the long endeavour to deny the revolutionary significance of the political crises of 1649 and 1688 has been carried to the point of declaring England to be an *ancien régime* in the eighteenth century.[4]

If the sources of revisionist historiography were not so disparate, it would be tempting to see in it a conservative conspiracy to completely remodel the main lines of economic, social and political development in the early modern period. Its full implications may be perhaps be seen in the view that the French Revolution broke out at 'a moment of rare economic crisis', when France was already making discernible and irreversible progress towards modernity.[5] Most of these views are rejected in this study in favour of an insistence on the qualitatively different paths of development followed by France and England which were manifest in every domain: economic, social, cultural and political. In the early modern period England was both a paradigm of capitalism and the benchmark of institutional modernity. When put to the test against Britain, the *ancien régime* proved devastatingly vulnerable and incapable of reform. Whatever was achieved by monarchical absolutism, it did not prepare France to withstand the pressures of Europe's major capitalist power nor open up the prospects for capitalist development. On the contrary, as is shown by both the French and English cases, absolutism was increasingly incompatible with economic progress – and perceived to be so.

A further purpose of this study is to move away from the economic reductionism which is still visible in attempts to explain the nature of the French state by reference to class antagonism, the balance of class forces or the mode of surplus extraction. Whilst taking issue with those who deny the reality of class in this period, and defending the proposition that the French state like other states was an instrument of the dominant class, my approach places as much emphasis on conflicts within the ruling class as on conflicts between classes. Without recognising the intensity and significance of these it is impossible to explain the formation and particular physiognomy of French absolutism. Throughout the analysis, therefore, class is treated both as a structure– defined by relationship to the means of production – and as an agent of historical change involved in its own making. The antithesis between the two approaches on which some cultural Marxists have insisted is more apparent than real. With similar pragmatic intent I have implicitly, and sometimes explicitly, placed my entire analysis within the framework of the classic Marxist conception of the relationship between political superstructure and economic base; though the base–superstructure model has frequently been dismissed as a form of economic determinism, my conviction remains that it is compatible with non-reductionist interpretations of political power.

The overriding belief which permeates all that follows is that theoretical issues, which have caused much philosophising amongst left-wing theoreticians and armchair politicians, are not actually amenable to theoretical resolution. Problems raised by the use of the base–superstructure model, the difficulties of relating class as structure to class as agency are, in the final analysis, manageable only at the level of empirical demonstration. As Marx and Engels noted, the abstractions employed 'to facilitate the arrangement of historical material' when 'divorced from real history' have 'in themselves no value whatsoever'.[6]

Thus, although this study does comment directly on some questions of theory, the amount of theoretical elaboration is limited. I have also tried to avoid writing 'jumbo history' because no matter how stimulating the attempts to provide comprehensive Marxist views of centuries of human development, they invariably fail to meet the requirements of empirical investigation.[7] What is unavoidable, even when largely concentrating on a single century and a single country, is the need to range over economic, social, intellectual, cultural, and political developments. For Marxism has always assumed the structural interdependence of all facets of any social formation. I am, therefore, conscious of having pursued themes where my expertise is less than I would have desired. My debt to others of all historical persuasions will be manifest throughout. In return, I hope that the empirical complexion of what follows has enabled me to distil the findings of a variety of specialists for the benefit of readers who may not share the conclusions drawn from them.

The book opens with a discussion of interpretations of absolutism, both Marxist and otherwise. Chapter 2 is designed to show that any connection between absolutism and capitalism was largely incidental; neither was particularly dependent on the other. The most striking and fundamental feature of the French economy was in fact the stagnant state of agriculture which constituted a major obstacle to capitalist development. That itself is largely explained by reference to the burdens placed on the peasantry by both landlords and state rather than technical backwardness or demographic pressure. Investigation of the economic and legal position of the peasantry shows how – contrary to some other Marxist interpretations – their pauperisation and lack of independence acted as a brake on economic progress. The intense pressures felt by the peasantry also contributed to the unrest which tore the regime apart in the first half of the seventeenth century. Chapter 3 demonstrates the reality of class struggle and its relationship to sectarian, corporate and factional forms of conflict. The dynamics of emergent absolutism owed at least as much to the antagonisms which divided the upper classes as to those between classes. The next chapter none the less insists on the class nature of the French regime. This is demonstrated through a discussion of the relationship between status and wealth and of the ties which bound robe and sword together into a single ruling class. A brief discussion of the value and limitations of such structural analysis then prepares the way for Chapter 5 which adds an essential cultural dimension to the argument. Here the increasingly strident emphasis on Rank and Degree is placed in the context of the remarkable success of the aristocracy in reasserting their cultural domination of French society which, for a time, seemed to be under severe threat.

The full range of economic, social and cultural forces which shaped the 'absolute state' having been established, Chapter 6 returns to an exposition of the validity of this concept. Consideration is given to the ways in which absolute monarchy was legitimated, the degree to which it represented a bureaucratic and modernising form of government and the manner in which it served the interests of the ruling class. A contrast is drawn between the success of French absolutism in bringing political stability, together with an impressive flowering of aristocratic culture, and the immense long-term costs of this achievement which flowed from the irremedial entrenchment of vested interests inside the structures of the state. These observations prepare the ground for the explanation offered in Chapter 7 of France's defeat by England in the competition for global supremacy. The structural weaknesses of the *ancien régime* became fatally exposed by the competition with a country where the unmistakable development of capitalism produced both a degree of prosperity and a 'modernised' state which put her at a decisive advantage. The extended comparison with England confirms the increasingly divergent and qualitatively different nature of the two societies and their associated forms of government. The progress of agrarian capitalism in England also throws into stark relief the extent and significance of France's agricultural malaise. The comparison also adds weight to the emphasis placed on the role of ideas and culture in determining whether monarchs triumphed or fell. Capitalism may be seen to have done much better where the assertion of royal authority failed rather than where it succeeded.

Much of this has the effect of bestowing on my overall perspective an uncomfortable but unavoidable Whiggish flavour. It is compounded by the conviction which grew in the course of writing that the French ruling class, although constrained by circumstances, bore a heavy responsibility for the mismanagement of a potentially wealthy kingdom. This approach may add to the irritation of those French colleagues who have already bridled at assertions of England's economic superiority. It will certainly not find favour with some British historians who have enthusiastically agreed that England was neither very different nor more 'advanced' by the eighteenth century. It also cuts across the entirely legitimate observation of developmental theorists that there is more than one path to modernity. That may well be so. But Britain by the eighteenth century had become the benchmark of modernity. The transforming power of capitalism, for all the misery that it brought, was immense. If England was in the vanguard of this process and France could not stand the pace, the historical record should not be amended because it is irritating, embarrassing, or ideologically disturbing.

1

APPROACHES TO FRENCH ABSOLUTISM

HISTORIANS, SOCIOLOGISTS AND THE EARLY MODERN STATE

Marxist historians have had a lot of trouble with France's absolute monarchy; but they are not the only ones to do so. Historians and sociologists of every persuasion – whether Marxists, modernisers, structural functionalists, Whigs or just empirical observers – have all struggled to accommodate its hybrid, ambivalent and ambiguous features within their various conceptual frameworks. A manifestly aristocratic state which apparently brought the nobility to heel, a seemingly centralised and bureaucratic form of organisation yet riddled with venality and patrimonial interests, legitimised by a compound of divine right and a modern concept of legislative sovereignty, the monarchy of Louis XIV sat astride the path to 'modernity', like Janus facing both directions at once. Not surprisingly there is little agreement about its precise location on the path or the nature of the surrounding terrain. Some historians even believe absolutism to be a misleading term and that in reality the power of the great king was as 'limited' as that of his English counterparts.[1]

The idea that there was something recognisably modern about absolute monarchy appears in many different forms. At its simplest it rests on the conviction that centralisation and bureaucratisation were the essential features of the modern state. In this case absolutism might be thought to be a long way down the modernising path. Some historians have no difficulty in detecting the growth of bureaucracy in medieval times and its first flowering in the 'national and territorial' states of the Renaissance.[2] It is not too difficult to underpin an empirical and gradualist approach to the emergence of the modern state with a modest injection of Weberian sociology to give it a bit more precision. In assessing the development of the French foreign ministry between 1698 and 1715 John Rule appealed to explicitly Weberian criteria:

> the emergence of a hierarchy of offices and a chain of command . . . the appearance of specialised bureaus, recognition given by the

> head of the bureaucracy to tenure of office, payment of salaries and pensions, reliance on experts and the preservation of documents in a central archive or depot.[3]

Joe Shennan, writing more generally, has observed that the outcome of the political crises of the early modern period was 'the transformation of patrimonial regimes into modern bureaucratic ones'.[4]

Once made, however, such formulations demand an explanation of how the transformation from one condition into its opposite was effected. According to Roland Mousnier, it is to be found in Louis XIV's success in reducing 'all fealties to fealty to himself'; fealty was confounded with subjection to the state of which the king was the embodiment.[5] In similar vein, Sharon Kettering, more percipient than Mousnier about the material interests that governed personal ties of dependence, has argued that 'the recruitment and retention of provincial broker-clients by Cardinal Richelieu was a deliberate policy meant to establish royal control over the peripheral regions of France'.[6] Through the successful manipulation of clientage the royal ministers were able to 'integrate regional and national elites'.[7] In the process ties of personal dependence were transformed into something else and produced not just a stronger monarchy but one founded on more modern, administrative modes of operation: the emergent state became less identified with royal and noble households, its mode of operation more straightforwardly political, personal relationships less binding and more businesslike.[8]

The concentration of executive, legislative and judicial functions in royal hands which resulted from these processes was sustained, according to Mousnier, by the doctrine of monarchical sovereignty.[9] His approach here agrees with the analyses of many others who have pointed to Jean Bodin's definition of legislative in 1576, as a crucial moment in the transformation of monarchical rule. Bodin is rightly celebrated for his enunciation of the modern idea of sovereignty as the untrammelled and undivided power to make general laws. Without a clear locus of such legislative authority the state – whether democratic, aristocratic or monarchical in form – could not, said Bodin, be held to exist. Sovereignty did not depend on whether laws were just but on the power to make them. Not surprisingly his ideas are often seen as providing the basic ideological ingredients of monarchical absolutism. Richard Bonney finds their practical expression in the exercise of justice by commission. He suggests:

> The powers conferred by the commissions of the intendants and the decrees and supplementary *règlements* . . . completely transformed the nature of royal administration in France and gave the ideas of Bodin to which was added the interpretation of Le Bret their posthumous significance.[10]

Commissioned justice allowed the delegation of powers by the Crown which could then be recovered, a possibility which did not exist with the venal magistrates who comprised the corps of the sovereign and lesser courts.[11]

The idea that commissioned justice heralded a qualitative change in the nature of the French monarchy is reinforced by those political theorists and legal historians who relate its enhanced power to the impact of Roman law. It has recently been claimed:

> The decisive contribution of Roman law was the idea that somewhere in the Community whether in the people or in the province or in the Prince (or in both combined) there existed a supreme will that could alter laws to suit the changing requirements of society.[12]

According to De Lagarde a shift occurred from the 'balanced' concept of contractual or customary law, which governed the traditional position of groups and individuals, to one concerned with imposing a rational order on a human collectivity. The king became a legislator rather than a judge.[13] This process was helped, it is also argued, by the steady incorporation of seigneurial jurisdictions within the framework of public authority. Appeals from seigneurial courts became normal, their competence was clearly defined and, in some matters, limited. The *de facto* separation of fief and jurisdiction which occurred as fiefs became marketable commodities received theoretical approval in the notion that fiefs did not carry with them, as of right, powers of justice. According to this perspective the key figure was not Bodin but the celebrated sixteenth-century jurist Du Moulin. His work has been seen as the 'the first attempt to break with feudal ideas by stressing that all subjects were in a direct and equal relationship to the king'.[14] The feudal pyramid was dismantled, the king 'singled out as the holder of complete *imperium*, and all other members of society [are] assigned an undifferentiated legal status as his subjects'.[15]

There thus exists a body of ideas which emphasises not merely the enhanced power of the monarch but also its increasingly modern complexion. Bodin's definition of sovereignty, reinforced by the impact of Roman law, not only provides a secular, rational legitimation of royal authority, but is also held to erode the power of divine and customary law as the basis of civil society. Its political expression was the deployment of a new kind of salaried and dismissible royal agent who pushed the country along the road to modernity. A bureaucracy began to develop and the state as a distinct sphere of political activity began to separate out. It now existed over and above all the subjects who increasingly stood in an equal relationship to it. The outcome of all these developments was the replacement of personal rule by the domination of an impersonal state. It rested on a formal set of political and bureaucratic relationships rather than patrimonial ties binding members of the political elite to each other and to the Crown.

The idea of the separation out of the modern state is shared by historians and sociologists of many different persuasions. Depending on one's predilections, it can be traced back to Marx or to Durkheim and has been absorbed by many who would not recognise a debt to either. Yet from all quarters come notes of reservation about the rate at which the process was accomplished and its applicability to absolute monarchy. When Shennan returned to some of these themes in 1986 it was to dwell on the capacity of the 'possessory, dynastic idea of kingship' to survive the encroachments of administrative concepts and practices well into the eighteenth century.[16] There was, he observed, great difficulty in discerning 'signs of equality between subjects' as long as the highly personal contract between the Crown and nobility endured.[17] Moreover, it proved impossible for the idea of the impersonal state to take root before the hierarchical and corporate structures of the *ancien régime* were swept away.[18] Bonney also recognises the continued presence of powerful clienteles in the heart of the administration. He concludes that absolute monarchy atomised society into 'individual groups who were in direct relationship with the monarchy from whom it hoped to gain privileges and benefits'. This cautious formulation appears to consciously shrink from any suggestion that the sovereign state had reduced society to a mass of formally equal subjects.[19] Skinner, despite the bold formulations which have been cited, is acutely aware of the hesitant and contradictory evolution of modern political ideas. Most strikingly, he departs from the frequently expressed view that Roman law necessarily led to absolutist conclusions. Many Romanists concluded that 'the grant of sovereignty embodied in the original *lex regia* ought to be interpreted in a constitutionalist sense'. Power is delegated by the people.[20] What is more, the general renewal of interest in the law under the impact of Renaissance humanism had the effect of developing an understanding of feudal, customary and Germanic traditions with their emphasis on a contractual and limited exercise of authority.[21] Even for those who most wish to do so, the task of ascribing to absolute monarchy a precise location on an upward path to modernity is far from straightforward.

A different way of tackling the problem has been offered by functional modernisation theory which, rather than positing stages of development, is concerned with the attributes of modern society and an implied or explicit contrast with traditional society. Primitive subsistence economies with minimal levels of social stratification are counterposed to technology-intensive, industrialised ones with a high degree of structural differentiation and specialisation; closed, ascriptive status systems to open ones geared to individual achievement; social systems based on extended kinship to those associated with the nuclear family;

societies sustained by religious or magical ideologies to those dependent on secular and rational ones. In structurally differentiated modern societies individuals acquire multiple identities and political activity becomes one of many distinct spheres of human activity.[22]

The simplicity of the antithesis between traditional and modern society has been highly susceptible to criticism. It is not difficult to point out that traditional societies are neither static nor homogeneous, that historically they have developed in divergent ways and that they may use both 'rational' and 'magical' means of social control. Indeed, 'a unified and nationalised society', it has been said, 'makes great use of the traditional in its search for a consensual base to political authority and economic development'.[23]

A major attempt to produce a functionalist analysis which could cope with such criticism appeared in 1963 in the form of Eisenstadt's *The Political System of Empires*. Here absolutism is categorised as a historical bureaucratic empire along with the Ottoman empire, successive Chinese empires, the Inca and Aztec states, the Mogul empire, the Hellenistic, Roman and Byzantine empires and others, all of which were characterised by the limited autonomy of the political sphere.[24] Autonomous because developing social stratification had reached a point at which the Crown was able to act as an arbiter between all sorts of groups who were engaging in political activity; but limited because such groups had not yet detached themselves from traditional systems of stratification.[25] If a bureaucracy was clearly in the process of formation it had not yet acquired the characteristics of a modern, professional and salaried civil service, but very much remained the property of the social elites who staffed it. The competition for position and material rewards made it both possible and desirable for the king to maintain the contrary tensions in some sort of equilibrium. 'In sum', as Abrams commented, 'the historical bureaucratic empires were a balancing act.'[26] The ambivalence of such quasi-bureaucratic regimes still permeated by powerful patrimonial interests is further accentuated by the way in which Eisenstadt fastens on the contradiction between the political (modernising) goals of the rulers and the need to justify themselves in essentially traditional terms.[27] Sustained by the contradictions inherent in their own conditions of existence, such regimes might evolve into even more differentiated forms or conversely into less differentiated ones.[28]

Within six years of the appearance of Eisenstadt's remarkable synthesis, but without any reference to him, Norbert Elias published his own highly novel version of the royal 'balancing act' in his masterpiece of historical sociology, *The Court Society*. Looking at the elaborate rituals and etiquette of the French court he concluded that 'it is quite obvious . . . that these differences and petty jealousies between the most powerful elite groups were among the basic preconditions for the abundance of power held by the kings and denoted by the term "absolutism"'.[29] It was with telling effect that Elias cited Louis' admonition to those

> who imagine that all this is mere ceremony. The people over whom we rule, unable to see to the bottom of things, usually judge by what they see from outside, and most often it is by precedence and rank that they measure their respect and obedience.[30]

It was the function of the king to manipulate and control, elevating himself, by etiquette, by the pursuit of prestige and glory above the ruck. The whole of his carefully regulated existence, 'His getting up and going to bed, his love-making . . . all served equally to maintain his personal rule and reputation'.[31]

To the extent that Elias offered a wider explanation for the emergence of court society, it lay in the vast increase in the money supply which promoted inflation and made life particularly difficult for the aristocracy who were thrown into greater dependence on the king.[32] 'The court monarchy' was 'founded on money income' making it quite different from feudalism which rested on barter.[33] At the same time Elias placed the recovery of royal authority from the reign of Henri IV in the context of the antagonism between bourgeois and noble estates who 'held each other more or less in an equilibrium' and thus allowed the king, 'who apparently was equidistant from all groups, the chance to appear as a peacemaker'.[34] However, Henri IV was the last of the knightly kings whereas Louis XIV became the head of a court aristocracy.[35] As such, he had a rather different role in relation to the nobility. 'The double face of the court as instrument through which the king simultaneously dominated and supported the nobility as an aristocracy, corresponds exactly to the ambivalent character of the relationship between nobility and king.'[36] Elias noted in passing that, if the bourgeoisie were able for a time to buy their way in, the period of flux once over, an elite separated out and the 'roads leading from non-court strata into court society grew narrower'.[37] A distinctive court culture evolved which distinguished its members from outsiders. Despite these observations Elias was cautious about ascribing to the court society any great signs of modernity. On the contrary, it was 'the last relatively closed social formation in the west, the members of which did not work or calculate their offices in rational economic terms'.[38] The historical emphasis is thus significantly different from that of Eisenstadt, despite the evident similarities in approach. Whether either effectively explained the genesis of the developments they postulated is, however, a moot point. Both took as given a certain level of social stratification and economic development without which the Crown would have lacked the resources and the freedom of manoeuvre required to assert its own interests. To some degree both writers left the question of historical causation hanging in the air.

Eisenstadt did, however, point to the political objectives of rulers and their capacity to carry them through as a driving force in their own right.[39] This opens up the possibility of integrating his methodology with conventional modes of historical explanation. Shennan, for instance, contends that it was the very authority of the prince which 'fed a growing appetite for power'.[40] Any such synthesis would, however, override Shennan's own conviction that questions of social stratification are of secondary importance in explaining the evolution and configuration of the early modern state. He writes:

> Whether the threat was military, religious or economic, it remained true that external pressures rather than changes taking place in the domestic political, social or economic structure were decisive in the development of states, including the development of the modern state idea.[41]

Whilst accepting the view that the elevation of the state and the atomisation of society into a mass of equal individuals were inseparable facets of the same process, Shennan insists that it was the former through the enlargement of its own powers which gave meaning and substance to the latter; in the dialectical interplay between state and liberty it was the first which defined the second. Social as well as institutional change thus flowed ultimately from the external pressures which brought the modern state into being.[42] Shennan is far from alone in stressing this sequence of cause and effect. Mousnier has related the change from judicial to executive government, the establishment of a genuine bureaucracy, as well as the rise of new social groups, to the impact of foreign and civil war which he concluded was the 'most potent factor in the transformations that occurred between 1598 and 1778'.[43] For Braudel, who found the sixteenth-century 'corridors of political history . . . suddenly thronged with the long procession of those members whom we may conveniently, if anachronistically, call "civil servants" . . . a political revolution coupled with a social revolution' had already occurred.[44] 'The modern state', he declared, had just been born, but being still insufficiently equipped for its task, 'in order to make war, collect taxes, administer its own affairs, and conduct justice, it was dependent on businessmen and the bourgeoisie, hungry for social advancement'.[45] Modernisation theory's lack of clear causal dynamics has perhaps left the initiative with those who argue that it was the state itself, nurtured in the bellicose turmoil of the sixteenth and seventeenth centuries, which provided the dynamic for social change.

FEUDALISM, CAPITALISM AND THE ABSOLUTE STATE

Marxism shares with all the other currents of thought to which allusion has been made the notion that there was a dialectical relationship between the separation out of the modern state and the atomisation of society into independent individuals. However, the genesis of these twin processes, according to Marx, lay not in the quest for security or sovereignty but in the development of capitalism. It was economic development rather than the levelling activity of the state which subverted the hierarchies, ranks and corporations of feudal society and replaced them with a mass of formally equally individuals.[46] Here lay the basis of the novel distinction between the public domain and private interests, precluded under feudalism where private property and public authority were fused in a continuous hierarchy of privilege and dependence. A complementary notion, which has become almost a commonplace of Marxist history, is that feudalism was distinguished from capitalism by the way in which the surplus wealth was extracted from the labouring population. In the former it was done by extra-economic coercion, by direct legal compulsion through the exercise of feudal rights, whereas in capitalist systems domination is purely economic. The formal separation of economic and legal modes of domination made possible the appearance of the state. Some Marxists have given such weight to this line of thought that they have concluded that the state is by definition a bourgeois construction.[47]

This approach might be thought to be superior to modernisation and functionalist theories because the development of capitalism provides a dynamic for social change which can be clearly related to the emergence of the state.[48] However, for all their precocious insights and conceptual flair, the founders of Marxism did not escape the contradictoriness of absolute monarchy. Placing absolute monarchy on the capitalist rather than the modern road may, perhaps, delineate the historical problems more sharply but it by no means resolves them. Engels has become rather famous for his view that absolute monarchy rested on a balance of power between the burghers and nobility which offered it 'a certain degree of independence of both'.[49]

> The nobility – politically put in retirement – got as its share the plundering of the peasantry and the state treasury and indirect political influence through the court, the army, the church and the higher administrative authorities, while the bourgeoisie received protection through tariffs, monopolies and a *relatively* orderly administration of public affairs and justice.[50]

Sometimes Marx pressed the latter part of this argument to the point at which it seems that absolute monarchy, by sweeping away all manner of feudal relics, prepared the ground for the Revolution of 1789.[51] At other times, he laid much greater stress on the conservative role of absolute monarchy which defended nobles' interests and refused to let itself be 'bourgeoisified amicably'.[52] This produced a distinction between its progressive and reactionary phases. Yet in some of their earlier writings Marx and Engels had seemed uncertain whether absolutism rested on classes at all. In the *German Ideology* they had gone so far as to state that 'the independence of the state is only found nowadays in those countries where estates have not yet completely developed into classes'.[53] Elsewhere Engels even proposed that absolute monarchy might be better described as *ständische* or estate monarchy as this would more accurately reflect the nature of the social hierarchy.[54] This line of thought, however fruitful in its own right, sits none too easily alongside the classic schema of successive modes of production, generating specific class structures in which the state was the instrument of the dominant one.[55] Only Kiernan has endeavoured to apply the former to early modern French society and his remarks focus on the sixteenth century; his view of later developments reverts to Engel's hypothesis of a class equilibrium.[56]

Further difficulties flow from the conflicting approaches to the question of capitalist development which are also to be found in the Marxist classics.[57] In the *Communist Manifesto* and the *German Ideology* Marx and Engels painted a picture of the genesis, maturation and triumph of the bourgeoisie which flowed directly from the growth of towns, an accompanying advance in the division of labour and the subsequent expansion of commerce and overseas markets. Eventually feudal structures could no longer contain the new force within it.[58] Elsewhere, however, Marx stressed the indispensable need for the labouring population to be divorced from the means of production if capitalism was to fulfil its revolutionary potential. By this process, frequently described as one of primitive accumulation, unfree peasants together with independent producers were reduced to the status of 'free' wage labourers; left with nothing but their labour to sell and dependent on their wages they were simultaneously transformed into a potential market. Without such a transformation of productive relations, it was not possible for money and commodities, which could exist comfortably within the interstices of feudal society, to themselves be transformed into capital.[59] The corollary of this argument was the idea that whilst merchant capital may have encouraged production for exchange value 'its development . . . is incapable by itself of promoting and explaining the transition from one mode of production to another'.[60] The emergence of a new mode of production 'does not depend on trade but on the character of the old mode of production itself'.[61] It was around this notion that Maurice Dobb built one of the central themes of his renowned *Studies in the Development of Capitalism*; in this he sought to show that 'the degree to which merchant capital flourished in a country' in the sixteenth and seventeenth centuries 'affords no measure of the ease and speed with which capitalist production was destined to develop'.[62] On the contrary, the conservative nature of merchant capital was reflected in the way in which merchants simply battened on to the existing mode of production without transforming it, whilst seeking constantly to climb the existing social hierarchy. Dobb's influence may be detected in Eric Hobsbawm's seminal essay 'The General Crisis of the Seventeenth Century' in which he formulated the notion of the feudal–business economy and also in my own perceptions of the economic and social conservatism of the French bourgeoisie.[63]

A more positive view of the corrosive power of trade and commerce has endured in Immanuel Wallerstein's *The Modern World System*. According to Wallerstein the overriding feature of economic and political development from the sixteenth century was the emergence of a capitalist world order. This was made up of strong core states, less strong semi-peripheral ones and weak political formations in the peripheral areas which were thus dominated economically by those at the core. Wallerstein explained the transformation of feudal agrarian relationships in the strong core states – England and the Dutch Republic – by reference to their location in the world economy; for it was 'crucial that resources be used more efficiently in order to benefit from the central trading and financial position in the world economy'.[64] At the same time, he insisted that the regions of the semi-periphery and periphery still dependent on forms of coerced labour – the *encomienda* of Hispanic America, the *latifundia* of Spain, and the second serfdom of Eastern Europe – were also capitalist. Because the world economy was capitalist, relationships that bore certain formal relationships to feudal relationships must be defined in terms of the governing principles of a capitalist system.[65]

Such a tautological definition of the world economy will barely stand scrutiny. In the course of demolishing it, Robert Brenner returned to the necessity for a prior transformation of agrarian class relations without which a development of the market was not possible.[66] As long as coerced labour persisted, landlords would prefer to squeeze the peasantry instead of stimulating investment, thus imposing severe restraints on the expansion of the market. Even where commodities were produced for exchange, the consequence was likely to be an entrenchment of feudal relations and of obstacles to capitalist development. This is what occurred in Eastern Europe in those regions, notably Poland, which became suppliers of grain to the markets of Western Europe, and whose economy was strangled in the process.[67]

The shaky foundations of Wallerstein's position are nowhere better revealed than in his treatment of France. He placed the north of France with its commercialised agriculture in the core of the world economy and the south, where sharecropping predominated, in the semi-periphery. Sharecropping, he asserted, was a second-best option for the landed classes of an area which was poor in soils, and backward in technology. It was 'a partial response to the creation of a capitalist world economy, in the form of semi-capitalist enterprises, appropriate indeed to semi-peripheral areas'.[68] Wallerstein then sought to relate the endemic unrest of the outlying French provinces to the imperatives of the world economy. Brittany and Normandy were pulling away because they preferred to break into the Atlantic–Baltic trade rather than construct a state bureaucracy whilst the 'landed capitalists of the south sought a free international market'.[69] The rising of the Nu-Pieds in 1639 was an expression of discontent with the way the politics of the centre were depriving the Norman peasant proprietor and local bourgeois of the benefits of fuller participation in the new world economy. This revolt was followed by uprisings in other frontier provinces – Provence, Brittany, Languedoc and Poitou – which were seeking more economic progress.[70] Unfortunately, the entire argument rests on a series of highly implausible assertions, based on abstract categories of peasant proprietors and landed capitalists, without a jot of evidence to show that they had the aspirations attributed to them. The evidence that sharecropping had anything to do with the world economy is simply not offered; the extent and nature of the connections between overseas and regional economies are nowhere demonstrated. Not only is this part of Wallerstein's argument deeply suspect but it hardly appears essential to sustain his view of the French state which rests on little more than a revamped version of Engels' equilibrium thesis.[71]

A more powerful and coherent development of the idea of world economies and of the primacy of commerce is offered in Braudel's panoramic *Civilisation and Capitalism*. Here he suggested that world economies have existed since time immemorial and have been composed of overlapping modes of production. What held them together was the central role played by towns – 'outposts of modernity' which on the basis of liberty created 'a distinctive civilisation and spread techniques which were new or rediscovered'.[72] In this perspective the major transition was from city-centred world economies, notably that centred on Venice, to national territorial markets, most obviously in Britain.[73] But the British market was not created by the union with Scotland or the abolition of tolls; it 'was primarily the result of the ebb and flow of merchandise to and from London, a mighty beating heart, causing everything to move at its own rhythm'.[74] It was the power of London which enabled England to achieve an optimum level of market organisation, thus outstripping the Dutch whose prosperity depended on the last of the great city-based economies.[75]

Although Braudel followed Wallerstein in suggesting that these developments were more likely to occur at the centre of the world economy, after a prior expansion in foreign trade, he is careful to acknowledge that there was nothing automatic about the transition.[76] Drawing on the work of Sachs, he noted potential bottlenecks: a growth in population which might negate the benefits of economic progress; shortages of skilled labour; a propensity to industrialise in the luxury and sometimes the export sector because of low domestic demand; and most importantly the barrier of inelastic agricultural systems which cannot feed the population. This population then emigrates to the towns creating more poverty and little demand.[77] Whereas city states had avoided the 'heavy burden of the so called primary sector' . . . 'territorial states by contrast, as they grappled with their slow political and economic construction, long remained embedded in that agricultural economy which was so resistant to progress . . .'.[78] Whilst capitalism was on 'home ground' in the commercial arena, it was 'away from home' in production where progress was only made very slowly.[79] Here Braudel recognised the significance of the development of agrarian structures in England which hinged on the leasing of land to capitalist tenant farmers. The significance of this observation is, however, blunted by his view that similar structures could be found in parts of France and Italy. The difference between a region like the Brie and England was simply that in the former 'nothing changed in the shape of *technology* until the nineteenth century'.[80] Indeed, the 'agricultural revolution was a European phenomenon, just as much as the industrial revolution which accompanied it'.[81]

Inexorably, this observation pushed Braudel back towards non-agrarian explanations for France's comparatively slow economic development: most clearly its exclusion from the world economy as it lost out in turn to Venice, Antwerp, Genoa and Amsterdam.[82] Western France, which was well endowed with ports, specie and textiles, failed to maintain its early promise. This was possibly due to the way in which the regional economies of France were pulled about by the 'external conditions of the world economy' as its centre moved northwards.[83] In England, on the other hand, the power of London, by creating a national market, also produced the paradigm of the modern state. After 1688 the country fell under the 'domination of its merchants', producing a coincidence of political with economic power.[84]

Braudel's treatment of the connection between economic and institutional development in France is much less clear. Here it seems that it was the towns that were the beneficiaries of the efforts of the state to establish a national market rather than the other way round.[85] He suggested that 'as purchase of office became more widespread, a whole bourgeois class . . . came into its own'. However, venality of office led to a feudalisation of a section of the bourgeoisie and the *noblesse de robe* were an 'ambiguous' class.[86]

This untidy thread, which Braudel left trailing across his rich and evocative tapestry, is a telling pointer to the difficulties of defining the

French bourgeoisie and its relationship to the state. The most precise attempt to do this has been made by Lublinskaya who argued that the royal victory over the Huguenots in the 1620s was made possible by the growth of capitalism. For this enabled the government to gain the support of the towns by responding to their appeals for help in the competition with the English and the Dutch. The common interests of towns and Crown meant that the 'reactionary groups of grandees and of the old nobility of blood were obliged to fight against it so long and fruitlessly'.[87] Unfortunately, the effectiveness of this argument is substantially diminished by the fact that the defection of the Huguenot grandees to the Crown played a critical part in the royal victory. At the same time it took the full might of the royal army to bring the major towns to heel and some were never taken by force.[88] Certainly, their resistance was critically weakened by the social and political conservatism of bourgeois oligarchs. But this, I suggested in response to Lublinskaya, was more convincingly explained by the flight of the bourgeoisie from entrepreneurial activities into *rentier* and office-holding ones.[89] Elsewhere, curiously enough, Lublinskaya distanced herself from those who saw in the *noblesse de robe*, many of whom emerged from the urban patriciates, a rising bourgeois class. For her they were nobles according to income, to their place in the system of production and in public opinion.[90]

For Boris Porshnev, the conservatism of the bourgeoisie contributed directly to the victory of absolutism in a somewhat different way. His pioneering study of the massive popular uprisings, which prepared the way for the Frondes, revolved around the proposition that two opposing forces existed in French society: one represented by popular resistance to exploitation and the other by the repressive force that countered it. All other participants in the myriad of struggles and revolts which took place situated themselves by reference to the two fundamentally opposed forces.[91] Ultimately, the bourgeoisie, more frightened by threats to their property than by the oppressive behaviour of the state, abandoned the populace.[92] Whilst parts of Porshnev's interpretation have survived well, its effect is to transform absolute monarchy into little more than a response to the pressures of the lower orders, a system for keeping them in their place.[93] This approach, imbued with the sort of class reductionism widespread in Marxist circles throughout the Stalinist period, cannot do justice to the complexities of seventeenth-century conflicts or to the range of factors which gave rise to absolute monarchy.

A more sophisticated way of sustaining the essentially feudal nature of French absolutism has been provided by William Beik who declined to focus on the relationships between discrete classes as though they were historical actors or 'like counters on a chessboard'.[94] Instead, Beik turned to the idea that an essential distinguishing feature of feudalism was its reliance on extra-economic modes of domination and exploitation.[95] Thus the hierarchy of orders, the multiplicity of corporations, the entire officeholding bureaucracy through which the relationship of Crown and aristocracy was mediated in the absolute state were not incidental to it. They reflected the organisation of power necessary to extract wealth from the land in a 'late feudal' society.[96] French society was hybrid. Its foundations were still 'sunk deep in the land and it was built around a class of nobles whose fundamental existence was based on the domination of units of peasant production'; but, at the same time, royal power had opened up membership of the ruling class to new groups.[97] Provincial aristocrats could become *officiers*, rich merchants state financiers. However, to make the system work it was necessary to overcome the inherent tendency to sectional and corporate rivalry amongst the upper classes and to enable them to cope better with popular disorder. This was made possible by a restructuring of their relationship to the monarchy which allowed them to benefit from the reflected glory of the monarch whilst 'submitting' to him.[98]

At first sight Perry Anderson's sweeping survey of the absolute state places a similar emphasis on the idea that political superstructures 'enter into the constitutive structure of the mode of production in pre-capitalist social formations'.[99] A major effect of this was that 'transnational interaction within feudalism was typically first at the political not the economic level'.[100] Anderson was thus able to explain the emergence of absolute monarchies in Eastern Europe by the need to respond to the armed might of more powerful western regimes. In sharp contrast his analysis of the western variant was strangely economistic for he found its genesis in the need to compensate the feudal lords for the loss of coercive powers at the local level consequent upon the disappearance of serfdom; 'the result was a displacement of politico-legal coercion upwards towards a centralised, militarised summit'.[101] Western absolutism was 'a redeployed and recharged apparatus of feudal domination designed to clamp the peasant masses back into their traditional social position'.[102]

In its own way this methodology is almost as reductionist as that of Porshnev, offering a view of the absolutist state in which its function is indistinguishable from its historical origins. It is, moreover, impossible to square his interpretation with the chronology of absolutist development in France – essentially an early modern process – even if it is conceded that the ending of serfdom was as definitive as such a view requires. In fact, as Anderson himself recognised, the ending of serfdom – never in any event the predominant form of seigneurial tutelage – did not mean the end of extra-economic coercion or the disappearance of feudal relations from the countryside.[103] There is an evident and unresolved contradiction between this observation and the argument that absolutism had its genesis in the loss of the direct coercive power of the seigneurial class.

It is curious that none of those who emphasise the feudal character of the French state have dispensed entirely with the rising bourgeoisie or the development of capitalism. Porshnev, quite unnecessarily, went much farther than the evidence will allow in describing the Fronde as an abortive bourgeois revolution which failed because of the 'voluntary withdrawal of the French bourgeoisie'.[104] As Beik observed, Porshnev saw 'his bourgeois as wavering between consciousness of their revolutionary role and subordination to the feudal regime, but only the latter is clearly demonstrated'.[105] Beik was clearly very aware of the difficulty of locating a significant and influential capitalist bourgeoisie and his interpretation requires one even less than that of Porshnev.[106] It is therefore remarkable that he finally closed his own book with the suggestion, albeit a tentative one, that this 'venerable though modified feudal society' was 'a society in transition, if you like, from feudalism to capitalism'.[107] Anderson's formulations are less tentative but more provocative. For, having insisted on the 'irreducibly feudal' nature of absolute monarchy, he immediately qualified this view with the statement that it was 'nevertheless constantly and profoundly over-determined by the growth of capitalism within the composite social formations of the early modern period'.[108]

Behind this rather bizarre usage of the Althusserian concept of over-determination lie several historical arguments. One brings him close to Lublinskaya. 'Economic centralisation, protectionism and overseas expansion', he wrote, 'aggrandised the late feudal state while they profited the early bourgeoisie'.[109] Such a development was, however, facilitated by the legacy of classical antiquity which bequeathed a comparatively high level of urban civilisation to medieval Europe. Moreover, the feudal mode of production with its 'parcellisation of sovereignty' allowed 'urban enclaves to grow as centres of production . . . rather than as privileged or parasitic centres of consumption or administration'.[110] Anderson also concurred with the idea that Roman law was used to enhance royal authority.[111] More distinctively, he argued that the revival of Roman law brought with it notions of absolute rights in property, unknown to medieval custom, but essential for the development of capitalism.[112] All this was helped by the fact that the fief – unknown outside Europe except in Japan – constituted a form of private property despite the conditional nature of the terms on which it was held; this made possible its transformation into 'absolute private property'.[113] Overall, 'what rendered the unique passage to capitalism possible in Europe was the concatenation of antiquity and feudalism'.[114] More specifically, it was the 'complex combination of feudal and capitalist modes of production . . . the intertwining of two antagonistic modes of production within single societies that gave rise to the transitional form of absolutism'.[115]

The shifting emphasis revealed by Anderson's successive formulations would be easier to cope with if they were not so resolutely abstract. Despite his proclaimed intent to bring Marxist theory and historical investigation together, the gulf between the theoretical and empirical chapters is wide. That on France reverts to a discussion of the series of prolonged conflicts from the Hundred Years War to the Fronde out of which absolutism emerged and concentrates subsequently on superstructural phenomena: sale of offices, the development of the intendants, the reaction to the revolts sparked off by fiscal demands, and the wars which 'from 1667 dominated virtually every aspect of the reign'.[116] Inasmuch as this chapter addresses the nature of the social formation, it focuses on the restructuring of the noble class into an aristocracy and its changing relationship with the Crown. There is, however, no real discussion of the towns or the nature of merchant capital, simply a fleeting allusion to the presence of a commercial bourgeoisie in Paris and elsewhere.[117] A few lines are devoted to Colbert's 'ambitious mercantilist programme designed to accelerate manufacturing and commercial growth' but no analysis is offered of its actual impact.[118] Likewise, there is no illustration of the way in which the different modes of production were intertwined, or even of the extent to which feudal landownership did give way to capitalist forms based on absolute private property. Nor is there any discussion of the reception and application of Roman law.[119] Most glaringly, Anderson fails to demonstrate the posited connection between the ending of serfdom and the concentration of power at the apex of French society. Indeed, it is difficult to see how he could do so, given the absence of a systematic empirical investigation of rural social relationships, agricultural production, the nature of the law and the role of the various legal agencies during the absolutist period.

Unfortunately, there has been little investigation by Marxists of the development of agrarian social relationships within the context of the absolute state. Robert Brenner's foray into this area produced some agreement about the poor performance of French agriculture but much discord about the reasons for it. The core of his argument was the proposition that the success of the French peasantry in securing their freedom constituted an insuperable barrier to economic progress. Partially victorious in the thirteenth century in resisting the demands of the landlords, the peasantry subsequently consolidated their independence in a system of petty proprietorship; this precluded capitalist development and was bolstered up by the state for its own fiscal purposes.[120] 'Strong peasant property and the absolutist state' thus 'developed in mutual dependence' and 'the state increased its own power by virtue of its ability to get between the landlords and the peasants' with centralised forms of surplus extraction.[121] In the ensuing debate Brenner was attacked from all quarters. Amongst other things he was charged with overestimating the independence of the French peasantry and underestimating the persistence of extra-economic forms of coercion. The state, it was suggested, was not an independent competitor of the nobility for the revenues of the peasantry. Moreover, it inflicted great damage on them. Brenner was further criticised for reducing class relations to the mechanisms of surplus extraction of which the absolute state then became an expression. In replying to his critics Brenner continued to stress the progress of centralised forms of surplus extraction whilst acknowledging that the new structures absorbed many of the casualties of the erosion of the seigneurial system. So the absolutist state 'came to express a *transformed* version of the old system' in which grant of office replaced seigneury and the relationship between state and ruling class was restructured. He also appeared to recognise the persistence of extra-economic coercion and the crushing burden imposed via the state on the peasantry despite the fact that it simultaneously maintained the juridical basis of peasant property.[122] Yet there was little change in the essential thrust of his argument or the reductionist methodology on which it rests.

George Comminel, in his study of the French Revolution, has arguably taken Brenner's methodology to its logical conclusion. During the *ancien régime,* he suggests, the surplus was extracted from the peasantry by means of a combination of rents and feudal dues. These were fundamentally different from those of true feudal manorialism, but also had nothing in common with 'the distribution of *surplus-value* through capitalist rent'.[123] The state and church also extracted 'surplus from peasants through taxes, fees and tithes'.[124] This line of argument, in itself not very different from that of Beik, leads to a sharply different view of the regime. 'If landed property and state office were the joint basis of class relations of exploitation in the *ancien régime,* the bourgeoisie and the nobility together made up the ruling class.'[125] The state of the *ancien régime* was neither feudal nor capitalist but reflected the distinctive combination of modes of surplus extraction. Here, once again, is a highly reductive methodology in which the nature of the state is deduced directly from basic class antagonisms, mitigated only by a passing acknowledgement that the relationship between rulers and ruled can react back on the nexus of exploitation.[126]

Ironically, the persistent reductionism of Marxist treatments of absolutism has left Marxism with very little to say about the formation and shape of the state. There is a huge gap between functional representations of absolutism and the real state which emerged out of the travails of religious war and the intense social and economic pressures of the early modern period. With the notable exception of Beik, Marxists have thus failed to offer an explanation for the precise political and social contours of the absolute state. Whether absolutism is considered to rest on or represent feudal or capitalist interests, one mode of production or the other, or even a mixture of the two, there is no obvious reason why Louis XIV's regime should have taken the shape it did. Even if Anderson's view of an upward movement of politico-legal coercion could be sustained, it does not in itself explain the extraordinarily intense preoccupation with privilege, precedence and rank which reached its apogee in the unprecedented concentration of power at Louis XIV's court. Its symbolism, elaborate etiquette and ritual, as fundamental to the nature of French absolutism as the concentration of military power, have no obvious place in such a schema. This weakness leaves it vulnerable to those would deny altogether the relevance of class to an analysis of the *ancien régime*.

MOUSNIER AND THE SOCIETY OF ORDERS

The multilayered dispositions of French status groups in this period lend themselves to a Weberian conception of status groups, membership of which may have brought material rewards but had little to do with the economic relationships. This view of the *ancien regime* is nowadays synonymous with the work of the late Roland Mousnier who spent the best part of thirty years in its elaboration.

Mousnier's point of departure was a rebuttal of Porshnev's insistence on the class character of popular revolts. Frequently incited by nobles, the widespread unrest, he argued, was based on the resistance of entire communities to the exigencies of the fisc.[127] Furthermore, the largely fiscal and limited social objectives of popular movements revealed a distinct lack of class consciousness.[128] Mousnier subsequently went on to develop a conception of French society which placed more emphasis on the vertical ties which bound people together than on horizontal ties of class. This meant that 'the peasant often had the attitudes of a *fidèle*, of a *dévoué* towards the seigneur'.[129] Peasant movements were not therefore directed against the seigneurial order. On the contrary, they were a response of the community to the pressures of the central state which was 'insinuating at every moment its justice, its law, its fisc, its army between the nobles and their men'.[130]

This argument, however, made it necessary to distinguish clearly between vertical chains of *fidelités* and feudal ties of dependence.[131] In 1963, Mousnier tackled this head-on with the argument that the main reason for the acquisition of seigneuries and fiefs was the status they brought. Such property was 'a source of fealty and hommage, of *cens* and dues', which were themselves a symbol of social superiority.[132] In addition, fiefs and seigneuries were the traditional reward for military service. The survival of the seigneurial regime was thus due 'above all' to the survival of military values and attitudes. As military rank and the social position which flowed from it were for so long tied to the hierarchy of landownership, so the latter had persisted as a source of social esteem and prestige. 'Thus', concluded Mousnier, 'the fundamental principle of a society dominated everything else, even economic activity.'[133]

Here, for the first time in Mousnier's published work, was the clear assertion that, in the society of seventeenth-century France, values determined the nature of the socio-economic structure and not the other way round. This then became the key element in his construction of an alternative model of French society, a society based not on classes but on Orders. Where social stratification takes the form of 'Orders' or 'Estates', he wrote in 1965, these were arranged:

> not according to the wealth of their members or their purchasing power, not according to their role in production of material wealth, but according to the esteem, the honour, the dignity bestowed by society on social functions which might have no relation to the production of material wealth. Thus in France during the feudal epoch and in France of the sixteenth and seventeenth centuries, social esteem, honour, status, were attached first of all to the profession of arms and to the aptitude to command and to protect which resulted from this.[134]

The location of all the lesser ranks was ingeniously related to this fundamental principle. The form of activity farthest removed from that associated with the profession of arms was manual labour and therefore those least tainted by the latter had the greatest status. Particularly prestigious was the cerebral work of those who gave legal expression to *de facto* power relationships, provided the juridical framework for social relationships, and maintained the equilibrium of society.[135] In this manner Mousnier thus endeavoured to explain the undoubted value placed on a legal career and the power and prestige of the magistracy. The principle at work was quite different from that in capitalist society where class position and status went together and both were determined by the role played in the production of material wealth and the money so earned.[136] In a society of Orders the prime function of wealth was to facilitate a style of life which would promote or confirm a family's status; it was not an end in itself.[137] This view permeated all Mousnier's subsequent works where forms of property and inheritance were presented as consequences of the need, as expressed by a certain nobleman, to have the 'means to sustain one's name and house'.[138]

Whilst Mousnier detected a shift in the dominant values over the course of the seventeenth century so that talent and intellectual work in the judicial, scientific, artistic and literary spheres were better rewarded, the organising principles remained those of a society of Orders.[139] A class society did not emerge until the last half of the eighteenth century when there was a decisive shift in attitudes and values. 'When concern for happiness through physical well-being, preoccupation with the production of material goods, became dominant in men's minds, there then triumphed in the court of public opinion the quiritarian form of property – absolute, exclusive, perpetual.'[140]

Mousnier's idealism was explicit. 'The social hierarchy is the result', he wrote in 1972, 'of the tacit approval of the people.' This itself 'flows from an ensemble of spontaneous value judgments about social behaviour which establishes a table of social values'.[141] The problem is that such value judgments turn out be those of the literate upper classes and the whole argument rests on a willingness to accept these as accurate representations of the society around them. Taxed by many for confusing reality with subjective perceptions of it,[142] Mousnier resolutely refused to yield. His first sketches of the society of Orders relied heavily on the writings of the jurist Charles Loyseau as did his last in which, despite a brief genuflection to his critics, he still insisted that 'for a society of Orders any social investigation must be guided by a search for social value judgments, explicit or implicit, resulting in the construction of a scale of dignities'.[143] The circularity of this argument which makes the society of Orders both premise and conclusion is glaring. Even when Mousnier began to treat the *noblesse de robe* as a distinct estate of the nobility, they were categorised as bourgeois on the grounds that this was the way in which they were regarded by the traditional nobility.[144]

As these observations make clear, Mousnier pushed his idealist methodology to the point at which it became exceedingly vulnerable to criticism. This is particularly true of his refinement of his conception of ties of *fidelité* which in his last works were transformed into emotional (affective), personal and voluntary bonds linking *maître* and *fidèle* in a relationship of protection and devotion.[145] His determination to largely discount the material considerations at work in such relationships has been attacked with devastating effect by Sharon Kettering. Her own elucidation of patron–client relationships as unequal yet reciprocal arrangements, in which the respective 'interests, resources and contributions' of the two participants were weighed against each other, constituted a frontal assault on Mousnier's tendency to create social models of French society from idealised constructions of social relationships.[146] For Kettering the expressions of devotion and loyalty utilised as evidence by Mousnier are secondary to the overriding material self-interest of the participating parties. Individuals frequently hedged their bets by entering into more than one relationship, and changes of allegiance were commonplace.[147] Clientelism encouraged factionalism and fragmentation.[148]

It would be relatively easy to dismiss Mousnier's work on the grounds that his hostility to Marxism, his ingrained idealism and his deep social conservatism profoundly distorted his historical judgment. Some of his claims – for instance that Marxists project into the past the social relations of the present – were so silly that they are best ignored.[149] His idealised constructs of social stratification and human relationships have been exposed to such criticism that they already seem remarkably dated despite their continuing influence on French historiography.[150] As formulated they are certainly incompatible with any sort of materialism. Yet for all that, Mousnier raised empirical and theoretical questions which should not disappear with the bath water. His insistence on the centrality of vertical social divisions – which Kettering also accepts albeit in a very different form – demands a considered response. So, too, does the related contention that the *menu peuple* lacked a consciousness of themselves as a class. It should also be recognised that, although Mousnier's treatment of upper-class perceptions of their own status was idealised and partial, such perceptions were none the less a facet of upper classness. They cannot be ignored.

SOME OBSERVATIONS

Marxist analysis of absolutism is far from resolving the question of its location on the road to modernity. On the contrary, the conception of the transition from feudalism to capitalism has reinforced the picture of a deeply ambiguous historical phenomenon. Coming to grips with it has not been helped by the uncertainty and disagreement over the genesis of capitalism itself; nor by the marked tendency to see the state in merely functional terms, as the direct expression of a class interest or a balance of class interests. For some, its social character is a simple expression of the system of surplus extraction, defined in the narrowest of ways. This approach leaves its proponents with very little to say about the genesis, evolution and precise shape of France's political regime. Only Beik's study, by virtue of its empirical style and his recognition of the specificity of political activity, offers an analysis in which the ruling class becomes an agent in its own making; and in which it is possible to recognise the state as a highly complex mechanism for ensuring the general social and political domination of the ruling class, as well as a wealth-extracting machine. On the other hand, the question of the relationship between political and economic change is not really pursued.

The conception of French absolutism which is offered in the following pages rejects the view that it was either an economically progressive or a modernising form of government. On the contrary, French absolutism was primarily an attempt to restore the structures of a monarchical regime which had been torn apart by decades of conflict. In monarchical absolutism a much shaken and divided ruling class found a means of renewing itself, but absolutism looked backwards rather than forwards.

Patrimonial mechanisms of rule remained more important than bureaucratic ones whilst the ideas which legitimated the regime were profoundly traditional.

Within the framework of this approach it is possible to bring together a number of seemingly antagonistic perspectives. A view is thus offered of the way in which class conflict interacted with the tensions which flowed from 'vertical' patterns of allegiance. It will be apparent that my picture of the state which emerged from these conflicts also owes much to the tendency, shared by writers of differing perspectives, to explain absolutism in terms of an equilibrium of contrary forces rather than as a monolithic structure. At the same time French absolutism was moulded by the intense preoccupation with rank and degree; this, it will be argued, is perfectly compatible with a class-based analysis.

It is perhaps harder to bridge the gap between those who make warfare the motor of political change and those who insist on the primacy of social factors. Empirically, however, there is little difficulty in bringing external and domestic pressures together. It seems sensible to proceed on the demonstrable assumption that the pressures of war were mediated by existing political and social structures rather than assert, at the outset, the primacy of one or the other. This approach is not incompatible with Anderson's theorising about the connection between feudalism and territorial conquest but his view of their interrelationship raises the issue at a higher level of abstraction than is attempted here.

The entire analysis is designed to demonstrate both the virtues and the limitations of structural definitions of state and class. These, it will be seen, remain very useful for their capacity to illuminate the mechanisms of economic domination and exploitation on which the rich and powerful depended. In this case they show only too clearly how the depredations of the absolutist regime, far from advancing the cause of capitalism, hindered its progress. None the less, without a recognition of the cultural dimensions of both state and class it is quite impossible either to explain the emergence of absolutism or to define it with real accuracy. The capacity of the monarchical regime to renew its cultural hegemony makes one of the most striking contrasts with England, where the ideological foundations of Stuart rule decayed steadily. Indeed, this contrast has much to do with the fact that it was in parliamentary England, and not in absolutist France, that capitalism really took off.

2

THE FRENCH ECONOMY

A case of arrested development

COMMERCE, CAPITALISM AND THE STATE

In view of the fact that absolute monarchies arose in countries with greatly varying social and economic structures and that they lasted longest in the most backward, it is odd that they have been so persistently linked to the development of capitalism. In the French case this association has depended in large part on two assumptions: first, that in return for the protection afforded by mercantilist policies the bourgeoisie became either an ally of the monarchy or at least a counterpoise to the nobility; second, that mercantilist policies themselves favoured the development of capitalism. There is no doubt that mercantilism was a key element in the making of French absolutism.[1] France was the country of state intervention *par excellence*. Its monopoly trading companies were state-inspired, state-financed and state-led to a degree unknown in either the Dutch Republic or England. The reinforcement and extension of the guild regime under Colbert were accompanied by a plethora of immensely detailed regulations enforced by a growing number of inspectors. However, if mercantilism strengthened the state, it is not clear that it significantly altered the pace and direction of France's economic development, much of which was simply beyond its power to affect.

Where mercantilist policies did have some effect it is doubtful that this was with the support, or to the benefit, of the bourgeoisie. On the contrary, the autonomy of French towns was one of the most obvious victims of the assertion of monarchical authority. From the settlement imposed on Amiens in 1597 to the forcible remodelling of the constitution of Marseille in 1661 there was a steady erosion of urban independence. Richelieu's ambitious plans for the development of France's maritime capacities were themselves forged in the context of the onslaught on La Rochelle whose economic independence was rightly seen as an obstacle to their implementation. Sustained by a fleet larger than that at the disposition of the government, its merchants were, at best, indifferent to and, at worst, hostile to government trading and colonial ventures. The sweeping away of La Rochelle's ancient privileges after a fourteen-month siege was the most dramatic moment in the extension of royal authority and a clear warning to less well-protected towns. Sometimes the government simply intervened to fix elections. More insidious was the remorseless fiscal pressure which contributed directly to increasingly unmanageable municipal debts.[2] To add insult to injury, the government then used the existence of these debts to justify the direct intervention of its agents. By the end of the century municipal finances were under the surveillance, sometimes close, of the intendants.[3]

By this time the towns, particularly in the north, were no longer under the control of merchants but of officeholders. Despite attempts to limit the practice, the growing number of venal officeholders were well placed to secure election (usually a form of co-option) to municipal bodies, often with royal assistance. Paris led the way.[4] From 1598 to 1715 all the now sadly misnamed *prévots des marchands* or mayors of Paris were either members of the royal council or *parlementaires*. Over the entire century only four Parisian councillors out of 236 were merchants.[5] Even in the commercial capital of Lyon, where the dominant group was undoubtedly its merchants, the wars of the later sixteenth century encouraged a distinct shift towards officeholding. Traditionally, the city council had been drawn from a narrow group of the wealthiest families who, by definition, were merchants, but between 1595 and 1610 twenty-four *échevins* out of forty were officeholders.[6] This process, replicated in one town after another, culminated in the decision of 1692 to transform major municipal offices, including those of mayor, into venal ones.[7] The only group of towns where merchant wealth retained the social and political edge seems to have been the smaller textile towns of the south such as Nîmes and Clermont-de-Lodève. Yet, even here, the attractions of office were not absent and the early eighteenth century saw determined and largely successful attempts to exclude merchant drapers from the first consulship of Clermont which brought access to the Estates-General. This office, it was claimed by the local notables, could only be held by '*gentils-hommes gradués* and bourgeois living nobly as is customary in all the towns of the province'.[8] It is true that the sale of office did enlarge the social foundations of the monarchy. It might even be argued that the flow of commercial money into office had the effect of tying the bourgeoisie to the regime. Yet, even if both these propositions were conceded, it would be necessary to turn officeholders into capitalists in order to sustain the idea that absolute monarchy in some measure depended on a capitalist class.

In any event, mercantilist policies were elaborated without the direct involvement of the commercial world. When Richelieu unfolded his plans in 1626–7 for an economic strategy designed to assert France's role as a major maritime power, it was to an assembly composed of great nobles, upper clergy, and leading magistrates.[9] It was not until the establishment of an advisory *conseil de commerce* in June 1700 that commercial interests in the form of representatives from eleven major cities and Languedoc secured a permanent presence at government level. Even then, together with the two representatives of the Farmers General, their lack of rank and status denied them the right to speak and they were obliged to elaborate their views in separate meetings with the government commissioners.[10] At the same time a dozen major trading centres were asked to establish chambers of commerce like those at Dunkirk and Marseille. Six responded by the time of the death of Louis XIV; La Rochelle, which was beset by squabbles over precedence and rank, did not do so until 1719, Bayonne in 1726, whilst Nantes and St Malo never did. Two towns – Lyon and Montpellier – not included in the plans did, however, set up such chambers.[11] This was fairly typical of mercantile reaction to government initiatives over the years. Efforts to involve merchants in trading companies had long met with a mixture of indifference and hostility. Colbert was obliged to find much of the finance for his companies amongst the court aristocracy and great financiers. Almost all the Parisian directors of the EIC were financiers rather than merchants despite the dispositions of its charter.[12] The lack of commitment amongst the merchant community to such companies certainly helps to explain why many, including those established by Colbert, were short-lived.

A major problem with the trading companies was their privileged character which was bound to irritate those who were excluded. Yet objections to them rarely went beyond sectarian resentment and there were few signs before the end of the century of a generalised opposition to the principle of state regulation as such. Herein lay a much deeper problem: the still highly localised basis of mercantile activity and the accompanying myopic attachment to particular interests. This was most plainly revealed in the contradictory and frequently hostile reactions to attempts to reduce the plethora of internal tolls and bring the customs boundaries into line with the frontiers of the realm. Nothing could have done more, as the proponents of a single export and import duty well understood, to achieve the triple objectives of stimulating inter-regional trade, lowering the cost of French goods on the international market and restricting imports of foreign manufactures.[13] Colbert managed to reduce the nineteen different tolls on the periphery of the *cinq grosses fermes* to one import and one export duty but that was the limit of his success. When the pressure for reform resurfaced in the *conseil de commerce*, with considerable backing from most of the deputies of trade, those from the Atlantic ports of Nantes, St Malo, Bordeaux and La Rochelle made it clear that their ports were determined to retain their privileges as *provinces reputées étrangères* outside the major custom boundaries. Similar anxieties led to cries of protest from the merchants of Lille and other northern towns. In 1703 they complained that the new tariff drawn up between France and Spanish Flanders meant that it would now be easier for foreigners to trade with France than for them. Strenuous objections came also from Hainault about the punitive duties imposed on the import and export of iron. The forge masters of Berry and the Nivernais, on the other hand, were equally vociferous in opposing any reduction of tariffs which would expose them to foreign competition.[14] In 1707 the deputies from Marseille and Bordeaux virtually came to blows over the tax concession enjoyed by the latter on its refined sugar.[15] Such lack of unity amongst the merchant deputies played straight into the hands of the Company of Farmers General which, as the lessee of all the major indirect taxes (*gabelle, traités, domaine* and *cinq grosses fermes*), was the real beneficiary of Colbert's limited rationalisation. In 1701 their opposition to proposals to reduce or abolish export and internal duties on six basic kinds of manufactures, including linens and cotton cloths, was sufficient to achieve its emasculation within a year.[16] Despite a growing litany of complaints from merchants about the bureaucratic and costly inconveniences involved in complying with tariff regulations, the network of tolls and tariffs largely endured until the Revolution. The merchant interest was never influential nor united enough to carry the day even when reform-minded officials led the way.[17]

The immaturity of the bourgeoisie notwithstanding, it might still be supposed that state policies were conducive to the growth of capitalism. Unfortunately, it is not possible to conduct the sort of controlled experiment required to calculate the difference made by government initiatives to economic development. Colbert came to power precisely at the moment when two of the three key sectors of the economy – agriculture and textile manufacture – were coping with a depression from which they were not to emerge for several decades. There is no way of knowing whether its effects were mitigated by Colbertian policies; but it was certainly not prevented. On the other hand, maritime trade continued to expand albeit it did so more hesitantly than during the preceding hundred years.[18] This was true even of Marseille, despite the ill effects of the deep economic crisis to which Spain and northern Italy succumbed and the depression which overtook the Languedocian cloth industry from the 1650s. Not only did trade with the Levant recover spectacularly in the 1690s but the Marseillais widened their economic horizons to embrace the Antilles in a significant way for the first time.[19] The power of the Atlantic economy can similarly be illustrated by the recovery of La Rochelle after the siege of 1627–8 which had reduced it to a quarter of its original size and ended its exemption from taxation. Despite the fact that the years of the Fronde were for Saintonge and Aunis years of scarcity, volatile food prices, famine and epidemics, La Rochelle's population recovered and its trade surpassed former levels. Largely as a result of the West Indian trade, shipping tonnage tripled between 1664 and 1682.[20] The figures from Bordeaux were equally positive: tonnage rose from 1,115 in 1672 to 1,919 in 1682.[21] What is particularly remarkable is that the wars of Louis XIV did not permanently reverse the upward trend.[22] The late 1680s and 1690s certainly witnessed a reduction in activity but the speed of recovery appears to have been rapid. In the years of peace between 1697 and 1701 Bordeaux dispatched a record tonnage to the New World and its wine exports, which had collapsed, also reached new heights.[23] The banking city of Lyon and the privateering port of St Malo may even have benefited from the wars.[24] During the War of Spanish Succession the Malouins, unable to maintain their trade with Cadiz, began to dispatch vessels directly to the Spanish Americas with highly profitable results.[25] French commercial activity, it has been said, followed much the same trajectory, albeit at a lower level, as that of the Dutch.[26]

This observation suggests that it is probably wiser to attribute the relative buoyancy of France's overseas trade to the power of the sea rather than to the efficacy of government intervention. True, there were moments at which it could help. Sugar refining, which had earlier succumbed to a lack of capital and expertise, certainly benefited from Colbert's endeavours; refineries appeared in Rouen, Nantes and Bordeaux from the mid-1660s and by 1683 France possessed a total of twenty-nine.[27] On the other hand, there were moments when success was achieved despite rather than because of government policy. Indeed, the ineffectiveness of government prescriptions may help to explain the limited effects of the long years of war. Attempts to impose embargoes on trade with France's enemies were persistently ignored. From the Bordelais came strident complaints that they could not sell all their wines and brandy without Dutch shippers.[28] It is difficult to see how such prohibitions could have succeeded given the fact that the tax farmers of the *gabelles*, the directors of the Asiento Company and the tobacco company, not to mention naval arsenals, were all, in some measure, dependent on Dutch ships and supplies. In 1708 404 passports were issued to the Dutch.[29]

The contrast between the performance of the maritime and domestic sectors of economic activity is a pointed reminder of the fact that there was no such thing as the French economy; only a number of regional ones and, within these, many local ones. These developed at variable rhythms which were only marginally affected by government policies. Virtually all of the really big French towns and the ones that grew fastest were 'scattered', as Jean Meyer observed, 'around the edges: Nantes, Bordeaux, Marseille, Toulon, Grenoble, Lyon, Strasbourg, Lille'.[30] As much under the pull of foreign trade as of domestic trade these centres drew entire regions into different economic networks which were, moreover, frequently controlled by others. Up to 1600 and possibly beyond, Lyon's import trade was dominated by Italian merchants. But, apart from booksellers and linen merchants, the Lyonnais largely failed to transplant themselves outside the realm.[31] Despite its presence at the heart of the great grain-growing region of the south, which constantly produced an exportable surplus, Toulouse barely boasted a single independent grain merchant. 'The entire Toulousain economy', it has been observed, 'was a prisoner of the Mediterranean grain market over which it had no control.'[32] Similarly, export of the higher-quality cloth produced at Carcassonne, Clermont-de-Lodève and the smaller textile centres of Bas-Languedoc, whose produce was hugely dependent on the Levant trade, was conducted through Marseille. However, although the influence of the merchants of Marseille reached Toulouse and Lyon it faded out beyond.[33] Montauban, only a day's ride north of Toulouse, was increasingly drawn into the orbit of Bordeaux, tripling its exports of flour to Canada between 1700 and 1763.[34] The natural markets of the western ports themselves also lay overseas rather than at home. This was particularly true for St Malo and La Rochelle which were without easy fluvial access to their hinterlands and in case of La Rochelle dependent on one dry land route across the salt marshes from which so much of its wealth had flowed.[35] Of 175 Rochelais merchants active in the period 1640–80, fifty-five were of foreign origin; of the remainder only seventeen came to the French interior.[36] Even for the less isolated merchants of Bordeaux and Nantes, the hazards of upstream navigation and a multiplicity of river tolls enhanced the attractions of maritime trade which became the foundation of their prosperity.

The unintegrated nature of French economic life was evident in the regional disparities in the way long-term trends unfolded as the rise in population, prices and land rents of the long sixteenth century ebbed away. Prices peaked earlier in the south than the north: in the 1590s in Provence, 1603 in Languedoc, but not until the 1630s in Beauvais, even later in the Ile-de-France.[37] Grain prices on the Toulouse and Paris markets also fluctuated to significantly different rhythms, confirming the effects of the space that separated them.[38] Nor was there any national pattern to the repeated subsistence crises which afflicted the French population. That of 1628, ushered in by the plague which devastated parts of the south, largely spared the Paris basin, Normandy, Brittany and the north-east. The subsistence crisis engendered by the Fronde did not extend to Brittany, Normandy, Languedoc or Provence.[39] That of 1661 largely spared the east, the south-east and lower Brittany; whereas the price of grain rose by no less than 116 per cent in the Paris region, at Toulouse the rise was a relatively modest 20.[40] Frêche notes that there was not a bad harvest from Provence to Aquitaine.[41]

Two major provinces stand outside the patterns followed in either north or south. One was Provence, where despite some acute cyclical movements in grain prices, population and production continued to progress, pushing the onset of depression back to 1700, if not to the end of Louis' reign. A decline in the birthrate is detectable from 1660 but it was not reflected in a significant drop in the population until the end of the century and there was certainly no sign of the collapse of agricultural revenues which overwhelmed Languedoc in the 1670s.[42] The other province which entirely escaped the acute demographic crises was Brittany. This was particularly striking given the high density of the population which, at fifty-three inhabitants per kilometre, rivalled that of the Low Countries. Moreover, there were only two years in the period from 1599 to 1624 when the province was completely free of plague and in 1639 it was struck by a wave of dysentery. Yet, of 108 parishes studied by Alain Croix, only eight declined in size between 1550 and 1660 and the overall population rose steadily before finally entering a period of relative stagnation. The net loss of 20 to 30 per cent suffered by communities of the Parisian countryside over the same period makes a remarkable contrast.[43]

None of the major provinces was homogeneous. Upper and Lower Languedoc, for instance, had virtually nothing in common. The one was overwhelmingly devoted to wheat of which it regularly produced a surplus; the other, constantly faced with a grain shortage, depended on the vine, the olive, the production of cloth and even the chestnut. The latter bestowed a highly particular character on those villages on the southern flank of the Cévennes where it was the principal source of revenue.[44] Whilst Lower Brittany was 'full of towns', harbouring 44 per cent of the province's urban population, Upper Brittany claimed less than a third.[45] Even more striking, despite the production of rural linens for export, was the physical and social gulf between the 'landlocked and Breton speaking world' of the interior and 'the commercial civilisation of the coast looking out to the ports of the Bay of Biscay, Spain, Portugal, the North Sea and the Baltic'.[46] In Normandy the relatively prosperous Carentan, with its dispersed villages much devoted to cattle-rearing, had little in common with the marshy lands of the Caennais coast and their high mortality rates; the *petit caux*, an area of rural textile production, was different yet again.[47] Even the Beauvaisis, where cereal cultivation was indisputably triumphant, was not without some local variety. For in the south the *pays de Bray*, blessed by river and streams, offered some rich meadowland which meant that it was noticeably better endowed with cattle than the endless arable zones to the north.[48]

Such diversity offered considerable potential for the growth of a lively regional and inter-regional trade. Unfortunately the natural, institutional and political obstacles to the development of internal trade were considerable. Perhaps nothing short of the advent of the railway could have overcome some of them. But such efforts as were made to improve the commercial capacity of the transport system either by central or local government were manifestly inadequate. It seems clear that the state of the roads barely improved over the course of the seventeenth century, despite the concern of some government officials. Horror stories were legion. In 1683 the coachmen of Beauvais drew the attention of the intendant to the impassable state of the road to Paris which could not be taken 'without loss of their horses and without risk to their lives'.[49] Even a hundred years later the road from the nearby château of Crillon was so bad that it proved easier to move a statue of Louis XIV across the fields.[50] Around 1700, the Dauphiné, despite its strategic position between Lyon and northern Italy, was endowed with only three adequate highways whilst local routes were no more than tracks; the entire province boasted only three stone bridges.[51] If Languedoc's long-distance communications were immensely improved by the completion of the *canal du Midi* in 1681, this triumph of engineering threw into sharp relief the inadequacy of the secondary routes such as that from Toulouse to Albi. Not until 1776 did Albi acquire its much-needed bridge over the Tarn. Traffic from Lyon took the long route around – down the Rhône valley, across the coastal plain of Languedoc, and up the canal to Toulouse. The smaller roads of the Toulousain had to wait even longer for systematic attention.[52]

Land transport was slow and expensive. At the end of the sixteenth century land transport moved at a rate of thirty to forty kilometres a day and there is no reason to suppose that times were significantly reduced during the course of the next hundred years.[53] Water transport was generally faster and cheaper. Nothing illustrates this better than the dramatic lowering of transport costs achieved by the *canal du Midi*. In the second half of the eighteenth century it was still seven times cheaper to take goods by canal from Narbonne to Toulouse than it had been by land prior to 1681.[54] Unfortunately, apart from the Briare canal which joined the Seine and the Loire in 1642, few of the other major projects for building canals or developing river transport had reached fruition by 1700. Most of Vauban's proposals for the improvement of navigation in the Lille region were not implemented for over a century; the Deule was navigable above and below the regional capital but not through it.[55] Of the major rivers, the Loire was the most used but it was impassable during the summer months and could be highly dangerous in winter. It was so unnavigable in its upper reaches that the rich coal mines of St Etienne were unable to ship their output to any of the glassmaking factories built along its banks.[56] For the considerable volume of traffic in transit between the Rhône and the Loire there was no way of avoiding the heroic struggle by land over the *col des sauvages* which marks the watershed between the two river systems.[57] Moreover, although it was possible to travel downstream at speeds much in excess of those over land, navigating against the current was another matter. Whilst it was not unknown to travel ninety kilometres a day descending the Rhône, boats going up the Saône, for example, were reduced to twenty-five.[58] Smaller rivers could prove even slower. It took no fewer than ten to twelve days to reach Rennes by river from La Roche Bernard during the six months of the year when the river was in fact open.[59]

If the authorities made little progress in eliminating the physical obstacles to the development of domestic trade, they seemed utterly powerless to deal with those created by seigneurial privilege. Whilst navigable rivers were part of the royal *domaine*, many concessions had been granted to seigneurs in relation to fishing, mills and ferries.[60] At Beauvais proposals for the development of the river Thérain met with strenuous opposition from the canons who owned the forty or so water mills from Beauvais to Creil which were a lucrative source of revenue.[61] There was a similar problem at Amiens, compounded by the bishop's imposition of a transit tax, as well as a boatmen's monopoly which the merchants did not succeed in breaking until 1724.[62]

Whether goods travelled by road or water, transport costs accounted for a large part of market prices. Those of grain carried from Amiens to Arras increased by 40 per cent.[63] That of coal arriving in Bordeaux from the mines of Carmaux and Quercy was doubled, as was that making the much shorter journey from the mines at Litry near Caen to Cherbourg.[64] Although Braudel may be right to suggest that toll charges were not the critical impediment to commercial activity, their weight and frequency, not to mention the paperwork they generated, certainly did not encourage it.[65] A boatload of cask staves incurred thirty-eight different levies at twenty-two different points on the trip from Lorraine to Sète in Languedoc.[66] Almost half the retail price of brandy exported via the river Charente and La Rochelle in 1730 was accounted for by tolls and taxes paid *en route*.[67] In 1749 a barrel of wine worth thirty-six *livres* dispatched from Toulouse by river and sea to Paris was sold in the capital for 500 *livres*, yet the owner still made a loss.[68] Given the need to surmount so many barriers to the development of the domestic market, the failure to achieve tariff reform was a costly one.

Despite all the factors conspiring against an easy development of commercial activity, local autarky was far from absolute. An estimated half of the agricultural produce of south-western France was finding its way on to the market by the eighteenth century.[69] Although much of this did not move far from its place of origin, some passed via the local fairs on to regional and national networks. It has been said that in Brittany, which could boast 500 fairs a year, there was not a single parish which did not export either grain or cattle.[70] Even in a less accessible region such as Lower Languedoc 'superior tinkers' were able to sustain a lively local market which met up with international trade at the fairs of Pézenas, Montagnac and even Beaucaire.[71] The pull of the Parisian market could be felt at some distance. In the 1670s the timing of the weekly cattle market at Neubourg in Normandy became a matter of urgent debate after Colbert established a market at Sceaux on a day which threatened to make it impossible for the local merchants to get their beasts there in time.[72] The growing reputation of the wines of the Beaujolais amongst a diverse Parisian clientele was reflected from the 1660s in the expansion of the *vignoble* and the increasing subordination of the *vignerons* to the demands of the merchants and their agents.[73]

Most important for the integration of local, regional and international commercial networks was the trade in textiles. By mid-century, for instance, Beauvais' most substantial merchant house was selling two-thirds of its linen cloth at Paris and Lyon – destinations which had not figured in the business of earlier merchants. Some part of this also found its way abroad.[74] Further expansion followed so that by the 1690s a third of the produce was going to Bordeaux, Toulouse and the towns of the Mediterranean basin, compared with the eighth which was sold on the local market.[75] Jean Pocquelin traded in goods from Rouen, Amiens, St Quentin and Paris, speculated in grain, wood, land and had debtors spread through 134 communities of the Beauvaisis. Three other members of the same family left for Paris where they became extremely successful, appeared in the entourage of Colbert and were associated with such major enterprises as the West Indian Company and the Glass Company.[76] Similarly, the family firm of *marchands-droguistes* headed by Jacques Galtié at Clermont-de-Lodève established a presence at Lyon where their cloth was dyed and finished; they also enjoyed reciprocal trade connections with Provence and the Mediterranean. An agent in Lyon acted as banker, also making regular trips to the cloth-making centres of northern France and the Low Countries.[77] However, it cannot be too strongly emphasised in the context of this assessment that the success of such merchant capitalists owed almost nothing to government intervention. On the contrary, their own perseverance and resourcefulness were at a premium.

It is also clear that they constituted a tiny elite. Most people described as merchants were in fact small retailers or shopkeepers. At La Rochelle the primary function of those who acquired *bourgeois* privileges was to act as middlemen; four-fifths of them in the years prior to the siege were *boutiquiers* involved in retail trade in the town.[78] In 1688 the 285 'merchants' of the medium-sized, albeit sleepy, Norman town of Bayeux consisted mostly of bakers, butchers, mercers, and other shopkeepers.[79] The term *négociant* used to describe wholesale merchants did not enter general usage until the second half of the century and in most towns, even those of some size, they long remained a tiny group. Despite the discernible development of their overseas markets, the majority of Beauvais merchants still limited their business essentially to the Paris basin up to 1730; perhaps twelve out of a hundred had overseas connections.[80] Vannes, the biggest town on the southern coast of Brittany with a population of about 12,000 in 1704, boasted ninety-five merchants of 'some importance'.[81] This proportion was not much different at Amiens, the major textile centre and regional capital of Picardy, with a population in the region of 35,000. The tax rolls for 1722 denote 138 merchants, probably a slight underestimate.[82] A major administrative capital like Aix-en-Provence, with a population of 29,000 in 1698, boasted only fifty-eight merchants and just three *négociants*.[83]

The organisation of commercial enterprises remained rudimentary. Those of any significance were invariably family affairs. Joint stock companies were not mentioned in the commercial ordinance of 1673. Although limited partnerships, in which investors could participate without assuming liability for the full debt, were recognised, these were much less common than the simple partnerships, in which all associates were jointly and severally responsible.[84] The difference between formal partnerships of this sort and family partnerships was far from clear. The latter were often a means of facilitating the entrance of sons and relatives into the family business. Both were flexible forms of organisation which through 'habit, kinship and friendship, and mutual benefit lent structure and permanence to relationships that superficially appeared to be unstructured and highly fluid'.[85] These advantages notwithstanding, associations were frequently of very short duration. Families moved through a series of such arrangements in the course of their lives. Permanent merchant dynasties were few. Less than a sixth of the principal merchant families in Amiens during the reign of Louis XIII survived to the end of that of Louis XIV.[86] Of the twenty-two Rochelais families active at one time or another during the course of the eighteenth century only six traded for more than fifty years.[87] Fixed assets were therefore few and considerable amounts of cash constantly lay idle. Even so, merchants frequently settled their debts by direct exchange of commodities. In part this was because of the lack of both paper money and an adequate banking system. But even letters of exchange were not used routinely by Beauvais merchants until the 1680s.[88]

It is is necessary to turn to textile manufacture in order to detect any measurable movement towards the concentration of either capital or the production process. In Amiens, by the 1690s, eleven merchants accounted for two-thirds of the finished cloths; their grip on the finishing processes was complete and it must be presumed that a number of them also controlled the previous stages of production. Soon less than a sixth of the masters owned over 40 per cent of the equipment.[89] Similar tendencies were also clearly visible at Sedan, at Elbouef and in the Languedocian town of Clermont-de-Lodève.[90] Here by 1732 twenty-two clothiers, mostly of merchant origin, more or less controlled the town's entire output. With fourteen or fifteen looms each, they employed an average of 300 people, depriving other industries such as hat-making of labour and causing widespread abandonment of landholdings in the neighbouring countryside. The seven dye houses were all owned by clothiers and leased to specialist master dyers.[91] During periods of prosperity there were a thousand or more textile workers in Amiens sustaining the activity of 2,000 looms. In Reims in 1692–3 there were 1,200 looms, over 700 at Caen, nearly 600 at Rouen and 500 at Beauvais.[92]

None the less, despite the visible signs of an incipient concentration of production, even in major textile centres the demarcation of each stage in textile manufacture was still clear. Combing, spinning, weaving, fulling, dying, finishing were all distinct stages and rarely brought together, each being executed by the appropriate master craftsmen and his *compagnons*. Those who sought to strengthen their position by integrating them provoked the same sort of objections as were aroused by the attempts of the producers to trade on their own account.[93] Moreover, in the generally depressed conditions between 1650 and the recovery of the eighteenth century, it seems that small producers were likely to fare better than larger ones. At Clermont, Thomson observed a return to the small-scale production of low-quality cloth which required minimal investment. Best equipped to survive in times of difficulty were the artisanal, family-based units which could utilise their own labour and sustain themselves from their own plots of land. Evidence from Beauvais and Amiens points in the same direction. In Amiens the emergence of a substantial number of masters with more than six looms was matched by a significant increase in the proportion of those possessing only one.[94]

It must also be stressed that, despite some concentration in major urban centres, textile production continued to depend enormously on the putting-out system. Goubert estimates that in Picardy the 5,500 rural workers outnumbered their urban counterparts by two to one.[95] Linen production occupied thousands of rural spinners in Picardy, Normandy, Brittany, Dauphiné and parts of the Lyonnais. Escaping the grip of the guild regulations, rural textile production was sometimes sufficiently threatening to arouse the ire of urban producers.[96] However, although the potential labour force was almost limitless, rural manufacture was frequently characterised by a low level of economic and physical concentration with one or two looms per household. These invariably lay idle during the harvest season.[97]

Even in iron and glass manufacture, where it might be imagined that the nature of the processes lent themselves to a greater concentration of both capital and labour, production remained overwhelmingly artisanal. Although the iron industry was able to take advantage of the reservoir of rural labour, this was a largely casual labour force of carters, miners and charcoal burners. A typical forge, employing three or four hundred people, would have perhaps ten skilled or semi-skilled workers amongst them.[98] Dark bottle plants employed between twenty-five and thirty-five people, ordinary glass production somewhat less. Many of those involved also worked in agricultural employment or were involved in the sale of wood. The smaller glass-making enterprises were frequently headed by rural nobles who displayed, says Scoville, little sign of capitalist rationality or knowledge of such techniques as double entry bookkeeping. The bigger firms were simple partnerships which ran for between six and fifteen years; this also applied to the giant amongst them, the Royal Plate Glass Company, which had thirteen partners in 1702. There were no joint stock companies. Additional capital could only come from new partners or borrowing.[99]

The capacity of the government to step up the pace of economic development was strictly limited. However, it is certainly possible to find some individual success stories. Sugar refining has already been mentioned. As far as textiles were concerned, state-sponsored and protected factories, notably those at Abbeville, Les Andelys in Normandy and Villeneuvette just outside Clermont-de-Lodève, survived and prospered, notwithstanding financial crises and the opposition of the less favoured. Even the strongly Protestant town of Montauban felt the benefits of Colbert's interest in the textile industry.[100] The military requirements of the state also gave a fillip to the developing iron industry. Le Creusot, Europe's largest munitions producer, founded in 1780, had its roots in the reign of Louis XIV.[101]

Yet, even in areas of apparent success, the effects of government intervention were always ambiguous and sometimes negative. Take, for instance, the Royal Plate Glass Company which by 1757 was producing half the world's plate glass. Without state support it would probably have succumbed to the acute liquidity crisis of 1702. But in order to protect its position, direct competitors, including Bernard Perrot who in all probability was the inventor of the glass-casting process, were refused production rights. Even the Parisian mirror merchants were forced into a protracted struggle to preserve their interests in the sale of glassware. This ended in an illuminating compromise by which they were allowed to polish small squares of glass provided that these were bought from the Royal Company; they also preserved their monopoly over the sale of silver mirrors to individuals in Paris whilst the Company retained the right to supply the king, provincial merchants and foreign purchasers. Although there was theoretically a free market in other glass products, manufacturers were not allowed to engage in retail selling which would have trespassed on the rights of a strikingly large number of guilds: notably opticians, glaziers and mirror, glass and pottery merchants.[102]

The negative aspects of the state's *dirigiste* policies are particularly well illustrated by the introduction of exclusive textile corporations to Languedoc. Here the net result was to encourage the tendency of entrepreneurs to transform themselves into merchants, landowners and *rentiers*. As Clermont's textile production emerged from the worst difficulties of the late seventeenth century another generation of substantial clothiers once again began to detach themselves from the smaller producers. In 1708 a new corporation was established and the mastership fee raised from a mere six *livres* to a whacking 450; apprenticeships were abolished for the sons of masters. The emergence of a protected elite of clothiers was reinforced by the government's decision to restrict the production of high-quality cloth to Clermont, Carcassonne and St Chinian. Enforcement of the regulations was the responsibility of Languedoc's inspectorate which grew from two to five by 1714. The apotheosis of state intervention was not finally reached until 1741 when annual production quotas were assigned to the various clothiers on the basis of the quality of their cloth. An attempt was also made to direct the labour force in accordance with the quotas. In these circumstances it was not surprising that successful clothiers became not only managers, as the size of their enterprises now required, but also manipulators of officialdom intent on exploiting their protected position to make easy profits. None of this sufficed to ensure the survival of the Languedocian cloth industry which, after the dismantling of the protective regime in 1754, proved unable to compete with England's relatively capital-intensive and technically advanced textile industry.[103]

Some of those who were encouraged by state patronage to invest in iron production seem to have been motivated less by the desire to develop a technically efficient industry than by the benefits of their monopoly position as suppliers of the state. This is nicely illustrated by the society founded in 1657 in Dauphiné by a number of forge masters and some merchants of Lyon. Although they brought together 100,000 *livres* of capital, the partners decided to shut down eleven of the sixty-eight forges and to limit the work of the remainder to nine months a year.[104] In a situation in which peasants were still using wooden hand tools and their ploughs were frequently constructed with wooden socks there was no more eloquent testimony to the structural weaknesses of the French economy.[105] The point is reinforced by the contrast between the success of the Plate Glass Company and the languishing state of ordinary glass and bottle production which, by comparison, needed only modest capital investment. Despite evidence of a slow recovery in north-eastern regions, traditional areas of glass production such as Normandy and Languedoc continued to stagnate if not decline into the eighteenth century. Glass windows were only found in the homes of the well-to-do whilst most wine, brandy and mineral water was exported in kegs rather than bottles.[106]

It was precisely the inflexible nature of the market which sustained the attachment of both state officials and producers to corporate and exclusive forms of organisation. State intervention was rooted in the fear that French goods, particularly textiles, were unable to compete, even on the domestic market, with those of their foreign rivals. The perceived solution was to raise quality through state control and direction. From the point of view of smaller producers and merchants, guilds were equally essential in order to preserve their share of a limited market and to prevent an excessive concentration of output in the hands of the wealthy. The introduction of guilds, therefore, did not necessarily require the helping hand of the state. There were already seventy-two in Rouen by the mid-sixteenth century.[107] At La Rochelle between 1580 and 1601, a period when it was totally outside government control, their number rose through the efforts of the *corps de ville* from twelve to twenty.[108] During the next hundred years attitudes seem to have changed little. Concern about illegal competition was expressed by the town's wheelwrights in 1704, cloth merchants in 1708, and pottery ware dealers in 1710.[109] Even the municipality of Lyon, a city traditionally free of guilds, was subject at moments of economic difficulty to intense pressure from a range of small producers and retailers (saddlers, needle-makers, locksmiths, cobblers, hatters, card-makers, and others) for the establishment of *jurandes*; these, it was hoped, by requirinq a formal apprenticeship, an entry fee or the production of a *chef d'œuvre* would reduce competition.[110] In response to the depressed conditions of the second half of the seventeenth century there was a tendency for guilds to become highly exclusive with a rising proportion of masterships going to the sons of masters.[111] In some towns there was also a renewal of municipal legislation limiting the number of looms to be operated by one producer; the authorities at both Amiens and Lille were still insisting – not always to great effect – on a maximum of six as the eighteenth century dawned.[112]

Larger merchants were more likely to find guild organisation both unnecessary and irksome. In Lyon the principal merchants remained strongly opposed to it.[113] On the other hand, corporate regulations provided a useful mechanism for maintaining the domination of masters over artisans and of merchant interests over those of the small producers. Sometimes this was blatant. In 1708 the most important of the cloth merchants of Amiens came together with some of the *mercier-épiciers* to form a corporation of fifteen *marchands négociants*.[114] Its statutes specifically forbade manufacturers to buy from other manufacturers; they were entitled to sell only their own produce.[115] Even in Lyon merchant attitudes were pragmatic rather than principled as their opposition to guilds coexisted rather uncomfortably with a determined defence of their own extensive privileges.[116] Silk production took root there precisely because of Lyon's monopoly of raw silk imports from Italy.[117]

Much of the mercantilist strategy adopted by the French government can be construed as a compensation for relative economic weakness rather than as an expression of strength; under pressure from its major rivals, faced with a commercial community that was often unresponsive and limited possibilities for rapid economic growth, the state was constrained to intervene. The policies adopted, however, failed to address the underlying problem of raising the level of domestic demand. It was not that goverment officials did not have some appreciation of the need to stimulate consumption. A prime objective was to retain and increase the amount of money in circulation by a combination of bullionist and protectionist measures. Unfortunately, this approach led to an almost exclusive concern with the production of high-quality cloth capable of competing in the export markets.[118] Production for the domestic market was sometimes sacrificed to this end. When the government limited the production of fine cloth to three Languedocian towns it actually forbade them to produce cheaper material. The inevitable consequence of such a policy was to accentuate the divide between the major textile centres, producing relatively limited quantities of quality cloth for export, and the smaller and largely rural producers who supplied local and regional markets with heavier and less well finished cloths. By the beginning of the eighteenth century Sedan, Elbouef, Abbeville and Carcassonne were producing a seventh of the total value of wool fabrics.[119] Languedoc accounted for half of the value but only one-sixth of the volume of national production.[120] Carcassonne alone produced half the province's quality cloth. The Cévennes and the Gévaudan, on the other hand, accounted for 60 per cent of its output but only a third of its value.[121] At Montauban, where in 1700 the production of broad cloths had been minimal, production increased eightfold by 1764, almost entirely squeezing out the traditional production of cheaper *droguets, burats* and *serges*.[122] Nîmes did continue to produce cloth for the home market but its real speciality was silks, socks and stockings; at the beginning of the eighteenth century 240,000 pairs of stockings were being produced largely for export, whilst the people of Languedoc rarely saw them.[123] In Normandy the picture was similar. Quality production was overwhelmingly concentrated on the estuary of the Seine, notably at Elbouef. Here the average value of each producer's output was over 70,000 *livres* compared with 12,500 for the *généralité* as a whole.[124]

Outside the major textile centres the regions of central France constituted 'a vast zone of mediocre or average wool manufacture' stretching from Paris to Nîmes.[125] Because much of this escaped the control of the guild and municipal authorities and was of little concern to the inspectors, a precise assessment of its economic significance is impossible. Not until the 1760s was rural production subject to official control and even then the amount of evasion remained considerable.[126] Markovitch thought that peasants used a fifth of their wool themselves but this can be no more than an estimate.[127] Given the nature of the records, the sort of highly quantitative analysis which he offers can only encompass the production of quality cloth largely destined for overseas markets.[128] Unfortunately, far from inducing a certain caution about their general economic significance Markovitch used the resulting figures to assert that the textile industry made a central contribution to France's position as the 'first industrial power in the world'. Such hyperbole reflects not simply an uncritical reliance on available records but an unqualified acceptance of the assumptions lying behind the Colbertian policies which generated them. Fundamental to these was the idea that the key to progress lay first and foremost in the battle for the foreign markets.

Now there is little doubt that France's long-term failure to compete successfully with the Dutch and the English in the export markets had serious consequences. It was indeed a factor in the renewed depression of the mid-eighteenth century and the deindustrialisation of Languedoc. The dependence of some of France's major textile centres on overseas markets made them exceedingly vulnerable. Foreign markets were prone to debilitating short-term fluctuations and, as Thomson points out, combined a slow turnover of circulating capital with heavy investment.[129] What French officials did not grasp was the fact that it was precisely this instability that made the domestic market the key to sustained growth. Interestingly enough a survey of Languedoc's trade, conducted by the intendant in 1698, showed how much, even in relatively depressed times, it depended on domestic outlets (see Table 2.1). Local sales in which grain and textiles were the two key commodities yielded over twice as much as exports.[130] Nor did the potential for further expansion go unremarked. An investigation into the Carcassonne industry in 1708 found that in the town there were 386 weavers with an additional 240 in the villages and hamlets of the nearby mountains; these would have been capable of producing 20,000 pieces a year if they could have been employed all the time.[131] The essential and unresolved problem was to unlock the potential labour force and simultaneously enhance the purchasing power of those involved.

The profound structural imbalances in the French economy cannot of course be directly attributed to specific economic policies. If the preoccupation with the export trade was unhelpful it does not, of itself, explain the lack of domestic demand. On the other hand, the general burdens imposed on the economy by the state were deeply damaging and, indeed, inconsistent with mercantilist policies. Protectionist and regulatory

Table 2.1 Value of Languedoc's local sales and exports in 1698 (in *livres*)

	Local sales	*Exports*
Grain	1,160,000	40,000
Wine		830,000
Eaux de vie		440,000
Silk	300,000	1,500,000
Leather	958,000	1,180,000
Textiles	12,875,000	1,985,000
Livestock	400,000	600,000
Fish	40,000	60,000
Other	2,860,000	1,440,000
Total	18,593,000	8,075,000

Source: Tilly 1986: 166

measures themselves all too easily degenerated into fiscal devices.[132] More critically, the financial requirements of the state led to a proliferation of venal office which constituted a permanent and immeasurable drain on the real economy. In town after town the wealth of merchants was outshone both collectively and individually by that of the officeholders. This was true not only of a great *parlementaire* city with a limited entrepreneurial culture such as Toulouse but also of a textile centre like Amiens which had no *parlement*. Analysis of tax impositions, marriage contracts and *inventaires après décès* from this city shows the superior levels of wealth that were attained by officers in the *élection*, *bailliage*, *présidial*, and even the *gabelle*. At the pinnacle of this elite were the *trésoriers de France* who left successions of upwards from 100,000 *livres* to over 200,000 in one case. Whilst it was not unknown for a few merchants to reach comparable levels, a majority of wholesalers left between 50,000 and 100,000 *livres*, putting them on a par with the officers of the *bailliage*.[133] Even in Bordeaux, where some colossal fortunes were to be made in the colonies, the social hierarchy in the early eighteenth century was headed by an array of financial officers, *parlementaires* and bankers, followed by the *négociants* in *toiles* and *dentelles* and then the smaller merchants.[134]

A significant element of the modest urban expansion of the seventeenth century particularly in cities with major law courts like Rennes, Dijon and Aix can thus be attributed to the growth in officeholding. As a result there may have been a certain quickening of demand for luxury articles. At Dijon cobblers, pastrycooks, leather workers, carpenters, tombstone carvers, wigmakers, pottery makers, carriagemakers, producers of combs, umbrellas and mustard and those in wine-related occupations all benefited from the presence of a well-to-do urban elite.[135]

On the other hand, sale of office accentuated the ephemeral quality of commercial capital, diverting it into usurious and *rentier* investments. The case of Master Serpe of Beauvais, who in 1645 discarded four of his five looms in order to concentrate on long-distance trade, is instructive. He also bought six houses valued at 15,000 *livres* in which he installed some textile workers as tenants. He began lending money to other merchants and bourgeois. His descendants became landowners, office-holders and *rentiers* and were styled *écuyers*.[136] Such transformations, of which there are countless exemplars, represented not just the forsaking of productive activity but a growth in the ranks of the tax-exempt. Between 1556 and 1643 the population of Dijon grew by 50 per cent; but the numbers of tax-exempt laity rose by nearly four times as much.[137] The obvious corollary was that the rising burden fell disproportionately on those who continued to engage in productive activity, many of whom hovered constantly on the brink of dire poverty.

Estimates of the proportion of poor in the urban population vary from between a fifth to a half depending on the criteria employed.[138] Those in receipt of public charity or registered as beggars with the municipal authorities undoubtedly represented only a proportion of those in need. Gascon estimated that in Lyon, in seventy-four of the years between 1475 and 1599, casual building labourers were below the poverty line; for twenty-five of those years semi-skilled labourers were in the same position.[139] Farr reckons that the wives of nearly all the journeymen of Dijon would have had to earn as much as their husbands in order to balance the family budget; in bad years even master craftsmen came perilously close to the poverty line.[140]

Most journeyman, humble craftsmen and textile and agricultural workers were paid less than ten *sols* per day. Assuming that the number of days worked might range from 200 to 270 and making some allowance for additional sources of family income, it is clear that, in common with the majority of peasants, labourers and artisans had annual net incomes of below 200 *livres*, frequently much less. A tiny minority of skilled workers in the major cities, notably carpenters and master masons or those engaged in luxury trades, could earn somewhat more; Parisian print workers received as much as 400 *livres*, comparable to the emoluments of a rural *curé*, and an income which, provided it was sustained, enabled them to think about other things than ensuring their daily bread.[141]

Not only were wages low but they were largely paid in inferior coin. Riots precipitated by the refusal of merchants to accept base coinage occurred in Marseille in 1602, 1636 and 1644 and in Rouen and Dieppe in 1643.[142] Sometimes wages were not paid in coin at all. In 1703 the authorities at Beauvais were obliged to authorise payments of wages in kind; in common with the rural poor, urban workers could be reduced to repaying loans with labour.[143] An embryonic proletariat was in the making; but its economic role, either as a productive force or as a market, was savagely reduced by the conditions of its own existence. The families of workers and poor artisans eked out their lives in a single sparsely furnished room; independent craftsmen may have had an adjacent workshop or boutique.[144] There were few extra comforts and the occasional luxury served to highlight the general impoverishment. Jean Gros, a Dijonnais armourer, had a total household worth a mere 125 *livres* in 1605; but amongst the fifteen *livres* of clothing there was a coat for his wife valued at six.[145]

The scale of urban deprivation obviously imposed severe limits on economic growth. The urban poor constituted both a potential market and a potential labour force but for much of the time were neither. Generation of greater mass prosperity was essential for the development of the small merchant elite, yet this was beyond its powers to achieve. As we have seen, merchant influence on government policy was limited and attitudes to government measures were inconsistent and ambivalent. Measures of protection were welcomed here, rejected there. Badly needed tariff reform ran into merchant opposition. Even when carried through, government action was ambiguous in its effects. The relative buoyancy of overseas trade owed as much if not more to the general expansion of the Atlantic economy and manufacturing seems to have been as much hindered as helped by the attachment to corporate regulation. This attachment was itself a reflection of the inflexibility of the market. Limited improvements to the transport system were inadequate to overcome the many obstacles to the development of the domestic market or achieve a general reduction in costs. Not surprisingly, successful merchants were all too easily tempted by the prospects of purchasing an office. So venal officeholding became a permanent drain on commercial capital and energies. The government's almost exclusive concern with the production of high-quality textiles for the export market did little to tackle any of these problems, above all the need to unlock the potential of the languishing domestic market.

As the physiocrats were to perceive, the key to the structural problems of the French economy lay not in the towns but in the French countryside. Although life in the towns was grim and mostly short, the reservoir of poverty was constantly replenished by a stream of rural immigrants. Indeed, urban mortality rates were so high that without a constant flow of newcomers French towns would have diminished in size. Dupâquier calculates that the annual deficit might have been as much as 10,000 per annum.[146] This influx was but one indicator of a growing rural poverty which counted for far more in the economic fortunes of France than did the prosperity of a small urban elite. It also has much more to tell us about the economic parameters of the state.

AN AGRICULTURAL IMPASSE

Explanations for the agricultural and demographic difficulties of the seventeenth century have largely been set in a neo-Malthusian framework in which falling population and prices are taken as indicators of stagnant or declining production. The latter is itself treated as both a cause and a consequence of the demographic difficulties. Jacquart emphasises the way in which the collapse of the birthrate in 1651–2 in the Ile-de-France ushered in twenty years of low agricultural output.[147] The decline in prices and rents in Languedoc, incipient by the late 1660s and severe from 1673, has been explained by Le Roy Ladurie in terms of a European-wide decline in population as well as a reduction of domestic demand; diminishing agricultural output affected not only grain but also wine and sheep.[148] Given the agricultural progress made in the Low Countries and in England during periods of relatively low prices the argument is barely watertight.[149] But even if the neo-Malthusian correlation between population and price trends is accepted, it does not, in itself, explain why French agriculture proved unable to meet the pressures on it. This is frequently explained by reference to its undoubted technical shortcomings.[150]

These have been so well documented that a brief enumeration of them here will suffice. Their most obvious manifestation was the high proportion of land that was left fallow, at least a half in regions of biennial crop rotation, possibly more. According to Molinier, in the Vivarais as little as 15 per cent of the land in any given year was under the plough and some was left fallow for ten or even twenty years.[151] In more fertile regions where the land was able to sustain two successive crops the attachment to the fallow was, none the less, reflected in the division of even the smallest tenures into three.[152] Whatever the amount of land under the plough it was overwhelmingly and increasingly devoted to grain: occupying over four-fifths of the rich land around Beauvais or Toulouse it also stimulated the clearing of totally unsuitable scrub lands of lower Languedoc and crept up the hillsides in the diocese of Castres where it displaced both *vignoble* and precious pastures. In the Beauvaisis meadows clung on to a mere 1 per cent of the land, a figure which makes the Lauragais with its 7 per cent of pastureland seem positively well endowed.[153] At Auriol in Provence householders complained in 1651 that they 'did not know where to pasture their cattle, the land being entirely cultivated'.[154] Even areas with a decidedly pastoral character such as the uplands of the Auvergne seem to have suffered from a relative decline in cattle-rearing from the end of the sixteenth century.[155] Given the balance of land usage, oxen and cows used for draught purposes were frequently more in evidence than dairy cows. A typical sharecropper of Gourgé in Poitou in 1676 had four pairs of oxen but only two calves, one bull and three cows. His flock of eighty-three sheep was decidedly more important.[156] Yet there is evidence from widely different regions to suggest that difficulties were also encountered in maintaining the size of sheep flocks.[157]

With insufficient grazing land to sustain the cattle necessary to ensure adequate fertilisation, French agriculture was thus locked into a vicious circle. Unable to increase yields significantly above their medieval levels of about 5:1 the only possible response to mounting population pressure was to make inroads into marginal land and extend cereal cultivation.[158] The unhappy result was not only to reduce the amount of pastureland available but also to exclude fodder crops, vegetables and artificial grasses, which would have both enriched the soil and improved the quality of animal feed. Particularly on medium and small holdings, peas and beans found only a tiny space alongside the spring grains.[159] Vegetables were cultivated for immediate consumption, their enriching power being inadequately exploited; although meadows of sainfoin were established they remained outside the rotation cycle.[160] Fallow, on the other hand, was perceived to be an indispensable part of the cycle without which the fertility of the land would be severely diminished. Leases were frequently prescriptive in this regard, obliging the tenants, as in one Norman example, to cultivate 'by fields and seasons . . . without taking the fields out of rotation'.[161] Given this combination of problems, access to the open fields, whilst they lay fallow and after the harvest, for the cattle was crucial for both beasts and fields; this in turn became an obstacle not only to enclosure but to any measures which would have facilitated the removal of land from the conventional cycle.

The impracticality and expense of other methods of fertilisation – by burning, marling or liming – meant that an improvement in the system of crop rotation was the *sine qua non* of agricultural progress.[162] The failure to make more than marginal progress in this regard is all the more striking given the fact that the technical know-how was available. Moreover, it had been successfully applied from the end of the Middle Ages in Flanders and adjacent parts of France. By the sixteenth century in many parts of Flanders the fallow land had disappeared entirely from the rotation cycle. It was replaced either by leguminous plants such as peas, beans and clover which provided both animal and human food as well as supplying the soil with nitrogen; elsewhere furze, buckwheat and turnips were introduced.[163] The continuous improvement of agricultural practice in Flanders makes a telling contrast with the arrival and then the disappearance of advanced techniques in the adjacent northern territories of France. In the Cambrésis yields had reached their highest point in the fourteenth century when leguminous plants had been sown between the oats. There was a also a tendency for fourfold crop rotation to replace threefold, with the leguminosae becoming the third rather than the second. But by the end of the fourteenth century the vegetable crops had been squeezed out and yields had declined significantly. Not until the suppression of the fallow and the introduction of artificial grasses, clover, sainfoin and carrots in the nineteenth century was progress renewed.[164] Neveux suggests that responsibility for this retreat lay with an increasing insistence on a strict sequence of sowing and the maintenance of the fallow which became general in the north of France by the end of the fourteenth century.[165]

Even so, progressive ideas and techniques did not completely disappear from the Cambrésis; cultivation of part or all of the fallow could still be found. Only half the leases stipulated a strict conformity to the general pattern and technically it would have been entirely possible to have removed part of the arable from the system as was done in England even on open field systems from the seventeenth century. Nor was the Cambrésis the only province where potentially fruitful practices could be detected. Breton agriculture, as Le Roy Ladurie has observed, with 'its insistence on fertilisers, hemp, vegetable growing and dairy animals had some striking similarities, at the beginning of the modern period, with that of Flanders'.[166] Around Paris the power of the urban market could be seen in the devotion of part of the fallow to vegetable crops and to sainfoin whose value as a fodder crop was widely appreciated and exploited by the *laboureurs* of the plateau of Longboyau.[167] In Normandy there were some areas in which communal systems never really existed and the right of proprietors to bar access to their land was accepted.[168] Similarly, in the Gâtine of Poitou the larger landlords engaged in a remarkable and successful consolidation of their domains throughout the sixteenth and seventeenth centuries: 'each piece of land having been enclosed and rigorously defended against the incursions of cattle, *vaine pâture* had become impossible.'[169] Yet nowhere did innovative practices or technical knowledge come together in a continuous endeavour to transform agricultural activity, nowhere did they lead to systematic experimentation with crop rotation cycles, the incorporation into them of artificial meadows or an interest in cattle-rearing. The only significant invasion of the fallow occurred in the Lauragais where from the 1650s the remarkable spread of maize broke its grip; however, the idea here was to exploit the abnormally high yields offered by maize to feed the people whilst wheat was grown for export.[170] If maize cultivation prevented starvation, the dietary benefits were non-existent whilst its labour-intensive character did little to raise agricultural productivity.

At the heart of the difficulties lay the preoccupation with corn. It was ever-present in all ranks of society from those whose survival depended on a chunk of hard bread to accompany their daily soup to those with responsibility for ensuring public order. The government's response to the crises of 1693 was to order proprietors to sow their land on pain of forfeiting the right to its produce to anyone willing to undertake the task; those who did were offered exemption from taxes and protection against the seizure of their harvest.[171] Such attitudes fitted in with those of the peasantry. As late as 1785 the intendant in Poitou, explaining their resistance to innovation, noted that 'for them custom was an inviolable law, particularly as artificial meadows demand a better soil which would consume all their *fumiers*, which they kept for their corn.'[172]

The persistent attachment of the peasantry to their customary rights and traditions was not just a manifestation of legendary peasant conservatism. It reflected the fact that their capacity to sustain themselves was in constant jeopardy as holdings became smaller and the pressures on dwindling resources grew. The proliferation of small peasant holdings is observable to a greater or lesser degree virtually everywhere. Le Roy Ladurie drew attention long ago to the decline in the number of substantial peasant holdings which occurred in Languedoc from the end of the fifteenth century. Between 1460 and 1690 they shrank from occupying half of the land to just a tenth whilst the smallest holdings, consisting of no more than a few parcels of land, doubled in number.[173] During the same years at the other end of the realm the Cambrésis was similarly affected as holdings of less than thirty *hectares* (seventy-four acres) started to fragment.[174] In thirty-five parishes of the lower Vivarais at the end of the Middle Ages only 2.9 per cent of peasant tenures were over ten *hectares*; seven in every ten were less than four and virtually a third less than one.[175] Nor did the pressures ease during the course of the sixteenth and seventeenth centuries. In the Emblavès, where the nobles were actively consolidating substantial farms, a fifth of the peasants were left with no land whilst a further three-fifths shared just under 12 per cent of the *terroir*, an average holding of perhaps two acres.[176] Even in those regions which escaped the worse vicissitudes of the seventeenth century and where peasant property stood up relatively well – Brittany, the Auvergne, Provence, Lorraine – the number of smaller properties appears to have grown.[177]

The pulverisation of peasant properties may be partly explained in neo-Malthusian fashion by reference to the damaging consequences of partible inheritance. It undoubtedly helped to reduce some holdings to pathetic proportions. In the Cévenol community of Assions between 1588 and 1633 the average size of tenures fell in exact proportion to the rise in population.[178] An individual but graphic illustration of the processes is provided by the fate that overwhelmed the two to three hundred *hectare* property of La Brouardière in the Mayennais, a region where both sons and daughters could inherit. In the twelfth century thirty *hectares* were leased to a certain Brouard for a substantial rent payable in kind and money, plus ten days of haymaking. By the end of the seventeenth century there were no less than thirty-three proprietors, sharing eighteen houses, seven cow sheds, two ovens, one press, and 118 parcels of land, occupying in all just under twenty-three *hectares*. Inevitably, there was some confusion about the proportion of dues owed by each tenant and, in 1694, legal proceedings led to the formal measurement of the properties by the royal *arpenteur*. After four days of effort the biggest was deemed to be three *hectares* and the smallest the equivalent of fifty square metres. The dues were allocated pro rata, with the smallest one estimated at 1/768 of a chicken and 1/348 of a labour service, no attempt being made to convert these into monetary obligations![179]

Clearly there was a connection between rising population, the pressure to grow grain, the reduction of the amount of land available for other purposes and the attachment to a rigid agrarian cycle. Once locked into a pattern of extensive grain cultivation and stagnant productivity it became virtually self-perpetuating. In the seventeenth century, according to some, the pressures of a rising population proved too much. France entered a period of demographic crisis, demand ebbed away and prices fell, further diminishing the incentive for innovation. Yet neither the impoverishment of the peasantry nor the accompanying lack of innovation were the inevitable result of the inner workings of a peasant economy. They were the entirely predictable outcome of the excessive burdens placed on it by both landlords and the state.

THE DISPOSSESSION OF THE PEASANTRY

Overall the peasantry in the early seventeenth century probably 'held' about half the land and worked most of the rest; the nobility had an estimated 20 per cent, the bourgeoisie about 15, the clergy possibly 10, leaving around 5 per cent of common lands.[180] In other words a minority of the population – maybe 5 per cent – owned most of the land as well as being the recipients of the rents, dues, tithes, and other obligations yielded by the peasantry on the land occupied by them. As one might expect, local variations were, however, considerable. The proportion of land in noble hands could vary over relatively short distances: from less than 5 per cent in the overwhelmingly peasant communities of the Vivarais it was as much as 22 per cent in the isolation of Emblavès in the Velay;[181] accounting for between 4 and 10 per cent at Draguignan in lower Provence, at Arles the nobles' share was a remarkable 50 per cent of the *terroir*.[182] Similar variations could be found in Languedoc, from over 60 per cent at Belbuze-lès-Toulouse but down to zero in virtually half of the communities in the dioceses of Castres, Albi and Lavaur.[183] The land held by the church was also subject to similar variations but the pattern was less random because ecclesiastical properties were heavily concentrated in the vicinity of the larger towns. Barely reaching 1 per cent in most Provençal communities, ecclesiastical estates occupied 15 per cent of the land in the vicinity of Arles.[184] The global share of the church in the Beauvaisis was around an eighth of the cultivable land but at Goincourt, on the threshold of the regional capital, a single abbey occupied nearly a third of the *terroir*.[185] In the communities of the *gardiage* of Toulouse, which covered a radius of ten kilometres, the church's share ranged from 12 to 23 per cent whereas in the Midi-Pyrénées as a whole it was rarely more than 2.5 per cent.[186] Where towns were dominated by ennobled officers the distinction between noble and bourgeois ownership lost all practical significance. The proportion of land in noble hands within fifteen kilometres of Toulouse rarely dropped below 30 per cent and in some villages accounted for two-thirds; this was a consequence of the purchases made by the city's *parlementaires* and other ennobled officers.[187]

The clearest feature of the situation was indeed the extent to which nobles, clergy and bourgeois together pushed back the extent of peasant holdings in the vicinity of the towns.[188] Within a radius of fifteen kilometres of Toulouse the property of the Toulousains never accounted for less than 75 per cent. In mid-century Cintegabelle-sur-Ariège, thirty kilometres to the south, seventeen Toulousains out of a total population of 731 owned over a fifth of the land. They included a *trésorier-général* of France, a priest, some other nobles and municipal big-wigs.[189] If the Toulousain was particularly marked by such developments it was by no means unique. Similar trends were discernible in both the Bordelais and the Lyonnais from the fifteenth century.[190] Perhaps a little slower to get under way in the Parisian hinterland, the urban invasion, when it came, was none the less irresistible. At Meudon, today a green oasis in the Parisian suburbs, perhaps a fifth of the land was already in bourgeois hands by the early sixteenth century.[191]

The corollary of the economic imperialism of the towns was the dispossession of the peasantry. In the Toulousain and the Lauragais although they constituted between 60 and 70 per cent of the population they held only a fifth or less of the land by the beginning of the eighteenth century.[192] South of Paris the picture was similar. In nine parishes of the Orge valley peasants held on average only a quarter of the land; where there were no vineyards their share was as low as 6 per cent.[193] At Avrainville it had fallen from almost half in the mid-sixteenth century to a fifth one hundred years later; nearer to the capital, at Antony, it was reduced from 25 to 15 per cent.[194]

Although not all urban purchasers of land were people of high status or enormous wealth, the urban colonisation of the countryside also meant a polarisation in land ownership.[195] At Avrainville by 1688 ten people held 1,150 *arpents* of arable land out of a total 1,690. All were bourgeois of Paris and ennobled officers.[196] On the other side of the Essonne valley at Fontenay-le-Vicomte a *conseiller-secrétaire du Roy et de ses finances* and the *receveur général des finances de la généralité de Rouen* had half the land between them.[197] Wherever possible, such ambitious landlords also sought to enlarge their holdings. By 1682 at Lapeyrousse on the outskirts of Toulouse, farms of one hundred *hectares* (247 acres) or more occupied just under 15 per cent of the territory, a proportion that was to double over the course of the next hundred years.[198] In the Parisian hinterland substantial farms of one hundred *hectares* or even more had long been common, particularly those farmed out by the great religious houses; they were joined now by increasing numbers of farms of between thirty and one hundred *hectares* through the assiduous process of consolidation carried out by a variety of bourgeois, religious and seigneurial owners.[199]

The counterpoint to this process was not merely a global decline in the amount of land left in peasant hands but a dramatic decline in the size of the tenures that survived. More than a third of the peasantry of the Toulousain had less than six-tenths of a *hectare* (1.48 acres) and 84 per cent less than three *hectares* (7.41 acres).[200] At Le Fossat in 1693 only four proprietors out of sixty-four possessed more than ten *hectares*, and only fourteen out of 1,258 at Lapeyrousse.[201] At Mennecy, near Paris, where the privileged 2 per cent of proprietors accounted for 70 per cent of the cultivated area, the *vignerons, manouvriers, charretiers* and *jardiniers* shared a tenth, just over two acres for the average household.[202] The contrast with the 650 *arpents* held by the Duc de Villeroy in the same commune was overwhelming, particularly as these accounted for only a quarter of his possessions in the region. His largest farm was 450 *arpents* and his smallest 130.[203] Evidence from the eastern provinces although more impressionistic points in the same direction. In 107 villages of the Dijonnais, Roupnel found that in over half there was not a single peasant who owned his land.[204]

Urban purchasers of rural properties strove to consolidate their position with privileges which put them on a par with the traditional nobility. Many of the larger towns had obtained blanket exemption from the *droit de franc-fief* for their citizens or at least for the bourgeois. They also succeded, after decades of litigation conducted by the inhabitants of Lyon, in obtaining exemption from the *taille*. Faced with widespread concern amongst the peasantry the government at first took their side;[205] but, by 1581, the perseverance of the Lyonnais brought them victory, on condition that the properties in question were registered and that the owners had been resident in Lyon for ten years. The responsibility for payment of the *taille* was transferred to their tenants, a situation which, broadly speaking, became the norm throughout the country.[206]

Urban domination of the countryside, particularly by the larger cities, was reinforced by an array of privileges. At Toulouse these included the right of the *capitouls* to levy taxes on food, wine and other produce brought into the *gardiage* whilst the citizens in general were advantaged by their exemption from all tolls throughout the region covered by the former *comté*. In addition, the municipality had complete control of the markets which were closely regulated to ensure that the town was supplied with food at the stipulated prices. In times of difficulty it was not beyond resorting to forceful methods to ensure that its needs were met. In the desperately lean months of 1652–3 it bought up stocks of grain from miles around, ordering the authorities in neighbouring burgs to provide the necessary transport; the consuls of Castelnaudary were threatened with arrest for obstructing the execution of these measures.[207] Corporate municipal responsibility for ensuring a supply of food at affordable prices sat somewhat uneasily with the interests of many leading citizens who as landlords hoarded grain in order to sell at the most opportune moment; this practice appears to have become increasingly systematic from the end of the sixteenth century.[208] Some privileges, however, were intended precisely to sustain the monopolistic aspirations of their beneficiaries. One of those most cherished by the Rochelais prohibited the import of any wine between the harvest and the end of November other than that produced in the *banlieu*, thus giving the town's vineyard proprietors a monopoly of both the local and overseas market.[209] The merchants of Lyon were similarly assisted by being able to bring wine – ostensibly for their own use – into the city without paying the *aides*.[210]

The economic imperialism of the urban elites should not obscure the fact that, although the process of consolidating large estates was most advanced in the hinterlands of the major towns, it is not entirely attributable to the activities of the high robe and urban oligarchs. The lesser nobility in the valley of the Essone who shared between them about 6.5 per cent of the cultivable land had farms of between eighty and 150 *arpents*.[211] Of the ten *métairies* farmed out by the Barons of Auneau in three villages in the Orléanais only one was less than forty acres and most were about seventy.[212] Moreover, holdings of this size have also been found at some distance from the great centres of population: St-Jacob observed their presence in Burgundy, whilst Merle has described in meticulous detail how the nobility of the Gâtine of Poitou engaged in a steady and systematic accumulation of parcels of land which they transformed into consolidated *métairies* protected by the carefully nurtured hedgerows of the *bocage*.[213] A similar process appears to have occurred in the Nivernais where peasant holdings were compacted into *domaines* of fifty to seventy or even one hundred *hectares* by both bourgeois and noble purchasers.[214]

The nobility, of course, did not share the burden of partible inheritance with their tenants. For this reason it can as easily be put in a class context as a Malthusian one.[215] Almost everywhere, nobles benefited from the *droit d'aînesse,* designed to help them keep their successions intact, and also from the privilege of *retrait féodale* which allowed them to recover by compulsory purchase properties alienated from their jurisdiction. Although a number of customs did extend the *droit d'aînesse* to non-noble proprietors of land, the claims of commoners to benefit from this custom were a source of considerable litigation and debate.[216] In any event, wealthy commoners had an equivalent of the *retrait féodale* in the *retrait lignager* which made it possible to undertake proceedings for the recovery of alienated family lands. For the poverty-stricken heirs of Brouard, struggling to survive on their atomised parcels of land, this was a manifestly meaningless right, a point which acquires additional force when it is noted that their seigneurs had been busy repossessing a number of their dependencies, in all probability by using the feudal right of *retrait*. They succeeded in recovering a third of the land at La Brouardière, rounding out the substantial *métairie de la Grange,* and enclosing the park with walls in order to create an avenue.[217]

Evidence of such use of feudal privilege comes from provinces as disparate as Brittany, Burgundy and Provence.[218] In the Gâtinais the persistent recourse to the *retrait féodale* over decades and even centuries was crucial to the endeavours of successive generations of seigneurial proprietors who slowly brought the task of consolidating and acquiring land to fruition.[219] Its use has been noted in the Bordelais in the fourteenth and again in the eighteenth century.[220] Forster has observed that the practice also seems to have become frequent in the Toulousain during the eighteenth century, being regularly employed in tandem with straightforward purchase and exchange;[221] but the number of significant cases brought before the *parlement* in the preceding century makes it clear that it was not a recent development. It is particularly noteworthy in a region where Roman law traditions had supposedly left an attachment to absolute property rights.[222] Apparently there was also frequent recourse to the *retrait féodale* in Berry, another province much influenced by Roman law.[223]

Despite the remorseless polarisation of landowning and the fragmentation of peasant holdings over the best part of two centuries, every community contained a small group of notables who stood out by virtue of their relative wealth and status: better-off peasants, small merchants, lesser officeholders, seigneurial agents and notaries – roles which frequently overlapped. Frequently contributors to, as well as beneficiaries of, the general impoverishment, such notables occasionally succeeded in founding farming dynasties which lasted into the mid-twentieth century.[224] However, as the figures for land distribution all suggest, they were few in numbers and their future frequently far from assured. No more than thirty-three out of 472 taxpayers in the nine communities examined by Venard south of Paris were described in 1717 as *laboureurs* rather than *vignerons, manouvriers, journaliers*.[225] In the Burgundian *bailliage* of Arnay-le-Duc only 329 out of 3,605 were thought to be comfortably or well off by the intendant in 1667; yet this was not a frontier region and was later to become renowned for its cattle-rearing.[226] In the Brionnais parish of Saint-Julien-de-Cray in 1683 forty-three of the sixty-nine taxpayers paid less than five *livres* in *taille*; just two *laboureurs* paid more than fifty.[227] Even within the ranks of the *laboureurs* there existed considerable disparities of wealth. Few matched the appropriately named Gille Laboureur who in 1700 was able to lease two farms from the Duchy of Villeroy totalling nearly 300 *hectares*; or Charles Auroy of Chavannes whose plough train alone was worth a stupendous 1,900 *livres*. In the Parisian region such substantial entrepreneurs were rare. More typical was Mathieu de Marseil of Baulne whose equipment was valued at eighty *livres*, his two horses at no more than 100 and his four cows at twenty each.[228]

Moreover, it should be borne in mind that the possession of equipment and cattle was no guide to the actual ownership of land, certainly in the grain-growing regions of the north. The most substantial peasants in the Beauvaisis, Goubert discovered, were the *gros fermiers*, the sort of people who with only five *hectares* of their own but with fifteen horses were able to rent a farm for 1000 *livres*.[229] Their capital lay in their ploughs rather than their land which they were frequently prepared to sell in order to take on larger farms as they moved from holding to holding. In 1690 a certain Michel Mercier was leasing both lands and the rights to tithes and *champarts* in the Parisian region; but he owed 2,850 *livres* in rent of which he had not got the first sou. He was obliged to surrender his harvest, sell part of his equipment, all his cattle, and some furniture and tools. He subsequently sold his house, meadow and vineyards. Three years later he was again to be found leasing land and succeeded in marrying his daughter into a comfortable family and providing her with a dowry of 150 *livres*.[230] Those less fortunate or those temporarily without a holding took on secondary employment as grain merchants, suppliers of inns, weavers or millers.[231] Sometimes there appear to have been no villagers with the means of taking on leases. The four extant leases – those for 1606, 1626, 1655 and 1687 – of the seigneury of L'Etoile in the Brionnais were all assumed by merchants of the neighbouring towns.[232] In the lean years of the mid-century the increasingly indebted *fermiers* of the Baronnie d'Auneau in the Orléanais became unwilling to accept leases. The response here was a marked transformation of rents in kind to money rents which in years of meagre harvests eased the problems for the *fermier* and thereby for the landlord. At the same time leases were concentrated in fewer and, Constant suggests, stronger hands.[233] In many parts of the country, however, leaseholders continued to struggle to meet their obligations. This was undoubtedly a factor in bringing an end to the long upward movement of rents.[234]

In some respects the *gros fermiers* were embryonic entrepreneurs; and sometimes it is misleadingly suggested that those of northern France approximated to the independent farmers of southern England.[235] Viewed from a different angle they were simply the most well-endowed part of a peasantry whose control over the means of production was rapidly being eroded.[236] When they survived and prospered it was frequently by hanging on to seigneurial coat tails. Genuinely independent proprietors – the *laboureurs* properly speaking – rarely had more than twenty-five *hectares,* frequently only ten. The most considerable observed by Goubert in the Beauvaisis owned 32.4 *hectares* (seventy-nine acres) of arable and two and half of woods, together with three *hectares* of pastures enclosed by cider trees and three houses; he had four horses, one foal, three cows, two heifers, two calves, two pigs, five piglets and some sheep. Able to sustain himself and his family, he was none the less in debt to the substantial tune of 2,900 *livres*.[237]

In some ways the developments which have been described were economically progressive. The expropriation of the peasantry was, after all, an essential precondition for the development of capitalism. So also, it is usually thought, was the concentration of landownership. A lively market in land, the proletarianisation of parts of the peasantry and flourishing local markets, sustained by those in receipt of cash wages, were undoubtedly present in many regions at the end of the Middle Ages. Brenner's view that further economic progress was impeded by the inability of the landlords to establish 'large' farms save on the worst land is not sustained by empirical observation.[238] Dewald is probably nearer the mark, if not completely convincing, with his observation that all the conditions that 'the Physiocrats thought necessary for agricultural progress' seemed to have been assembled.[239] Yet the transformation of France's socio-economic structures proved to be the work of centuries rather than decades. The polarisation of rural social structures led to stasis rather than capitalist social relations whilst, market pressures notwithstanding, agricultural techniques and productivity improved not at all. A closer look at the dynamics of agrarian relations is required.

AGRARIAN CLASS RELATIONS

Robert Brenner believes that the prime agents of capitalist development in England were the large landlords. Le Roy Ladurie, despite the conceptual divide which separates him from Brenner, has pointed in the same direction. In France he has suggested it was the seigneury which 'became the matrix of the capitalism of the big farmers' and that 'capitalism was . . . inserted . . . within the structures of seigneurial manors'.[240] The consolidating activities of sections of the seigneurial classes do seem – although the evidence is fragmentary and impressionistic – to have been accompanied by a slow growth of a more businesslike attitude. The extent and nature of assets were carefully recorded together with the obligations of tenants and dependants. Income was calculated more accurately and rights over mills, markets and woods administered with greater rigour. In 1566–7 the receiver of the Barony of Neubourg carefully listed the merchants trading in the local market: fourteen *merciers*, seven smiths, seventeen shoemakers, twelve drapers, fifteen bakers and so on.[241] The same attitude is revealed in the remarkable set of estate papers left by the judicial family of Daliès who acquired the Barony of Caussade in the Montalbanais at about the same time. In addition to the inventory of titles stretching back to the thirteenth century their activities are enshrined in the systematic ledgers of wheat sales, dues payments and arrears, and the comprehensive list of those who were infringing the seigneurial monopoly of ovens; amongst similar documents relating to the Barony of Bressols of which the Daliès were co-seigneurs, the register of dependants drawn up in 1675 runs to thirty-four pages.[242] Robert Forster has concluded, on the basis of information from Bordeaux, Toulouse and Rennes, that the provincial nobleman 'was actively engaged in estate management, leaving few stones unturned in his efforts to make the domain farms yield a maximum return'.[243]

However, the emergence of a commercial ethic was clearly a protracted and uneven process. Dewald's picture of the way the Norman Barons of Pont-St-Pierre managed their affairs reveals the persistent influence of non-economic considerations. They leased land just as much to secure the support of the petty nobles and families of the local notables, who were also frequently attached to the lord's household, as for profit. Most of the food and drink needed for the household came from the Barony and 'self-sufficiency seems to have remained a cultural ideal into the late seventeenth century'.[244] Moreover, the desire to increase administrative efficiency and maximise revenues did not necessarily hasten the commercialisation of landlord–tenant relations or promote capital investment as a means of raising productivity and profit margins. Account books make it clear that the central preoccupation was with global quantities.[245] This preoccupation can also be seen in the way that well into the eighteenth century, even amongst large landowners in advanced regions, the clearance of wasteland received a higher priority than experiments with artificial meadows or systems of cultivation.[246] Leases continued to impose on tenants the obligation to stick to the traditional system of crop rotation. Landlords probably feared the degradation of the soil at the hands of tenants on short leases.[247] Not even the success of English agriculture, which they greatly admired, sufficed to overcome the deep doubts amongst French commentators about the capacity of mediocre land to sustain more intensive cultivation. In the relatively fertile Cambrésis as late as 1782 criticisms could still be heard of the new practice of sowing 'a forced and premature crop be it flax or rape seed'; allegedly this not only reduced the fallow but also undermined the production of wool and cattle.[248]

Pushed towards extensive rather than intensive cultivation by their own technological limitations, the key problem for landlords who had succeeded in assembling sizeable *domaine*s was to find tenants capable of taking them on. The optimum size of holdings was, in fact, determined essentially by the technology and labour available to the family units who worked them as well as by the quality of the soil. In the Parisian hinterland a family fortunate enough to possess them might manage three ploughs. With sufficient horses these could take on a farm of around 400 *arpents*.[249] Most *laboureurs* and *fermiers*, however, were not in this happy position and, even if a taker could be found for such a large farm, the costs of transporting manure and employing additional labour were critical considerations. Whilst the sowing and cultivation of the crops, together with the care of the cattle and general upkeep, were undertaken by the tenant and his family, harvesting and associated tasks required additional paid labour as did the flocks of sheep.[250] In the Essonne valley a farm of 100 *hectares* demanded a permanent household of eight to twelve with a supply of additional labour for the harvest.[251] Bois felt that the optimum size at the end of the Middle Ages in Normandy was twenty to thirty *hectares* and that further expansion meant the employment of marginal land, increased labour costs, and declining productivity.[252] In the Ile-de-France exploitations of the same order which were manageable with one plough were those that multiplied most rapidly, whether as a result of the creation of *domaine*s by the Parisian bourgeois or by the bringing together of different leases by the tenants.[253] In less prosperous regions extensive *domaine*s were necessarily leased out in multiple small holdings. The huge *domaine* de Rochefort in Brittany, covering 5,000 *hectares*, was broken up into 400 holdings.[254] From Normandy come examples of substantial farms of seventy acres or more being leased in separate strips of land, none of which was larger than eight.[255] The largest part of the Seigneurie de l'Etoile in the Brionnais – 450 of its 620 hectares – was composed of peasant *censives* which in most cases did not exceed eight *hectares*; even the seigneurial reserve did not appear to have an individual exploitation of more than eighteen. Here it seems that the *charrue à versoir* possessed by prosperous peasants from the twelfth century was unknown, let alone the heavy ploughs introduced into maritime France by the Dutch in the course of the seventeenth century. The *laboureur* of the Brionnais managed with a light wooden plough (*aireau*) and a few spades and forks.[256] One way of compensating for technical backwardness in poorer regions was through the maintenance of extended families which could provide additional labour. These were common in large parts of central and southern France. In the Nivernais a direct correlation has been observed between those localities with a higher proportion of larger farms and the presence of extended, particularly joint families, to whom they were leased. In striking contrast to the situation in the Ile-de-France, a farm of thirty to forty *hectares* required two plough teams because of the need for repeated ploughings in order to prepare the fallow for sowing.[257] As we have seen, finding tenants capable of sustaining a reasonable farm appears to have grown generally more difficult towards mid-century, possibly earlier in some areas.[258]

Exceptionally, proprietors elected to manage their desmesne farms directly, using paid labour. Commonly employed in some areas for gardens, small enclosures, parks and woods, it was likely in other instances to have been no more than a device for claiming exemption from the *taille*.[259] Overwhelmingly, landlords opted either for *fermage* or *métayage*, the former predominating in the Paris basin, and in the northernmost provinces, the latter throughout most of the rest of France where its usage became increasingly widespread from the fifteenth century onwards. Inevitably this broad picture risks oversimplifying some significant regional developments: in the Beaujolais, for instance, *fermage* predominated in the north, *métayage* in the centre whilst in the south the position varied from village to village.[260] Moreover, larger *domaines* and seigneuries leased in their entirety to a *fermier* were frequently sub-let on a sharecropping basis or by combining leases of both types.[261] What all the leases had in common was the brevity of their duration. Leases for life, even three lives, and twenty-year leases, relatively common in the fifteenth century, became a distant memory. Now they rarely exceeded nine years, and were commonly for five or six, not infrequently three and sometimes just one.[262]

Fermage is generally regarded as a crucial stage in the development of agrarian capitalism depending as it did on the leasing of medium and larger farms to tenants who paid a money rent and assumed responsibility for marketing of the produce. *Métayage* by contrast depended on the proprietors providing the farm and a proportion – traditionally a half – of the grain, equipment and cattle and taking in return half the produce. It was attractive to small as well as to big proprietors for it offered a means of acquiring produce for the urban household which was not normally available.[263] It might also provide a countryside retreat. Leases at Aix frequently gave the proprietor a right of accommodation and sojourn in the sharecropper's dwelling, the use of the garden and stable, hay for his horses and even milk for his family when present.[264] Amongst the invariable obligations to provide a number of *convois* for the transport of produce, one required the sharecropper to collect his proprietress and take her to mass! Use of *métayage* to ensure the provisioning of the landlord's household was not, however, confined to leases drawn up by urban proprietors.[265] Those of the Gâtinais typically required the tenants to make one or two journeys per year to collect barrels of wine.[266] In the Vivarais a tenant might be required to provide, in addition to half of the harvest, specified amounts of cheese, butter, milk, and a number of chickens; he might also be required to bake the proprietor's bread and carry firewood to his house.[267]

Yet, the almost universal presence of *métayage* makes it clear that this was not simply a device employed by the urban bourgeoisie to satisfy their domestic needs. Such systematic calculations as have been done suggest that *métayage* left the landlord with a significantly larger share of the produce than *fermage*.[268] It was, moreover, a mode of exploitation made possible by the poverty-stricken state of the peasantry which left them denuded of the material resources required to maintain their economic dependence. Its advance in many regions had clearly been facilitated by the devastation of the Hundred Years War and again by the civil strife of the sixteenth century.[269] In the Gâtinais *métayage* leases rose from constituting 5 per cent of all leases to an overwhelming 90 per cent in the century after 1580 with the significant periods being the last decades of the sixteenth century and then the years after 1640. Here the extension of sharecropping went hand in hand with the consolidation of noble *domaines*.[270] The resulting reduction in the sharecropper's independence was reflected in the steady move away from a position in which the provision of the indispensable draught animals was a shared responsibility to one in which they were provided entirely by the landowner; more startling is the fact that it was not long before the sharecropper's sheep, once entirely his own, suffered the same fate. This appears to be true even of the Parisian region where *fermage* was commonly supplemented by sharecropping arrangements for sheep and cows.[271] Needless to say, the sharecropper was often required to bear the loss if flocks diminished rather than grew. Pressure on the tenant could be further increased by requirements to provide pasture for the owner's cattle, restrictions preventing him looking after the cattle of third parties, using his cart and animals for others or even lending them without permission.[272]

Not surprisingly, the extension and intensification of *métayage* appear to have induced a growing instability with many tenants leaving their properties before the termination of the lease, a situation which persisted in the Nivernais well into the nineteenth century.[273] The position, noted by Sicard, at the end of the Middle Ages when families stayed for twenty or thirty, even one hundred years had certainly changed.[274] Sharecroppers frequently became little distinguishable from wage workers who had an interest in the harvest. In much of Languedoc there seems to have existed a mixed system, part *métayage* and part exploitation by servants paid by the year in kind.[275] At Aix sharecroppers were often described as *travailleurs* or *journaliers* and were accustomed to moving from holding to holding.[276] Sharecroppers more or less everywhere were subject to the tightest instructions about the manner of cultivation. Invariably required to leave their holdings as they found them and to complete a full rotation cycle, the leases might also prescribe the colour of grape to be cultivated, prohibit the planting of root crops in the gaps between vines, impose restrictions on the use of wood and so on.[277]

In a macro-economic perspective sharecropping was deeply contradictory. On the one hand, the remorseless pressure on the peasants was creating an embryonic rural proletariat. On the other, their survival was required by the immediate need of proprietors for produce and labour. Furthermore, sharecroppers rarely entered into market relationships either as vendors or consumers whilst short-term leases and the impositions imposed on them destroyed any incentive to make improvements. Wedded to the values of self-sufficiency, the proprietors also distanced themselves from the market, at least as consumers. By comparison, *fermage* left more of the surplus to the tenant, allowed him greater economic freedom, and potentially offered greater possibilities for economic progress.[278]

Yet the degree to which *fermage* shared the disadvantageous characteristics of *métayage* should not be overlooked. Both were characterised by short leases which remained a major disincentive to investment and a barrier to the capital accumulation that this required. Lack of incentive for the tenant was aggravated by the unwillingness of many landlords to maintain their properties.[279] Second, *fermage* leases were often as restrictive as those for sharecropping. They were likely to prescribe that the soil should be tilled, manured, sown and cultivated following the custom of the *pays*, according to the seasons, that all straw should be converted to manure, that hemp was to be excluded and that the fallow was not be used for the growing of vetches.[280] Third, tenants did not necessarily enter as fully into market as is often suggested. Even in the environs of Paris, where rents were rarely paid wholly in kind, *baux mixtes* were common and much produce thus found its way by this route on to the Paris market or the tables of bourgeois proprietors.[281] In some instances it was the pressure from tenants that brought the introduction of money rents which, particularly in times of bad harvest, suited them better. Yet, even in Picardy, where the *laboureurs* were normally in a position to retain a proportion of the surplus grain for sale, their ability to fully exploit the market was circumscribed by their lack of storage facilities.[282] Fourth, the relationships between the tenants themselves and their own farm workers were not necessarily commercial ones. It was commonplace for farm workers to be paid in kind, even in the north. Debts were frequently repaid in grain, wine or with labour.[283]

It is not surprising that, in some parts of the country, the formal distinction between *métayage* and *fermage* was barely made and they were simply lumped together as *baux à ferme*.[284] Virtually everywhere, both types of lease were subsumed in seigneurial structures with the effect that the difference between the forms of exploitation became very indistinct. This might be because the landlord farmed out the right to collect the dues to a tenant as part of the lease; some of the most prosperous *laboureurs* were those who acted as seigneurial receivers.[285] In sharecropping arrangements the landlord normally retained his seigneurial prerogatives but, where he himself had obligations to meet on the leased *domaine*, these became part of the contract and the burden was shared by both parties.[286]

Even when rents were not conflated in this way the difference between a commercial and seigneurial rent might be hard to discern when the payment was in kind rather than money. If there was a legal difference between paying a proportion of the harvest under a sharecropping arrangement, as part of a *rente foncière*, or as a feudal due, in practice the distinctions could be so blurred that the legal commentators themselves became unsure of their basis. The fact that the Custom of Paris explicitly recognised that the *droit de champart* might be held by other than the seigneur led the jurist Bacquet into some fine distinctions about when it was considered to be a commercial and when a feudal perquisite.[287] Nor was it always clear whether the *cens* – usually an insignificant amount – was a feudal or quit rent.[288] Sometimes these were deliberately confused in order to retain seigneurial perquisites as in some of the areas subject to the *droit écrit* between the Charente and the Gironde.[289] The uniquely Breton and hybrid *domaine congéable* almost made the tenant into a proprietor of any buildings, if not the land, by providing compensation for improvements. In practice this advantage was offset by a proliferation of obligations and of rents in both cash and kind. Historians, as well as contemporaries, have experienced difficulty in defining the *domaine congéable*. It has been recently described as 'a cross between *métayage* and feudal tenure'.[290] There was, in fact, a whole spectrum of forms of surplus extraction running from money rents through a variety of payments in kind to strictly feudal perquisites of all types: tolls, market dues, forests rights and *banalités*. Larger landlords combined some or all of these forms, if not within single leases, then across the management of their properties as a whole. The essential preoccupation was with the capacity of the tenant to pay, not the forms of tenure which were rarely differentiated in a systematic way.[291]

It is apparent that the commonplace equation of *fermage* and *métayage* with bourgeois rent considerably oversimplifies the situation. So does the associated assumption that a reduction in the proportion of revenue yielded by strictly seigneurial mechanisms heralded the arrival of modern forms of property ownership.[292] For, in the context of the petty mode of production which has been described, the replacement of feudal tenures with terminable contracts did not, in itself, transform the dynamics of the system. Seigneurial rights were not only instrumental in reinforcing the economic domination of the great landowners but, together with the *retrait lignager,* impeded the growth of a free market in land. Moreover, even if current estimations of the weight of seigneurial revenues are accepted, it is not clear that they had become as insignificant as is sometimes suggested. There were, of course, enormous variations in the level of dues not only from one province to another but from one custom to the next.[293] Where feudal dues were particularly low, as in Provence, the ecclesiastical seigneurs might extract a heavy tithe.[294] Le Roy Ladurie thinks that the 23 per cent of the gross income of a typical seigneury in the Hurepoix drawn from feudal perquisites was 'not very considerable';[295] but given the low return on land – normally not more than 5 per cent – such revenues must have constituted a welcome additional source of revenue and reduced the incentive to make commercial improvements. It is perhaps also worth noting the admittedly fragmentary evidence suggesting that seigneurial revenues withstood the post-1650 depression much better than other forms of income.[296]

It also seems that the importance of seigneurial dues increased with the size of estates.[297] This was partly because the larger landlords were more likely to have the necessary administrative and legal machinery to organise and secure payment of a multitude of small dues. The range of dues and rights associated with the Duchy of Villeroy created in 1663 makes the point. Tenants paid either a *cens* or a *champart* or both; in some parishes a heavy tithe of one eleventh of the harvest was imposed. The tithes and *champart* at Ballancourt were farmed out for 1,200 *livres* plus three *muids* of grain and an amount of hay. At Corbeil, road and river tolls and various other perquisites like the *droit de tabellionage* and the *lods et ventes* were leased for a further 2,400. These were supplemented by revenues obtained from leasing such rights as 'la chasse pour l'enlèvement et la mouture des grains', the 'forage, persage et rouage des vins', and the 'pesage, mesurage et aulnage' of cattle on market days at Mennecy. Perhaps the most curious was the monopoly of the 'jeu de la quill à baston qui se joue à Mennecy le jour de foire'.[298] Although the precise sum is not known, a significant part of the Duchy's revenues of 20,000 *livres* came from this carefully managed array of seemingly antiquated rights and dues. A further example is offered by the Duc de Rohan's seigneury of Beauchastel in the Vivarais where, out of a total of 2,200 *livres* yielded by farming a similar range of dues and rights, 1,000 came from river tolls alone.[299] Such revenues were certainly on a par with the commercial proceeds from the sale of grain which a well-organised and substantial estate might achieve. They were dwarfed by the 15,000 *livres* of corn tithe collected by the abbey of Saint Sauveur d'Aix.[300] Some rights bestowed advantages which cannot simply be represented in financial terms. At Lyon the canons of St Jean held the *droit de banvin* which gave the church the monopoly of retail wine sales in August. The market was thus reserved for the tithe wine – a twelfth or a thirteenth of the harvest – giving the collectors a real advantage over the producers to whom they could even sell their own produce.[301]

Larger landlords were also advantaged because significant revenues came not only from the largely honorific *cens* but also from the *lods et ventes* (*rachats* in the case of fiefs) which were payable on the succession or alienation of dependent land. Worth usually one fifth or a sixth of the sale price, or sometimes a year's revenue, the proceeds from such rights were obviously of much greater concern to those with substantial seigneurial dependants.[302] Antoine Périgord, a judge at the *présidial* of Poitiers and a dependant of the Maréchale de Meilleraye, paid 600 *livres* in 1706, 1,200 in 1747 and 2,400 in 1760 on three different estates. Peret estimates that the *redevances casuels* were worth between 5,000 and 6,000 *livres* a year to the Marshall.[303] It was also still possible to make some money from rights of jurisdiction. The parlementary seigneurs of Largouet-sous-Vannes, where the court presided over 1,000 cases a year, collected 1,000 *livres* in the process, a sixth of their revenues.[304]

There were, of course, many nobles dependent on a few payments in kind or some truncated rights of justice whose position was much less happy.[305] Goubert estimated that a third of the nobility of the Beauvaisis were *pauvres honteux*. He found seventy families who shared a total revenue of 81,000 *livres* and amongst them twenty-three *écuyers* who had less than 500 *livres*.[306] Some of the Norman nobility appear to have been so poor that they were in danger of slipping into the peasantry. Alexandre de Bailleur de St Crespin-du-Buquet, *chevalier seigneur du Mesnil Tournant*, had only two wigs, a pair of breeches, four shirts, a sword and a pair of pistols plus a broken hunting gun with which to sustain his impressive title. His only furniture was his bed.[307]

Such poverty was a reminder of the constant need to exploit the opportunities provided by the seigneurial system. Every aspiring landowner sought to acquire a seigneurial title and every ambitious seigneur strove to consolidate his estates into blocks of territory sufficiently impressive to justify their transformation into a *fief de dignité*. An accumulation of effectively administered feudal perquisites was both desirable and valuable. It would indeed be difficult to explain the ferocity and length of the legal disputes which they provoked between rival seigneurs if this had not been the case. A concern with maximising feudal revenues was certainly more in evidence than an interest in raising agricultural productivity. Nor did the widespread decline in the proceeds of justice stimulate a change of attitude. Sometimes the response was indeed the opposite of what might have been expected, as in 1585, when Pierre de Roncherolles, Baron de St-Pierre in Normandy, sold all his arable and meadow land, retaining only his seigneurial rights. It was a strategy which was not reversed until the middle of the eighteenth century. By then 'virtually every element in the Barony reflected the Roncherolles' failure to maintain and improve their property'.[308]

What helped the Roncherolles and many others through this period was partly the steady rise in income from customs and tolls and partly the exploitation of woods and forests. Market revenues at Pont-St-Pierre rose sevenfold during the course of the seventeenth century.[309] At Neubourg, also in Normandy, the seigneurs benefited from a threefold rise between 1601 and 1631.[310] Whilst this suggests some growth in commercial activity it was also a reflection of the capacity of the seigneurial administration to use its privileged position to benefit from – and contribute to – the inflation of agricultural prices. The Roncherrolles, sustained by the *parlement* of Rouen, remained opposed to freedom of trade within their jurisdiction down to the end of the *ancien régime*.[311] Their barony, Dewald observes, 'stood as the local embodiment of the regulated economy'.[312] The exploitation of woodland, of which the nobility possessed a highly disproportionate share, yielded even more than market dues. Dewald notes a sevenfold increase in the value of woodland over the first two-thirds of the sixteenth century, followed by a further trebling by the 1570s and a doubling by 1730.[313] The Roncherolles, in common with other seigneurs of western France, obtained over half their income in this way. For a period in the late sixteenth century the proportion rose to 70 per cent.[314] A substantial part of the income was derived directly from privileges and rights over woods rather than their commercial development.[315] But the cutting and selling of wood did not, as Gallet observes of his Breton seigneurs, indicate a profit-making mentality.[316] Certainly, the capacity to plunder a natural resource in order to benefit from price inflation was hardly conducive to agricultural investment.

The attachment to seigneurial dues and rents in kind may also have been reinforced by the upward movement of grain prices which enabled large profits to be made simply by playing the market. Gascon estimates that the profits made by Lyon grain merchants rose from about 10–20 per cent in 1518–20 to 96 per cent by 1580–9.[317] In these circumstances it was not surprising that there was a tendency to limit the share of produce left in peasant hands and/or to demand higher rents. The imposition of the harsh forms of *métayage* observed in Poitou from the sixteenth century have already been discussed. In Lorraine down to 1605 the *baux de vignes* stipulated a rent of one quarter of the harvest; subsequently it rose to a third.[318] Rents in western Normandy appear to have quadrupled between 1535–40 and 1575–80.[319] Whilst the rise of rents recorded during the first half of the sixteenth century in the Ile-de-France was reversed during the wars of religion, the upward movement was resumed with a vengeance from the turn of the century; between 1600 and 1650 rises of anything between 125 and a staggering 445 per cent were recorded.[320] In Languedoc increases of up to 150 per cent during the same period meant that by mid-century rents had reached unprecedented levels.[321] Taking France as a whole it is estimated that rents, feudal dues and tithes took away around 30 per cent of the net agricultural produce.[322]

Much of this flowed into the towns from which, as we have seen, growing numbers of acquisitive landlords dominated the neighbouring countryside. The vastly increased tax yield went in the same direction, sometimes into exactly the same pockets. By 1675 taxation was probably taking a fifth – perhaps as much as a third – of the total grain harvest.[323] The yield of state taxes had tripled, perhaps quadrupled, since 1600.[324] Tilly calculates that the average hours of work required to sustain this burden rose from about fifty to 120 a year. Even if the actual amount reaching the Treasury was not as great as is assumed the upward trend was dramatic (see Figure 2.1).

The fiscal demands of the state were compounded by the direct military burdens imposed on many rural communities. The accumulated effect of the repeated visitations of the soldiery in the frontier regions is difficult to quantify but the impressionistic evidence is plentiful. In 1692 the Provençal community of Auriol borrowed 5,500 *livres* for the sustenance of fifty dragoons with sixty horses who stayed from November to February. In 1642 twelve villagers were called up. Ten years later the community was given three days to mount a militia of seventy-two in conjunction with a neighbouring village. In 1674 sixteen men went to fight and in 1688 a further twenty-eight. In 1692 the Consuls claimed to have provided five companies of fifty men each.[325] Such inroads into the able-bodied population, although certainly serious, were insignificant by comparison with the effects on the population of those regions most affected by the constant fighting. Of 126 Burgundian villages surveyed in the 1660s, fifty-three had alienated their communal lands in whole or part since 1600 frequently in order 'to pay for their garrisons and royal taxes' as the representatives of Chazilly complained.[326] Soldiers also brought the plague. Of eighteen communities in the Vivarais ravaged by troops and plague in the period between 1628 and 1632 seven renewed their population quite quickly, five by the late seventeenth

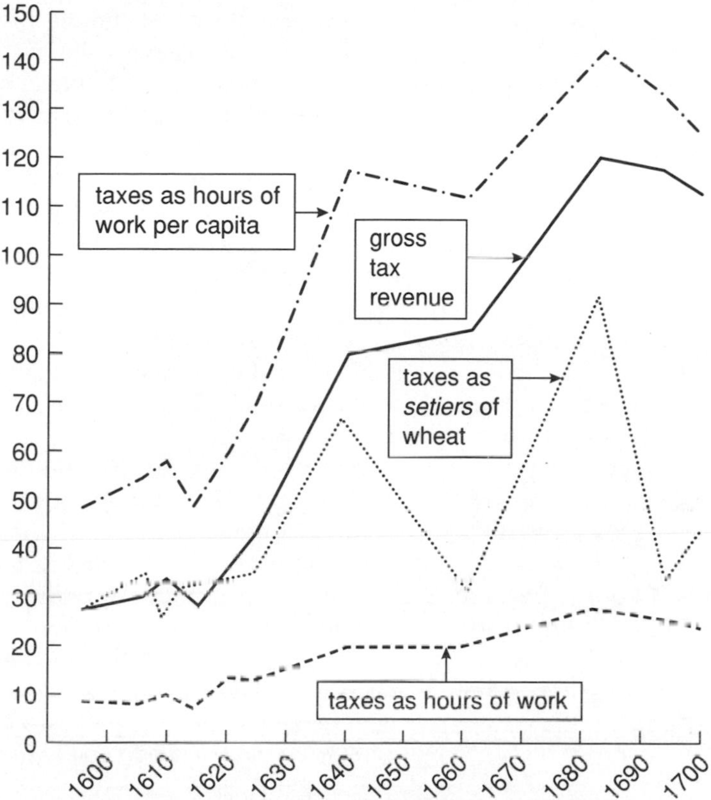

Figure 2.1 The burden of gross tax revenues

Source: Tilly 1981: 120

century, two in the eighteenth, two in the nineteenth whilst two never recovered at all. After the sacking of Privas its population fell from 2,500 to less than 600, a catastrophe compounded by the expulsion of its remarkably resilient Huguenot community in 1664. It did not recover until 1800.[327]

The loss of the population by death or flight accentuated all the regressive features of the picture which has so far been drawn. Alienation of the commons, involving the loss of yet more forest and pastureland to seigneurs and landlords, or recourse to further borrowing were frequently the only options left.[328] Vacant holdings were either abandoned or acquired by those notables in a position to take them on. Faced with a shortage of labour they then resorted to attempts to revive old obligations or impose new ones on the remaining tenants and their communities. Roupnel long ago remarked on the exceptional vigour of the seigneurial reaction carried through by the urban notables of the Dijonnais.[329]

It is a testimony to the resources and resilience of the rural population that in some areas some of the peasantry may have benefited from rising prices; but everything depended on local custom, the size of holding, and the nature of their contracts.[330] By mid-century, as production faltered, the capacity to meet the insatiable demands of their landlords gave out. Everywhere there were signs of mounting arrears, growing peasant indebtedness and a falling away of rents as proprietors adjusted to the harsh realities. The ebbing tide exposed a thoroughly indebted rural population. Goubert's well-known calculations for the Beauvaisis show that, by the time all dues, tithes, taxes, and contributions to the parish had been taken into account, the average family had less than half their produce with which to feed themselves.[331] The lower prices and improved real wages of the second half of the century were only a marginal compensation. Nor did the decline in interest rates help much because, as inflation turned to deflation, the size of debts was little diminished. In any event there is some fragmentary evidence to suggest that whilst interest rates fell in mid-century to around 4 or 5 per cent, peasants were charged somewhat more.[332]

The accumulative effect of these process was well observed by the royal commissioners sent to investigate the collection of taxes in the Orléanais and Le Maine in 1687 who observed that:

> there are hardly any peasants that own property . . . there are only small farmers who own nothing. The proprietors must furnish them with cattle, advance them money on which to live, pay their *tailles* and take in payment the peasant's entire portion of the harvest. Even this is sometimes insufficient to cover his debts. Thus the small farmers earn nothing; they leave the land as destitute as they came to it . . .

What cash was left they said went into paying taxes so that 'there was almost no money left for individuals; from this comes the decline of commerce . . .'.[333] Such coins as were to be found in the hands of artisans and peasants were sometimes considered so worthless by traders that they refused to accept them; those fortunate enough to acquire silver or gold coins were as likely to hoard as to spend them.[334] Even in 'advanced' regions like Artois and Picardy cash payments were still rare at the beginning of the eighteenth century.[335] So denuded of specie were the villagers of the Andance valley by the end of the seventeenth century that even their small dowries – 250 to 600 *livres* – were frequently paid in instalments over a period of two to five years.[336] Yet this represented relative affluence: at least one in twenty, and sometimes as many as one in ten, villagers were totally indigent and dependent on charity or begging to survive.[337]

Deprived of the means to survive as independent producers, the peasantry were thus also prevented from becoming consumers. Even in those areas most under the pull of the market such as the Lauragais or the Essones valley in the Ile-de-France the peasantry had virtually nothing to show for their years of toil: a single, probably windowless, room adjacent to the shelter for the animals, with a floor of beaten earth and containing some basic items of furniture and kitchenware: a table, benches, one or possibly two beds, some earthenware or iron pots, pewter utensils, a chest for the few precious items of linen and clothing, the whole lot not worth much more than 300 *livres* at the end of a lifetime. The average *vigneron* of the Essonne valley might have twelve sheets, six napkins, six shirts, two pairs of breeches, a jerkin and coat, and some skirts and headscarfs for the women. The household linen seems plentiful compared with that to be found in the peasant households of the Lauragais. Here socks and stockings were unknown; sometimes wool or linen gaiters were worn and clogs were available from the local shoemaker but many simply went barefoot. Most of the king's subjects thus bought little or no copper or silver ware, no glass, little or no linen which was not produced locally; they were unlikely to have a plough and if they did it was made largely of wood as were other rough and ready tools. Those requiring much metal, notably sickles, were prohibitively expensive.[338] Essential equipment, however, together with any cattle, usually constituted the largest part of these meagre fortunes. When Seguin, *journalier-vigneron* of St Julien de Cray in the Brionnais, died, his furniture was not worth more than ten *livres*, his tools fifty-six and his cow forty-nine.[339] Gallet's analysis of 276 Breton inventories shows that virtually half of the peasantry even in this relatively favoured province, where plough trains and a surplus of grain were common, left possessions worth no more than 200 *livres*; even those with inventories estimated at 300 or 500 lived in the same humble fashion, for half of this was represented by their equipment and cattle.[340]

It might be thought that despite the lack of domestic comforts the peasants would at least have eaten well. In fact, the staple diet for most homes was a soup thickened with peas, beans or other vegetables and bread. Although the quality of the bread varied from province to province, in most it was brown or black, being made with barley or rye. It could be very hard. In Dauphiné it was prepared twice a year and lasted eighteen months. In the mountains of the Vivarais and the foothills of the Cévennes, bread was displaced by chestnuts as the basic element. Potatoes were unknown until the last quarter of the eighteenth century.[341] The limited amounts of dairy produce were either sold for much-needed cash or went in rent or dues. Apart from the occasional rabbit poached from the seigneurial reserves, meat was a rarity. Even in a regional centre like Castelnaudary it was said in 1734 that there were only fifty families who regularly ate meat from the butchers.[342] In general the diet of the populace was no better and possibly worse than it had been in the fifteenth century. It is worth noting Le Roy Ladurie's suggestive picture of the decline during the course of the sixteenth century in the nutrient value of the wages received in kind by the *fermier* of the ecclesiastical seigneurs of La Bastide-Redonde near Narbonne: more bread but of worse quality, the partial substitution of plonk for better-quality wine and less oil.[343] There were some significant exceptions to this grim picture: for coastal populations where fish was available; in Normandy where white bread and dairy produce were more commonly found; and, above all, in Brittany where meat, butter, fish and fruits filled out the basic provision of bread.

Given this situation it is not surprising that, overall, half the children brought into the world by the inhabitants of rural France did not survive beyond their tenth birthday.[344] Once past the vulnerable years of young childhood the chances of survival increased significantly; but only about half of those who attained their twentieth birthday were likely to survive beyond the age of 50. Even when the mortality rate ebbed somewhat in the eighteenth century life expectancy at age 20 was only 36½.[345] It was not, however, just the high rates of mortality which were responsible for the demographic stagnation of the seventeenth century. The capacity of the population to renew itself after the recurrent demographic crises was in some ways quite extraordinary. During the crisis of 1693 mortality rates in the Paris basin soared from 175,000 per annum to 214,000; but by 1696 they had fallen back to just 150,000 whilst births – normally equal to the number of deaths – reached 201,000. By 1704 the balance had been restored. This outcome appears to have been the result of a combination of factors: an increase in the number of marriages, particularly amongst women who might otherwise have remained celibate but who now found partners amongst the bereaved; a rise in pre-nuptial conceptions; shorter intervals between marriage and the arrival of the first child. In other words there occurred a seemingly collective mobilisation of unused reproductive capacities.[346]

What such crises did not induce was a reversal of the steadily rising age of marriage which had the effect of shortening the period of female fertility. Commonly around 19 years of age in the mid-sixteenth century, the average age of marriage for women rose to 22 or 23 and even more. In the Paris basin under Louis XIV it reached 24½. In Normandy a rise from around 21 to over 25 has been suggested.[347] There were some exceptions, most notably Brittany. Here the rise in marriage age was lower than throughout most of France and the birth rate consequently somewhat above average.[348] Alain Croix explains this by reference to the relative prosperity and security of the province, sheltered as it was from the direct effects of warfare and the worst effects of the plague. This view is given credence by the fact that the buoyancy of the Breton population began to ebb with the onset of the Dutch War in 1672. The province was also affected for the first time by the full force of state fiscalism. Declining economic opportunities and expectations gradually brought the province into line with the reproductive behaviour of France as a whole.

The key question for young couples throughout most of France was their ability to sustain an independent household. Again the exceptions prove the rule; for in those areas where the newly married immediately became part of the household, with access to all its resources, marriage age remained low. In Bigorre and the Lavedan where the oldest child regardless of sex inherited, most women appear to have married before their twentieth birthday. Women also continued to marry at an early age in the Limousin – a province with many extended family communities.[349] In most regions, however, marriage was deliberately delayed. 'It happens only too often,' declared the consuls of Arles in 1716, 'that fear of misery prevents people from marrying.'[350]

France's demographic stagnation thus reflected not just the direct impact of war and plague. It flowed from an increasingly widespread collective 'auto-regulation'. This was itself bound up with a petty mode of production in which the disappearance of the parents was the normal precondition for the establishment of a new household. The inflexibility of the system was compounded by the polarisation of property structures as the contradiction between the demands of large farms for labour and the ability of that labour to sustain itself became unmanageable. Deprived of their surplus, in many cases unable to survive as independent producers but not yet wage-earners, millions of French peasants teetered on the brink of complete expropriation. Here was a proletariat in the making but one so denuded of resources that its capacity to act as a generator of demand was negligible – a point well understood by many royal administrators even if it was couched in empirical rather than theoretical terms. This impasse was the inevitable result of the remorseless exploitation of the peasantry rather than a reflection of the technical inadequacies of French agriculture or Malthusian blockages. Despite its capacity for 'auto-regulation' the countryside could not sustain the people it produced. As Dupâquier has wryly noted, had 'the entire French territory been divided into micro-exploitations of one or two *hectares*, and cultivated with spade and hoe as in Flanders, the realm could have nourished possibly forty or fifty million people' – a fanciful idea but a telling point.[351] Inasmuch as the seigneury was an agent of consolidation and reorganisation it served only to deepen all the contradictions without making any positive contribution to the growth of new practices.[352] Indeed, there was little incentive to do this. With an array of feudal mechanisms at their disposition, the opportunity to plunder extensive reserves of timber and to profit from playing the market in grain, landlords took a very short-term view of their economic interests.

The distress of the peasantry was deepened by the fiscal and military demands of the state. Some spasmodic efforts were made to prevent soldiers and tax farmers depriving peasants of their cattle but these were little more than gestures when set against the overall picture. If some government officials showed an awareness of the need to raise purchasing power, this was more than negated by the state's own financial needs. To the extent that the state entered into a competition with the landlords for a share of the agricultural surplus it simply aggravated the plight of the rural world. To the extent that it was itself tied to the seigneurial and officeholding elites the chances of significantly reducing the pressures on the peasantry were minimal. Yet, without resolving the contradictions in the heart of the French economy, without improving the conditions of the 85 per cent of the population that lived and worked in the countryside, there was no way that the strivings to boost trade and manufactures could generate more than a limited amount of growth, still less a significant development of capitalist structures. Indeed, capitalism made little progress during the course of the seventeenth century and the economy was largely listless.

Whatever character is ascribed to the economic foundations of French absolutism, capitalism is largely irrelevant. Moreover, the fiscal demands of the state by contributing directly to the depression of the home market probably did more to impede than promote capitalist growth. They also provoked some of the biggest popular revolts in French history and simultaneously fostered a bitter competition amongst the privileged for power and influence over the processes by which wealth was extracted from the labouring population. It is in the dynamics of political and social conflict, rather than of capitalist development, that the genesis of the absolute state is to be located.

3

THE ROOTS OF CONFLICT

A TIME OF TROUBLES

From the assassination of Henry IV in 1610 to the revolt in lower Brittany in 1675 French society was beset by debilitating and destabilising internal conflict. These decades, so often viewed in terms of the triumph of its great rulers and the onward march of monarchical authority, were in fact marked by brooding uncertainty, constant political tension and acute social antagonisms. As the king's assassination in 1610 made brutally clear, the menace of renewed religious strife still hung over the realm; Catholic fervour was not satisfied nor the threat of Protestant rebellion liquidated until 1629, at the end of a decade in which almost all the financial and military resources at the disposition of the young king had been consumed in the endeavour.

This victory only momentarily obscured the perpetual aristocratic intrigue which beset the court and government. The tone for the entire reign had been set in 1617 when the young Louis, ordering the murder of the court favourite, Concini, swept his mother Marie de Médicis from power. Taking up arms against her son in 1620 only to be defeated at the skirmish of the Ponts de Cé and compelled to renounce 'forever' all cabals and factions, the queen mother none the less continued to be a focus for all the resentment and jealousy of those excluded from power.[1] She was exiled in 1631. But there was no such remedy for the equally damaging disaffection of Louis' brother Gaston d'Orléans. From the Chalais affair of 1626 to the Cinq-Mars conspiracy of 1642 this erratic and wayward prince was implicated in a series of plots aimed at the king and his first minister. Whilst Richelieu's entry into the royal council in 1624 had brought an end to seven years of ministerial reshuffling, the cost of sustaining him against his enemies was enormous. Forced into open conflict with members of his own family, forced to arrest and imprison childhood playmates, betrayed by favourites and advisers of his own choosing, Louis XIII presided over more political executions than any other ruler in French history. In addition to the queen mother, the list of those who died in prison, in exile or on the scaffold was impressive: it included the king's half-brother Alexandre de Vendôme, the Duc de Montmorency, the Keeper of the Seals, Michel de Marillac, and Gaston's governor, Marshall d'Ornano; Louis' cousin, the Count of Soissons, died helping the Spanish to invade France in 1641.[2]

Extraordinary survivors though they were, the king and his chief minister pushed themselves to the limit. By early 1643 both were dead, prematurely worn out by the constant struggle. They bequeathed to Cardinal Mazarin all their responsibilities, an aristocracy close to open revolt and a 4-year-old heir to the throne. This potent legacy was compounded by Mazarin's foreign and upstart origins. His political survival owed much to his relationship with the Regent, Anne of Austria, whom, it was rumoured, he had married. The Cardinal's accumulation of power and wealth, together with his endeavours to secure a base in the French nobility through the marriage of his nieces, inevitably aroused hostility. He was even willing to contemplate a marriage alliance with the treacherous house of Vendôme. This earned him the bitter opposition of the Prince de Condé who, resentful about the government's failure to reward him for his services in the war against Spain, was anxious to consolidate his own network of alliances.[3] Arrested by Mazarin in January 1650, Condé led the resistance to the cardinal in the ensuing civil war before passing into Spanish service.

The capacity of aristocratic rivalries to destabilise the regime was enhanced during the 1630s and 1640s by the simultaneous threat of widespread revolt amongst the population at large. As the campaigns against the Huguenots passed their climax the Crown was confronted by a series of major provincial uprisings. The first came in September 1630 at Aix-en-Provence when a powerful combination of militant *parlementaires* and elements of the populace made the provincial capital unsafe for the intendants and those suspected of colluding with the government's plans for fiscal reform. It required the presence of the Prince of Condé and 5,000 troops to restore order. Next it was the turn of Languedoc where the provincial Estates, galvanised by the government's erosion of its financial powers, momentarily lent its support to the ill-fated aristocratic rebellion of 1632 which cost the Duc de Montmorency his life. In 1635 a new tax on wine provoked the first of an almost continuous sequence of uprisings which swept through the western provinces. They began in Bordeaux where for two months the authorities battled to retain control of the popular quarters of the city, recovering them by dint of superior firepower only after prolonged bouts of fighting. Unrest broke out almost immediately in Périgueux and Agen leading to the death of fifteen notables in the latter. Further north, in the southern regions of Saintonge and Angoumois resistance to mounting fiscal burdens culminated in the summer of 1636 in a massive peasant insurrection remarkable for its high degree of organisation and cohesion. A series of popular assemblies, announced in advance and summoned by the tocsin, mobilised between 12,000 and 40,000 inhabitants. Rotas were devised, which ensured that the call to arms did not impede cultivation of the fields. From Angoumois the revolt spread to Poitou, Limousin and as far as Berry. The following year a comparable movement swept through Périgord, involving an assault on the provincial capital itself and the occupation of Bergerac by contingents of peasants. As the revolts of the central western provinces ebbed away, the ground was being laid for perhaps the most celebrated uprising of the century – that of the Norman Nu-Pieds of 1639; for over four months a large part of the Cotentin peninsula slipped from royal control, whilst major revolts also occurred in Rouen and Caen. A well-organised army composed largely of salt-workers and wood carriers assumed control of the region between Avranches and Coutances. Only with the arrival of crack troops in December was the peasant army finally dispersed.

It is doubtful whether the repression which followed was effective. From 1643 to 1645 revolt was endemic throughout the west and south and some parts of the north. It took ten months and a general amnesty to pacify the peasantry of Rouergue after they had invaded Villefranche in protest against the rising burden of taxation.[4] At Montpellier in June 1645 streets were barricaded and the houses of a number of fiscal agents and their relatives sacked, several being killed in the process.[5] Although this revolt lasted for only four days, the authorities were greatly alarmed about

> the perilous consequences for the authority and affairs of the king . . . for in a town where there is a citadel, a company of sovereign officers, treasurers of France, a *présidial*, and the presence of the governor of the province the people dared to take up arms and resist by force.[6]

It is against this turbulent background that the Frondes of 1648–53 must be set. Precipitated by the magistrates of the *parlement* of Paris, followed by those of Bordeaux and Aix-en-Provence, the Frondes drew into revolt members of every social stratum from the highest ranks of the nobility to the lowest ranks of the Third Estate. Whilst the great princes raised the standard of revolt in pursuit of their claim to a share in government and to achieve the departure of Mazarin, the lesser nobility came together in a series of assemblies seeking the restoration of their 'ancient prerogatives and immunities'.[7] Although Mazarin suc-cessfully deflected their demand for the summoning of an Estates-General, assemblies of the nobility continued throughout the 1650s. In Anjou and Normandy in 1656–7 a remarkable organisation appeared which divided these provinces into cantons, each of which elected two deputies charged with collecting information about the violation of noble privileges. A government ban appeared to have little effect. It was not until 1659 that noble agitation faded away in the face of ruthless repression and news of the forthcoming peace with Spain.[8]

Whilst dukes and *gentilshommes* strove to preserve the rights of the noble born, Bordeaux gave birth to the most radical movement of the century. In June 1651 a popular organisation known as the Ormée suppressed both municipality and *parlement* to seize effective control of the city. At its height the Ormée probably had the active support of a quarter of the population; it did not succumb until July 1653, nearly a year after the government had regained control of Paris. Even when the Ormée was finally destroyed violent resistance to the tax collectors remained endemic in much of the south-west throughout the 1650s and barely diminished with Louis XIV's assumption of power. In 1664 simmering discontent with government efforts to extend its powers of taxation over the privileged salt trade of the Pyreneen foothills erupted in open but guerrilla-style resistance. Unable to get to grips with the small bands of men who melted away into the mountain valleys, the government was eventually forced to issue a general amnesty and to abandon its plans to introduce the *gabelle* into the *pays redimés*. Furthermore the petty noble, Bernard d'Audijos, from whom the revolt took its name, was not only pardoned but in 1675 given permission to command a regiment drawn from his followers.[9] Perhaps the government's forgiveness had something to do with the renewed popular agitation which afflicted Bordeaux for six months of that year, and which was only finally quelled by yet another compromise and the billeting of soldiers on the unfortunate city. Some 6,000 troops were also required to deal with the simultaneous and brutally anti-seigneurial uprising of the Breton peasantry.[10]

Such a selective summary can do no more than indicate some of the moments of greatest disaffection; only inadequately does it convey the almost permanent state of tension which threatened at any moment to erupt into open unrest. Pillorget counted 103 insurrectional movements of diverse social character in Provence between 1596 and 1635 and a further twenty-seven which he classified as 'marginal'.[11] For the entirety of the *pays d'oc*, 300 or so specifically popular revolts have been recorded for the century as a whole.[12] Goubert deduced that the total number of popular *émotions* throughout the realm must have been in excess of 1,000.[13] Despite the fact that only a handful of these blossomed into large-scale armed resistance the figures highlight the enormous gap between the theoretically sovereign powers of the monarchy and the fragility of its control over the population. As discontent was not confined to the poor and dispossessed, there existed an ever-present possibility that their grievances might be harnessed to the opposition of the rich and powerful in an overwhelming movement of resistance. Diverse though the sources of opposition to the Crown were, they did appear to share a common interest in the destruction of the system of war finance, soaring fiscal burdens and a ruthless exercise of authority widely perceived to be nothing short of tyranny. The demand of the magistrates of Paris for a 25 per cent reduction in the *taille* certainly met up with popular sentiment and, together with its success in obtaining the suppression of the intendancies, directly encouraged the ensuing and almost universal strike of tax payers.[14]

It is, in fact, remarkable that the multiple sources of opposition to the government never combined in a challenge capable either of achieving the overthrow of the hated cardinals or of obtaining a significant modification of the aggressive foreign policies which were widely perceived as being the source of France's misery. In the Fronde, the Estates-General, though promised, never met and the intendants were quickly restored. Mazarin died in 1661, perhaps the richest and most powerful man in Europe as well as one of the most reviled. Louis XIV retained the cardinal's administrative personnel including Colbert, whilst making it clear that he intended to rule in person. Decades of strife gave way not only to a long period of political stability but to the unfolding of one of the most remarkable, and certainly the most systematic, assertions of royal grandeur in the long history of the French monarchy.

It is possible to point in many directions to explain the return of political stability and why it was that such intense and endemic resistance failed to open up an alternative path of political development. The answer, some have suggested, lies partly or wholly in the nature of conflict itself. According to Porshnev the bourgeoisie ultimately abandoned the populace and stood firm with the feudal rulers of France; class confronted class. For Mousnier the dynamic of revolt was provided not by class at all but by chains of *fidelité* which enabled the notables to involve the lower orders in their own resistance to royal authority. Louis XIV's power came from his success in making himself the fount of all patronage and concentrating all the chains of *fidelité* in his own hands.[15] At the heart of these apparently irreconcilable viewpoints is the problem of the degree of autonomy to be ascribed to popular revolts and their relationship to those of the notables. One particularly well-documented and studied rebellion – that of Aix in 1630 – provides an exceptionally clear picture of the social forces at work. A brief account of this episode makes a useful starting point for a more extended analysis.

A CASE STUDY: THE CASCAVEOUX REVOLT[16]

In the years immediately prior to 1630 Provence was tormented by a classic combination of inflation, plague, troop movements and the rising fiscal exigencies of the Crown. Between 1625 and 1630 bread and wheat prices, additionally inflated by the demands of the troops for provisions, rose by perhaps 75 per cent; the bourgeoisie of Aix expelled numbers of the poor suspected of carrying the plague, whilst the *parlement* protested at arbitrary increases in salt prices. In October 1629 the *parlement* resolved to leave Aix because of the plague; for practical reasons the magistrates divided into two groups, one sitting at Salin and one at Pertuis, though in practice most retreated to their country houses leaving no more than ten judges in session in each of the towns.

Social and political tensions were already mounting when news broke that it was the government's intention to introduce royal tax officials – *élus* – into the province, thus undermining its fiscal autonomy, and possibly opening the way for the destruction of the provincial Estates. The privileges of the notables were at stake. Simultaneously, in common with all royal officers, the *parlementaires* faced a demand for a forced loan equivalent to a quarter of the value of their offices in return for a renewal of the *paulette*. This threat was only lifted on condition that the magistrates made a hefty loan to the king. In unison with the provincial Estates and the Assembly of Communities the *parlement* resisted the royal demands. In July the intendant d'Aubray was compelled to adjourn the Estates which had been summoned and the atmosphere deteriorated. Unrest amongst the peasantry, clashes with the troops and attacks on corn convoys were reported.

In Aix itself, to which the *parlementaires* returned at the beginning of September, disturbances grew. On the 8th the first consul (the mayor), Gaspard de Forbin, sieur de la Barben, member of one of the wealthiest families of the region, fled for safety. When the intendant arrived on the 19th he was met with what Pillorget describes as a classical type of charivari and he too was forced to flee. At the head of the opposition and now emerging as a leader of some stature was de Coriolis, president of the *chambre tournelle* in the *parlement*. For some time de Coriolis had been conducting a bitter feud with the first president, d'Oppède, who, like the first consul, was also a member of the Forbin family. During the enforced separation of the *parlement* the two rivals had each presided over one section, allowing de Coriolis to build up support. These divisions in the midst of an apparently united resistance were of profound significance. D'Oppède was suspected of collaborating with the government and de Coriolis certainly regarded himself as a defender of provincial liberties. News that the *cour des aides* and the *chambre des comptes* were to be transferred to Toulon provoked renewed agitation; on 13 October it was the turn of the president of the *comptes*, whose highly ambivalent attitude had aroused suspicion, and of d'Oppède himself, to hastily depart from the town. Assemblies of the three orders were held and they unanimously proclaimed their opposition to the royal demands; the *parlement* authorised the towns of the region to raise arms. In Aix itself one of the nephews of de Coriolis, the seigneur de Chateauneuf, organised elements of the populace into a militant party. Those who joined received a little bell attached to a leather strap or white ribbon. Peasants encouraged by Chateauneuf flocked into the town. Unrest also spread outwards into the countryside.

On 3 November – a Sunday – an influx of peasantry from a group of communities adjacent to the lands of the first consul, Gaspard de Forbin, arrived. These communities had been engaged in continual and bitter disputes with Gaspard as a result of his refusal to allow them to gather wood on his lands. He had also used his office to prevent the citizens of Aix doing likewise and, to boot, was suspected of grain hoarding. After subjecting the bourgeoisie to a night of terror, and pillaging the properties of some tax officials, the following morning a sea of peasants and artisans streamed out of Aix and marched for half a day to the château La Barben. There was some pillaging of outbuildings and destruction of trees before the peasants dispersed to their villages laden with firewood, furniture, sacks of salt and wheat.

But when the artisans returned to Aix they found that a bourgeois militia had been mobilised. The reaction had set in. For a moment the city divided on social lines. On 8 November the *parlement* prohibited night meetings and the carrying of arms. Measures were taken to expel 'vagabonds' and other *gens sans aveu* from the town. These somewhat belated measures were, however, insufficient to prevent further attacks on the houses of those suspected of involvement in the sale of the new tax offices. A compromise party under a new first consul, the Baron de Bras, gained strength. On 6 December a violent clash between the partisans of Bras and de Coriolis left the *parlement* as a sort of arbiter and increasingly concerned to press for law and order. Many of the well-to-do left the city in fear of the populace. *Parlement* and municipality were still technically in revolt but uncertainly so; frequently only half the *parlement*'s complement of sixty or seventy judges were present. The towns of Arles and Marseille refused help. News came early in 1631 of the approach of an army under the Prince de Condé. In March negotiations were opened, the Estates summoned, and a settlement rapidly concluded. In return for a payment of 1.5 million *livres* the installation of the *élus* was abandoned. Later Condé's army occupied Aix which resulted in a handful of deaths at the hands of the soldiers. Some twenty-five or thirty rebels were condemned *in absentia* but only one insignificant fellow paid with his life. De Coriolis was subsequently condemned to death for participating in Montmorency's revolt in Languedoc; he returned from exile in 1640, dying in gaol shortly afterwards. His nephews, the Chateauneuf brothers, although similarly excluded from the general amnesty of July 1633, later quietly returned to Provence. The Aixoise courts suffered a short exile in various small towns whilst Aix spent two months under military occupation for which it had to bear the costs; until 1637 it was also deprived of its right to municipal elections.

One actor is conspicuously absent from the above account: the Duc de Guise, governor of the province and admiral of the Levant.[17] Son of Henri de Guise who was murdered at Blois in 1588, Charles had been appointed to these positions at the age of 23 in 1594 as part of Henri IV's settlement with the nobility.[18] Guise quarrelled with every rival authority, notably with the general of the galleys, first Philippe de Gondi and then his son Pierre, Duc de Retz. The *parlement* of Aix supported Gondi. It also obstructed Guise's ambition to turn the governorship into a hereditary office by refusing to verify the royal letters of September 1615 appointing Guise's son as governor of Provence *en survivance*. The feud intensified in the years prior to 1640 as the *parlement* came into conflict with Guise over his claims to powers of taxation for military purposes, to criminal jurisdiction over military personnel and other matters. It did not help that the magistrates were largely supported by Richelieu. In August 1629 Guise blockaded Aix during the outbreak of plague, disrupting commerce, paralysing the provincial administration, and riding roughshod over such privileges as the inhabitants' traditional exemption from billeting and the right to cut wood within five leagues of the city. The following January he was finally compelled by the king to abandon the blockade and accompany him on the campaign to Italy. Although he returned to the province in November he was by then embroiled in the Queen Mother's conspiracy against Richelieu and stayed in Marseille. A few troops were dispatched to ravage the lands of those rural communities which had participated in the attack on the Château Barben but the governor studiously ignored the requests of the *parlement* and municipality to restore order in their restive city. Instead, he wrote to the magistrates announcing the fall of the cardinal. Learning that like the other conspirators he had been deceived, the Duke prevaricated for a few months before opting for exile in Italy where he died in 1640.

The revolt of the Cascaveoux ended in the sort of compromise that became characteristic of the next twenty-five years. Forced to back down on the central question of the *élus*, whilst extracting some immediate financial compensation, the government contented itself with an immediate assertion of its authority before resuming normal relations with the provincial courts and the families that wielded power in the region. The most significant casualty of these years in Provence was the Duc de Guise who, despite his opposition to Richelieu, was completely isolated from the other mainsprings of resistance. Indeed, his desire to extend his authority within the province brought him not into alliance with, but in opposition to, the other loci of authority, notably the *parlement*. Unwilling to respond to its appeals for assistance, he forfeited this unexpected possibility of consolidating his own position; as far as the government was concerned he compounded his sins by failing in his prime duty to maintain law and order.

From this brief account it should be readily apparent that the revolt at Aix was a complex affair. Involving widely differing social groups and a diversity of political interests, it evolved at different levels which sometimes meshed in an unpredictable way. What is beyond dispute is that the multiple causes of disaffection, and the continuous interplay of different interests and motives, make it impossible to confine such events within simple explanatory formulae. Porshnev's observation that 'this was at first a typically plebeian uprising' is manifestly untenable.[19] Equally inadequate is Mousnier's insistence that the populace were simply 'auxiliaries' in 'a rivalry between factions of officers and nobles'.[20]

Amongst the many elements at work in this uprising the following stand out. First, the economic and social dislocation caused by rising prices, the plague and the demands of the soldiery. Second, a widespread hostility to the demands of the fisc and a defence of provincial privileges which for a time achieved a measure of unity. Third, the presence of acute rivalries within the urban oligarchy, between the notables and amongst the provincial-wide authorities. Lastly, a tumultuous and frightening intervention by the lower orders which threatened to get out of hand. These elements reappeared time and time again during the course of the seventeenth century, sometimes in isolation but mostly in combinations of varying proportions. A closer look at them therefore seems worthwhile.

THE MISERY OF THE PEOPLE

It almost goes without saying that material deprivation was a constant factor in the lives of millions of peasants and artisans. Bread absorbed at least half of a typical family's income. A bad harvest, the arrival of the plague or troops could unbalance the precarious equilibrium of the local economy and, with that, of countless households. If harvest failure was followed by famine the poor died in their thousands whilst the marginally more fortunate sold their tiny holdings for a pittance or simply abandoned them. Such crises then spilled over into the towns which were reservoirs of poverty at the best of times. Virtually all the regional capitals – Aix, Amiens, Bordeaux, Dijon, Grenoble, Montpellier, Marseille, Rouen, Rennes – were afflicted at one time or another by significant disturbances. So were a number of secondary towns such as Angers, Caen and Agen and numerous small textile centres.[21]

Those with little to lose defended it with desperation. 'We have neither work, nor bread, we prefer to die' was the cry heard at Amiens during the violent disturbances of the textile workers in April 1636.[22] At Montpellier in 1645 Marshal Schomberg, struggling to restore order, encountered a women hastening with her son to join a group of rioters. Asking why she hurried so he received the reply that it was 'to die once and for all in order that they cannot kill us every day by taking away our bread'.[23] Possibly embellished in the retelling, this incident is entirely compatible with the reactions of those who were present; the intendant Bosquet concluded that the uprising was due in part to the great 'distress and misery of the people'.[24] From distant Grenoble, where the Montpellier affair evidently aroused considerable anxiety amongst the authorities, the Duke of Sully was moved to warn the government that 'the misery and necessity of the people of this province have almost caused a revolt in this town . . .'.[25]

Sometimes the correlation between economic conditions and unrest seems fairly obvious. The uprising of the Nu-Pieds in 1639 erupted in a less well-endowed part of Normandy. They were dependent on the production of inferior grain and on the activities of poor salt-workers and wood burners, so it is little wonder that the inhabitants of the Cotentin littoral fought for what privileges they had. For more than a decade grain shortages had been endemic. Disturbances, encouraged by rumours of grain hoarding, affected several of Normandy's main towns.[26] Textile manufactures, particularly in Caen and Rouen, were struggling to compete with English and Dutch competition. A dramatic decline in paper production also affected the smaller centres of Viré and Mortain close to the heart of the rural revolt.[27] Four years later similar economic pressures probably contributed to the uprising in the Rouergue, a region of limited agricultural capacity where a bad harvest had pushed prices to two or three times their previous level.[28] At Marseille in 1644 a shortage of grain, exacerbated by the refusal of traders to accept the inferior coinage offered by the populace, sparked off a riot which required the intervention of the governor.[29] On the other hand, the comparative economic stability of Provence as a whole may explain why such explosions of discontent never blossomed after 1630 into the large-scale, months-long, mass movements typical of the western provinces. Pillorget suggests that the calm of the 1650s was possibly due to good harvests and low prices.[30] It might also be that Provence and Languedoc benefited from the relative diversity of their economic activity; the cultivation of Mediterranean fruits, vines, olives and nuts complemented that of grain and was further supplemented by some rural textile and mining activities.

Yet, beyond a certain point the correlation between economic conditions and unrest is far from clear. In neither Provence nor Languedoc were their relative advantages sufficient to prevent the repeated outbursts of violent disorder which affected their principal and smaller urban centres. Nor is it obvious that all the major western epicentres of revolt were areas of particular economic distress. The rebellious communities of Saintonge and Angoumois not only produced wine and hemp but were also able in most years to send a grain surplus to the urban markets. It is certainly impossible to establish a precise correlation between grain prices and large-scale unrest. This is true even of Normandy where, after the bad year of 1630, prices dropped by as much as a third in the period prior to the revolt of the Nu-Pieds.[31] In Provence before 1635 Pillorget is emphatic that 'the chronology of insurrections was on the whole clearly independent of the cyclical rhythm of prices' and likely to occur on the downward slope as at the peaks.[32] Bercé's study of the revolts in the south-west led him to a similar conclusion, notwithstanding their greater scope and larger popular base. Recognising the full effects of the acute agrarian crises which engulfed the poor in 1595, 1628–31, 1662, 1694 and 1709, he noted that the major waves of revolt may have come near them but they did not flow from them. They occurred in 1594, 1635–7, 1639–43, 1648–53, 1658–62 and 1702–7.[33] Analysis of the incidence of revolt in the towns of Languedoc between 1625 and 1660 has also shown the difficulty of establishing a clear correlation with the price of basic commodities.[34]

A closer correlation may be made between the geographical pattern of revolts and the distribution of taxation. The western provinces were certainly more heavily taxed than the relatively protected provinces of the south. Although the figures for government revenue must be treated with caution, because they both exclude money raised and spent locally and also exaggerate the amount actually levied, all the evidence suggests that Normandy together with *généralités* of the south-west – Poitiers, Limoges, Bordeaux, Montauban – contributed an excessive proportion. In 1639 these provided virtually a quarter of the *tailles* – a heavy burden for regions which outside the Bordelais were amongst the most sparsely populated in France. Normandy, although more densely populated and generally regarded as a rich province, provided between 20 and 25 per cent of the government's income. In the 1630s and 1640s Normandy and the south-west were contributing over 40 per cent of the revenues. In 1639 the single *généralité* of Caen paid 1.66 million compared with Provence's 1.33, a sum which by 1647 had actually fallen to under 1 million. Languedoc paid somewhat more; but at their peak in the early 1640s its total taxes did not exceed 6 million and they were normally less than 4 million.[35] There was, however, a measure of correlation between some of the most serious outbreaks of disorder in this province and tax increases. The intensification of unrest which occurred in the period 1643–6, including the Montpellier uprising, came in the wake of accumulating fiscal burdens which reached their highest level before 1691.[36] The distribution of taxes within regions was also significant. Although nominally they bore some relation to ability to pay, inertia or vested interest could produce a highly arbitrary distribution. In 1636 the creation of the new *généralité* of Alençon threw additional burdens on to that of Caen which was significantly reduced in size. The *élections* of Viré, Mortain, Valognes, and Coutances were particularly affected and these areas proved to be at the heart of the revolt of the Nu-Pieds.[37] Of the five *élections* within the *généralité* of Bordeaux that of Périgord bore just under a third of the fiscal burden and within this *élection* the *sénéchaussée* of Périgueux itself carried two-thirds of the taxes; this may well have contributed to its notably turbulent character.[38] On the other hand, the Bordelais, which managed to steadily reduce its share, was no less prone to open resistance.

These examples suggest that revolts were precipitated not just by the sheer weight of the tax burden but also by threats to increase it. Resistance came from both the already heavily burdened regions and those which were more lightly taxed. Moreover, although complaints about the *taille* abounded, particularly in the revolts of the western provinces, it was nearly always the impact or the threat of new indirect taxes which precipitated trouble despite the fact that these accounted for less than a quarter of the royal revenues in the 1630s and 1640s.[39] The chain of urban and rural revolts which began in Bordeaux in 1635 and then spread into the neighbouring western provinces and up the valley of the Garonne were sparked off by the imposition of a tax on wine sold in inns; violent confrontations over similar taxes continued for many years.[40] Two years later, the catalyst for the dramatic events in Périgord was an illegal levy of grain, ironically imposed by the provincial governor in order to raise troops to deal with the deteriorating situation.[41] At Amiens in 1635 it was the imposition of a sales tax on linen and woollen cloth which provoked the strike of merchants and led to the subsequent uprising of the carders.[42] In Normandy taxes on leather, playing cards, cloth and wine prepared the way for the conflict of 1639. In Rouen itself the inflammatory spark was provided by the arrival of an agent to impose a new tax on the dyeing of cloth and in upper Normandy by the threat to extend the *gabelle* to the privileged coastal regions of the Cotentin peninsula.[43] Similar fears about the extension of the *gabelle* into privileged regions were responsible for the Audijos revolt of 1664.[44] There were also fiscal devices which were little different in their effects from indirect taxes. At Montpellier in 1645 the precipitating factor was a compulsory tribute marking the *joyeux avènement à la couronne*, paid to preserve the privileges of the town. Artisans, it was rumoured, were to be taxed individually as well as through their guilds.[45] Thirty years later, the resort to a tax on pewter utensils and tobacco in order to finance the Dutch War precipitated the last major revolts of the century by the people of Bordeaux and Brittany.[46] Virtually all the taxes mentioned here were those on basic items of consumption – clothes, drink, salt, tobacco, and common utensils. Although care must be taken not to confuse underlying causes of revolt and the triggers which set them off, a common thread is evident: the arrival or suspected arrival of fiscal agents with yet another new tax with savage implications for the daily life of a population already existing on the very margins of survival. In this situation rumours of new taxes abounded. Some, such as the frequently voiced fear of a tax on births, never materialised. Yet this was perhaps less fantastic than it might seem. For in 1690, long after the great endemic of tax revolts had faded, the public registrars of funerals and burials sought to collect taxes on all aspects of phases of funeral arrangements – on the graves, the caskets, transportation and so on. Some women of Dijon complained that the bodies of their children and husbands had been seized in order to extract fees.[47]

These observations begin perhaps to cast light on the geographical pattern of revolt with its heavy concentration in the west and south. Some of these regions undoubtedly suffered from a combination of heavy burdens and local inequities in their distribution. However, the suggestion that it was not just the weight of taxation but its aggressive imposition on these regions brings into focus a larger issue: the way in which the fiscal depredations of the central state violated long traditions of provincial, urban and communal autonomy.

LIBERTIES AND THE DEFENCE OF COMMUNITY

There can be no doubt that the antagonism between centre and periphery was a basic element in the conflicts of the seventeenth century. Only with the virtually total collapse of effective government during the Fronde, when the ravages of civil war came to the Ile-de-France, was this polarity obscured. In part the prolonged bouts of revolt in the remoter regions of the realm simply reflected that very remoteness. At a time when large concentrations of troops were deployed along the northern and eastern frontiers, maintaining order in the distant parts of Normandy or Brittany and the heart of Languedoc was far from easy. Marshal Schomberg, lieutenant-general of Languedoc, had only forty soldiers at his disposition at Montpellier with which to confront an armed and hostile crowd, 2,000 strong.[48] It took the arrival of Marshal Gassion with 5,000 troops from Picardy to crush the armed resistance of the Nu-Pieds.[49] To cope with the Breton rising of 1675 eight companies of infantry from Brouage, Ré and Oléron were brought together with 350 musketeers, the French and Swiss guards, the regiments of Couronnne and Navailles and the regiment of dragoons of Tessé.[50] But, as the Duc de Chaulnes made clear to Colbert, the terrain, with its many raised dykes and enclosures, was unsuitable for cavalry. He also felt unable to guarantee the security of the soldiers if they were billeted in the tiny and dispersed hamlets of the Breton countryside.[51] The dragoons dispatched to deal with the Audijos revolt in 1664 spent several frustrating months in a vain endeavour to come to grips with the terrain, the weather and the elusive guerrilla band.[52]

The problems posed by the topography of these remote regions were not simply physical ones. The coasts of the Normandy peninsula, the dispersed hamlets of the west, the mountainous regions of the Pyrenees, the forests of the Périgord and the uplands of the *Midi* evidently sheltered communities which were at once more cohesive and more volatile than those of the grain-growing regions of the north. Bound together in varying degrees within the framework of patriarchal family networks and self-regulating communities, the villages of the *Midi* and the mid-west were well equipped to resist the pressures from outside. Many of the remoter regions also sheltered numbers of masterless people – the salt-workers and wood carriers of Normandy, the boatmen of Agen and the mountainmen of the Pyrenees who 'preferred smuggling to politics'.[53] The rhythms of work, the life and culture of these distant villages and towns, so different from region to region, were none the less quite distinct from those of the physically concentrated, hierarchically organised villages of the northern and eastern grain-growing regions. In the next century, as the peasantry of these areas lost respect for their masters, the epicentres of revolt shifted towards them; but for the moment the key issue was the burden which an expansive state endeavoured to impose on remote and independent regions.

This constituted a threat not only to the tax-paying populace but to the local rulers of France's provinces and cities. The uprising at Aix shows this very clearly because it arose not from a specific tax but from sweeping fiscal reforms which threatened provincial institutions. Efforts to undermine the autonomy of the *pays d'états* went back to the days of Sully and eventually bore fruit in Dauphiné, Guyenne and Normandy where the last meetings of the provincial assemblies took place in 1628, 1635 and 1655 respectively. However, the resistance in Provence, Languedoc and Burgundy was sufficient to induce the government to compromise in return for substantial cash payments.[54] Survival of the Estates was also an issue in the Audijos revolt. Some months before the revolt the Bishop of Tarbes, President of the Estates of Bigorre, wrote to Colbert, pointing out in no uncertain terms that 'this poor country' was under his protection. 'By the duty that is attached to my cross', he informed the minister,

> I would have you, sir, consider freely that the king's service may one day receive some harm from the suppression of these Estates

and of those of Foix and all the others that border the Pyrénées and enjoy their privileges from time immemorial.'[55]

Even in Normandy, where ancient privileges had largely been gutted of substance, the manifesto produced by its literate and perhaps well-to-do leaders declared that Normandy would either preserve its charter or lose its heart. The charter was that granted in 1315 by Louis X, decreeing that no extraordinary taxes would be levied.[56] To similar purpose the Breton peasantry associated their demands with a defence of *'la liberté armorique'*.[57]

It was, however, in the urban rather than the provincial context that a defence of traditional liberties made most sense. Many towns entered the seventeenth century with a remarkable degree of political, financial, legal and military autonomy. For the most powerful this included legal rights which prevented their citizens being tried elsewhere and exemption from garrison and governor. In the west La Rochelle's economic privileges guaranteed not only almost total exemption from royal taxation but the right to trade freely even with the enemies of France; the mayor acknowledged no superior save the king and royal authority was felt only indirectly through the small body of officers attached to the *présidial*. It was to take a fourteen-month siege, after a decade in which La Rochelle – partly because of its importance to the Huguenots – had been at the centre of French politics, to achieve the reduction of the town and its subjection to the royal will. In the south Marseille, whose privileges outshone those of La Rochelle, preserved its autonomy until the accession of Louis XIV. One of his first acts was to descend on the town and impose a new constitution. Even then it retained the inestimable advantage of being a free port. If few towns had such a wide range of privileges as La Rochelle or Marseille, nearly all possessed some on which they continued to insist. Arles, for instance, possessed its own salt marshes and various associated privileges which went back to a charter of 1251 obtained from Charles d'Anjou. This guaranteed a supply of cheap salt for inhabitants whilst generating an illicit trade with the surrounding regions. From 1596 various attempts to destroy the marshes met with determined opposition which brought into play another treasured right – that of not being removed from the city for trial.[58]

Even smaller rural centres were not without important rights. This was particularly so in Provence which, says Pillorget, can be considered as 'ensemble of 650 to 700 communities.'[59] They elected their consuls, constituted the basis for the provincial *assemblée des communautés* and were represented in the permanent commission of the Estates by two *procureurs*. The Treasurers of the Estates needed their authorisation to make payments, they had some control over roads and no military force could enter Provence without their written approval, a privilege supplemented by the power to determine its itinerary. But the *procureurs* themselves could not make any fiscal imposition without the assent of the full assembly of the communities.[60] If the communities of western France lacked the same elaborate superstructure, they too had a powerful sense of their own collective identity. This manifested itself in the disciplined series of assemblies, summoned at the sound of the tocsin, which organised resistance in 1636, sent deputies to regional gatherings and facilitated communication between the parishes.[61] As the movement developed, mass assemblies gave way to gatherings of the parish leaders and notables which were duly authorised by the anxious royal authorities. One brought together as many as 600 syndics from throughout Saintonge.[62] The leaders in these assemblies came from the more substantial members of the rural community: well-to-do peasants, small merchants, priests, officers of the local seigneurial courts and, quite possibly, the occasional royal *officier*.

Many royal *officiers* from the humblest *commis* for the *taille* to the dignitaries who headed the provincial *parlements* came to feel that they were as much victims of royal policies as beneficiaries. For as the Crown's financial plight grew more desperate so did its efforts to wring more cash out of the officeholding system by multiplying the number of offices and by imposing forced loans on the *officiers* themselves. In Normandy the general climate of unrest owed much to their resistance to the demands of the central government. From the beginning of Louis XIII's reign the *parlement* rejected edicts creating new officers – from those of presidents to humble clerkships – by the hundred.[63] They were, however, unable to prevent the transformation in 1636 of the lesser jurisdictions of Normandy into *vicomtés principales* with an array of the additional offices. The same year saw the creation of a new *généralité* based on Alençon, bringing with it a *bureau des finances*. Additional alternative and triennial offices were also established in the administration of the *eaux et forêts*.[64] The *parlement* of Bordeaux likewise found that it had to resist similar threats to its material and political interests, represented most notably by the creation of a *cour des aides* at Agen in 1639. Such initiatives, however, paled into insignificance when put alongside the intention of introducing *élections* into the major *pays d'états*. In Provence ten new bureaux were envisaged with a complement of 350 offices.[65] Although the government retreated on this issue, in the years that followed the *parlementaires* were obliged to battle against an array of new offices: two new *sénéchaussées* in 1632, an additional *chambre des requêtes* in 1641 and finally in 1648 the imposition of a *semestre*. This involved the creation of ninety-five new offices in the *parlement* and contributed directly to the fact that Aix became, yet again, a major centre of unrest.[66]

Invariably, the more important provincial officers were also local landlords which compounded the mounting conflict of interest. In Quercy in 1644 an official in the *cour des aides* ordered an attack on the musketeers sent to levy the *tailles* on his lands. For similar reasons in 1656 an *élu* of Brive, mounted and armed, led his peasants against the tax agents. The most striking case of this sort involved Leonard Daignan, Baron de Castelveil, treasurer of France at Montauban, who with three brothers – one of whom was a councillor in the *parlement* of Toulouse – organised the seizure of an agent and two soldiers sent to demand tax arrears from the little community of Orbessan. One of the brothers was shot as he called on the peasantry to resist a contingent of troops who intervened. In retaliation three of the soldiers were captured and handed over to the *vice-sénéchal* who ordered their execution that very day. When justice finally caught up with Daignan he was banished for three years and fined 31,750 *livres*; but he did not even forfeit his office.[67]

Subjects of the Crown fortunate to live within the protection of those with status and influence could certainly hope to avoid some of the burdens placed on others. The Duc de la Trémoille invoked his status to prevent soldiers billeting in the bourg which carried his name and impeded the collection of the *aides* at Taillebourg.[68] The Comte de Blénac, *sénéchal* of Saintonge, *maître de camp* in the cavalry, encouraged violent resistance to the agents of the *convoi et comptablie de Bordeaux* as well as taking legal action against them for attacking one of his dependants. In August 1658 Louis Chabot, Comte de Jarnac, with his brothers and twenty-four horseman recovered by force the cattle which had been seized by tax officials and taken to Cognac.[69] More legitimate methods were employed by the Duc de Gramont, governor of Béarn and Bayonne, during the Audijos revolt, both to protect his own property at Hagetmau where the uprising began and to ward off the threat to the general privileges of the region.[70] Bercé, who offers many more such examples, concludes that the institution of the seigneury 'appeared as one of the most formidable obstacles encountered by the modern fisc'.[71]

As this reference to the modern fisc indicates, Bercé places tax revolt in a wider conceptual framework. The motor of conflict was the antagonism between the central, bureaucratic, modernising state and the traditional relationships, customs and traditions of provincial society which still bound men to men.[72] Bercé elaborated this idea through a demonstration of the correlation between the rhythms of existence, the pastimes and *fêtes*, the myths and images of an illiterate populace and the forms which violence could assume. For a start unrest was more likely to occur on Sundays (as at Aix) and on saints' days. It is undoubtedly true that the celebrations of the *confrèries* and carnivals which gave the people an opportunity for a short time to make mockery of kings, bishops and authority in general could all too easily get out of hand; at Dijon in 1630 *mère folle et son infanterie* were implicated in the rising against the imposition of the *élus*.[73] Eighteen years later the dissident magistrates of

Aix took advantage of the *Mardi gras* to intimidate their opponents who were confronted by thirty masked men in red and blue hats.[74] At Montpellier in 1645 crowds of women were summoned by a child beating a drum.[75] Even a crowd aroused to kill would pass through the motions of a popular form of justice to legitimise their acts. Their enemies were hung in effigy in splendid imitation of the way their betters did such things; some historians have even argued that in throwing victims into a lake or river insurgents were performing an act of purification. Certainly the notion that in expelling a *gabeleur* a community was performing a ritual act of purification seems to have some ground in fact. Bercé has shown that towns were given a feminine personality and placed under the protection of the Holy Virgin. Uzerche had the motto *non polluta* and Bayonne *nunquam polluta*. In 1625 the consuls of this town complained to Richelieu that agents of the tax farmers were 'ravishing this maiden whom our kings have honoured with title of *impolue* and using fragile pretexts to corrupt the Virgin given to David . . . given to our kings in splendid virginity'.[76] Bercé also offers a vivid picture of the rich symbolic significance of the wisps of straw carried in the hats of the peasants who rose throughout Périgord in 1637. Straw in a variety of forms might be

> mistaken for a *mai* which marked the limits of a jurisdiction, or perhaps its seat (a local judge holding court in an inn or on common land) or even the site of its gallows. Planted straw might mark the suburbs of a city, the limits of a seigneurial jurisdiction, of a sanctuary from the law, or a region exempt from taxes. Elsewhere it could be associated with the bung (of a barrel or ale pot) which was used as a sign for a tavern. . . . Yet again straw might be associated with the blazing torches of First Sunday of Lent (*fête des brandons*) made from gathered weeds and burnt in a celebratory fire. By approaching the fire it was felt that one's bodily ills would be cursed. And lastly straw was associated with the 'brandons' – a kind of justice pole which served notice of legal confiscation of crops. . . . More generally a wisp of straw pinned to a hedge or a tree trunk marked a boundary, indicating perhaps the limits of an area of communal rights, the land where cattle could be freely grazed.[77]

Through this description of what he terms the *fondamentalisme populaire* of provincial communities Bercé conveys a powerful impression of their inherent unity and cohesion. It would be foolish to dismiss this simply as an idealised picture of an imagined pre-industrial past. However, Bercé, like Mousnier, tends to gut his rural communities of tension and to eliminate conflict and exploitation. For him, as for Mousnier, popular violence was an instrument which 'the urban elite knew how to wield, of which they did not fear the outcome, understanding the secret both of its explosion and of its disappearance'.[78] They 'feared only the threat to their properties, the intrusion into the town of the *petit peuple.*' What is more, 'the only enemy of the collective conscience', says Bercé, 'was the *gabeleur*', and he was primarily an institutional figure not a social one.[79] The objectives of the populace were thus conservative, limited to non-subversive, anti-fiscal protest and without serious implications for the social order. They expressed themselves in repeated outbursts of anger which were limited in their objectives, profoundly conservative, and ritualistic. 'It is possible,' he has summarised, 'to speak of the functions of revolt as a routine social occurrence . . .'.[80]

CLASS CONFLICT AND CONSCIOUSNESS

It seems almost self-evident that, had vertical chains of allegiance and traditional bonds of communal solidarity been as powerful as Mousnier and Bercé have argued, they would have carried all before them. It is true that both, in different ways, recognise the ultimate failure of the ties which bound men to men to withstand the pressure of the centralising state. What neither has acknowledged is the degree to which class and social antagonisms played a part in this outcome. For these had the simultaneous effect of dividing resistance to the Crown and of reinforcing the conservative attitudes of the notables.

This is more easily appreciated once it is understood that the defence of traditional liberties largely meant the defence of upper-class privileges. In some instances the two were synonymous and nowhere more obviously than in relation to fiscal issues. Seigneurial encouragement of peasant resistance in many instances reflected no more than a self-interested concern that their tenants would be unable to pay their dues and rents. Moreover, those nobles in a position to do so were not above accepting the largesse of the state as long as it derived from the misfortune of others. The Duc de la Trémoulle's objections to royal fiscality, for instance, have to be put alongside the complaints of lesser nobles about his own acquisition of tolls along the river Charente. Similar observations may be made about the defence of provincial liberties even where these were embodied in and protected by representative institutions. For the latter were essentially the preserve of the upper classes who used them for their own ends. The Estates of Languedoc were dominated by the twenty-two bishops who 'represented' the First Estate. The twenty-two barons of the Second Estate represented nobody in particular and were extremely bad attenders. The Third Estate, which had double representation, could make its presence felt but – although royal officers were excluded – its members were drawn exclusively from the urban oligarchies of the chief towns.[81] In Provence the First Estate was composed of the Archbishop of Aix, ten bishops and two abbots;

fief-owning nobles of whom there were over 200 made up the Second; whilst thirty-seven communities were represented in the Third. There were, in addition, separate assemblies of the three Estates but only that of the Communities continued to meet after 1639. Even in this unusually autonomous province its affairs were subsequently conducted for much of the time by a small permanent commission; this was dominated by the archbishop or his representative and those from the municipality of Aix.[82]

By the seventeenth century urban oligarchies had devised remarkably elaborate procedures for excluding or severely reducing popular participation in municipal government.[83] At Bordeaux where the original *jurade* of fifty had been reduced to six by the mid-sixteenth century and where the office of mayor had disappeared, the jurats were elected by twenty-four electors; these electors were themselves selected by the outgoing jurats from a body of notables known as the *cent et trente*, thus excluding any form of popular participation. Other big cities, such as Toulouse, had developed even more complicated procedures for ensuring the reproduction of the ruling oligarchy. Here the eight outgoing *capitouls* (reduced from twenty-four in the sixteenth century) selected eight each, who were reduced in number to twenty-four by a panel of officials and former *capitouls*. The *viguier*, who represented the Crown or the king himself, then chose the final eight.[84] There was an almost endless variety of such constitutional arrangements. Even where the lesser bourgeois and artisans were not entirely excluded, as at Montpelllier, it was likely that they would be nominated rather than elected. This situation meant that the frequent appeal to ancient rights was often little more than a means of securing the privileges of the few.

It is true that, in highly protected enclaves like La Rochelle or Marseille, or in areas exempt from the full *gabelle*, the entire population benefited indirectly from fiscal immunities. Yet even here the benefits were unequally distributed and were not always fully passed on by local authorities who needed to raise taxes themselves. In a major provincial centre like Toulouse the privileges so persistently upheld by the *capitouls* had little relevance to the interests of the population at large. The instructions given to the deputies dispatched to Paris to obtain their confirmation in July 1643 make it clear that they were primarily con-cerned with the preservation of their own authority *vis-à-vis* both the populace and rival bodies.[85] The *capitouls* claimed responsibility for the security of the city, civil and criminal jurisdiction, authority in matters pertaining to the guilds, control over the supply of food and cloth, weights and measures, and the right to levy certain taxes; they also claimed that the principal royal officers in the *sénéchaussée* should swear an oath to them to preserve the liberties of the town; more importantly, they asserted that the right to judge differences between themselves and the *parlementaires* over their respective honours and pre-eminences was theirs alone.[86] General privileges such as the freedom from the *droit d'aubaine* for foreign immigrants or the immunity against being removed from the city for trial accounted for only six of the twenty-six articles. Even the traditional exemption of the city from the *taille* was effectively subordinated to the insistence that the *capitouls* had sole authority over the levying of the sums required for the annual payment of 2,500 *livres* which the Crown accepted in lieu.

Partly because of the gulf that separated oligarchs and populace, class feeling was particularly intense in the towns. It did not require a major political crisis for it to surface. Resentment about a toll placed on a bridge at Arles exploded into a violent attack on the consuls after 160 people were drowned as a result of its being overladen.[87] The arrival of plague was almost guaranteed to heighten social tensions because the well-to-do endeavoured to save themselves at the expense of the poor and defenceless. At Amiens in 1632 the priests were given the responsibility of tending to the sick but without the necessary resources. Themselves resentful of the town council, their inability to cope in turn aroused the anger of their parishioners. Passions were further heightened by the suspicion that the *aireurs*, appointed to oversee the evacuation and burning of houses, were profiteering from their grisly trade. All this contributed to the atmosphere in which the major uprising of 1636 was to occur.[88]

When matters did get out of hand, municipal prisons where tax debtors frequently languished, together with the persons and properties of the municipal authorities, were at risk. The mayor of Dijon, who refused to hand over the keys to the gates to the leaders of the 1630 uprising, had his house burnt down only to be accused by the government of being to blame for the disorder![89] In May 1635 d'Aguesseau watched helplessly whilst an estimated 3,000 people made up of *'la plus basse partie du peuple'* besieged the town hall at Bordeaux, freed the prisoners and forced two municipal councillors to beg for their lives, compelling one to remove his hat in order to assume the proper posture.[90] At Périgueux the hostility of the inhabitants towards the mayor took a particularly curious turn when they more or less compelled the intendant to dismiss him and his consuls and to assume the mayoral functions himself.[91] Six years later an insurgent crowd of between 500 and 600 penetrated the fortifications of Bayonne and seized the castle and the town hall, releasing the prisoners they found there.[92] Making up the largest part of such turbulent crowds, and most prominent amongst those condemned in their wake, were poor artisans, day workers, and peasants. The list of the guilty – cobblers, dyers, carders, wineworkers, leather workers, wood burners, shoemakers, locksmiths, boatmen, ploughmen, carters, coachmen and labourers – constitutes a veritable roll-call of the labouring population.[93]

Exceptionally, the latent power of the urban populace was harnessed to more organised and durable forms of opposition to the municipal oligarchs. In 1613 the lesser bourgeois of La Rochelle seized control of the principal gates and fortifications; the following year they compelled the *corps de ville* to accept a new constitution by which each of the parishes elected a *procureur* with a deliberative voice in the council, and which allowed these representatives to assemble the people as they saw fit. They also obtained a measure of control over the town's fortifications and artillery as well as the right to scrutinise the official accounts. At the same time a parallel organisation based on the eight militia companies also emerged, securing in the years that followed a powerful influence over the stance adopted by the town in its prolonged conflict with the Crown.[94] Not until 1626 was the government in a position to insist on the restoration of the old municipal forms. These developments are thus worthy of comparison with the Ormée which, whilst entailing the effective replacement of both *parlement* and municipality with its own popular organisations, survived for only three years. If such movements were exceptional they pinpointed with great accuracy the social and political divisions which constantly threatened to sap the cohesion of communities great and small. Of the 130 Provençal insurrections noted by Pillorget between 1596 and 1635, the most common were those directed against either the consuls or the local judicial officers. Revolts directed at royal taxation accounted for only twelve whilst those against other forms of royal authority made up a further five.[95] Conflicts which divided communities were thus more common than those which united them against a threat from outside.

Moreover, despite the evident opposition of many provincial office-holders to the fiscal policies of the Crown, the generalisation that they also consistently failed to do their duty cannot survive careful scrutiny. Fear, if nothing else, was a powerful inducement to take action. At times of crisis urban authorities were particularly apprehensive about an influx of the turbulent crowds who inhabited the suburbs and environs. They could move with rapidity to shut the city gates. This happened at Dijon in 1630, Agen in 1635,[96] Caen in 1639,[97] and at Rennes[98] and Morlaix in 1675.[99] At Moulins in 1640 the refusal of the guards to allow the inhabitants from the suburbs to enter the town to attend Sunday service provoked an immediate threat of violence, followed by a doubling of the guards in order to prevent the crowds 'pillaging the houses of the bourgeois'.[100] In May 1637, so apprehensive were the local rulers, a three-day fair at Angoulême was cancelled.[101] Nor did tardiness in mobilising the urban militias always mean that the authorities were sitting on their hands, still less fomenting trouble.[102] Sometimes they were paralysed by fear and uncertainty as appears to have been the case at Amiens in 1636; sometimes they simply lost control of the militia companies which were largely composed of artisans.[103] In 1635 one sacked the municipal prisons at Périgueux which it was supposed to be guarding; but the intendant had no complaints about the valiant efforts of both the municipal and legal authorities, together with 'some other principal residents', to prevent worse befalling.[104] Bosquet reported in similarly favourable terms on the way in which the consuls of Montpellier, and the officers of the *cour des comptes, aides et finances,* had endeavoured to restore calm to the troubled town in 1645.[105] The significance of such commendations from intendants, often quick to detect the surreptitious hand of the local notables behind any disturbance, is a salutary reminder of the dangers of trying to push dynamic social relationships into theoretical straitjackets.

In the *plat pays* beyond the city walls class antagonism was less acute. The lifestyle of the poorest nobles was sometimes little different from that of their tenants and their own hostility to the truly rich and powerful could be just as great. Yet this did not make nobles in general either willing or effective champions of the populace. Whilst landlords were quite capable of inciting resistance to the demands of the fisc, they did not rush to put themselves at the head of insurrectionary movements. Where such involvement did occur the nobles concerned were nearly always of humble means or on the criminal fringes of society. The exceptions stand out. Amongst them was the Sieur de la Mothe et de la Forest, a respected nobleman of ancient stock who commanded the peasant army in Périgord in 1637.[106] Also involved in the prolonged disorders which flowed from this uprising was the Marquis d'Aubeterre; but his status only belied his penchant for intrigue and adventure which he seems to have acquired from his father. He was disinherited in favour of his younger brother, and his prime concern was to recover some of his lands in Périgord. Then there was the Baron de Madaillon, a noble of some military capacity but woeful reputation who was executed in 1645 on the orders of the *parlement* of Paris.[107] Virtually all the other names of nobles who plunged into revolt were those of obscure people who have only come to attention because of their violent ways. Some were executed or deprived of their rank, some became the victims of their own murderous activities and others disappeared without trace. In this respect the success of Bernard d'Audijos in obtaining a military command was extraordinary. Invariably lacking in the sort of wealth and influence that gave those like the Duc de la Trémoulle a certain immunity, petty noble leaders risked all.[108]

This made them uncertain allies. Not beyond attaching themselves to a revolt when it was already under way, they were also likely to abandon it when the going proved difficult. In Normandy a minor noble, Jean Quetil, Sieur de Ponthebert, played a part in the initial agitation but later withdrew, declaring that 'he had not thought that his speech would have opened up such a large wound'.[109] More strikingly, La Mothe, having led the successful assault on Bergerac but conscious of the military difficulties, entered into negotiations with the Duc de La Valette who was approaching with royal forces. Not only did he relinquish Bergerac but he shamefully sanctioned the murder of the popular leader Doctor Magot who sought to continue the struggle. 'The apparent ambiguity of La Mothe's role', noted Bercé, 'corresponded to that of the French nobility as a whole when faced with popular unrest'.[110] In fact, it is clear that the overwhelming majority of the local nobility did not respond to the calls for support, even in the Périgord and despite La Mothe's own respectability. This was also true of the revolt of the Nu-Pieds, notwithstanding the undoubted participation of those nobles engaged in salt smuggling whose profits were threatened by the proposals to extend the *gabelle* into the privileged area of the *quart bouillon*. Only a handful of the 500 nobles known to have been resident in the *vicomtés* of Coutances and Avranches rebelled.[111] In general, such collective movements of the lesser nobility as did occur took the form of quasi-illegal assemblies which concentrated on drawing up formal *cahiers* of grievances. Although ultimately suppressed, such assemblies had little direct connection with popular agitation.[112] The gathering of the nobility of Saintonge and Angoumois at Lusignan in 1643 appears to be an exception and it was forcefully dispersed by other members of the noble Estate.[113] Many nobles, indeed, not only declined to participate in seditious activity but fulfilled their obligation to maintain good order. When intendant Foullé appeared in Gascony to suppress the revolt of L'Astarac in 1640 he found fifty nobles to join with him.[114] At Villefranche it was the arrival of some of the local nobility with 200 armed men which rescued the beleaguered town from its peasant invasion.[115]

It is also worth pointing out that if matters did get completely out of hand large forces under the command of the governor or other magnates would eventually arrive. Condé was dispatched to Aix, the Duc de la Valette to Périgord, the Duc de La Force to the west in 1636, Marshal Gassion to Normandy, the Duc de Chaulnes to Brittany in 1675, whilst the Duc d'Epernon was constantly involved in keeping Bordeaux and its region in some sort of order. In 1637 the revolt in the Périgord was dealt with by the Comte de Roure and Marshal Lebret.[116] Two years later the Comte de Matignon, lieutenant general for lower Normandy, assumed responsibility for the pacification of Rouen helped by both nobles and *officiers*.[117]

There were, it is true, some moments when princes and people did momentarily make common cause. One can single out the alliance between the house of Rohan and the people of La Rochelle during the Huguenot rebellions of the 1620s or that between Condé and the Ormée of Bordeaux. Yet, in both instances, they were formed out of a curious compound of deference on the part of the people for the great and good and the characteristic opportunism of the princes which could all too readily give way to a fearful disdain. Condé recommended that the Ormée should be supported because 'it is much the stronger party and as we have been unable to bring it down through either guile or force'.[118] His brother's adviser had no compunction whatsoever about describing these valuable allies as 'lowly riff-raff'.[119] In similar fashion the Duc de Rohan eventually made plain his contempt for his Rochelais allies whom he found 'in keeping with the humour of the people to be as insolent in prosperity as cringing in adversity'.[120] Perhaps the most effective links between aristocratic intrigue and popular disaffection were those forged by de Retz, coadjutor to the Archbishop of Paris. Even after his arrest in 1652 and subsequent flight to Rome, de Retz commanded extraordinary support from the assemblies of the Parisian *curés*. These continued to regard him as the legitimate incumbent of the archdiocese of Paris and frightened the government by their capacity to arouse their congregations. Apart from his links through the clergy, his clientele included key personnel such as Miron, *maîtres des requêtes*, colonel of the *quartier* St-Germain, and Martineau, *conseiller aux requêtes*, captain of the rue St Jacques.[121] Yet, like nearly all other aristocratic leaders, de Retz was never able to trust his followers, nor even to make common cause with the other exiled Frondeur, the Prince de Condé. By the time Louis XIV came to power de Retz was as isolated as the Duc de Guise had been thirty years earlier.[122]

Reliance on the people was in any event a risky business. When Marie de Médicis, who was governor of Angers, arrived in the adjacent stronghold of the Ponts de Cé in 1620, her preparations for resisting the king merely provoked panic and hostility. As the royal army approached she felt it safer to make the inhabitants surrender all their arms and impose a rigid curfew whilst emptying the gaols so that the prisoners could serve in her army![123] For all their social deference and sometimes misplaced enthusiasm for the benefits of upper-class leadership the common sense of the people was ever likely to surface. In Paris the famous Day of the Barricades (27 August 1648), when the people had successfully secured the release of the radical *parlementaire* Broussell, gave way in the autumn of that year, as the authorities failed to keep bread prices in check, to serious anti-*parlementaire* riots.[124] Some of those involved may well have remembered the rapidity with which the *parlement* had distanced itself from the populace and, on Broussell's own advice, forbidden 'all vagabonds and *gens sans aveu* to carry arms on pain of punishment'.[125]

The idea that seventeenth-century uprisings flowed from a permanent community of interest or from the capacity of the upper classes to provoke, direct and lead the *menu peuple* is thus unsustainable. Outside small egalitarian rural communities, the cohesion of which is rightly stressed by Bercé, French society was characterised by stress, division and conflict, including a significant measure of unmistakable class antagonism. Even the inhabitants of such communities displayed a sharp perception about the precise source of their misery, accurately ascribing it to those who occupied a privileged position in the towns from which they dominated the neighbouring countryside. Such hostility was already noticeable at the end of the sixteenth century. In 1594 the Third Estate of Périgord complained bitterly about the failure of the *messieurs de justice*, the governors, mayors and consuls of the towns, to alleviate their distress. On the contrary, those who robbed the people 'having access to the towns came and went more freely than the *gens de bien* who feared that they would be imprisoned for the *tailles* and their arrears'.[126] Writing to the consuls of Domme for the release of those imprisoned for failure to pay, the peasants' leaders demanded that the officers of the *taille* be replaced; arrangements should be made to pay the king directly, 'without letting the money pass through the hands of so many people who have made themselves rich at the expense of the king and the people'.[127] Such sentiments re-emerged in the 1630s amongst the peasantry of Angoumois who sought the removal from the administration of the *tailles* of those rich inhabitants who were responsible for the ruin of the people.[128] Furthermore, it was well understood by the peasants that those in a position to manipulate the *tailles* benefited because they were simultaneously important landowners. The insurgents of Angoumois in 1636 complained that the '*officiers, sergeants, notaires,* and *gros bourgeois* hold all the best land without paying the *taille*', the burden of which was then placed on the poorest members of the community.[129] These then became indebted to the very people who were the cause of their distress. The rebel leaders complained to the governor and intendant that:

> If one considers ecclesiastics, nobles and *privilègiés* have many domaines exempt from the *tailles* ... one can clearly see that nothing remains for the poor supplicants and that in order to feed themselves and pay the *tailles* it has been necessary for ten or twelve years to borrow or mortgage their property to the inhabitants of the towns and the said *privilègiés*.[130]

What was clearly at issue was the unjust distribution of the burdens which, by a variety of mechanisms, the privileged were able to deflect on to the less fortunate.

Most of the victims of popular violence were *partisans*, tax farmers, fiscal agents and their associates. Conservative historians use this fact as confirmation of the view that the essential conflict was between the central state and the provincial community and to deny its 'social' character. But the typical victim of popular fury was not, as Bercé claims, simply an institutional figure but also a social one. He was likely to be an important member of the local or regional financial administration with a certain status and, invariably, a local landlord. Thus the villain of the piece at Aix in 1630, the first president d'Oppède, not only was suspected of collusion with the government's fiscal reforms but had a reputation as an unsympathetic landlord and grain hoarder to boot. It is worth looking at the victims of the major upheavals in this light.

The revolt at Agen in 1635 was one of the most violent. Amongst those murdered was David Codoing, *conseiller* in the *élection*, and receiver of the *tailles*; his town house was pillaged and his country estate ruined by the peasantry. Etienne Cunolie was receiver and treasurer of the domaine of Agenais and Condomois. His son was *assesseur criminel* in the *présidial*; he escaped from his burning house by the skin of his teeth. All their lands less than three miles from the town were burnt and their cattle killed.[131] Madeleine Foisil has analysed the forty-three victims of the Nu-Pieds with meticulous care but this makes it all the more difficult to share her emphasis on the role of the outsider.[132] Three were officers of justice, eight were in the *élections*, five were receivers of the *taille*, thirteen were agents of tax farmers. A number had their country houses attacked. Amongst these were the château of the Vicomte de Mortain, treasurer of France, *conseiller* in the *cour des aides*. His family had been ennobled in the reign of Henri IV and his brother held important military posts. There was also Mesnil-Garnier, *trésorier de l'Epargne*, who had to defend his castle near Coutances with eighty armed men. His father was of bourgeois stock and had married the daughter of a bourgeois of Caen where he had made a fortune as *trésorier général*.[133] At Montpellier in 1645 the rising began with an attack on the house of a local merchant after he had been accused of being a *partisan* by a crowd of children. Subsequently the house of the *procureur du Roi* in the *chambres des comptes, aides et finances* was pillaged together with that of the receiver of the *droits d'amortissement*. Although the attack on some agents of the *partisans* staying in a local inn indicates the presence of unwelcome 'outsiders', most of the victims were not in that category.[134] Somewhat surprisingly Bercé's conclusions about the social character of the *gabeleurs* of the south-west are very similar. They came, he said, from

> families who had married amongst themselves, heirs of merchants who, having rounded out their patrimony in the previous century, became owners of *métairies* in the nearby countryside, and who in the century of absolutism increased their prosperity thanks to the acquisition of the sub-farms of the *élection* or of the province beyond the city walls.[135]

It is impossible to reconcile this picture with Bercé's own statement that the *gabeleur* was simply the representative of a cold and distant bureaucracy. On the contrary, the wrath of both urban and rural poor, like that of the rural nobility, was concentrated on those in their midst who had grown visibly rich at their expense, and who were evidently prepared to risk life, limb and property in order to profit from the opportunities created by the expansion of the venal bureaucracy. Moreover, it was not just royal taxation from which the urban notables sought to profit and which provoked unrest. In 1656 the city council of Angers farmed out all the city's taxes to one of their number. When he tried to extend them to include all foods entering the city violence erupted and the guardhouse at the gates was destroyed. Members of the crowd which invaded the council meeting threatened to 'kill and exterminate all the profiteers, starting with those on the city council'.[136] A slightly different but equally illuminating episode occurred at Bordeaux. Here, in 1673, the populace displayed scant concern about a new tax on legal documents which affected them little; but two years later when a similar burden was placed on pewter utensils and tobacco uproar ensued. A *parlementaire* who tried to reason with the crowd was killed, one president and his wife beaten and another imprisoned.[137] Porshnev was absolutely right in arguing that popular resentment about taxation could all too easily overflow into a wider onslaught on the well-to-do. There is no reason to doubt the conviction of the Ormists that 'the actual cause of the sedition is the excessive wealth of the few'.[138] Nor should one dismiss the implications of the bitter sentiments of the Aix pamphleteer who, invoking Lazarus, besought God that 'the rich man should die and be buried in hell'.[139]

The contention that class consciousness was absent in the turmoil of these years is thus woefully wide of the mark. On the contrary, the populace and its leaders frequently displayed both a general antipathy to the rich and a close perception of the way in which the privileged were able to impose ever-rising burdens on the poor and weak. What is true is that the populace were not demanding a recasting of the entire social order but a redistribution of burdens. Inasmuch as their class consciousness reflected itself in a political outlook the latter was indeed backward-looking, conservative and royalist, showing at times a sad faith in the capacity of the king to save them from their oppressors. Precisely because these were mostly identified with the local notables, the world beyond the parishes most immediately involved rarely came into focus. If it did this was quite likely to be through an awareness that other parts of the country were more privileged; thus at Saintes in 1636 a demand appeared for wine tolls on the Charente to be brought into line with those on the Garonne.[140]

Limited though the political consciousness of the *menu peuple* may have been, their betters lived in a constant state of anxiety about their unpredictable and melancholy humour. During the last years of the religious wars, as the wrath of the populace descended on municipal elites, seigneurs and tax agents alike, so the aristocratic assumption that men were naturally unequal received ever more widespread expression. The naturally servile *menu peuple,* said Pierre Dampmartin in 1585, existed to feed, clothe, and serve nobles and princes who 'owed their status to their human perfection'.[141] Many were not so confident that the people would conform to their designated station in life. The erstwhile Catholic Leaguer, Jean de Saulx-Tavanes, wrote in his *mémoires* that a major impediment to the re-establishment of a more representative form of government based on the nobility was the danger of sliding into a popular regime.[142] In similar vein the *robin,* Michel Hurault, felt that in order to keep the people in their place the nobility were obliged 'to stick together and to attach themselves to kings'.[143] This, however, was easier said than done.

THE DISARRAY OF THE PRIVILEGED

The privileged groups in French society were locked in an almost perpetual competition to maximise their own power, influence, status and share of the wealth extracted from the labouring population. Its clearest expression was the willingness of some of the nobility to encourage resistance to the fisc which we have already encountered. Their demands for an easing of taxation on their dependants was linked either explicitly or implicitly to the claim that the depredations of the fiscal officers were eroding the basis of noble wealth and prestige. Without hesitation they attributed their own difficulties and the ruin of the realm to the useless, 'monstrous and unrestrained multitude of new officers both of justice and finance'.[144] The remedy was to abolish venality of office, reduce the number of officeholders, and grant the nobles a monopoly of offices and ecclesiastical benefices.[145] Fiscal officers were accused of interfering in the administration of justice, charging and discharging parishes without reason, and verifying tax edicts without careful consideration because of their own interest in them.[146] Not only had venality of office undermined honour, valour and pedigree as the foundations of true nobility but it meant that the wealth of the realm was being bled dry.[147] Demands for a reduction of taxation thus fused with a defence of the corporate identity of the Second Estate.

That identity itself was, however, far from assured. For the middle-ranking nobility, so crucial to any concerted opposition to the Crown, could at times barely contain their animus towards the grandees of the sword, let alone upstart officeholders. Though they were strenuous in defence of their own exemption from taxation, the pensions, concessions and honours bestowed on the rich and influential provoked ever-increasing hostility.[148] Bemoaning their own loss of military authority, the *gentilshommes* simultaneously attacked the military abuses of the soldiery and their commanders.[149] By the time of the Fronde so deep were the antagonisms that Mazarin was able to exploit them by allowing the lesser nobles to assemble in 1649 in order to present their grievances. Indeed, when the faction around the Duc de Beaufort attempted to use the assembly for his purposes it was made plain that 'they did not want anything to do with Princes and even less the chief of the Frondeurs'.[150] A further assembly held in Paris in the spring of 1651 brought together 459 nobles, mostly of ancient stock, who challenged the growing differences within the noble Estate by insisting on undifferentiated seating arrangements.[151] The extent of the growing antipathy between the magnates and their lesser brethren was confirmed when the Prince de Marsillac, about to become the Duc de la Rochefoucauld, together with the eldest son of the Duc de la Trémoille – both of whom had been the subject of considerable resentment – attempted to raise the western provinces. At Cognac the nobility formed an alliance with the municipality, obliging Marsillac to besiege the town.[152]

This episode also points to the diminishing capacity of the grandees to arouse whole provinces. If, in 1632, the revolt of Montmorency in Languedoc did momentarily secure the support of the provincial Estates, the deputies were rapidly disavowed by their communities; the rebellious Bishop of Albi was even expelled from the town.[153] On the outbreak of the Fronde the clientele of Condé's brother-in-law, the Duc de Longueville, governor of Normandy, had a presence in the *parlement* of Rouen as well as in the provincial military strongholds. Yet it proved to be extremely fragile, collapsing rapidly in the spring of 1650 in face of royal injunctions for loyalty.[154] The apparent disinclination of the city of Rouen to follow the lead of the provincial governor is remarkable given its history of disaffection.

All this might simply be construed as lending weight to the contrast between an emergent modern, centralising state and an increasingly divided and disempowered nobility. Certainly, the ultimate triumph of the monarchy owes something to their evident disarray. However, such a simple antithesis fails to take account of the fact that the state apparatus was itself rife with conflicts of interest. Officers of every rank, angered by the threat to their material interests, status and authority, were frequently to be found either inciting disorder or failing to act to prevent it. Opposition inside the *parlement* at Rouen overflowed on to the streets.[155] At Dijon in 1638 the officers of the *bureau des finances* refused to allow the collection of taxes imposed on officers. Two years later the head of the legal corps at Périgueux, sword in hand, provoked a riot by calling on the people to chase away the *gabeleurs*. Near Domfront in Normandy financial officials were directly responsible for the deaths of four agents who came to levy taxes.[156] The root cause of such violent antagonisms was clearly revealed by the agent responsible for the tax of *franc fief* in Angoumois who felt constrained to seek the appointment of judges from outside the province. 'Most of the ordinary judges', he complained, 'have an interest in the taxes because of the fiefs held by them and their relations.'[157]

Patrimonial interests were compounded by corporate rivalries. The determination of the *capitouls* of Toulouse to preserve the powers of financial administration and taxation granted them by the Crown led, for instance, to bitter disputes with the *parlementaires*; the latter not only were jealous of any diminution of their corporate rights but strenuously resisted the municipality's demand that they should avoid paying their share of the annual *abonnement* for the *taille*. In 1640 the *capitouls* complained of the difficulty in raising the sums required because of the number of persons claiming exemption 'such as the officers of the *parlement, présidiaux, trésoriers de France, sécretaires du roy, docteurs régents* in the university, monks, nuns and others who make up the better part of the town'.[158] Municipal agents and their creditors engaged in an endless stream of litigation against non-payers and were in constant danger of harassment and worse.[159] Disputes also arose with the officers of the *sénéchaussée*. These challenged the jurisdiction of the *capitouls* over the *ban et arrière-ban*, which carried with it the authority to receive declarations from fief-holders, collect the taxes and to grant exemptions. Naturally the *capitouls* claimed that they themselves were exempt. This led the lieutenant-general of the *sénéchaussée* to effect legal seizures of 'fiefs belonging to the said sindic, *capitouls* and inhabitants of Toulouse'.[160] Even the *capitouls'* control of the food supply caused difficulties. During the dearth of 1652 they ordered the consuls of the neighbouring towns of Beaumont and Grenade to release grain which they claimed was destined for Toulouse and took action to obtain the arrest of two consuls of Castelnaudary.[161]

Effective administration appears, at times, to have come close to breakdown during the years of minority rule. In March 1646, the *chambre des comptes, aides et finances* at Montpellier imprisoned the treasurer of the provincial Estates for his failure to pay his fee for tax collection in the previous year.[162] In the early 1650s the *parlement* of Toulouse and the provincial Estates engaged in a prolonged dispute over the authorisation of royal taxes, each countermanding the orders of the other with the greatest of vigour.[163] Similar issues at a national level divided the *trésoriers* and the *élus* as both stridently claimed to be the best and most loyal servants of the Crown. Throughout France the *élus* refused the treasurers access to their bureaux, resisted the execution of their orders and appealed against them to the *cours des aides*. These were only too willing to provide support because of their own objections to the claim of the *trésoriers* to 'sovereign' powers.[164] Sectarian disputes dragged on into the personal rule of Louis XIV. In Quercy in 1662 the *commis des tailles* in the *élection* of Rivière Verdun was attacked by the clerks of the judges in the *cour des aides* who were aggrieved about non-payment of their salaries.[165]

Corporate rivalries were invariably deepened by ties of kinship and patronage. At Aix-en-Provence Kettering has identified five family networks in the *parlement* which sustained the opposition to royal demands in the 1640s. One of these was connected to a wealthy merchant family, the Valbelles of Marseille.[166] The Valbelles had emerged from the intense disputes over the distribution of taxation, which plagued Marseille in the early years of the century, to dominate the municipality throughout the 1620s and 1630s. They also controlled the lieutenancy of the Admiralty which brought them into conflict with the Duc de Guise and his successor as provincial governor, the Duc d'Alais. The wrath of the merchant community was further aroused by the Valbelles' interest in a much-disliked import tax which had been imposed in order to liquidate the municipal debts. In the 1640s mounting tension flared into open street violence. The Duc d'Alais, whose supporters included nearly all the former creditors of the town, finally managed to oust the Valbelle clientele. Alais, however, was increasingly disliked by the *parlementaires* of Aix which directly contributed to the fact that Provence became one of the provincial centres of the Frondes. It did not help that Alais was a cousin of the Prince of Condé.

The quarrels of the great and the good served all too easily to inflame local disputes. In Bordeaux, the rivalry between Richelieu's client, Archbishop Sourdis, and the somewhat maverick Duc d'Epernon led to an undignified public confrontation for which the governor was later obliged to apologise. Seething with resentment, he seized the chance during the uprising of 1635 to accuse the municipal councillors, who owed their position to the archbishop, of cowardice and to replace them with his own clients.[167] The installation of Orléans as governor of Languedoc in 1644 precipitated a whole series of conflicts within the towns of the province. At Toulouse it stimulated a bitter struggle for municipal power between two factions within the municipality and involving a number of *parlementaires*. This became intertwined with disputes over taxation. The resulting legal procedures undertaken by the town council against one of its recent treasurers went on for nearly ten years. A similar rivalry for control of the town hall at Béziers, fanned by the paper warfare between the two intendants of Languedoc who had each been 'ostentatiously nullifying the decrees of the other', was also given renewed vigour. Victory went to the Orléans clientele.[168] At Albi, the ancient conflict between municipality and bishop was given a boost as the consuls, exploiting the change of governorship, sought to shift the balance of power by obtaining the creation of a *présidial*.

Defeated on this issue, they led the popular resistance to the taxes made necessary by the town's indebtedness whilst the Estates lent support to the bishop. In the event the bishop's influence in higher places proved its worth.[169] In Brittany, another province which required the most careful handling, rivalry between the houses of Rohan and La Trémoille led in 1651 to the *parlement* of Rennes naming the Duc de Rohan as president of the Estates contrary to the wishes of the Estates themselves. In this case the decisive intervention of the acting governor, the Maréchal de la Meilleraye, a nephew of Richelieu and ally of Rohan, prevented matters getting out of hand.[170]

These episodes convey something of the unpredictable effects of conflicts of jurisdiction, honour and faction and the way in which they might, or might not, interact with the agitation of the lower orders. Even where the notables did not deliberately arouse the populace, the potentially dangerous consequences of their own divisions were clear. Sometimes this received explicit recognition. In August 1644, the intendant at Valence carefully explained to Chancelier Séguier that, whilst the disorders in the town 'certainly had their source in the misery of the people, their development resulted from the divisions amongst the most powerful people who ought to have been dealing with them'.[171] In the midst of the upheavals at Montpellier in 1645 the intendant Bosquet observed in similar vein that the rivalries between the treasurers and the officers of the *présidial* as well as the cathedral chapter could only serve to 'weaken the respect of the people towards the officers and diminish their authority . . .'.[172] Occasionally, the intendants took steps to at least ensure an outward display of solidarity. At Périgueux in June 1635, Verthamont summoned the mayor to his house where he ordered him to 'embrace the son of the *juge criminel* . . . who had much credit amongst the people, both of whom then delivered a few words in the public square . . .'.[173] In the event, as noted earlier, both Bosquet and Verthamont went out of their way to express satisfaction with the efforts of the principal citizens to maintain order.[174] Not that such commendations necessarily saved local notables from the wrath of the central government. In 1675 the intendant at Bordeaux wrote to Colbert saying the *parlement* had done everything that one could have wished to control the insurgent populace. It was none the less exiled to the small town of Condom.[175]

TOWARDS THE ABSOLUTE STATE

The restoration of political order in France was in part achieved by default. The divided and sectarian nature of opposition helped the government to survive the worst moments of crisis. Not surprisingly, it proved unable, as will be seen, to open up an effective and unifying political perspective. Popular discontent also ebbed as the soaring and provocative fiscal demands of the pre-Fronde years gave way to more restrained fiscal policies. Their benefits were enhanced by the tailing off of rents and prices after decades of inflation. Yet the Crown did more than survive and it is unwise, given the lack of a clear correlation between the patterns of revolt and prices, to make too much of marginal improvements in living conditions. In any event, grain riots did not disappear and desperate bouts of economic and social crisis were yet to come. The famine of 1693–4 cost two million lives.

The experience of decades of popular disturbance, however, had left a powerful imprint on the attitudes of the French upper classes. A mixture of contempt and fear with which they viewed the people expressed itself in attitudes and policies across a spectrum of concerns. They were, perhaps, most tellingly displayed in the stream of legislation directed at the significant numbers of young men in domestic service. One might expect this relatively comfortable and secure group of the population, some of whom undoubtedly prospered as a result of their masters' patronage, to have exemplified the power of vertical ties of *fidélité*. Yet the relationship of the well-to-do with their servants was profoundly uneasy. Legal checks on their movement and employment multiplied. It became necessary to furnish a *congé* from the previous master, whilst the employment of *gens inconnus*, vagabonds, and those of ill repute was forbidden.[176] Legislation 'forbidding all pages, lackeys and valets of lowly condition from carrying swords, daggers, knives, sticks or any other arms' was constantly reiterated.[177] The guild regime, reinforced and extended by Colbert for much larger reasons, provided anxious masters with a further means of ensuring the respectability of their apprentices.[178]

Anxiety was also manifest in the increasingly repressive attitude displayed by urban elites towards popular festivities. Fears of social disorder reinforced by an austere reforming Catholicism gave rise in Hoffman's words to an ethic which 'condemned idleness, sexual license, insubordination and disorder, a morality that extolled diligence, abstemiousness, obedience to authority and social and political order'.[179] Participatory processions were transformed into parades of the urban big-wigs and the crowd into spectators; unseemly wakes, celebrations of saints' days and processions were curbed; religious fraternities brought under episcopal control. Clerics and lay moralists alike pontificated against the sexuality which pervaded much of traditional folklore. Dancing, the wearing of masks, the activities of travelling players, and even walking to the market place during divine service became subject to municipal regulation. The repressive reflexes of the well-to-do are also discernible in the confinement of the poor in the municipal hospitals established from mid-century. Genuine concern for the poor became almost inseparable from a desire to cleanse the streets of vagabonds and the potentially criminal. These attitudes have not unreasonably been seen as a manifestation of the domination of town over countryside, of institutionalised piety over popular religion and as evidence of a widening gap between the culture of the masses and the culture of the elites.[180] Whatever the perspective, the desire to discipline and control the populace was unmistakable and hardly surprising. It lent itself admirably to the wider purposes of the monarchical state and contributed directly to its cultural complexion.

On the other hand discipline and repression alone cannot explain the ebbing of the great tides of revolt after 1675. What was striking during the crisis of 1693–4 was the way in which the central government, *parlements* and municipalities, despite differences of interest, largely pulled in the same direction to ensure the flow of grain to where it was most needed: the biggest cities, the most distressed rural areas, and the 300,000 soldiers stationed on the frontiers.[181] That this was achieved with the minimum of popular unrest was testimony both to the enhanced administrative capacity of the regime and to its careful exercise. The flexible and speedy reactions of the intendant at Orléans almost certainly prevented disturbances provoked by the passage of grain along the Loire from getting out of hand.[182] Even more important was the commitment of the municipal authorities, particularly in the larger towns, to close control of the supply and sale of grain. The years of dearth and disorder fostered an attachment to regulation and the 'moral economy' which was to endure, despite the physiocrats, down to the end of the *ancien régime*.

The upper classes thus reacted in a number of ways to popular unrest – or the threat of it – all of which helped in the restoration of social order. But care must be taken not to compound the error made by Porshnev of elevating class dynamics above all others in order to explain the emergence of the absolute state. This is not to deny that Porshnev was right in making class antagonism a central feature of his picture; the anti-fiscal character of popular revolts pinpointed precisely the divide between exploiters and exploited. They also revealed a sharp perception amongst the poor of the mechanisms by which those with privileges and influence were able to deflect the burdens on to them. Porshnev was, however, surprisingly blind to the significance of the acute divisions amongst the privileged and so failed to grasp their relationship to his primary conflict. For these divisions flowed, in large part, from an increasingly bitter competition for a share of the vastly swollen revenues extracted from the labouring population or for a protected niche within the bureaucracy itself. A perpetual striving for office and influence divided robe and sword, lesser *gentilshommes* from the greater and the robe itself. The struggle was at times so intense that it overflowed into a willingness to encourage and participate in anti-fiscal riots and movements.

However, the dynamics of these were not dependent on upper-class leadership; indeed, they could become quite uncontrollable and threatening. What is true is that the sectarian rivalries of the notables set a very bad example to the *menu peuple* whilst simultaneously opening up the political space into which the crowd could erupt. The dangers of discord amongst the notables was clearly understood; both by the government which never ceased to berate local authorities, even when blameless, and by many of those who found themselves confronting angry crowds.

The essential problem facing the privileged orders, therefore, was not that of disciplining the populace but of disciplining themselves. Without doing the latter the former was unlikely to be effective. Up to a point the resolution of this problem lay in the nature of upper-class discontent itself or, more precisely, in the 'vertical' chains of allegiance which sustained it. Not only were they likely to rupture at critical moments but, as long as the Crown had sufficient resources at its command, it could create its own clienteles with which to outflank those of its opponents. Furthermore, Louis XIV's assertion of his role as the fount of all patronage was not unwelcome to those who had grasped the need for an effective regulation of the disorders which beset the body politic. At the same time the intense competition for place and status fostered a preoccupation with rank and degree which was ultimately to bring shape and cohesion to his regime.

This, however, is to anticipate. If hindsight makes it possible to discern the potential for order in the seemingly interminable disorder, much more was required for its realisation. The dynamics of revolt alone do not explain their own exhaustion nor the triumph of the monarchy. Indeed, the former was as much a consequence of the latter as the other way round. The emergence of monarchical absolutism depended on the convergence of a number of conditions, both structural and conjunctural, which have yet to be considered.

4

ORDERS AND CLASSES

STATUS AND WEALTH

Enough has been said to show that class and class consciousness were social realities in seventeenth-century France. Class conflict was endemic whilst the intense exploitation of the productive classes was the principal reason for the contrast between France's poor economic performance and its considerable economic potential. By modern standards, of course, class consciousness was rudimentary but this was to be expected given the lack of economic integration. As Marx was to observe, even in the nineteenth century the French nation was formed by the 'simple addition of homologous magnitudes' like 'potatoes in a sack' and divided as much as united by the mode of production.[1] This imagery actually provides a point of contact with Bercé's view of the *'fondamentalisme populaire'* of autonomous rural communities. But whatever imagery is employed, there is no doubt about the antagonism of rural communities towards the privileged burghers of the nearest town or city. The fact that so many of the latter were, at one and the same time, landlords and royal officeholders suggests that it is not unreasonable to locate the French state by reference to this set of class relationships.

Roland Mousnier attempted to deny the class nature of these relationships by arguing that seigneuries were not sought for material gain and that officeholders possessed fortunes which 'played no role at all *in* [my italics] production but consisted of a vast accumulation of consumer goods'.[2] But officeholders clearly did have a relationship *to* the means of production from which they benefited enormously. It expressed itself in the *rentier,* fiscal and usurious forms in which the wealth produced by the labouring classes was channelled upwards. Indeed, in his pioneering study of venal officeholding Mousnier himself recognised that the corps of fiscal officers 'became a gigantic mechanism for raising cash and throwing it into the royal coffers', constituting a huge burden on the productive sectors of society.[3] If more recent research requires this observation to be modified it is only to emphasise the extent to which the sale of office spawned a spoils system which diverted a significant proportion of the revenues raised into the pockets of the officials themselves. At Valognes in Normandy the *bureau des élus* increased in size from four in 1540 to twenty-one a century later; but, over roughly the same period, the proportion of the tax revenue taken as remuneration rose from 1.8 per cent to 7.1.[4] At Montpellier the number of officials rose from 111 to 441 but the nominal wage bill multiplied seventeenfold, a dramatic increase even when set against a sixfold rise in wheat prices.[5] Taking Languedoc as a whole, Beik has estimated that in 1677 about 30 per cent of the revenue levied by the Crown found its way into the pockets of the principal figures in the provincial institutions and into those of their creditors.[6] Collins reckoned that in general between 7.5 and 10 per cent of money raised in each *élection* was consumed by the costs of the officers themselves.[7]

Not only did the greatly expanded bureaucracy have to pay for itself but it also serviced the state debt. In fact the two functions can hardly be separated as many tax officials doubled up as private financiers. Moreover, an extremely high proportion of the debt was serviced in the form of *rentes* and *droits* which did not appear in the central accounts.[8] The most important of these after 1616 were the *droits aliénés*, a surcharge on the *tailles*; initially set at about 10 per cent of their value, this had risen to 50 per cent by 1634.[9] Between 1616 and 1633 they had an estimated aggregate value of 100 million *livres*.[10] In form a forced loan imposed on the *officiers*, the *droits* were in practice borne by the taxpaying population.[11] *Droits* were even levied on other *droits* and the rights to these could be sold. For instance, in 1630, in the *élection* of Figeac those in possession of *droits* included the *commissaire des vivres* and the multiple holders of the post of *greffier ancien, alternatif, triennial*; one of these was simultaneously a councillor in the *parlement* of Bordeaux and another the *trésorier général des bâtiments du Roi*. In 1634 the government restructured the system of *droits* so that their cost would rise less rapidly. But, at the same time, a million *livres* of *rentes* were established on the *tailles* and three million on the *gabelles*.[12]

As many of those who profited from the proliferation of such devices were themselves exempt from taxation, the labouring population sustained an increasingly disproportionate share of the growing burden. For example, between 1556 and 1643 the relative contribution of Dijon's artisan community to the fisc grew nearly fivefold and the legal establishment's by just 50 per cent. Yet, in this period, the number of artisan households had actually declined whilst legal households had more than tripled. In the parish of St Médard, which housed the administrative and legal elite, a third of the residents were tax exempt compared with only 3.3 per cent of the inhabitants of the popular quarter of St Philibert.[13]

Mousnier's earlier appreciation of the exploitative function of the officeholding system became obscured in later years by his predilection for deducing the nature of the social system from upper-class perceptions of it. For him, contemporary value judgments were the determinant of social position and preoccupation with status, rather than wealth, its prime driving force. Whilst the increasing attachment to distinctions of rank does raise a real problem about how to relate status to class, Mousnier's approach barely recognised the problem at all. It was, moreover, dependent on a highly partial reading of contemporary views. For these by no means sustain his view that the social hierarchy was simply the product of value judgments about status in which class, economic location or wealth counted for little. Although the tripartite division of French society was often depicted as an emanation of an idealised metaphysical cosmos, it also represented a division of labour. It had evolved from the ancient categories of clerics and laymen to which were later added those of the warriors and the Third Estate. The first description of the three categories as Orders dates from around 1175, being given force by the need to bring order to a very turbulent world and to justify the emergent seigneurial regime.[14] In medieval times wealth and status were generally seen as going together.[15] Terms such as *ordre, rang* and *état* had clear economic connotations representing an amalgam of perceptions about social, political and economic position.[16]

Clouatre suggests that it was only from the sixteenth century that these terms acquired a more abstract socio-legal resonance.[17] But the effect of defining rank and status by reference to abstract personal attributes was to make it plain that the majority of the population did not possess them. Charles Loyseau was explicit: the Third Estate as such was not an Order at all. Most of those who belonged to it neither occupied, nor had the aptitude to occupy, a position of public authority which he made the benchmark of rank. Merchants were the lowest element of the social hierarchy to receive epithets of honour and to assume municipal office.[18] Domat made a comparable observation when he noted that, although agriculture was the foundation of human society embracing the 'greatest part of mankind', those employed in it were the farthest 'from the use of rank and precedence'.[19] Not only did the literate upper classes believe that 'artisans had no honour or rank' but their attitude to those engaged in manual labour was suffused with class undertones as the contemporary synonyms for *mécanique* make clear: *avide, avare, pauvre, mesquin, grossier* and *vil*.[20]

It was of course possible to attribute 'qualities' to the lower orders so that artisans were recognised for their manual dexterity, merchants their financial skill, and peasants their love of animals and land.[21] Yet this barely disguises the fact that the social location of those who stood outside the ranks of polite society was defined quite differently, that is by reference to economic function. Moreover, the growing social differentiation within the Third Estate had long made it difficult to treat it as homogeneous. At the beginning of the sixteenth century Claude de Seyssel had divided it into the *peuple gras* and the *menu peuple*.[22] Loyseau, having first modified the traditional tripartite model by a general distinction between those who command and those who obey, proceded to identify *'vocations particulières'*.[23] At the head of the Third Estate he placed the professions and after them in descending order: merchants wealthy enough to employ others; skilled tradesmen (apothecaries, goldsmiths, drapers); *laboureurs* (whom he thought oppressed); artisans; wage labourers; and finally the sturdy beggars. The divide between the liberal and mechanical arts – the latter depending largely on manual labour – was a critical one.[24] Loyseau's picture of French society was thus just as much a reflection of the division of labour as a hierarchy of status groups. As such, it was a fair approximation of social reality. For, inasmuch as the bulk of the population had any sort of social standing, this was inextricably bound up with occupation. A glance at the role of the *états et métiers* eligible to participate in the election of the municipal officials of Beauvais makes this clear (see Table 4.1). In the countryside too, despite regional variations in usage, the terminology employed to describe those who worked the land – *laboureur, métayeur, closier, brassier, travailleur de*

Table 4.1 Role of the *'métiers'* and *'états'* required to assemble in 1636 for the nomination of the mayor and councillors of Beauvais

Officers of the *Présidial*	Pastry, butchers, fishmongers
Officers of the *Élection, grenier à sel,* receiver of the *aides*, receiver of the *tailles*	Goldsmiths, pewter makers, lead-workers
Officers of the seigneurial and ordinary courts	Masons, carpenters, roofers
Barristers and doctors	Hardware merchants, armourers, needlemakers
Prosecutors, clerks, notaries	Iron workers, nailmakers, toolmakers
Ushers, sergeants, constables	Dyers, hatmakers, painters, glaziers
Wholesale textile merchants	Tanners, glove makers, furriers
Mercers, haberdashers, button makers	Shoemakers, curriers
Apothecaries, surgeons	Cobblers
Drapers, wool merchants	Sadlers, ropemakers
Teaselers	Joiners, barrelmakers
Shearers	Tailors, embroiders, tapestry makers, jewellers
Weavers	Woodturners, basket makers
Serge makers	Tenant farmers, wine-growers, market gardeners
Combers	
Innkeepers, vinegar merchants, brewers	
Bakers	

Source: Goubert 1960: 267–8

terre, manouvrier – was an indication of both material position and status.[25] Of course worthy commoners might seek to describe themselves as *honorable homme* or *noble homme* as the first step towards entering the ranks of the privileged.

A major reason for seeking such status was the prospect of achieving some protection from the depredations of the fisc. Even where this was not the prime attraction, the material benefits of status, particularly at a time of intense fiscal pressure, were obvious. Conversely, wealth was not only a reliable indicator of economic and political power but also the most crucial element in sustaining the lifestyle and the visible symbols of status to which so much importance was attached. Whilst the correlation between social rank and material prosperity may not have been exact, any analysis which fails to recognise their reciprocity is grossly deficient.

Most people stood no chance of acquiring either public office or authority. For at least a third – maybe a half – of the population, the only prospect was of an endless and unremitting struggle to survive. Vauban's estimate that one in ten of the French population were beggars and a further three near beggars has certainly withstood the scrutiny of modern scholarship.[26] Millions earned so little that their accumulated possessions were never worth much more than a couple of hundred *livres*. Spare cash was non-existent and such as passed through their hands was of inferior quality. Parisian inventories suggest that only where the value of personal possessions exceeded 500 *livres* was silver coin likely to be present.[27] Even at this level gold, silver and jewellery were largely absent. Better-off artisans accumulated pewter instead. Jean Piot, a master tailor of Dijon, left household possessions worth 731 *livres* in 1605 of which no less than sixty-two *livres* was accounted for by pewter utensils. Such resources did, however, permit an accumulation of linen. The homes of master craftsmen would commonly boast perhaps a dozen sheets and blankets, several dozen napkins and a half-dozen tablecloths.[28] Expenditure on clothes also became more significant. A modest Parisian master candlemaker, who left 680 *livres* worth of possessions, had clothes valued at 200 *livres*;[29] Jean Tatibouet, a Breton *laboureur*, with total wealth of roughly of the same order, must have been proud of his twenty-four white shirts.[30]

Movable wealth valued at 1,000 *livres* or more was an indication of real comfort and a significant disposable income; clothes accounted for a smaller part whilst tapestries, pictures, silverware, grain and cash reserves were correspondingly more important.[31] The only members of the popular classes who could conceivably aspire to this sort of wealth were domestic servants. These probably constituted between 5 and 10 per cent of the urban population and were thought by Vauban to be 'the most comfortable *état du Royaume*' given their lowly status.[32] Whilst wages were not high, lodging was assured and it frequently proved possible to save for a reasonable dowry. In 1700 the average patrimony of Parisian domestics was 4,279 *livres*, about four to six times as large as those of apprentices and journeymen. Their provincial counterparts were probably much less well off but they too found it possible to accumulate liquid cash and consumables.[33] However, even with the help of their masters, domestic servants found it difficult to move up the social hierarchy. They were firmly bracketed with the artisans and wage labourers for tax purposes and even *valets de chambre* tended to marry within their milieu well into the eighteenth century.[34]

In some ways the difference between poverty and modest security was not enormous. It might be no more than that between ten acres and twenty-five or one loom and three or four. The wealthiest textile entrepreneurs of Amiens at the end of the seventeenth century possessed an average of no more than eight looms. Yet there only sixteen of these entrepreneurs. They would bequeathe over 2,000 *livres* worth of succession and their houses had many rooms, courtyards and well stocked grain stores; linen was present in substantial amounts together with silverware, and gold as well as silver coin.[35] Such success was in reality beyond the reach of all but a handful. The result was a pyramidal socio-economic structure resting on a very broad base and narrowing rapidly to its apex. Tax assessments confirm this picture. In 1722 not a single one of 2,270 domestics, *compagnons* and *manouvriers* at Amiens paid more than five *livres*; indeed, all but five of them paid only one. Equally striking is the fact that 78 per cent of the master craftsmen in the building, textiles and clothing trades also paid five *livres* or less. Paying between six and twenty-five *livres* alongside the textile entrepreneurs were master masons and carpenters, goldsmiths, apothecaries, drapers, mercers, the lesser members of the legal profession and most of the 138 merchants. Just a handful of these together with some *rentiers* and non-exempt *officiers* paid more than forty *livres*.[36]

In rural communities the distribution of wealth replicated, if somewhat less dramatically, that of the towns. Their domination by a tiny minority of *laboureurs* or rural notables, at a time when the smallest holdings were proliferating, has already been observed. Everywhere, there was an unmistakable and significant gap between the penurious state of the vast majority of peasants and the relative comfort of a small number of families. In the extensive arable regions of the north the *laboureurs* reinforced their economic superiority through the acquisition of positions as seigneurial receivers or as *officiers* attached to the royal *domaine*. Some developed ties with the merchants of neighbouring country towns and enlarged their incomes by acting as creditors of parlous neighbours. If the more egalitarian communities of the south and west boasted fewer substantial *laboureurs*, inter-related groups of notables did exist. Entry into them frequently came through small-scale commercial activity which characterised pastoral and mountain regions. The artisans of St André-les-Alpes in Provence combined their trades with sheep rearing, cultivation and tax collecting. The members of some families spanned the whole social spectrum from cobbler to ecclesiastical canon, from tailor to lawyer; nevertheless, the concentration of wealth and authority in the hands of a few of these families was clearly visible.[37]

Whilst the divide which separated the poor from the petty bourgeoisie of town and countryside was a formidable one, it paled in comparison to that between the comfortably off and the super-rich. The largest capital fortunes amongst the *gros laboureurs* of the Ile-de-France were between 20,000 and 30,000 *livres*; the largest known dowry 8,300.[38] Yet such assets, despite exceeding those of the majority of provincial nobles, came nowhere near to matching the fortunes amassed by members of the higher nobility or those of the most prosperous merchants. This is demonstrated in Table 4.2.[39]

Such fortunes were the accumulated product of prodigious annual revenues. Those of the *parlementaires* of Aix ranged from 5,000 to 20,000 *livres* per annum; even these look modest compared with the incomes of the *ducs et pairs* which ranged from 40,000 to 100,000. Two years prior to his death Richelieu received an annual income of no less than one million *livres* – 5,000 times as much as a skilled craftsmen. On his death a fifth of his estate consisted of cash. The contrast with the villagers of the Andance valley, paying their meagre dowries in instalments, is so enormous that it almost defies comprehension.

There is, therefore, no reason whatsoever to suppose that disparities in wealth and class were any less obvious to the people of seventeenth-century France than they are to those of the twentieth. They were

Table 4.2 Some examples of estimated wealth

Person or office	*Wealth in livres*
Parisian wine merchant (mid-century)	2,000 to 6,000
Amiens wool merchants and *épiciers* (pre-1650)	50,000 to 100,000
Amiens *trésoriers de France* (pre-1650)	100,000 to 200,000
Amiens *trésoriers de France* (post-1650)	100,000 to 500,000
Aix-en-Provence *parlementaires*	100,000 to 400,000
Toulouse *parlementaires*	100,000 to 1,000,000
Ducs et pairs	1,000,000 to 3,000,000
Claude de Bullion, *Surintendant des finances* (1640)	8,000,000
Cardinal Richelieu	20,000,000
Condé family (early eighteenth century)	31,000,000
Cardinal Mazarin	35,000,000

reflected in the size of dwellings, dress and even in the contrast between the tanned skins of those who tilled the land and the pallor of upper-class complexions. In towns and cities the rich were fairly obvious as they passed by in their coaches or, if on foot, accompanied by servants or bodyguards in numbers which corresponded pretty well to both their wealth and their status. Equally evident was the growing geographical demarcation between the popular and the well-to-do quarters of the larger towns.[40] By the end of the sixteenth century Rouen's most disfavoured parish boasted not a single lawyer or *officier*; the only three merchants of any substance who lived there were wine sellers. In mirror image, the Beauvais parish of Basse Œuvre was almost entirely inhabited by those attached to its dominating cathedral and by members of the legal profession; it contained only five textile workers, one textile merchant, one inn, but no tailor nor even a butcher. At Toulouse the southern *capitoulat* of the Dalbade was steadily colonised by an elite of *parlementaires*, nobles and bourgeois, with clusters of houses being swept away to accommodate the imposing and secluded hotels which replaced them; by the end of the seventeenth century its formerly popular character had been lost. In such administrative centres the spaciousness and elegance of the upper-class quarters, frequently located near the law court or cathedral close, and refreshed by fountains, were in marked contrast to the twisting streets and overcrowded dwellings of the poorer quarters. Houses in Aix contained an average of over nine persons at the end of the seventeenth century; but in the poorest quarters this rose to as high as forty.

Not surprisingly, such social differences manifested themselves most cruelly in the differential effects of subsistence crises and effects of the plague. As Alain Croix has clearly demonstrated in the case of Rennes in 1605, the plague did not strike in a socially random fashion.[41] Similarly, at Gien in 1693–4 the plague carried off 45 per cent of the artisans and labourers whilst the number of *nobles hommes* was reduced by less than a fifth.[42] In the crisis year of 1709 whilst three-quarters of the population of Lyon were without corn or flour, those families with servants had enough to provide seventy-two loaves for each member of the household.[43]

Not only were differences of class obvious but they were also fairly rigid. For those without the wherewithal there was no escape from the social milieu into which they were born. Virtually every social group was affected by a powerful tendency for its members to marry within it and frequently into the same occupational group. Of 146 master craftsmen in Paris in 1634–6 half were sons of masters; three-quarters of them followed the same craft as their fathers and a half married daughters of other masters. A quarter married well-dowered daughters of merchants; significantly these grooms came from the most steady occupations in food, clothing and textiles. In contrast, those in poorly paid and little-considered trades, such as masons, soap makers, barrel-makers and potters, tended to marry daughters of fathers *sans qualité*.[44] Where choice was restricted – as with some groups of rural artisans or notables – marriages with blood relations became quite common.[45] Social mobility was further reduced by the consciously exclusive policy adopted by those with a position to defend. An analysis of 196 wives of Parisian *parlementaires* in the last decade of the century shows that, overwhelmingly, they came from the families of the high robe and officials in the royal household. Only two of them were daughters of merchants.[46] Cabourdin's investigation of 457 marriages celebrated in the Toulois between 1550 and 1635 suggests that at least 61 per cent and possibly as many as 77 per cent can be described as endogamous. Amongst the nobility the proportion rose to 95 per cent.[47]

Much of the explanation for this situation lies in the fact that, for those with any assets, marriages were business arrangements. There was a presumption that the input from the groom's family would be in proportion to the dowry; it typically involved both a cash contribution and the expectation of an inheritance.[48] Of course, as Farr has emphasised, this did not mean that the cash contributions were always evenly balanced, as financial considerations might well be tempered by the availability of partners as well as the more intangible concern to 'secure networks of solidarity'.[49] However, in making this observation he perhaps overlooks the possibility that where brides brought substantially more in cash than their partners this reflected not just a disparity in wealth but an estimation of the assets and skill brought by their craftsmen spouses. This was almost certainly a factor in the apparent willingness of masters to marry their daughters to poorer masters. Any journeyman, on the other hand, who wished to marry a master's daughter needed to mobilise considerable resources.[50] At this and every other level of French society the accumulation of wealth was essential if the barriers to upward social mobility were to be surmounted. Yet by the same token, for those with the means and a modicum of good fortune or determination, upward social movement was far from impossible. It is, however, also clear that, given the generally endogamous character of marriage arrangements and the need for substantial resources, few short cuts were available. Almost by definition, social and political success was the product of the assiduous accumulation of wealth, status and influence by family endeavour over several generations.

LINEAGE AND PROPERTY

Notwithstanding a pervasive and authoritarian paternalism, there was no such phenomenon as the 'self-made man' in seventeenth-century

France. This is readily illustrated by reference to some of France's most illustrious and powerful individuals.

The d'Aligre family produced two Chancellors of France – one in 1624 and the second in 1674. Its origins can be traced back to fifteenth-century Chartres where it had almost made a family preserve of the *grenier du sel*. By the early sixteenth century the head of the family had acquired municipal office and his four sons then branched into the law, the army and the finances. One of these, Etienne I, returned home from the Faculty of Law at Orléans to obtain a position in the *bailliage* and to preserve the family position in the *échevinage* of Chartres. Of his sons one became a canon at the cathedral and acquired the lucrative post of *receveur du domaine de Chartres*; a second distinguished himself at the battle of Pavia in 1515, before entering the royal household and becoming one of the *cent gentilshommes du Roi*, a position of noble status. A third, the father of Etienne II who became Chancellor in 1624, occupied a legal office and inherited the post of receiver of the cathedral *domaine*; he acquired land both by purchase and marriage assuming the style of *écuyer*. His daughter married the president of the *présidial* of Chartres. This office was subsequently acquired by his son *en route* to membership of the *grand conseil* and the chancellorship itself. The assistance provided by the family's well-entrenched position amongst the local officeholding elite was almost certainly reinforced by the presence of his uncle at court. Membership of the *grand conseil* came within a year of his uncle becoming one the *cent gentilshommes du Roi*.[51]

Like the d'Aligres, the Colberts go back to the fifteenth century when some of them were probably masons, and others, peasants who had branched out into the carting business. By the early sixteenth century the first generation of merchants was beginning to emerge and a residence was established at Rheims. Here, Gérard Colbert (1493–1571) became an *échevin* and 'bourgeois'; he was involved in tax farming and married a daughter of a *notaire royal* who was also receiver of the Archbishopric of Rheims (see Figure 4.1). In the next generation a Colbert became a canon of the cathedral. Most of Gérard's seven children, however, stayed in commerce. Amongst them was a merchant banker, who combined long-distance trade with retailing, tax farming and the possession of municipal office. There also appeared the first lawyer in the family who became successively *lieutenant-général* of the *présidial* at Rheims and of the ducal *bailliage* of Rethellois; he 'slid into nobility' by purchasing land and styling himself *écuyer* or *noble homme*.

One of Gérard's grandchildren was in turn the grandfather of the great minister. He stayed in Rheims, married the mayor's daughter and became *contrôleur-général des gabelles de Bourgogne et de Picardie*; his younger brothers went to Amiens and Troyes and developed links with the Lyonnais banking community. His elder brother established the

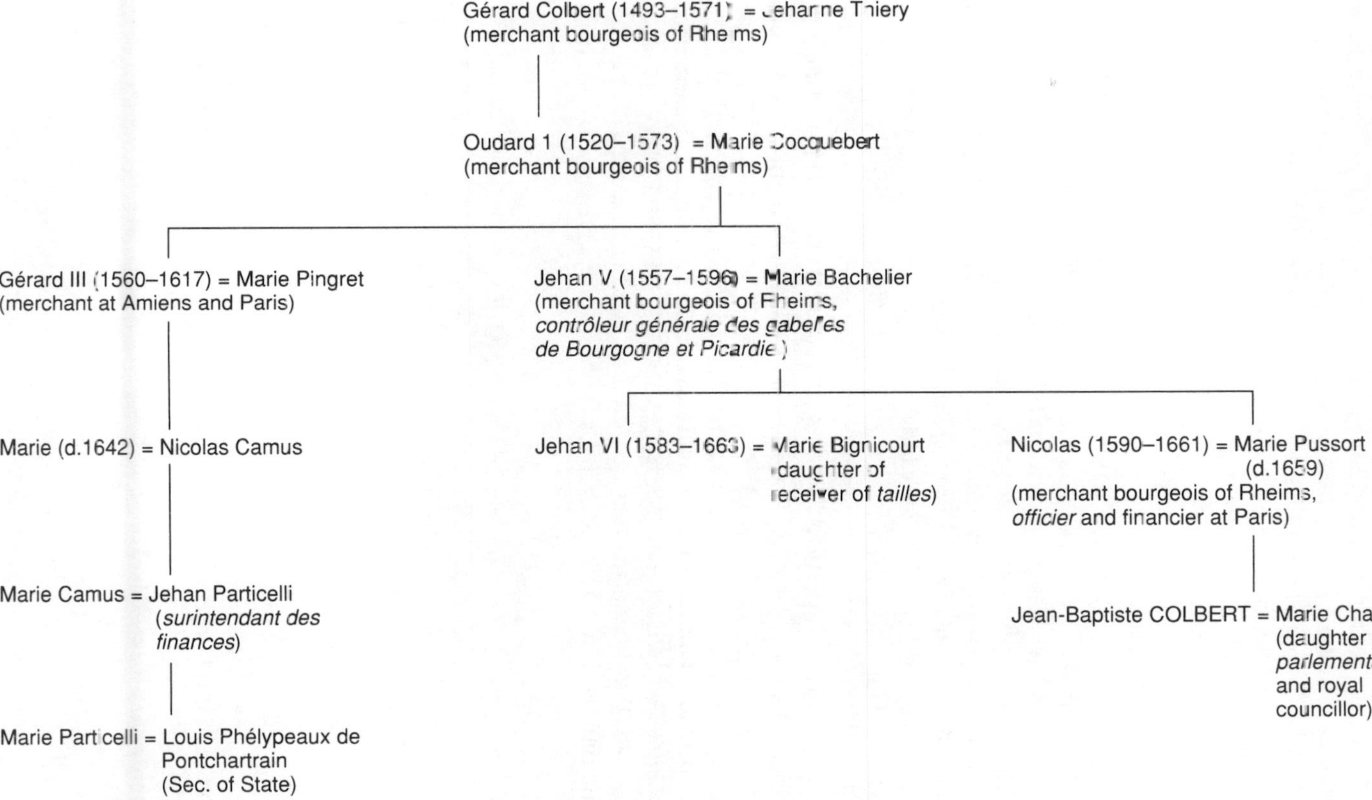

Figure 4.1 The ancestors and some relations of J.-B. Colbert

Source: Bourgeon 1971

family at Paris and married his daughter into that of Nicole Camus, the great financier. The granddaughter produced by this alliance, and therefore the great Colbert's second cousin, was Marie Camus. She eventually married Jehan Particelli, brother of the future *surintendant des finances* at the time of the Fronde. Her own daughter, Marie Particelli, married the Secretary of State, Louis Phélypeaux, in 1635. Thus in 1628, when Colbert's father, who at first devoted himself to the family's now considerable commercial interests, decided to move to Paris his relations there were already thriving. The cousins included a councillor in the *parlement* of Paris, the wife of Nicolas Camus, a third who was on the verge of buying an ennobling charge of secretary of the king, and a fourth about to cement another key family alliance by marrying Claude le Tellier, daughter of the future secretary of state for war.

It was this impressive family network which put Colbert's father in a position to become *conseiller et maître d'Hôtel ordinaire du Roi*. Styling himself *noble homme*, sieur de Vandières (after a fief he had acquired), he became deeply engaged in the financial affairs of the king, experiencing both the immense rewards and the moments of crisis which afflicted the lives of *partisans*. These preoccupations were shared by two cousins and a brother; the latter was a merchant banker who had acquired the lucrative office of *receveur général* of the Archbishopric of Rheims and of the Abbey of St Rémy before also moving to Paris. The way was thus well prepared for Jean-Baptiste Colbert to acquire an office of *commissaire ordinaire des guerres* in 1640. It was not long, however, before his father began to shed his financial interests; in 1652 he became a councillor of state. This may well have been a consequence of Jean-Baptiste's own service in the entourage of Le Tellier and Mazarin which placed him on the threshold of real power.

Perhaps the only person whose social standing has been more generally misunderstood than that of Colbert was Nicolas Fouquet, the *surintendant de finances* whose downfall the great minister himself engineered. He was, in fact, no more of a social upstart than his rival; the similarity in social origins is striking (see Figure 4.3). He was descended from a merchant family already rich in the fifteenth century; by the sixteenth his ancestors had integrated themselves through the purchase of land into the world of the provincial nobility. There was a simultaneous move towards the world of law and office, including municipal office, by younger brothers and through the marriages of the daughters. Well before the end of the sixteenth century the family was firmly implanted in the upper reaches of the robe with representatives in both the *parlement* of Rennes and that of Paris. A Fouquet also secured a position as canon in the cathedral of Langres and then as almoner to Henri IV. When the Parisian Fouquets were stricken by a series of deaths their Breton cousins came to the aid of François, the young and now bereaved representative

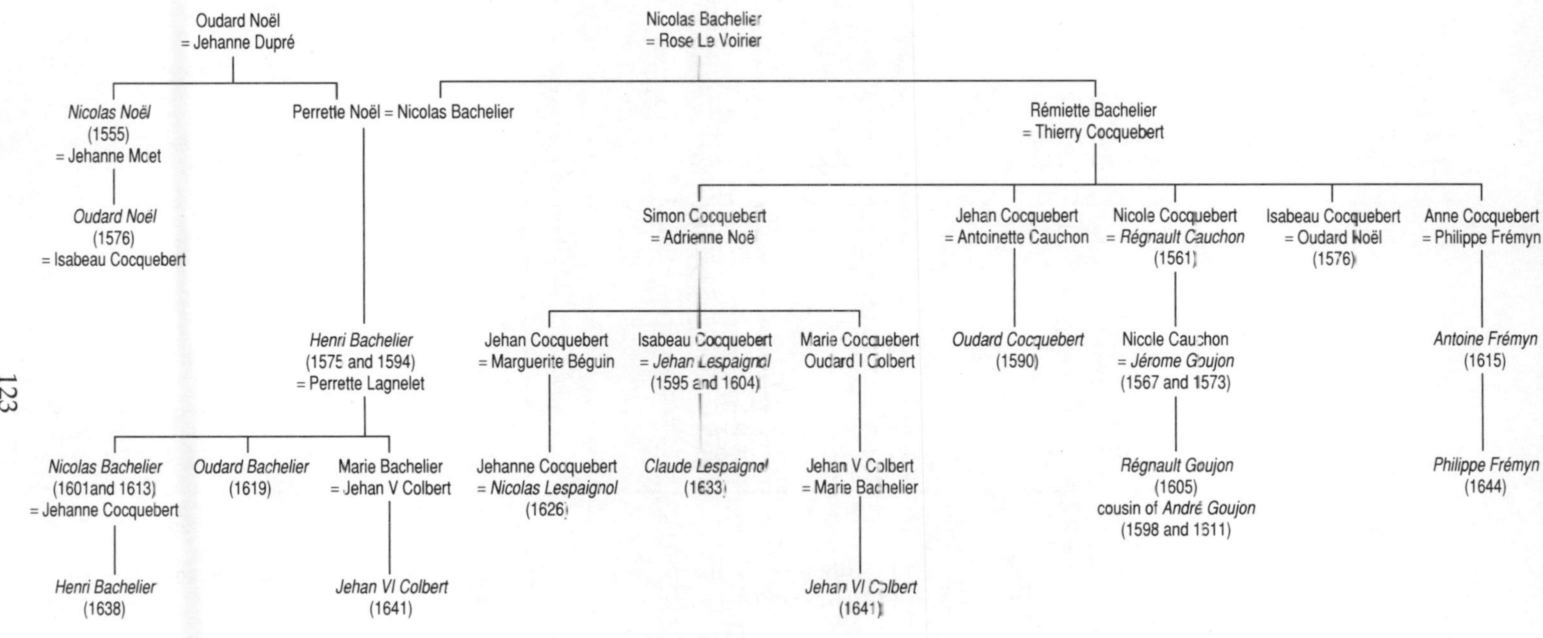

Figure 4.2 The mayors and their relations of Rheims

Source: Bourgeon 1971

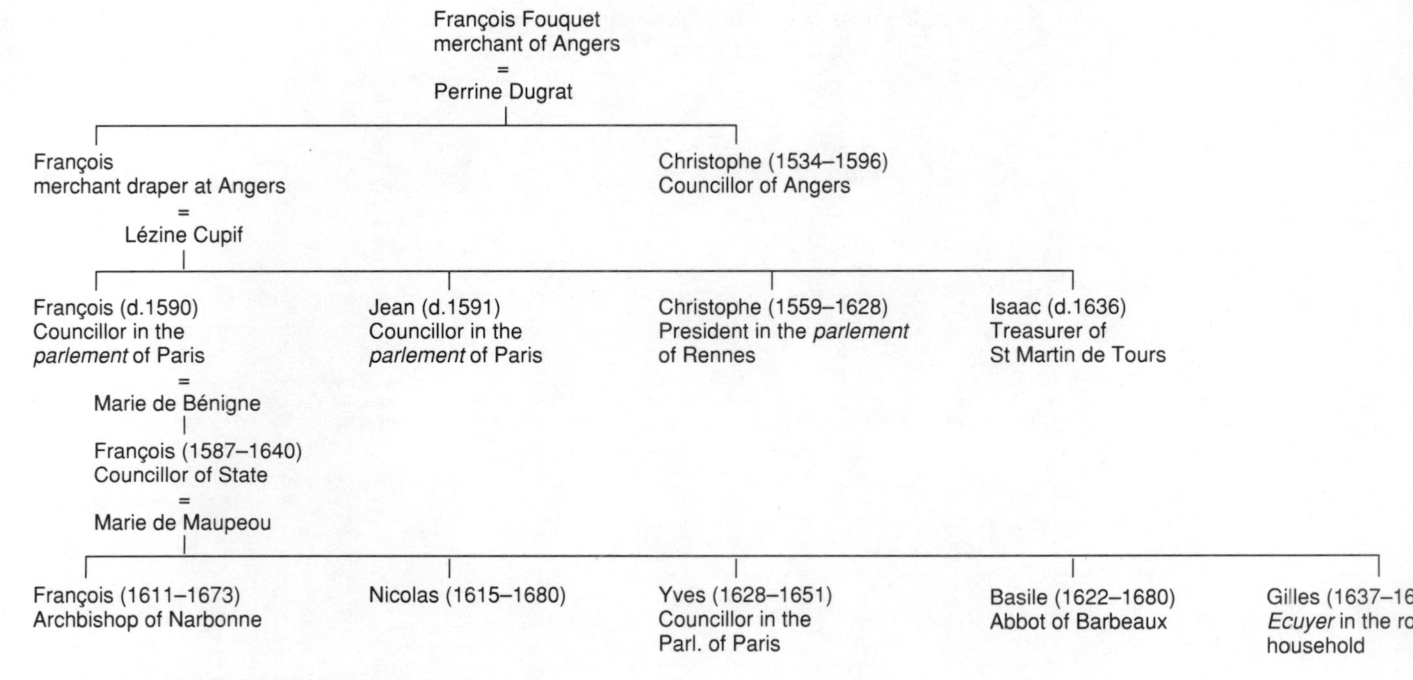

Figure 4.3 The ancestors of Nicolas Fouquet

Source: Dessert 1987

of the main line. His uncle assumed the family office in the *parlement* of Paris, reserving the office of judge at Rennes for the youth. François occupied this for a year before claiming his place in the *parlement* of Paris in 1609.

A year later he married Marie de Maupeou whose father had been appointed *contrôleur général des finances* in 1607. Her uncle was treasurer to the Duc de Joyeuse and had been ennobled in 1596. Apart from her substantial dowry, Marie also bestowed on François a brother-in-law who was a future councillor in the *parlement* of Paris, and through him a further relative in the *grand conseil*, two in the *cour des aides*, one treasurer in the Parisian bureau and last, but not least, one *maître des requêtes*. In 1615, the same year in which Nicolas was born, François sold his position in the *parlement* and acquired an office of *maître des requêtes* for himself. He was a judge in the Chalais affair, participated in investigations into financiers and presided over the notorious *chambre de l'Arsenal*. Like so many his cause advanced with that of Richelieu. The way was well and truly prepared for his son to achieve the highest financial office.[52]

Such accounts show the extent to which the rise of 'great individuals' flowed from the steady social ascent of their families over several generations. They also illustrate a number of other social phenomena. One is the crucial part played in sustaining family position by ecclesiastical office, particularly in the cathedral chapters. This interest continued as the families prospered. Etienne III d'Aligre, chancellor in 1674, had a brother who became *commendataire* of two monasteries in 1624 and in one of them he was succeeded by three more Aligres; Colbert's sons and cousins included three bishops, one archbishop and one abbot, whilst no less than four of his sisters became abbesses. Two of Nicolas Fouquet's brothers acceded to the episcopacy, a third became an abbot whilst all six sisters became *religieuses*. Equally important in consolidating family position was a grip on municipal office. It is nowhere better illustrated than by the situation at Rheims where, for a crucial period, the Colberts, in conjunction with a handful of related families, dominated the mayoralty (see Figure 4.2). The progress of all three families further exemplifies the drift, observed in other contexts, away from entrepreneurial activities into *rentier* and officeholding ones.

The part played by wives and daughters in furthering and consolidating family fortunes is also very clear. At first sight this may seem surprising in view of the lack of female legal autonomy and the increasingly ferocious deployment of the law in order to ensure the subordination of both young men and young women to the dictates of their parents in matrimonial matters. Clandestine marriages were outlawed in 1556 and the age of majority pushed up from twenty to thirty for men and from seventeen to twenty-five for women. From 1579, even widows under twenty-five required parental consent to marry. In 1639, children of clandestine marriages were disbarred from inheriting the estates of any of their relatives and, in 1697, this was extended to include even the *légitime* portion of an inheritance. The corollary of these developments was draconian punishments for concealing pregnancies.[53] Such measures certainly reduced the formal legal independence of women (and young men); but they were also an eloquent testimony to the real and perceived importance of the part played by women in the maintenance and furtherance of family interests. Advantageous marriages, as Denis Richet has remarked, allowed the transfer of wealth, the accumulation of property, and access to wider social milieux.[54]

It is also important not to exaggerate the effects of the legal restraints on women from the propertied classes. For, although they passed directly from the tutelage of fathers to that of husband, the law did provide some protection for their material interests. The principle of the inalienability of the dowry, derived from Roman law, the evolution of customs which allowed women compensation for losses suffered through their husbands' alienation of property, the ability to renounce the succession and associated debts, together with an increasing application of measures to ensure that widows enjoyed a life interest in the income from their dead husband's estate, all helped to offset their lack of legal autonomy.[55] Moreover, the legal incapacity of women did not apply to those engaged in business on their own account.[56] This was a not insignificant concession given the increase in single female headed households which occurred between the mid-fifteenth and the mid-sixteenth century. In the customary regions of the north between 12 and 20 per cent of households were headed by women; in the Roman law regions of the south it was less but still between 5 and 10 per cent. Whilst it is true that most of these represented unmarried women and young widows who lived in abject poverty, they also included a leavening of the comfortably and even well off. Women, often but not always widows, ran farms and businesses; they constituted a significant element of some guilds and played independent roles as *rentiers* or property owners. Noblewomen were prominent as managers of large estates and households, a necessity perhaps in view of their husbands' frequent absences.[57] It was also not unknown, despite the general presumption against women holding fiefs, for a noble house to survive the interruption of the male line as a result of patrimonies being passed through a female heiress to her children.[58] Noblewomen could also exercise considerable powers of patronage in their own right as heads of large households, heads of religious houses, and through their influence at Court.[59]

It is not surprising that Bodin's view of the Commonweal as nothing less than the 'rightly ordered government of a number of families . . .' long continued to command universal assent.[60] According to the *Encyclopédie*, 'A people or nation' was 'nothing more than an entirety compounded of several families'.[61] Generally speaking the family envisaged did not resemble the modern nuclear and 'private' family, although the possibility of a narrow definition was increasingly recognised. Seventeenth-century definitions vacillated between an emphasis on 'household' and 'lineage', from 'all persons who live in the same household under a common head' to all those who were of the same blood in the male line. *Famille* could be synonymous with *race* or *maison* or *lignage*.[62] The distinction between family and domestics was very blurred. In aristocratic households the domestics included intendants, secretaries and other personal attendants who were themselves commonly nobles. Unlike the *serviteurs* – lackeys, valets, coachmen, cooks and so on – not all superior domestics were paid wages. Socially the *serviteurs* were on a par with artisans and boutiquiers.[63] Viewed in this way the concept of the family was profoundly upper-class; some commentators denied its applicability to the *ménages* of the *menu peuple*.

The size of upper-class households alone justified such an attitude. That of a grand seigneur would have perhaps thirty domestics. If he was married, his wife would have her own personal servants and the children a governess, nurse and tutor. In such circumstances a household might reach fifty-five or even more.[64] That of the Duc de Gramont, governor of Bayonne, Basse-Labourd and Basse-Navarre, swollen by its forty military personnel, totalled 116. By way of comparison the household of a president of the Paris *parlement* reached thirty, that of his counterpart in Aix twelve whilst the average for the judges of that city was five. As might be expected there was a definite correlation between the number of domestics employed, social standing and wealth.[65] Less well-to-do households sometimes included servants or apprentices and labourers who lived in for all or part of the year but their role was essentially functional.

The orbit of households was further enlarged by the way in which interlocking networks of kinship and patronage extended far beyond the immediate family. Alliances were constantly forged between different branches of the same lineage, particularly through the uniting of cousins, whilst different families were brought together by double or sometimes triple marriage ties. This upper-class practice seems to have been emulated by the rural notables of central and southern France where extended and deeply patriarchal families were common.[66] Godparents frequently played a central role in linking kinship networks to wider patron–client relationships and were clearly regarded as a critical element in the claim to social standing. Just as the well-to-do robe families of Paris sought godparents for their infants amongst the *grands* so the master craftsmen of Dijon sought them from their social superiors amongst the nobles, officers and members of the legal profession.[67] Marriages constituted a key moment in the fashioning of social ties and lists of witnesses to these occasions constitute an invaluable guide to the formation of both clan networks and broader clienteles.

Looked at in one way the concern with family, lineage and kinship was divisive; it certainly underlay many of the factional rivalries which so destabilised French society. Intense and interminable legal battles over property, marriage alliances, successions, debts, and possession of office made French society one of the most litigious in Europe, sometimes tearing families apart. On the other hand, *lignage* provided all members of the propertied classes with a common set of social, legal and economic structures.[68] The dominant social groups were brought together not only by networks of family, kin, and their extension in social and political clienteles but in a shared nexus of ideas about family and property. This was true despite the insuperable regional and local variations in legal practice. Both legal practitioners and litigants, whether subject to the customary traditions of northern France or the Roman ones of the *Midi*, shared certain basic objectives. The first was to enable family patrimonies to be passed on relatively intact; the second was to try to reconcile this primary consideration with the need to ensure that all members of the family were treated reasonably fairly. In the regions of *droit écrit* this was achieved according to Roman principles by giving the testator and head of the household the capacity to dispose freely of the family property, reserving only for the younger children a specified proportion of the estate. In the customary regions of the north the same objective was attained by reducing such freedom so that only a small proportion of the patrimony – usually a fifth – could be alienated. The bulk went as of right to the next of kin. In some regions the eldest child was also allowed to select the best part of the inheritance. Derived from feudal custom, this practice was quite widely used by the seventeenth century for noble properties in the possession of commoners, for non-noble properties in the possession of nobles and increasingly for patrimonies which had no claim to nobility at all. Although frequently resisted by jurists concerned about the rights of all the children, such developments were further facilitated by increasing testamentary use of the device of *fidéicomis* or strict entail which allowed a family patrimony to be retained in the male line.[69] Nothing perhaps illustrates more the concern with preserving the patrimony from one generation to the next than the right of *retrait lignager*; this allowed members of a lineage who had been deprived of their inheritance to recover alienated properties on payment of compensation to those by whom they had been acquired. The *retrait lignager* served an analogous purpose to the *retrait féodal* which, as has been seen, was frequently used by those with seigneurial rights to consolidate their estates. It is noteworthy that, despite its incompatibility with the freedom of the testator, the *retrait lignager* was common throughout large parts of the romanised south; so too was the customary practice of excluding dowered females from any share in the succession, another device which served to ensure its integrity.[70]

A moment's reflection is required to grasp the full ambiguity of a system in which so much emphasis was attached to lineage both as an institution and as an ideal. It was simultaneously a cause of factional division and a medium for the construction of an upper-class identity. It certainly does not sustain the view that French society was divided 'vertically' rather than 'horizontally'. The rivalries of the upper classes were precisely that: rivalries between members of a wealthy elite who shared a common relationship to the means of production, who were united as well as divided by family and kin and who increasingly shared a common set of assumptions about the nature of the family and property. Lineage, clienteles and their accompanying rivalries were themselves an upper-class phenomenon. Suggestions that vertical ties served to unite the privileged with the labouring classes have rarely been sustained by clear evidence. The best examples relate to master craftsmen or household domestics who clearly benefited from their association with great houses. Farr cites the embroiderer Claude Rebuilt, later *valet de chambre* to the Duchess of Lorraine, and Martin Maupoi, shoemaker to the Duc de Mayenne; both were well rewarded by their patrons, securing respectively exemption from municipal taxation and from service in the night watch.[71] For journeymen, however, this sort of protection was virtually impossible. In any event, as Farr himself observes, such relationships were as much to do with ensuring deference and the maintenance of a paternalistic system as with the creation of a dynamic clientele.[72] Whilst lowly domestics might well tend to identify their interests with those of the household and even endeavour to use their savings in impeccable *rentier* style, such relationships certainly lacked the reciprocity of upper-class ones which Kettering has identified as an essential ingredient of clientelism. Furthermore, as has been shown, they were fraught with tension, mistrust and class feeling which could erupt into open hostility. There was absolutely no guarantee when disorder loomed that the bourgeois captains of the urban militias could enforce their orders on the artisans who served in them. Relationships between landlords and tenants were similarly uncertain.

ROBE AND SWORD: A SINGLE CLASS

The preceding analysis lends perspective to the much discussed question of the social character of the robe and its relationship to the sword. For one of the most obvious features of the family networks described above is the remarkable range of social, economic, financial, clerical, administrative, military and political interests that they encompassed. It is only possible to sustain a clear demarcation between robe and sword by emphasising, as Mousnier has done, the endogamous tendencies of the principal male line and by arguing that it was the marriages of the men that determined social status.[73] Such a mechanical and formalistic approach, however, is unable to encompass the fluid social dynamics which have been described. It fails to recognise the role played by women and younger sons in consolidating both the material assets and status of families. In this context Carolyn Lougee's fascinating analysis of the marriages of the women who dominated the Parisian salons is of considerable significance. She shows quite clearly how these centres of high society 'functioned as a melting pot which blurred distinctions of birth and profession'.[74] The most striking feature to emerge is the extent to which women without title married the titled, and the extent to which those from newly ennobled families managed to secure partners from those with significantly longer pedigrees. Despite upper-class concern about *mésalliances* these may well have been more common than is often supposed. Numerous alliances between court women and financiers seem to have been accepted without commotion or adverse comment.[75]

In some parts of the realm the distinction between robe and sword was pretty meaningless, as families of ancient stock had never found it demeaning to acquire office. At Aix-en-Provence they shared offices in both *parlement* and the *cour des comptes* with those recently ennobled. By the seventeenth century a quarter of the *parlementaires* of Aix belonged to sword families ennobled prior to 1500.[76] Bohanan, observing that the nobility of Aix were much more akin to an Italian patriciate, suggests that the explanation may lie in the non-feudal origins of the southern nobility. However, it is striking that in a highly feudal area like Brittany 144 families of ancient lineage are known to have served in the *parlement*.[77] In fact the divide between robe and sword was already blurred by the early seventeenth century. Members of the upper classes frequently moved from one to the other without fuss; conscious and considered decisions were also made about which career path was most suitable for their noble offspring.[78]

The younger sons and daughters of the greatest robe families developed significant ties with other socio-professional groups. Take for instance the thirty-two brothers and younger sons of the councillors of state in 1658; ten were clerics, six belonged to the sword and nine to the robe.[79] The orientation of the brothers of those *maîtres des requêtes* appointed between 1661 and 1677 was very similar: half of the younger brothers went into the church and ten bishops, including the celebrated Bossuet, were to emerge from their ranks. A further fifth passed over to the sword.[80] The younger sons of the *maîtres des requêtes* produced four bishops, four abbots and twenty nobles of the sword.[81] The tendency for brothers and younger sons to enter the church or become soldiers increased towards the end of the century. Of the brothers of the *maîtres des requêtes* appointed between 1688 and 1704 over 30 per cent were clerics, 10 per cent sword nobles, whilst 40 per cent remained in the robe.[82] Of their younger sons nearly a third entered the church whilst as many as 45 per cent joined the ranks of the sword. Mousnier also noted that an analysis of the marriages of eldest daughters 'shows a clear increase in the number of marriages into the sword'.[83] These observations seem to point in the same direction as Labatut's breakdown of the marriages of the *ducs et pairs*; after 1660 the proportion of them marrying into the robe rose from 10.5 to 26.8 per cent.[84]

Misunderstandings about the relative social positions of robe and sword have arisen in part from a failure to appreciate that social status was determined not simply by professional occupation or function but also by the number of generations of nobility that could be claimed. Perfect or complete nobility was generally associated with those considered to have possessed it from time immemorial; in practice that meant long enough to exceed the memory of the oldest witnesses, broadly speaking for three generations.[85] Moreover, as noted in relation to the Aixoise nobility, length of pedigree was not a sure guide to occupation. Whilst most of the more recently ennobled had legal or mercantile origins it remained possible to achieve nobility through military service or the ownership of fiefs.[86] Wood's study of the *élection* of Bayeux offers particularly valuable evidence of the processes at work in the critical social space at the lower end of the noble hierarchy. Here new nobles contributed to military life in numbers that equalled or even exceeded their general numerical importance; in the mid-sixteenth century a quarter of the sword nobles were recently ennobled and almost one in five of those who went to the relief of Amiens in 1597 were in the same category. By 1666, on the other hand, the officeholding nobility of Bayeux was composed overwhelmingly of those with more than a century of nobility behind them.[87] In the Beauce, another region for which systematic evidence exists, it could take several generations for *anoblis* to win their spurs; some 14 per cent of them none the less took up arms, a not insignificant figure when it is generally considered that perhaps only a quarter of all sword nobles actually fought.[88]

Even well-established robe families did not disdain a military career. At Montpellier increasing numbers of robe sons entered the army as commissioned officers after 1640.[89] By this time some of the most prestigious *parlementaire* families – like the Potier and Talon – had already acquired military experience. Although army careers became less common after 1675 as far as Parisian magistrates were concerned, their provincial counterparts retained a military profile. Those of Rouen apparently 'colonised' the regiment of Guards.[90] Of 164 *lieutenants-généraux* under Louis XIV whose origins can be discerned, eight came from bourgeois or robe backgrounds; it was even possible to find the son of an intendant and of an *avocat-général* amongst the thirty-two French-born marshals of France.[91] Those at the pinnacle of the robe – ministers, secretaries of state, presidents of the *parlements* – were also admitted by the king to the exclusive and venerated Order of the Holy Spirit where they rubbed shoulders with sword nobles of the most illustrious stock.[92]

The social and family ties which bound robe and sword were underpinned by their common relationship to the means of production and the similarity of their revenues. Despite differences in rank and function, the economic interests of newly arrived members of the upper orders were indistinguishable from those of their social superiors. Like them their wealth was represented by land, houses, offices and state loans. The overwhelming predominance of these four types of investment, in which all the constituent elements of the ruling class – sword, robe, finance, ecclesiastical – participated, gave it an underlying economic unity. All derived their revenues from an amalgam of feudal dues and perquisites, commercial rents, state investments and other forms of usurious activity. Newly arrived members of the robe elite frequently took great pains to establish their credentials as landowners in traditional seigneurial style. Claude le Bouthillier, Secretary of State from 1628, appears to have inherited no lands from his family but on accession to office felt it appropriate to acquire some. On his estate at Pont-sur-Seine he constructed a fine house and bestowed gifts on the parish. Portraits of his family are still visible in the church and castle.[93] Claude de Bullion made a prodigious fortune in the service of the state, holding the lucrative post of *surintendant des finances* from 1632 to 1640. *Maître des requêtes* by 1605, he had already begun to purchase numerous seigneuries; but the real expansion of his landed estates was almost contemporaneous with his elevation to the rank of royal councillor and the victory of Richelieu over his enemies in 1629 to 1630. In 1628 Bullion was able to buy a seigneury worth more than all his previous purchases put together. By 1642 just under half of his assets were in land, 30 per cent in state offices, and just 12.5 per cent in *rentes* on individuals. Despite the size of his landed interests and the necessity for farming out the administration and collection of the revenues, Bullion's relationships with his dependants preserved their feudal character, with regular declarations of faith and homage. In December 1639 he infeudated the manor at the hamlet of Gastines which was dependent on the seigneur of Grange de Bois. The contract was concluded in strict conformity with the custom of the *bailliage*; Bullion received the homage of his new vassal, and allowed him to establish his manor as a noble house and have a dovecote there. He also felt it important that one of the many seigneuries should bear his name and obtained Letters Patent to this effect. Later he founded a school in the parish for thirteen children of the poor.[94] When Louis II de Phélypeaux, seigneur de la Vrillière and the real founder of his family's fortunes, became Secretary of State in

1629 he possessed but one seigneury and the bulk of his capital was invested in offices. A successful marriage and persistent endeavour meant that by 1678 he had accumulated a fortune of 2,400,000 *livres* of which 1,800,000 were in landed estates. He personally received faith and homage for his fiefs, erected new properties into fiefs, and in 1660 obtained Letters Patent authorising him to establish the feudal dues and payments dependent on them. When he died he ensured that the division of his properties was made in accordance with feudal practice.[95] These illustrations expose the inadequacy of treatments of the robe either as bourgeois newcomers breaking down traditional social relations and attitudes or as remote and impersonal agents of a modernising government.

It is true that the economic assets of some members of the robe reveal a different pattern, reflecting the vast increase in the flow of usurious money. Louis Boucherat, Chancellor from 1685, possessed only two or three small seigneuries and the largest proportion of his capital was invested in *rentes* and loans to individuals.[96] This was even more so with Henri Pussort, uncle of the great Colbert and councillor of the king from 1649. *Rentes* on individuals, including members of his own family who required funds for the purchase of office, constituted 63 per cent of his fortune of over 1,300,000 *livres*.[97] It is also important to note that even where land constituted the major part of a family fortune, this was not usually reflected in the character of its revenues as the return from land was comparatively poor. Despite the fact that the Phélypeaux capital assets were preponderantly in land, something like 60 per cent of their revenues came from offices.[98] Yet this in no sense makes it legitimate to describe them as bourgeois.[99] Their fortune and revenues were little different in character from those, for instance, of the ancient and princely family of Condé. In the first decade of the eighteenth century two-thirds of the Condé fortune was in land; but revenue from their estates was 783,000 *livres*, only fractionally more than the 750,000 which came from royal offices and pensions.[100] Nor were the Condé unrepresentative of the higher ranks of the traditional nobility. Labatut has concluded that, in general, offices and *rentes* accounted for about two-thirds of the revenues of the *ducs et pairs*, despite the fact that the largest part of their capital was invariably invested in land.[101] He also anticipated the more recent findings of Daniel Dessert by showing – aristocratic pretensions notwithstanding – that their revenues could include some of the grubbiest, such as those derived from tax farms or customs. Dessert's brilliant illumination of the murkier recesses of high society has established that behind many of the financiers in whose name transactions were conducted stood some of the greatest families in the land: Sully, Séguier, Condé, La Trémoille, Bullion, Montpensier, la Rochefoucauld, the Archbishop of Avranches, the Bishop of Toulon and so on. Of fifty-two investors in the salt farms between 1635 and 1663, twelve were nobles of the sword, eighteen of the robe, four held high financial office while five were *sécrétaires du Roi* (a sinecure for those with money to lend).[102] Towering above them all were Mazarin and Richelieu. By 1642 the investments of the latter in the royal domain and *rentes* were producing an annual revenue of over a quarter of a million *livres*; this came primarily from immensely lucrative rights in the salt of Brouage and its region, supplemented by substantial proceeds from the weights and measures of Le Havre and Rouen, and the fruits of relatively humble clerkships in Beaufort, Chinon and Loudun.[103] If Richelieu was both enormously greedy and remarkably successful, he was not atypical, merely representing at the pinnacle of French society the apotheosis of trends to be found lower down. Thus amongst those who lent money, for instance, to the municipality of Toulouse in mid-century were not only well-known regional financiers but principal *parlementaires*, the secretary of the provincial Estates and members of the clergy and religious foundations.[104]

THE ARGUMENT THUS FAR

The argument so far has been intended to show that it is perfectly possible and quite fruitful to construct a model of French society based on class. Such a model makes no less sense of French society than one based on Orders; it actually makes more complete sense of the social hierarchy depicted in the writings of Loyseau and his contemporaries. For they recognised that status was an attribute of its upper echelons which differentiated them from those who worked. Wealth and status generally went hand in hand. The ruling class – those who 'commanded' in Loyseau's terminology – was composed of an amalgam of robe and sword and can be defined not only by a common relationship to the means of production but also by a corresponding set of ideas about property, lineage and family. Moreover, the fact that upper-class relationships were so overwhelmingly mediated by lineage, kin and clienteles informs and illuminates both the rivalries that divided them and also the common interests which bound them together. Clienteles were an upper-class phenomenon and did not extend in any meaningful way across the divide between the privileged and non-privileged. The rivalries between them were to a large degree a manifestation of sectional struggles for the benefits of the surplus wealth generated by the labouring population. Whilst a common antipathy to the fisc sometimes united landlord and tenant in rebellion and reciprocal relations of dominance and deference brought together municipal oligarchs and aspiring artisans in formal acts which legitimised those relations, the antagonism of the poor and powerless for the rich and influential was ever likely to rupture the social harmony.

It is also clear, in a general way, that the state served the interests of the ruling class which has been identified. This is not surprising given that so much of the royal administration had literally been bought up by the seigneurial officeholding elite, many of whom became enormously wealthy in the process. If one was looking for a state apparatus which conformed to the vulgar Marxist notion of an instrument in the hands of the ruling class it would be difficult to find a better example. It can be seen that a structural analysis does help to illuminate both the nature of the ruling class and the mechanisms by which wealth was appropriated and distributed.

Yet the net effect of such observations is to delineate the limitations as well as the virtues of this mode of analysis. Whilst offering an acceptable general explanation of the socio-economic underpinnings of the state it does not explain either the precise character of absolute monarchy or the mechanisms by which political stability was achieved. Indeed, the entirely reasonable insistence on the common-class location of sword and robe makes all the more problematic the contradiction between the community of their material interests and the bitter social antagonisms which frequently divided them. If, as suggested, these were manifestations of an intense competition for place and position, it remains to be explained how the ruling class succeeded in getting its act together. This cannot be done if this class is defined only in economic terms; its cultural and ideological dimensions also require consideration. Nor can these be conveyed solely by reference to a static model; the specifics of a changing situation have to be brought into play.

5

THE NOBILITY

A hegemonic *tour de force*

SOCIAL MOBILITY AND THE RENEWAL OF TRADITIONAL VALUES

There was a widespread belief amongst the nobility that the traditional order had been subverted by *nouveaux riches* upstarts, that virtue had been displaced by money, and that valour and honour were no longer publicly recognised. It went hand in hand with a gloomy conviction that the political regime was being recast at the expense of the nobles. Such feelings were not confined to the provincial nobility or those in danger of sinking into the ranks of the peasantry. In the last decades of Louis XIV's reign, long after the years of greatest tension had passed, they were taken up and articulated by members of the high nobility. Foremost amongst these were Archbishop Fénélon, the Duc de St Simon, and the Comte de Boulainvilliers, a descendant of the House of Croy which had once known more glorious times. They differed in some of their specific propositions but their common desire was to restore the authority and reassert the distinctive status of the nobility as an estate of the realm. This they believed had been usurped through the combined effects of money and the need felt by those of lowly birth to please the prince.[1]

One of the most striking expressions of noble resentment can be seen in the common stereotype of the financier as the archetypal self-made man, of lowly, if not base origins, who had insinuated himself into high society. In fact, as Dessert has shown, the essential prerequisite for embarking on a financial career, as on any other, was a network of family contacts among the well-to-do and the wherewithal to exploit them. Thus Jean Thevenin, accused by his detractors of being nothing but the son of a poor peasant, was in fact descended from a proud Rochelais family which produced several mayors for the town and whose grandfather had been Master of the Mint at Poitiers and ennobled in 1652. Not a single one of the 534 financiers investigated by Dessert came from lowly domestic service; only a tiny minority of them had graduated from the ranks of the merchants and even in these cases one is dealing with the *bonne bourgeoisie*. Most in fact emerged from the royal administration itself. Moreover, just under a third of them inherited titles of nobility and 79 per cent of them achieved that status ultimately.[2]

The gulf between noble perceptions and reality was so wide as to suggest that, in extreme cases, they were the product of a curious blend of social myopia and hysteria. The aristocratic foundations of French society were clearly not about to crumble at the hands of Louis XIV. Dessert's explanation for the ill-founded stereotyping of the *laquais financier* stresses the desire amongst members of high society to obscure the extent to which they themselves were benefiting from the financial operations on which the state depended. The widespread use of *prête-noms* and other subterfuges to conceal their activity may well have been a measure of the ambivalence and guilt of those involved. Yet these attitudes cannot be reduced to a straightforward conspiracy. They reflect a much wider anxiety about the threat to noble values, the roots of which lay in the last half of the sixteenth century.

Down to the middle decades of the sixteenth century the lack of an absolute divide between noble and non-noble seems to have caused little problem. It had been possible to slide from one to the other, particularly through the purchase of a fief, and the assumption of the epithet 'noble homme'. As noble status was usually confirmed on the mere oral evidence of witnesses, who could vouch for the lifestyle or military prowess of the family concerned, it was often only necessary to live like a noble to become one. Three generations of officeholding also sufficed for assimilation into the nobility despite the fact that, in strictly legal terms, office was not deemed to ennoble. Members of the robe acquired *de facto* nobility long before the principle of ennoblement through office was embodied in the edict on the *tailles* of 1600.[3] It was even possible in a maritime province like Brittany for nobles to engage in trade without suffering an irrevocable loss of status.

However, what was tolerable in relatively stable conditions was to become less so as inflation and commercial growth, combined with the proliferation of venal offices and recurrent political crises, vastly increased the opportunities for upward social mobility. At Dijon the number of merchant households grew from forty-two to seventy-four between 1556 and 1643. Yet this was totally overshadowed by the more than threefold increase in the number of legal households which expanded from sixty-nine to a staggering 222. Thus, in a period when the overall population of Dijon grew by a half, the merchants' community increased by 76 per cent and the legal one by a massive 222 per cent.[4] At Amiens lesser merchants and shopkeepers were able to achieve municipal office with relative ease and the move from commerce to the highest legal office was accomplished by some in one or two generations.[5] At

Rouen in 1543 the son of a humble attorney was the leading candidate amongst fifteen for parlementary office.[6] In the *bailliage* of the same city no less than a quarter of 254 fiefs examined between 1530 and 1580 changed hands, either through sale or marriage or exchange.[7] Ennoblement by office, through the purchase of fiefs or by military service, as well as by the simple dispensation of *lettres d'annoblissement*, became increasingly widespread.[8] Whereas in the early sixteenth century the officeholding families possessed only 11 per cent of the seigneurial holdings in the Beauce, by 1640 they accounted for half.[9] An estimated three-quarters of the Parisian nobility in 1696 had acquired their status since 1560.[10] In the *élection* of Bayeux a combination of population growth, immigration and upward mobility generated an additional 250 noble families between 1540 and 1598, an increase of 81 per cent.[11]

Although a complete ascent of the social hierarchy invariably took several generations, the scale and nature of upward social mobility made it highly visible. Whereas Francis I had ruled with the aid of perhaps 12,000 *officiers*, by Louis XIV's reign their numbers had at least quintupled. Chaunu estimates that, including the lesser officials of the tax farms, there were no less than 80,000 *officiers* by 1665. With their families they thus accounted at a conservative estimate for about 1.8 per cent of the population.[12] Given the overwhelming concentration, particularly of the more prestigious, in the towns, their presence and influence were felt much more sharply than this figure suggests. Overall, perhaps one in ten of the urban population belonged to an officeholder's family. In major administrative centres the proportion rose to one in five or six. Roupnel estimated that at Dijon officeholding familes accounted for 6,000 to 8,000 people out of a population of 25,000.[13] Even in an essentially commercial town like Amiens there were no less than fifteen officer corps sharing the administration of justice. Nationally, the officers were headed in wealth, status and influence by representatives of many institutions which had not even existed at the beginning of the sixteenth century. There were, at that time, less than half Louis' thirteen *parlements* (only four prior to 1475), none of the one hundred or so *présidiaux*, or the twenty-three *bureaux des finances*. No wonder that Cardin Le Bret, observing the 'prodigious multiplication' of offices at the beginning of the seventeenth century, was under the erroneous impression that out of 500 citizens half were officers.[14] To add insult to injury, from the reign of Henri IV the great nobility of the sword were virtually excluded from the royal councils. The perceived threat was made all the worse because it was underpinned by money. Whilst a slow assimilation of newcomers into the nobility might in itself have caused little concern, the ability to buy status certainly did. Hence the insistent demand – temporarily met between 1618 and 1621 – for the suppression of sale of office.[15] The fact that money could buy position also challenged the cherished belief that service ought to be personal and immediate, determined by the king's choice of those with merit.[16]

At the same time, the nobles of the sword had to contend with pressure from those who argued not only that the robe was worthy of equal consideration but also that nobility should be a personal attribute.[17] Towards the end of the sixteenth century some critics were even making the *robins* superior to the *épée*.[18] Turquet de Mayerne, whose treatise *De la monarchie aristodémocratique* was written around 1591 and published in 1611, took such views to their logical conclusion. He envisaged a personal nobility based on merit and equality for which the aptitude to undertake public functions, enter trade and the liberal professions would carry more weight than military activity. This bourgeoisification of the nobility was to receive its political expression in the creation of an Estates of 200 *'agripossesseurs'*, also ennobled by virtue of office. It would have legislative and administrative authority, control the royal council, change its composition, and call it to account. The king would not have the power to dissolve the Estates which would also control an army.[19]

In retrospect it is all too easy to conclude that such extraordinary ideas, whose implementation would have destroyed the *ancien régime*, amounted to no more than wishful thinking by one rather precocious writer. The political structures of seventeenth-century France offered no means of achieving an effective public platform for the articulation of such a radical and comprehensive programme. Yet Turquet undoubtedly drew on contemporary attitudes towards the nobility. His ideas may, perhaps, also be seen as a manifestation of the dynamic economic and social impulses of the sixteenth century before they faded away. Moreover, the underlying issues continued to arouse controversy for many years, notably in the highly mobile social milieu of the salons with their correspondingly heady intellectual atmosphere. Here it seemed that the values of traditional society were on trial. Rightly or wrongly the women who dominated the salons were associated with feminist writers who propagated a Neoplatonic concept of love that 'cut across the boundaries of marriage and contradicted demands of marital fidelity', applauded *mésalliances*, venality and luxury and proclaimed the superiority of virtue over birth.[20]

By this time the noble reaction was well under way. Disquiet had already reached intense proportions during the last fifty years of the sixteenth century when an ever-mounting litany of complaints were directed at those elevated without merit.[21] From the Edict of Amboise of 1555, which threatened noble usurpers with a fine of 1,000 *livres*, a series of edicts endeavoured to stem the erosion of noble distinctiveness.[22] Demands for an end to ennoblement surfaced at the Estates-General of Orléans in 1560 and the resulting royal ordonnance threatened those who engaged in trade with loss of their privileges and subjection to the *taille*.[23] Although the petty nobility of Brittany and some other areas continued to trade, this law became the norm throughout the realm.

Apologists for the nobility did not simply adopt a defensive posture; they also engaged in a vigorous intellectual reconstruction of the concept of nobility itself. This rested partly on a reassertion of military values but also, and with increasing emphasis, on birth and lineage as the essential prerequisite of nobility and of virtue. For whilst the defenders of the nobility were prepared to concede that a bad upbringing could subvert an inherited capacity for virtue, they remained adamant that a good upbringing could not compensate for lowly birth. Hard work and application may have been necessary to bring noble virtues to fruition but such endeavour could only perfect what nature had endowed in the first place. Whilst making allowance for the possibility that God might implant superior souls in people of low birth, defenders of noble status were fond of analogies between various human races and species of animals in order to sustain the emphasis on blood.[24] By the mid-sixteenth century the first formulations about the *noblesse de race* and the *noblesse d'ancienne race* had made their appearance.[25] In 1605 Clément Vaillant defined nobility as an 'honorific preeminence deriving from *race* by which some men or women are distinct from, and given precedence over, others'.[26] Such ideas were sometimes bound up with claims that the nobility as a whole descended from the Franks, a conquering race who had brought liberty to the Gauls.[27]

The impact of this nexus of ideas could be seen in the increasingly restrictive approach to ennoblement. Oral evidence of noble stock became less acceptable and written proof was required in the form of parish registers, marriage contracts, wills and records of successions.[28] In 1579 the Norman custom of ennobling those who had held a fief for forty years was suppressed; in 1634 ennoblement through the holding of military office followed suit.[29] Although the Edict of the *tailles* of 1600 gave legal force to the already common practice of ennoblement through office, it also stipulated that the title of *écuyer* could only be held by those whose grandfather had been in the profession of arms or had held an ennobling charge.[30] It was, of course, another matter to make a reality of such legal dispositions given the inevitable resistance to any attempt to deprive those who falsely claimed nobility of their fiscal privileges. With the exception of Normandy, Dauphiné and the Parisian region, investigations into the usurpation of noble titles did not occur until 1666–8 when they were extended to the entire realm. Although their practical effect, measured by the numbers of those deprived of their title, varied from province to province, their very occurrence confirmed the now general requirement for proof of three generations of nobility; in fact nobility going back to 1560 was required and without any trace of anterior commoner status.[31] From the time of Colbert each family was theoretically required to register its coat of arms with the Armorial General. Such requirements, however much they upset the fraudsters and those mistakenly accused of being so, undoubtedly reflected a general concern to preserve distinctions of rank and status. In Burgundy the provincial Estates declined in 1712 to admit anyone whose father's noble ancestry could not be traced back for at least sixty years.[32]

One of the most striking features of this prolonged noble offensive was not just the increasing insistence on the distinction between noble and non-noble but on degrees of status within the nobility itself. The *ducs et pairs* conducted a long and determined campaign to assert their pre-eminence over all others.[33] In March 1664 they commissioned a major work to demonstrate the historic roots of their prerogatives as the heirs of the ancient feudal barons. Although it was not officially published until the mid-eighteenth century the issues it raised were not merely of academic interest. Precipitated by their objections to removing their hats when speaking in the *parlement* of Paris whilst the *président* remained covered, this seemingly petty dispute heralded a major social and constitutional controversy. By the end of Louis XIV's reign the peers were claiming not only access as of right to the principal offices of state but also an existence as a distinct Order with the right to determine the course of the regency. In March 1716 they complained that the *parlement* had prevented them from performing their 'essential functions' which were 'to counsel and assist the king in his most high, great and important affairs'. Such exclusivity rapidly provoked an assembly of the court nobility in defence of the formal equality of all nobles. 'Nobility once recognised,' they declared, 'admits no internal distinction.' It was not a view which would have appealed to Louis XIV. By legitimising the bastard royal princes and attempting to give them a leading role at the coronation ceremony Louis took the emphasis on blood and lineage to a logical if controversial conclusion.[34]

The attempt to reinforce social distinctions was helped from around 1650, or even earlier in some parts of the country, by the changing economic and social climate. Ebbing economic vitality and the consolidation of social conquests by those who had profited from the dynamism of the long sixteenth century meant that the opportunities for upward mobility were sharply diminished at all levels. Master craftsmen, for instance, responded to the deepening depression by severely restricting access to their ranks. At Amiens a relatively fluid situation was transformed so that apprentices who were not sons of masters found they were virtually excluded from their ranks.[35] Similar developments at Clermont-de-Lodève were formalised in 1708 with the introduction of regulations exempting the sons of masters from the need to serve an apprenticeship, pay a fee or complete a *chef d'œuvre*.[36] At Paris the formal obstacles to upward mobility could be even more elaborate; by 1680 the

152 masters of the Parisian guild of ribbon makers were divided into no less than ten grades.[37] Farr's pioneering analysis of the fortunes of the artisans of Dijon points in the same direction. Master craftsmen increasingly married within their own ranks, as did their daughters, the size of their wedding *apports* revealing the social distance that had opened up between them and the journeymen. The genesis of this situation lay in the fifty years after 1561 during which the wages of master craftsmen had risen continuously whilst those of the journeyman moved not at all.[38] Even in the small and relatively egalitarian rural communities of Provence it seems to have definitely become more difficult for newcomers to put down roots after the mid-seventeenth century. Family solidarities, succession in the strict male line, resort to the privilege of *retrait lignager* – all discouraged acquisitions by outsiders.[39]

Just as master craftsmen asserted their socio-economic dominance *vis-à-vis* the mass of artisans, so merchants were gradually eclipsed by the legal profession in one town after another. At Montpellier this process has been traced with particular clarity. In the sixty-year period ending in 1575 just over a fifth of Montpellier's *officiers* themselves came from robe families. During the next fifty years this percentage doubled whilst the number of merchants' sons acceding to the robe on the other hand declined in almost exactly inverse proportion. The number of *officiers* who were grandsons of *officiers* rose from three to twenty-five. Dowry payments also suggest that an economic divide had opened up between them and the merchant community. Similar developments have been detected at Amiens, Dijon, Lyon, Marseille and Poitiers and even in a stagnant backwater like Chateaudun which had a tiny corps of magistrates.[40]

Restrictions on upward mobility were reinforced by the way in which those with the means accumulated offices. In Normandy by 1622 seventeen people possessed a total of 969 posts of *commissaires des tailles*.[41] Once *in situ* the officeholders tended to close ranks against newcomers; as has been seen, some of the most determined opposition to the creation of new offices came from existing officeholders. Within the legal world differentiations became more marked. Everywhere magistrates cut themselves off from notaries and lawyers.[42] During the course of the sixteenth century, for example, the *parlementaires* of Rouen had been drawn largely from the sons of lawyers and lesser officials. Yet by 1619–38, six out of ten came from the upper robe, the soaring cost of their offices making access to their ranks even more difficult. Whereas in the early sixteenth century the annual revenues of the magistrates had been in the region of 500 *livres*, by the 1570s over 5,000 was the norm and over 10,000 not rare. Average capital assets increased in value from about 15,000 to around 100,000; those of 200,000 were not unknown.[43] By the end of the seventeenth century the tendency to endogamy at the highest level of the robe had become overpowering; of 196 wives of Parisian *parlementaires* who held office between 1685 and 1690, only seven were from sword families and just two were daughters of merchants.[44]

For all these reasons the number of newcomers who penetrated the upper levels of French society after 1650 or 1660 declined. Constant's penetrating studies of the nobility of the Beauce leave no dubiety. Whereas in 1500 the families with a noble pedigree of less than 100 years had accounted for over a half of the total, by 1600 they were down to just over a third and a century later to a mere 10 per cent. This was clearly linked to a marked decline in ennoblement through the acquisition of fiefs and military service.[45] In the *élection* of Bayeux in 1666 only twenty-eight of its noble families were recently ennobled compared with seventy-one in 1598.[46] A marked decline in the rate at which newcomers were able to penetrate the ranks of the nobility during the course of Louis XIV's reign has also been found in distant Provence.[47] Of those who did manage to acquire a major office a decreasing proportion were in any sense upstarts. By the end of Louis XIV's reign a half of the new magistrates of the *parlement* of Paris were considered to belong to the old nobility, that is, to have had a pedigree of three to five generations behind them.[48]

Despite its responsibility for the tide of venal offices the government itself contributed to the reduced opportunities for upward social mobility and to the renewed emphasis on rank. After 1634 assimilation into the nobility through the purchase of land or military office, which had accounted for perhaps three out of every ten *annoblissements,* was severely checked.[49] Lesser military personnel such as those in the royal bodyguards found their aspirations curtailed whilst the possession of middle-ranking posts, such as the presidency of a *bailliage,* was no longer axiomatic with noble status.[50] The government even vacillated over the status of the *parlementaires*. Having been accorded complete hereditary nobility in 1644, the Parisian judges were reduced to personal nobility in 1669 before the Crown accepted the reality of the situation in 1690.[51] These hesitations may have flowed from Louis XIV's conviction that 'distinctions of rank were the first motivation of all human action'. He was certainly more cautious than his father in the promotion of newcomers. One of the consequences was that the *ducs et pairs* became a more exclusive body, carefully selected from families of ancient lineage and of proven military capacity.[52]

The government's ambivalent policies – on the one hand, fostering social mobility through the sale of office and on the other lending support to the aristocratic and noble reaction that this provoked – reflected the contradictory nature of the processes at work. This contradictoriness helps to explain why noble anxieties seem to be out of proportion to the threat that they faced. With the benefit of hindsight and a deeper understanding of the social and economic dynamics of the seventeenth century it is possible to see that, after 1650, the feared subversion of the noble Estate and its values was unlikely to materialise. However, if by the reign of Louis XIV the fears of subversion of the aristocratic order seem to be wildly exaggerated, this was the somewhat paradoxical result of the very success of the prolonged endeavour to reinforce distinctions of rank. The strident emphasis on status and order became an essential ingredient in the restoration of social stability so that it is now difficult to imagine the regime of Louis XIV without this ideological characteristic. In response to mounting pressures the upper classes did succeed in redefining the basis of noble pre-eminence and domination. Drawing on a highly idealised past, the apologists of noble supremacy breathed new life into the body of ideas which legitimised it. Even writers like Loyseau who despised the petty nobility of the countryside and sought to place the great magistrates of the robe on equal terms with those of the sword never questioned the need to define and refine the hierarchical disposition of the manifold ranks of the body politic. The growing attachment to rank and degree was thus the product of a complex dialectical dance. Beginning as a reaction against the fluid social currents of the sixteenth century and shaped by intense sectarian rivalries, it was subsequently sustained by the deepening stagnation of the seventeenth.

FROM NOBLE WARRIOR TO *HONNÊTE HOMME*

The restoration of order required more than a reassertion of the social pre-eminence of the nobility and of hierarchy in general. As has already been observed, the essential problem facing the privileged orders was not that of disciplining the populace but of disciplining themselves. Forced to face up to this issue by unavoidable social and political pressures, the nobility experienced a major crisis of identity.

The Fronde made it absolutely clear, if it was not clear before, that the day of the anarchic grandee was at end. The theatrical withdrawals from court ostentatiously employed during the wars of religion and the minority of Louis XIII became meaningless in the post-Fronde world.[53] Whilst some of the remoter parts of the realm remained notorious for noble lawlessness, resulting most famously in the holding of the *grands jours* in the Auvergne in 1665, the nobility as a whole was obliged to come to terms with the need for self-discipline. The heroic assertion of the will so vividly portrayed in the great tragedies of Corneille slowly gave way to a noble stoicism which could be portrayed as a form of virtue. Those, in Krailsheimer's perceptive words, 'who had tried to act like Corneillian heroes in real life, willing their way to glory, and others who had seen them fail, were no longer in the mood' for passions stronger than love.[54] Krailsheimer is here dealing with that arch-intriguer de Retz who in pursuit of *gloire* and his cardinal's hat acted out a typically Corneillian conflict between his ambitions and his passions.[55] Ironically enough Retz in his own limited contribution to France's dramatic tradition confirmed the point exactly. His play *The Conspiracy of the Fieschi,* based on the attempted Genoese *coup d'état* of 1547 but in reality a commentary on events much nearer home, offers a fascinating insight into the evolution of Retz's own attitudes. John Salmon has drawn particular attention to the changing descriptions of the hero in the successive versions of the play written between *c.* 1629 and 1682.[56] The original version concluded that: 'His high and elevated conduct was such that he would have regarded his actions in the same light whether they lifted him to the throne or bore him to the scaffold.' This then gave way in 1665 to:

> Posterity might have placed him amongst the great heroes of the century, inasmuch as it is true that success or failure are the usual criteria we adopt to apportion praise or blame to extraordinary actions . . . there was nothing lacking in count Jean Louis Fiesque for the achievement of glory save a long life and more lawful occasions.

Finally the audience of 1682 had to make do with the almost laconic attribution of 'a grandeur of soul which made nothing too difficult'.

The same tone of resignation and self-discipline is manifest in the celebrated self-portrait produced by another equally turbulent participant in the Frondes, the Duc de La Rochefoucauld. Steering carefully between an insistence that his passions were moderate and sufficiently under control and an assertion of his sense of honour, La Rochefoucauld claimed that:

> Hardly ever have I been seen in a temper and I have never entertained feelings of hatred for anybody. Yet I am not incapable of taking revenge if I am wronged and it is a matter of honour not to let an insult past unnoticed.

Feelings of pity, he continued, 'should have no place in a noble soul for it only makes one soft-hearted'; but one could admire those noble passions which 'denote greatness of soul, and although the emotional stress they involve us in is hardly compatible with wise moderation, yet they are so conducive to austere virtue that they cannot rightly be condemned'.[57]

With Racine the tone of resignation became overwhelming. Whereas Corneille's tragedies had come from a 'clash of wills', those of Racine flowed from the 'subjection of mankind to the will of the Gods'. Suffused with an Augustinian sense of human inadequacy, they are characterised by 'predestination and the pitiless nature of divine judgment'.[58] This is nowhere better expressed than by Œdipe's widow Jocasta as she cries:

> This is the justice of the mighty Gods
> They lead us to the edge of the abyss
> They make us sin but do not pardon us[59]

Upper-class anxieties can in part be traced back to the disgust with noble mores which flowed from their comportment during the long years of civil strife. Claude Haton in 1576 castigated those who were formerly those nobles of virtue for having degenerated into *'gens pille-et-tue hommes*, heretics, infidels, irreverent, idolatrous, crazy, cruel, proud, arrogant, violators of the property of others, sacrilegious, oppressors of the *peuple'*.[60] Loyseau, expressing the animus of many towards the *'menue noblesse des champs'*, described them as 'savage animals' and 'birds of prey'.[61] Some of the nobility themselves quickly recognised the need to move away from an insistence on courage in battle as the prime element in noble conceptions of honour. It was even suggested that, without a greater emphasis on virtue, the very survival of the nobility was at stake.[62] 'There is no true Nobility but that which derives from virtue and morality,' declaimed Pierre de la Primaudaye in 1577.[63] The great warrior La Noue, recognising that exclusive emphasis on courage was harmful, suggested that in times of peace nobles should be the agents of 'piety, temperance and justice' and become 'professeurs de vertu'.[64] Reminding the nobility that they could maintain their position only through virtuous actions, La Noue went so far as to suggest that merit should govern the choice of officers.[65] Concepts of honour thus began to lose some of their belligerent overtones. According to Nicolas Pasquier in 1611, honour 'consisted in serving and honouring one's God, king and country, and in not allowing others to gain an advantage over one in such matters'.[66] For those seeking to flee the unpleasantness of public life and behaviour, honour became no more than 'the personal satisfaction of a duty accomplished in all probity'.[67] By mid-century it was possible to suggest that true honour consisted in remaining an *'homme de bien'*. Some defined virtue in almost the same way.[68]

Had honour or virtue been reduced to this sort of universal morality it would, as Devyver has observed, have been impossible to discern what distinguished the nobility from other *hommes de bien*.[69] What in fact happened was that virtue became more dependent on birth.[70] But it was also increasingly acknowledged that, by comparison with the upper ranks of the robe, the old nobility of the sword were an uncivilised and uneducated lot.[71] Innate qualities, it had to be accepted, required good breeding and education to bring them to perfection.[72] This, however, was not an insuperable problem, if one shared the conviction of the noble poets of the Pleiad that literary capacities arose from the same generosity of spirit as military prowess.[73] In similar vein, fighting with courage and dispensing justice were presented as two effects of the same generosity of soul.[74] Ronsard felt that 'it was honourable to bring together arms and learning'.[75] 'Nobility is not complete in its vocation', it was suggested in 1584, 'if it does not employ good letters with arms: learning discretion, and knowledge of histories along with valour and dexterity.'[76]

Changing attitudes expressed themselves in demands for the establishment of noble academies. These, it was hoped, would rectify the perceived deficiencies in the education of the nobility but without replicating the sort of education offered in the universities and colleges. For the conventional emphasis on grammar, rhetoric, humanities and philosophy was deemed to be both pedantic and irrelevant.[77] Indeed, it was frequently urged that the academies should be financed by taking money from the universities and colleges which were accused of producing too many lawyers and officials. The first and most celebrated of the noble academies was that established by Antoine de Pluvinel, a nobleman who had studied under a famous Neapolitan riding master before beginning a career at the French court. It was followed in the course of the next century or so by the establishment of seven or eight at Paris and between eighteen and twenty in the provinces.[78] Licensed but not financed by the state, the academy, comments Motley, was a 'vector for the code of graceful behaviour derived from the Italian Renaissance'.[79] Concentrating on horsemanship, dancing, fencing and military mathematics, it cultivated grace, controlled movement and good posture. A small minority of noble sons of unquestionable noble pedigree could aspire to receive a similar education at court through service as pages in the royal stables.[80] Richelieu, who strongly believed that a humanist education would contribute to political and social stability, made a determined effort to encourage the nobility of the sword to extend their education to embrace philosophy, geography and history. He founded an academy for this purpose but it collapsed on his death. For the rest of the century the sword nobles who did not attend the academies were left with the choice of an exacting but unsuitable classical education or the employment of a private tutor.[81]

Apparently, only a fifth of the nobles educated in the largely Catholic provincial colleges completed the secondary curriculum. Their essential objective was to acquire Latin grammar and an introduction to history or maths. With the partial exception of younger sons who were considering a career in the church, noble students displayed little interest in pursuing the courses offered in the humanities, rhetoric and philosophy.[82] Some colleges, however, adapted their offerings to include supplementary subjects such as history, geography and chronology. Private masters were often brought in to provide the necessary instruction in writing, dancing, music, fencing and drawing.[83] For the many young nobles educated entirely at home the emphasis was placed on an early acquisition of Latin grammar followed by the development of reading and writing skills in French with a focus on history, geography, mathematics and modern languages.[84] Despite the short-lived nature of Richelieu's grander plans for the education of the nobility, the intention of harnessing an education in the liberal arts to a concern with social comportment was not lost. The advantage of a home education was that the family could ensure the desired balance between the two.[85]

Ideally a noble education should steer between the extremes of ignorance and pedantry, providing for a formation in virtue on which honour depended. 'The main goal', some thought, 'in the education of a young noble should be teaching him how to converse well in society.'[86] Antoine Malet, one-time chaplain of the Duc de Lorraine, felt it was from both natural advantage and education that nobles acquired the 'gestures, vocabulary and manner of speaking of the court'.[87] The heavy stress on discourse and oral communication was further reinforced, notes Motley, by the way in which letter writing was almost seen as a form of conversation.[88] Translation work was also designed to perfect skills in reading and writing Latin and 'in speaking elegant French suitable for courtly society'.[89]

The retreat from an unqualified emphasis on courage and military reputation towards an emphasis on virtue, modesty and a generally civilised mode of behaviour had a feminist dimension. Women played a central role both as role models and as agents for the transmission of the new culture through the salons. It was here that the aspiring courtier could acquire the final touch of urbanity and polish for success. Poulain de la Barre said:

> If they wish to enter the *monde* and play well their role in it, they are obliged to go to the school of ladies in order to learn there the politeness, affability and all the exterior which today makes up the essence of *honnêtes gens*.[90]

The ideal which emerged from these processes was that of *honnêteté*, a concept rendered immortal by Nicolas Faret in his *L'Honneste homme ou l'art de plaire à la cour* which appeared in 1630 and went through seven editions by 1660.[91] Endowed by background with certain natural advantages, shaped by military experience through which nobility was achieved, but capable of conversing with women, educated in the ways of the world, the courtier soldier brought both good taste and knowledge to the leadership of French society.[92] 'Grace, ability and self-control' were, suggests Dewald, his main attributes, combined with 'a respected position in the wider world'. For Magendie the key words were 'sobriety, modesty, fidelity to one's word, self-control, justice, and generosity'.[93] Above all the *honnête homme* had a sense of that most slippery of French abstract nouns – *bienséance* – a feeling for the appropriate comportment for all times and occasions.[94]

It has been suggested that a strict insistence on noble birth tends to disappear from the conception of *honnêteté* revealed in post-Fronde writings.[95] None the less its predominantly aristocratic character remains unmistakable. Both the Chevalier de Méré and Charles de Saint Evremond, whose writings made a significant contribution to its elaboration in the 1660s, had a military formation and their views are replete with aristocratic assumptions. Acknowledging the competence of the robe in the specialised sphere of politics and administration, Saint Evremond showed explicit disdain for their ability to comprehend the wider roots of the human condition. The *gens de robe* were, he thought, frankly laughable 'as soon as they wish to move outside their profession'.[96] The inability of scholars to fully understand the nature of past civilisations resulted from the fact that they were unused to the company of *gens de qualité*.[97] Only the latter possessed true insight into nature of human society and civilisation. In similar vein the dramatic theorist La Mesnardière argued that tragedy was not likely to be appreciated or understood by the common herd for it had a moral purpose, dealing with 'state revolutions, the rewarding of good princes and the punishing of the bad'.[98] In theory, if not always in practice, tragedy was designed to deal with noble themes and characters whilst comedy was thought more suitable for representations of 'people of humble condition'.[99] Such observations, although not novel, served to rationalise the widespread view that *bienséance* and *connaissance* were the preserve of the upper classes whose education was precisely intended to minimise the possibility of corruption by contact with the gross habits of the lower orders.[100] In Furetière's *Roman bourgeois* the nobleman, polished and refined by the salons through contact with the fair sex, is contrasted with the clumsy and dull bourgeois.[101]

In developing the concept of *honnêteté* the nobility found a means both of reconciling themselves to the need for self-discipline and of subsuming what might be thought of as incipient bourgeois values, particularly about education, in a recast but distinctly aristocratic ethos. Taking the idea of virtue out of the hands of their critics they succeeded in anchoring it to the concept of honour. Both were underpinned by the belief that a combination of birth and good breeding was the essential ingredient in the formation of those who were destined to lead. In Gramscian terms the French nobility had accomplished a hegemonic *tour de force*.

INDIVIDUALISM AND THE LIMITS OF BOURGEOIS IDEOLOGY

The insistence on rank and hierarchy which was central to all these developments may be placed in an ideological context as well as a social one. For it met up with and helped to sustain the religious and neoplatonic cosmology of which the earthly hierarchy was still held to be part. It was not, however, surprising that the traumas suffered by the body politic were reflected in potentially subversive currents of thought. For some, the conventional imagery no longer adequately conveyed their perceptions of the workings of the social order. In the 1670s the Jansenist Nicole was able to represent society as made up of little bodies which as they

> unite their forces and movements . . . form great masses of matter . . . called whirlpools, which are like estates and kingdoms. Since these whirlpools are themselves crowded and confined by other whirlpools, as by neighbouring kingdoms, little whirlpools form in each larger one, which while following the general movement of the larger bodies propelling them, do not cease, however, to have a movement of their own, which in turn forces smaller bodies to revolve around them. Similarly great personages of state, while following the general movement, have their own interests providing centres for quantities of people attached to them. Finally, as all little bodies propelled by whirlpools also turn around their own centres, so little people, who follow the fortunes of the great and those of the state, do not cease in all other duties and services they perform for others to think of themselves and to have their own interests continually in view.[102]

Such a view of social dynamics clearly had a much greater affinity to Descartes' mechanistic universe than to the cosmic harmony depicted by Bodin or Loyseau. As a piece of social analysis it offers a telling picture of the social tensions which afflicted the body politic. Moreover, it moves beyond a representation of corporate and factional rivalry to assert the powerful presence of self-interest. Fascination with self and human motivations penetrated every aspect of French culture from the frivolous conversations of the salons to the high tragedies of Racine. It has recently been suggested that one of the manifestations of this preoccupation was the driving ambition of great nobles which, reinforced by a growing attachment to material and sensuous pleasures, directly threatened the values of a patriarchal society. Money and a capacity for political manoeuvring became the requisites for worldly success. A modern culture was in the making. The resulting antagonism between the interests of the individual and those of family or community provided the inspiration for many of the tragedies of Corneille and Racine.[103]

These, of course, were still noble dramas expressing noble sentiments, fascinating to audiences who found in them heightened representations of themselves and their own dilemmas. If there was a modern culture in the making here, the vehicle for its transmission remained profoundly aristocratic. This was perhaps less true of the precursors of the eighteenth-century novel which, according to Erica Harth, heralded a significant move away from the traditional *roman à clef* epitomised by d'Urfé's *L'Astrée*.[104] The turning point, she says, was Furetière's *Roman bourgeois* of 1666. Despite its form as a *roman à clef*, in its treatment of people of all conditions and its subordination of marriage and sex to money this work heralded a new realism.[105] It prefigured the classical and moralising portraiture of La Bruyère whose *Caractères* of 1688 'mark the final modification of the seventeenth-century portrait before its incorporation in the realistic novel'.[106] Harth also sees a process of cultural bourgeoisification in the emergence of fictional narrative in the *nouvelles* or *petits romans* of the 1660s and in the development of engraving techniques for the depiction of architecture, sculptures, plants and animals. Whilst *nouvelles* were essentially the work of outsiders – disaffected nobles, bourgeois and adventurers – it was the Academy of Sciences itself which promoted a much more accessible and scientific representation of the physical and natural world.[107] These lines of thought meet up with Apostolidès' suggestion that the eruption of the quarrel between the ancients and the moderns created a fissure in the general attachment to 'mythhistory'. By doing so it opened up the possibility of liberating the writing of history from ancient mythology.[108]

It is not surprising that the stresses to which the social fabric was subject stimulated new ways of looking at the world. Cultural developments which were subsequently incorporated within a dominant bourgeois ideology were apparent. But that moment had not yet come and it is all too easy, with the benefit of hindsight, to overestimate their progress. The appointment of Racine as a royal historiographer is a sharp reminder of the distance to be travelled before history writing was liberated from the obligation to provide an elegant literary vehicle for the representation of worthy royal actions. Racine, who learnt to write history on the job, took his inspiration from classical authors rather than the not insignificant achievements of earlier French history writers. Whilst his reverence for the accomplishments of antiquity restrained the tendency to heap excessive praise on those of Louis XIV, the net result was none the less a classical form of prose writing intended to be 'read as far into the future as the works of those ancient historians whom he [Racine] so admired'.[109] The esteemed Bossuet produced history of the most providential kind which often amounted to little more than a literal reading of the Bible in search of justifications for monarchical rule.[110] His view of monarchy was also profoundly patriarchal. As Dewald acknowledges, if alternatives to patriarchal ideology were explored it was not because its hold was weakening but because it was so strong.[111]

Even the power of money was insufficient to transform either social relationships or cultural values. Its intrusion, although disturbing, did not mark, as Harth asserts, the replacement of an old elite based on privilege by one based on wealth. This misconception leads her to identify in changing cultural forms a 'bourgeois challenge to authority and tradition'.[112] Yet their progress, as she herself points out in the context of her appraisal of Sorel's *Le berger extravagant*, was hesitant, contradictory and hardly challenging. Published in 1627–8 and revised a few years later, Sorel's pastoral tale was both a satire on *L'Astrée* and a rehabilitation of the nobles. The comic hero, albeit 'ridiculous in his noble disguise as a shepherd . . . finds sanity in living nobly in the end'.[113] Interestingly enough, Sorel was himself a member of an upwardly mobile judicial family who attached himself to aristocratic patrons. Corneille (1625–84), also of legal stock, found this no impediment to his unrivalled depictions of the heroic ideal which wayward nobles seemed to emulate during the turbulent years of mid-century. Faret (1596–1646), who taught them how to behave at Court, was the son of a shoemaker; he progressed through administrative and military service to the Bishop of Bordeaux and Duc de Lorraine before acquiring the office of *conseiller secrétaire du Roi*.[114] Even La Bruyère (1645–1696) was profoundly ambivalent towards an order which he vehemently criticised but still aspired to join. He became secretary to the grandson of the great Condé and bought an ennobling office.[115] Harth's ultimate explanation for the ambivalence of contemporary attitudes is 'the hiatus in the development of the bourgeoisie as a class and of capitalism' which 'was filled by a period of enchantment with nobility'.[116] If such it was, the hiatus was a rather long one.

What is certainly true is that, even in the hands of the most disenchanted thinkers, the widespread fascination with self and *amour-propre* did not overflow into a systematic critique of the existing social and political order. At first sight this seems surprising because some came close to envisaging a society founded on the free play of individual interest. Dewald observes that Nicole's view of the social benefits of greed resembled that of Adam Smith. Nicole also thought that the market network offered a more efficient way of meeting material needs and comforts than the noble household.[117] Amongst merchants there were to be found a few whose opposition to mercantilist regulation led them into quite large statements about the desirability and necessity of liberty of trade.[118] Towards the end of the century the noble economist Pierre Boisguilbert produced a picture of the natural order which clearly prefigured the ideas of the Enlightenment. Nature herself – with which men and their governments should not interfere – would serve to combine the competitive instincts of individuals into a harmonious whole.[119]

There was, however, no question of Boisguilbert winning the government over to his view. On the contrary, he was briefly exiled and obliged to promise to hold his tongue. More significantly, such views were clearly far from understood in the commercial world. Sectarian opposition to regulation, monopolies and privileges did not lead to a clearly founded defence of individual freedom. Nothing illustrates this better than the attitudes of those who came together in the resuscitated Council of Commerce at the end of the century. Whilst it occasionally turned down requests for exclusive manufacturing rights there is nothing to suggest that this was a matter of principle. Some new privileged enterprises were created and virtually all the existing ones had their privileges renewed.[120] The Council also stuck firmly to bullionist principles.[121] A deep conservatism was further apparent in the way in which the deputies combined opposition to proposals permitting noble participation in trade with a demand for titles of nobility for those whose families engaged in overseas trade for three or four generations. What is more, they thought that those engaged in wholesale trading should be forbidden from retailing.[122] Sectarian rivalry, rooted in an attachment to corporate privilege and distinctions of social rank, meant that the representatives of France's merchant communities were a long way from providing an alternative vision of the social order. The French bourgeoisie had acquired neither a sense of its own identity nor the desire to create a world of competing and equal individuals.

That might have occurred more readily had the attachment to patrimonial forms of property spawned a sense of absolute property rights. Theoretically such a development was entirely possible; but it did not happen. The principle of no land without seigneur, carrying with it an assumption about the conditional nature of property rights, was the norm outside the romanised south. Even here where land was deemed to have once been freely held, the seigneurial regime had made deep inroads. Although there was much dispute about whether or not fiefs were compatible with the principles of Roman law, few denied their legitimacy as a form of property. However, in 1629 when Louis XIII sought to extend the principle of no land without seigneur to all parts of the realm as a means of asserting his own title to all land without one, this spurred the *parlementaires* of Toulouse to a defence of the allodial traditions of Languedoc.[123] Four years later their chief propagandist, Caseneuve, published his *Le franc-aleu de Languedoc* which charged that fiefs, introduced to remedy the disorders attributable to the fall of man, had 'reduced our properties to a formerly unknown servitude'.[124] Yet he made no attempt to assert the universality of absolute property rights, merely insisting that in the regions of the *droit écrit* seigneurs must be able to show written title; otherwise, the presumption was that property was freely held. Whilst Caseneuve did suggest that the feudal hierarchy added nothing to the king's authority which was complete without it, the *parlementaires* of Toulouse, so many of whom were seigneurs, were hardly likely to abandon their own prerogatives over lands dependent on them by attacking the feudal hierarchy as such.[125] The Berrichon legist Thaumas de la Thaumassière went so far as to declare that seigneurial rights were contrary to 'natural liberty and the *droit des gens*'. However, he also made a sharp distinction between noble and commoner allods which meant they were treated very differently when subject to succession. What is more, said Thaumas, citing several other authorities, although the *franc-alleu noble* possessed rights of justice, it should not be imagined that justice was allodial. It could only be held in fief.[126] Jurists were seemingly unable to envisage property rights independent of a system in which nobility, rights of justice and property were interwoven in a hierarchy of domination and dependence. The *parlementaires* of Languedoc got little further than a defence of customary exemptions from feudal obligations.

These observations may help to explain why, as Keohane remarks, French individualism was much more an attitude of mind than a theory.[127] Given the absence of a responsive social and political environment, its capacity to reshape conventional assumptions about the relationship between the public and private *domaine*s was limited. In the context of the seigneurial system in which the two were fused together in a hierarchy of dependence, individualism had little meaning. Despite the theoretical distinction commonly made between fief and jurisdiction, there existed no conception of a class of formally equal landed proprietors sharing a common relationship to the state. Even in the commercial sector *laissez-faire* tendencies were offset by the belief that the necessary but selfish activity of merchants required their close regulation and social subordination. In parallel fashion the preoccupation with *amour-propre* as a rationale for individual actions was blunted by the enduring conviction that, without love of God and genuine charity towards others, self-interest also remained deficient as a rationale for social behaviour.[128] Fénélon's view of *amour-propre* led, as did those of Domat, not to a recognition of individual interest but to the need for 'self-denial and immersion in the love of God'.[129]

The internalisation of French individualism was most apparent in the writings of the *libertins* whose disquiet about the state of the world led them to make a sharp demarcation between the private and public domains. Even Jean de Silhon, who perhaps came nearest to Hobbes in his deduction of the need for a powerful state from the nature of individual human beings, left this dichotomy intact. For him honour and virtue – the ultimate aims of human activity – were an attribute of the former whereas the objectives of public authority were essentially utilitarian.[130] Pierre Charron, from whom the *libertins* took much of their inspiration, was assiduous not only in promoting the separation of public and private life but also in accepting the need for outward conformity and the desirability of an overriding authority to maintain order. Explicit in his contempt for the common man 'who had no better pastime than to speak ill of the great and rich', he held that the pursuit of wisdom was reserved for the great and good.[131] Were his study 'to be popularly received and accepted it would have completely failed in its intentions'. The most appropriate means for instilling both admiration and fear in the people was 'a great authority, a brilliant and striking power which blinds them with its splendour and gravity. . . . There is nothing grander in this world than authority, which is an image of God . . .'.[132] Preoccupation with self thus ended up in a conservative, introspective and elitist cul de sac. Dewald suggests that the 'most vigorous cultural contribution of the nobility lay . . . in an autobiographical literature that sought to display the continuity of self'.[133] This is a much more tenable proposition than his suggestion that French nobles in general 'viewed society as a society of competing individuals rather than an organic whole'.[134] Had this been truly the case, the way would have been open for a recasting of the entire social order. As far as it is possible to pinpoint the concept of 'the individual' as distinct from a concern with *amour-propre,* it appears to be still rooted in an Aristotelian cosmology. It is not surprising that Charron, writing at the beginning of the century, employed a conventional microcosm of the macrocosm approach in which the individual was composed of contrary elemental forces; his social location was also determined by quite conventional criteria relating to rank and degree.[135] But the last edition of Silhon's *Le ministre d'état,* published two years before his death in 1667, continued to depict the relationship between rulers and ruled by means of conventional body politic imagery.[136]

With Domat, in the 1690s, virtually all the strands of thought to which allusion has been made were brought together in a remarkable synthesis. It was imbued with a Thomist view of the higher purposes of government, the organisation and operation of which should be based on the principles of natural and divine law.[137] Within this framework Domat strove – not entirely successfully perhaps – to reconcile a functional division of labour, and a recognition of its role in determining status, with a depiction of the state as composed of families united by religion, humanity and the social Order.[138] All the Orders ought to contribute to the public good and to the order and providence of God.[139] *Amour-propre* was to be tempered by the injunction to place love of God and therefore the love of others above all else. The 'individual' was thus subsumed within a divinely ordained Order, each being assigned a rank and put under a moral obligation to do nothing which would disturb the dispositions of God.[140]

It is significant that, although Thomas Hobbes spent eleven years in France during which he wrote *Leviathan,* this work aroused little interest.

Whilst his 'geometric' science of politics held a certain appeal for the scientific circle associated with Mersenne with which he was in close contact, it is not surprising that his political philosophy achieved little resonance.[141] For his world of 'appetitive' individuals contained no vestiges of the traditional social hierarchy. His materialist treatment of human nature and the purposes of government would have made him very uncomfortable reading for most French intellectuals. The same was even truer of Locke whose assertion of natural equality and rights presupposed an entirely different world view from their own. Domat had actually emphasised the natural and personal equality of human beings as early as 1669; but he had immediately made clear that, because 'the multitude' could not exist in conditions of equality, God had established the superiority of fathers over their children and princes and judges over the people.[142] Some passages of his later work suggest that he may have become aware of Locke's views on natural equality but, if so, it was insufficient to impinge in any significant way on his belief in a hierarchical disposition of power and privilege.[143] Assumptions about natural inequality, associated with a belief in the divine source of all authority, precluded the elaboration of an alternative construction of the social order.

In the absence of such an alternative it was the traditional and backward-looking constitutionalism of the aristocratic reformers associated with Fénélon which offered, at the turn of the century, the most clear-cut challenge to the existing regime. Reiterating demands that had surfaced in noble protests for many decades they sought the abolition of venality, the suppression of the intendants, the restoration of conciliar government together with traditional governorships, the Estates-General and provincial Estates.[144] The fact that a revival of representative institutions was central to such a programme should not deceive. There was no suggestion here of following the English road. Nor was there any echo of Turquet de Mayerne's proposed bourgeoisification of the nobility.[145] This was a project for a monarchical regime tempered by the power of a traditional nobility. As such, it shared with the proponents of absolute monarchy a common ideological framework. If some Frenchmen came close at times to the idea of a king in parliament, dependent on the common consent of all three Estates, the latter did not represent, in Jouanna's words, the 'sum of individuals' who had elected them.[146]

In retrospect it can be seen that French thought and culture were full of half-way houses. Disquiet, dissatisfaction and even disaffection with the regime can be found. The social and political tensions which gnawed at the social fabric were mirrored in the behaviour and attitudes of French intellectuals. For some the traditional chain-of-being imagery no longer made sense of the fractured society they saw about them. But they were unable to refashion the ideas that lay to hand into a new world view, and the result was frequently a retreat into self. Not until *amour-propre* was transformed by ideas of natural equality and *laissez-faire* into a thorough-going individualism would the ideological underpinnings of the monarchical regime be in real jeopardy. The limitations of French individualism, however, cannot be attributed solely to its own internal logic. It was dominated, deflected and absorbed by the cultural adaptability of the upper classes. Fashioning a renewed sense of hierarchy, order and self-discipline out of the disarray into which they had fallen, they reshaped their own aristocratic identity. In the process they also gave shape to the absolutist regime.

6

POWER, IDEOLOGY AND THE FRENCH STATE

ABSOLUTISM

It is more than odd that Perry Anderson, who made the impact of large-scale warfare the primary cause of the rise of absolutism in Eastern Europe, did not extend this argument to the western variants. For it is extremely difficult to deny the claim of Roland Mousnier and others that war was probably the major factor in promoting the development of the French state. Even a cursory appraisal of the institutions through which the absolutist regime governed makes this clear. The first embryonic ministries to slowly acquire a degree of coherence under the direction of specific secretaries of state were not surprisingly those of finance, war and foreign affairs. Equally obvious is the direct correlation between the number of offices sold and the intensification of large-scale warfare. It was precisely in 1635, the year of France's entry into the war against Spain, that the sale of offices reached its highest point with a massive flooding of the market with every sort of financial and judicial office from presidents of *parlements* to sergeants and clerks in the lesser jurisdictions. Two entirely new *bureaux des finances* were created. By mid-century there were about 500 principal officers attached to the *bureaux des finances*, around 5,000 in the *élections*, sustained by perhaps 4,000 receivers, payers and controllers and an estimated 20,000 within the tax farms.[1]

The same period also saw the full institutionalisation of the intendants, partly, indeed, so that they could keep an eye on the proliferating and frequently unreliable venal *officiers*. The *prima facie* case for assuming a causal link between this development and escalating military need is further borne out by the easy and continuous manner in which the intendants moved between civilian and military duties. From 1643 to 1648 no commissions were issued to intendants which did not confer some military responsibilities.[2] In 1638 they became responsible for raising the subsistence – a tax imposed in cash or kind for maintenance of the troops – and eventually acquired complete administrative control over any armies billeted in their jurisdiction during the winter season.[3] Although the intendants were given an impossibly comprehensive brief, their prime function was to find the resources with which to sustain the royal armies. In 1642, as a result of the government's dissatisfaction with the performance of its *trésoriers* and *élus,* the intendants were given overall responsibility for the raising of the *taille*.[4] During the reign of Louis XIV they were also increasingly preoccupied with bringing the debts of the municipalities under control. In the 1680s their correspondence with the *contrôleur-général* suggests that this concern was matched only by the need to ensure a proper supply of wheat to the royal armies and, in time of military activity, to find lodgings and pay the suppliers.[5] Thus, in its broadest outlines, the shape of the French state with its unique combination of centralised ministries, commissioned royal agents, venal officeholders and private financiers was overwhelmingly determined by the exigencies of warfare. The most significant exception to this observation is provided by the development of the guild regime and the elaborate system of inspection put in place by Colbert in order to enhance the quality of French manufactures; but in terms of the overall deployment of the state's energies and personnel, regulation of the economy was a secondary preoccupation.

There is no reason to doubt that these developments involved a concentration of power at the centre and apex of the regime. This point is worth emphasising given the tendency in some quarters to carry the revisionist critique of the concept of monarchical absolutism to the point at which it is simply seen as a particular type of 'limited' monarchy. Of course, the idea of a single person wielding complete and effective power is absurd in any context and certainly in *ancien régime* France. None the less, there did occur, over the course of the seventeenth century, a visible diminution of the institutional restraints on the exercise of royal authority; it stands in sharp contrast to the limits imposed on royal power not only in England but also in the Spanish peninsula or, even more clearly, in Poland. The Estates-General, which had long lost any capacity to limit royal powers of taxation and had never acquired a law-making role at all, was insufficiently powerful to constitute either a threat or a help to the Crown. At the last session in 1615 the delegates, many of whom owed their presence to royal influence, had not even secured a response to their *cahiers* before the government locked them out of their meeting place.[6] A number of provincial Estates, notably those of Guyenne and Normandy, also disappeared in the half-century that followed. In Provence they were effectively replaced by a truncated commission; in vain did the *assemblée des communautés* request its recall. Although Louis XIV kept some representative assemblies alive, particularly in the frontier regions, 1672 saw the last meeting of those of Basse-Auvergne, 1675 those of Quercy and Rouergue, 1683 those of Alsace, and 1704 those of Franche-Comté.[7] Major Estates survived in Brittany, Languedoc, Burgundy and Dauphiné but perhaps only the first two retained a significant degree of political clout. Urban autonomy, as we have seen, was also eroded, sometimes by direct government intervention, sometimes by fiscal depredation, or simply by taking advantage of the tendency for local government to fall into the hands of royal officeholders.

The *parlement* of Paris made a strong effort to fill the institutional vacuum by claiming the mantle of the dormant Estates. But despite the right to register fiscal edicts, it was unable to stem the flow of new taxes, devices and loans. Under Richelieu these were implemented more at less at will and with frequent recourse to *lits de justice*. Firmly told by Louis XIII to keep out of politics, the *parlementaires* were none the less sufficiently powerful to achieve the withdrawal of the intendants in the Fronde. However, these soon reappeared in another guise and, with the assumption of power by Louis XIV, it was impossible to turn the clock back. From the outset of his reign Louis XIV made it plain that the *parlement* must defer to decrees of the royal council and limited its capacity for judicial review. In 1667 and 1673 measures were taken to reduce the power of remonstrance to a formal procedure, only undertaken after contentious edicts had been registered.[8] The political superiority of the royal council was thus asserted and recognised.

The *parlement* also struggled to preserve its judicial autonomy. It certainly failed to block the use of commissioned and arbitrary forms of justice. The 1640s and 1650s witnessed incessant parlementary complaints about the *évocation* of cases to the *conseil privé* and the annulment of parlementary decrees. These 'were sought', claimed the *avocat général*, Omer Talon, in 1645, 'with the same abandon as appeals from a village court'. He also attacked the practice of diverting cases to the *requêtes de l'hôtel* with powers of sovereign decision which served only to encourage the *maîtres des requêtes* to abuse their authority in the provinces.[9] Even more galling was the way in which the *conseil privé* used its power to actually annul decisions of the sovereign courts in instances which were normally without appeal.[10] Although, as will be seen, Louis XIV compromised on some of these issues there was no sense in which the *parlement* possessed legislative or fiscal powers comparable to those of the English Parliament.

These developments must further be placed in the context of the concentration of authority which occurred at the highest levels. The process of reducing the influence of the great nobility of the sword inside the royal councils began with Henri IV. This was carried on in the 1620s and 1630s with attempts to limit membership and systematise procedures particularly by giving precedence to ordinary members of the council as opposed to those whose presence was a consequence of their rank. Although much of the work appeared to be undone during the turbulent days of the Fronde when the numbers of *conseillers d'état* rose to 120, under Louis XIV they were rapidly reduced to about thirty. Precedence inside the council was determined by date of appointment. The inner council was never larger than five; over the entirety of the reign only seventeen ministers were ever admitted to it.[11]

Underpinning all these changes was the irreversible decline in the independent military capacity of the great nobles. With the destruction of Protestant military and political strength in the 1620s the nobility lost their potential for organised resistance. Factions, which for fifty years or more had torn France apart, disintegrated. The Duc de Guise fled ignominiously from Provence whilst Montmorency's ill-judged attempt to raise Languedoc against the king in 1632 led to his execution in front of the town hall at Toulouse. Even when the minority of Louis XIV gave the dissident princes an opportunity to exploit the intense passions aroused by the ministerial 'tyranny' of Richelieu and Mazarin, they were unable to create a durable movement of opposition.

The undoubted growth of royal power was also sustained by a body of ideas which may legitimately be described as absolutist. The argument that such a description of monarchical ideology is only comprehensible in the context of the contrast drawn in the nineteenth century between 'absolutist' and 'constitutional' forms of government fails to recognise the extent to which these choices had already opened up and were, indeed, passionately debated.[12] During the wars of religion the idea that kings were made for the people and not vice versa secured a significant presence in French thought. Moreover, although contract theories tended to be associated with Protestant movements of resistance and in France are particularly associated with the *Vindiciae Contra Tyrannos* of 1579, there was nothing exclusively Protestant about them. On the contrary, by the turn of the sixteenth century anti-absolutist views had largely become the property of pro-papal factions. It was to the Jesuit, Suarez, that the English lawyer Robert Mason appealed for his conclusion that 'the extent and limits of the king's power . . . depend on human will and on the ancient agreement or contract between the kings and the kingdom'.[13] During the Fronde strong Catholic convictions came once again to the fore. Listen, for instance, to the author of the deeply Catholic *Maximes morales* of 1649 who asserted that as 'the soul is more precious than the body, and Salvation of greater moment than fortune, our religious maxims should govern the rules of government'. It followed that, if kings command things which are contrary to the achievement of salvation, 'it is simply not possible to render obedience to men to the prejudice of that which we owe to God'.[14] Claude Joly, the most celebrated theorist of the time, was quite unambiguous in his view that kings received their power from the people by means of a contract imposing on them an obligation to rule justly and provide protection. This was then ratified and approved by God who bestowed on it 'all the power required for its execution'.[15]

Religiously based contract theories were buttressed by historical/constitutional arguments which, if different in detail, were similar in nature. The idea of an ancient constitution which had subsequently been corrupted, although perhaps most effectively elaborated by the English common lawyers, was also a significant component in French political thought; and if the most famous and systematic treatise – Hotman's *Franco-Gallia* – had a Huguenot parentage, his historical views were readily taken up by his religious opponents. The Catholic League of 1576 declared its intention of restoring the 'rights, preeminences, franchises and ancient privileges as they were in the time of Clovis'.[16] Moreover, there were dozens of French legists who assumed along with Guy Coquille that 'our customs are our true civil law'.[17] Claude de Bauffremont, addressing the king on behalf of the nobility at Blois in January 1577, said: 'The French nobility only request of you what they asked of Charlemagne . . . that is that you let us live and grow old in the ancient laws, customs and ordonnances of France.'[18]

As Jouanna points out, this approach endowed the laws with an autonomous existence and was linked to the distinction which some writers made between the *état du Roi* and the *état du royaume*. The distinction between the person and the office of the king had of course been long expressed in the notion of the *corps naturel* and the *corps politique*.[19] Sometimes it was linked with the views which bestowed on bodies like the *parlements* or the Estates-General a restraining power or even attributes of sovereignty. In 1576 the Estates of Blois requested that where there was unanimity between the three orders this should be sufficient to make an inviolable law.[20] Coquille believed that laws made by the king in the Estates were irrevocable without their own consent, although he was obliged to acknowledge that, in practice, kings had dispensed with them.[21] Some ascribed similar characteristics to the *parlement* of Paris. Amongst the responses evoked by the government's annulation of *parlement*'s condemnation of Mazarin for *lèse-majesté* appeared the claim that it had its origins in the assemblies of the Franks.[22] At least one pamphleteer came very close to granting the *parlement* powers superior to those of the Crown, arguing that since it was 'the most important and considerable body in the state' it was only reasonable for it to take 'cognizance of the affairs of the realm which it governs . . . Senatus immortalis est, Princeps vero mortalis'.[23]

Such views were reflected in more specific constitutional ideas. The principle of consent to taxation, for instance, was very much alive whenever the Estates-General called. Bodin's attachment to this principle at the meeting of 1576 cost him his political influence. At the Leaguer

Estates of 1588 both clergy and nobility demanded the transformation of all provinces into *pays d'états* so that taxes could not be raised anywhere without consent.[24] Even the largely ineffectual Estates of Normandy continued to reiterate the principle right down to their last meeting in 1655.[25] The related notion that the king ought to live off his own was also to be heard in the middle years of the century.[26] Constitutional ideas survived into the rule of Louis XIV to surface at the end of the century in the entourage of the king's grandson.

Many of the ingredients required for a fully fledged justification of resistance to an abusive use of royal power thus seem to have been present in French thought. They were brought together at the time of the Fronde in the work of Claude Joly. His celebrated *Maximes* constituted the finest summation of all the strands of thought – religious, historical, contractual – which might be used to justify resistance. Kings derived their power from the people and were not above the laws of the state.[27] Misuse of the soldiery, the abuse of *chambres de justice*, arbitrary taxation and interference with the sovereign courts were illegitimate.[28] Justice was the essential foundation of states and the royal judges were 'no less officers of the people than of the Prince'.[29] As for the Estates themselves, to which he accorded an authority higher than any other body, these had their origin in the first assembly which put the crown on Pepin's head. They should be called with the aim of re-establishing with 'firmness and vigour our ancient customs, laws and ordonnances'.[30] Moreover, the king needed their consent not only to raise taxes outside his domain but also to wage war.[31]

In the event the French Crown was obliged to sacrifice none of its ministers and none of its prerogatives. It retained the *de facto* power to tax without consent and successfully asserted the supremacy of the royal council over the *parlements*. These never acquired the legislative powers of the English Parliament or, indeed, the *cortes* of Catalonia. Royal ordinances were considered to be superior to customary law and the king had the power to override custom if he wished. It was generally accepted that the king was accountable for any misdeeds to God and to God alone. Some writers thought it was inconceivable that the king could do wrong; things were not just or unjust in themselves but rendered just by the mere fact of royal command.[32]

In the conflicts of the 1620s those who sought to justify their right to defend long-cherished liberties were roundly informed by government propagandists that the king was not bound to the ordinances of his predecessors, nor even his own, but must have the power to change them according to the necessities of the moment. As the king could not be subject to himself he was clearly above the law.[33] Replying to the manifesto of the rebellious Huguenot leader, the Duc de Soubise, in 1625 the government bulletin, the *Mercure français*, declared that:

> One cannot say that it is unjust for him [the king] to extend the limits of his authority. . . . He is obliged to do so by *raison d'état*, by the laws of Majesty. Subjects should regard such changes as originating in heaven.[34]

The Huguenots once defeated, these precepts were then deployed in defence of the government's aggressive anti-Spanish foreign policy which caused such disquiet amongst significant and influential sections of the political classes. Only those on whom God had bestowed the responsibility for affairs of state were blessed with the necessary insight into their mysteries, which were beyond the grasp of mere subjects. It was therefore impossible to subject the actions of rulers to the same criteria as those that governed the behaviour of subjects.

Such arguments were reinforced by an increasingly strident insistence on the personal qualities of the king which began to obscure the distinction between him and his office. As Louis XIII set about the destruction of the Huguenot 'state within a state', innumerable careerists, royal propagandists and hack writers had every opportunity to extol his divinity, his invincibility and his clemency.[35] 'God had placed the king on his throne, having first put the Crown on his head, the sceptre in his hand and royal virtues in his heart . . .'.[36] Giesey thinks that such ideas may have their root in Bodin's notion of *majesté royale* which encapsulated a new symbiosis of ruler and office.[37] He has also pointed to the significance of the way in which the funeral and coronation ceremonies were displaced as the central rites of monarchy. By legitimising the transfer of power from one holder of office to the next they sustained the idea that although the king died the power of his office never faded.[38] Seventeenth-century theorists, however, offered a much simpler view of the process with the adage that 'the king never dies' which nicely confused the two bodies.[39] The transference of power became instantaneous.[40] In 1610 a *lit de justice* was used, despite Sully's objections, to transfer power within hours of the assassination of Henri IV. The declaration of a regency was made not only before his successor had been enthroned and anointed but before Henri IV had even been buried. The president of the Paris *parlement* defended the procedure with arguments which concentrated on blood, lineage and dynastic right; a genealogical tree was produced tracing the king's ancestry back to Louis IX.[41] When the coronation finally took place at Rheims five months later the idea that 'the king never dies' was built into the proceedings.[42]

Under Louis XIV the symbolic importance of state ceremonies declined even further. This was true not just of the coronation and funeral ceremony, the utility of which diminished simply because Louis lived so long, but also of the royal entries and the *lit de justice*.[43] The last time he sat on the throne of Parliament was in 1673, his legislation having made the *lit de justice* redundant. Versailles provided, for the first time, a permanent throne outside the *palais de justice*. From 1683 it was to be found in the salon d'Apollon. Apollo himself adorned the back of the throne with reclining representations of Justice and Force on either side.[44] For the last forty-two years of his life Louis undertook no state ceremonial occasions whatsoever. Whilst victory celebrations, processions and Te Deums, together with festivities hailing the arrival of a new royal infant, continued throughout his long reign, the fabulous royal entry into Paris on 26 August 1660 turned out to be the high point of that form of state ceremonial. Such events, which had legitimised royal authority by associating it with the formal representation of all the orders of the realm, faded away as the king travelled less and less and in face of a court etiquette designed to elevate him above everyone.[45] Whereas state ceremonies were designed to serve an anonymous king, court ritual served a particular person.[46] The medieval concept of the two bodies gave way, suggests Apostolidès, to the *corps symbolique* which in turn was confounded with the machinery of state.[47]

For a significant moment at least, monarchical absolutism triumphed in both practice and theory over more limited conceptions of the power of kings. As long as absolutism is conceived as a process or tendency and not as an immobile structure, it usefully conveys the success of the French monarchy in asserting the fullness of its power; it also distinguishes it from others where royal power was subject to formal restraints imposed by representative institutions with significant legislative and fiscal powers.[48] It must, however, be acknowledged once again that, up to a point, French absolutism was achieved by default. The Parisian *officiers* on whom so much depended in 1648 were not capable of sustaining their early display of unity, whilst the sectarian corporatism of the Parisian *parlementaires* diminished their support for the demand that the Estates-General should meet. For a while they achieved a modest degree of cooperation with their counterparts in Aix and Bordeaux but this also faded. Mazarin did not suffer the same fate as Archbishop Laud and his fears for the monarchical order proved unfounded.

What stymied all the movements of opposition to the Crown in France was their own acceptance of the royalist assumption that kings were divinely appointed and could be punished only by God. Resistance was resistance to the divinely ordained order and, indeed, to God himself. The impact of this belief was nowhere more clearly seen than in its demoralising and divisive effect on the Huguenot community.[49] With the return of a measure of peace and stability under Henri IV the Protestants hastened to disavow their past espousal of resistance theories; indeed, their political ideas increasingly resembled those of their most determined opponents. One of the most paradoxical but significant moments in religious history came in the aftermath of the Estates-General of 1614 when the Huguenots made a central issue of the government's failure to endorse the celebrated first article of the First Estate with its trenchant Gallican defence of the divinely bestowed and unlimited authority of the French monarchy. Badly repaid for their loyalty and pushed into rebellion in 1620, the Huguenots adopted a strikingly defensive posture. When the Protestant assembly of 1621 published its manifesto it proved to be little more than a list of specific grievances, accusing the Jesuits of plotting their destruction, complaining of events in Béarn, of troop movements in Poitou, about the removal of tax bureaus from Protestant strongholds and so on. Throughout the 1620s only one Protestant writer, de la Milletière, produced any rationale of a philosophical sort justifying resistance to the king. His bold defence of the Huguenots cost him some years in the Bastille. But even he did not challenge royal sovereignty. Moreover, he was eventually excommunicated for proposing the reunification of the two faiths.[50] Protestant attachment to hierarchy and order went so far that from the beginning of the seventeenth century there were pastors who began to suggest that, in principle, bishops were not a bad idea. This clearly distanced the Huguenots from the English Puritans whose anti-episcopal sentiments were a vital ingredient in the assault on the entire establishment. With alarm but considerable accuracy, the synod of Charenton in 1644 condemned the Independent movement in England as prejudicial not only to the word of God but also to the state.[51] During the Fronde the Protestants as a group remained aloof from rebellion. In 1652 this was recognised by the government which lifted all the restrictive applications of the Edict of Nantes as a sign of royal pleasure at the 'affection and loyalty' displayed by the king's Protestant subjects.[52] But the royal pleasure did not last long. Under Louis XIV, as persecution became ever more intense, the Huguenots responded by retreating into a stoical acceptance of their fate, frequently attributing their misery to a Godly retribution for their own shortcomings.[53] They certainly did not blame the king who, in the words of one pastor, was 'the true image of that great God who presides over the world. Like God, he has no superior nor equal. He alone is greater than all. He concentrates in his person all the majesty of the state'.[54]

Similar reverence for the person of the king also sapped the resistance of the *parlementaires*. Despite their constitutional pretensions they never went beyond a defence of their juridical role to claim legislative sovereignty and they never challenged the ultimate authority of the king. The lack of bite in the *parlement*'s claim to parity with the royal council was revealed in 1645 when it acknowledged the legitimacy of conciliar encroachments on parlementary functions which had been personally authorised by the king.[55] Attacking ministers during a Regency was one thing, attacking the king another. When, at the end of 1651, the *parlement* found itself directly confronting the now fully empowered Louis XIV over its condemnation of the Cardinal for treason, they had come to the end of the road. Without challenging the king himself there was no way forward, and the claim that all acts committed in the king's name were really tyrannous measures of his minister carried less and less force.[56] The magistrates undoubtedly agreed with Claude Joly who despite his own powerful elaboration of the limits of royal authority was insistent that only God can punish kings who transgress.[57]

The inconsistency in Joly's thought was more apparent than real. His views simply hinged on the conventional distinction between tyranny and lawful monarchy. The latter was an expression of both divine and natural law, implying an acceptance of God's universal Order and a proper distribution of authority, which itself is ordained of God. As St Paul had made clear in the much-quoted letter to the Romans, ' every soul must be subject to higher powers'. It was 'therefore indubitable that any man who resists' higher authority 'resists the order . . . and the will of God'.[58]

Given that magistrates were themselves a crucial element in this Order their ambivalence was hardly surprising. If they claimed a restraining role *vis-à-vis* the monarchy it was in order to preserve the integrity and justice of the monarchical order itself. Opposition could not, therefore, diminish the prestige of the Crown.[59] This position, together with the assumptions about the nature of authority which lay behind it, led logically not to the subversion of the monarchical regime but, on the contrary, to demands for its renewal and regeneration. The essential problem, as one pamphleteer explained, was that Richelieu and Mazarin were usurpers of royal authority who had undermined the *parlements*, subverted the 'ordinary course of justice' and stolen the wealth of France. The conclusion was self-evident. Mazarin should be exiled and replaced by a 'council of experienced, virtuous and generous people'. Then the 'title and function of First (or rather the only) Minister' should be abolished. 'For this is an office which leads to tyranny . . . and . . . dethrones the supreme lineage of our kings. . . .'[60]

These arguments place Louis XIV's decision to dispense with a First Minister in an interesting light. Viewed in one way it represented a further assertion of royal authority, flowing from the most obviously absolutist tendencies in French thought; from a different angle it was also a response to some of the most articulate critics of the regime. In one sense Louis' personal rule was a culmination of processes put in train by the two cardinals; in another, his assumption of personal responsibility was an acknowledgement of the widespread desire to bring the years of ministerial tyranny to an end with the restoration of a lawful and just monarchy. The result was a regime which may reasonably be described as absolutist but one which was still deeply rooted in traditional notions about the nature and purpose of monarchy.

ROYAL AUTHORITY LEGITIMISED

In considering the ideological underpinnings of French absolutism it is important not to be misled by the nastiness of Richelieu's regime into imagining that the moral traditions of the French monarchy had been swept aside. The brutal assertion of the interests of the state could certainly be seen in a range of practices – from censorship of the 'press' to the flagrant abuse of judicial procedure in order to deal with dissidents. Yet *raison d'état* was more of a mood than an ideology; it did not herald the elaboration of a modern or secular legitimation for monarchical rule. *Raison d'état* in its French form, although frequently disturbing to the Christian conscience, was invariably harnessed by the propagandists to more conventional assumptions about the public good. Just as conceptions of individual interest embodied in *amour-propre* were constrained in their development by powerful religious impulses, so too was the idea of reason of state. Although Richelieu's propagandists sometimes struggled to accommodate the moral purposes of government to the necessities of state, particularly in justifying the long war with catholic Spain, the bottom line remained the conviction that it was the divinely bestowed nature of royal authority which gave kings unquestionable insight into the mysteries of government.[61]

The increasingly strident emphasis on the personal attributes of the king, far from representing an attempt to subvert the traditional order of things, was intended to restore it. Those who sought, as Louis XIII set about the destruction of the Huguenots, to raise him to the level of an invincible demi-God did not imagine that this was in any way inimical to inherited views of the body politic. On the contrary, the 'elevation of the king was perhaps the most crucial aspect of the attempt to recover the integrity of the social order and the divinely ordained harmony of which it was part'.[62] Always implicit in the ideological onslaught on the Huguenots, this was sometimes explicit – nowhere more so than in one of the tracts written just after the fall of La Rochelle. Having described the order to be found in the universe as the essence of God, 'which is not to be found in disorder and confusion', the author immediately went on to describe the magnificent order and, indeed, symmetry to be seen in the disposition of the forces which had reduced the rebellious city to obedience. Had the German prince who was so impressed with the order and discipline of the Roman Army under Tiberius witnessed the siege of La Rochelle he would have agreed with all those who 'have seen this miracle, and these works of Archimedes . . . that our king was a living God who commanded there'.[63] This constituted a remarkable appeal to an audience sensitive to Neoplatonic as well as religious conceptions of Order, not to mention the military achievements of the Romans.

As the turbulent middle decades of the century receded it became apparent that the traditional intellectual foundations of monarchical rule had survived well. The two key elements were, as they had been for at least two centuries, Religion and Justice. It was on these, said Bossuet, that the health of the body politic depended. Justice itself flowed from God who was the judge of all judges and who bestowed on kings the authority to judge on his behalf and 'in accordance with his eternal laws'.[64] Jean Domat expressed almost identical views; kings, who received their power from God, were obliged to govern according 'to his will which is no other than justice'.[65] The king was expected to use his power for the 'maintenance of justice and public tranquillity'.[66] Both Domat and Bossuet would have appreciated the attitude of the sixteenth-century jurist who had been at pains to declare that of all the titles bestowed on French kings – August, Conquering, Invincible, Hardy, Victorious, Debonair, Wise and so forth – only the epithet Just distinguished them from the other princes of the world.[67]

The persistent preoccupation with Justice is not helpful to those historians who have associated absolute monarchy with a shift away from the idea of the king as judge to that of sovereign lawmaker. This interpretation is based partly on Jean Bodin and partly on the impact of Roman law.[68] There was undoubtedly an assertion of royal sovereignty from at least the fifteenth century in which some of the principles of Roman law were useful; and Bodin's definition of sovereignty as the undivided and untrammelled power to make general laws opened up the possibility of a break with traditional concerns about the higher purposes of government. Laws, according to him, were laws regardless of whether they were just or not. Yet, it is all too easy to exaggerate the modernity of these ideas by taking them from their context and also to overestimate their contribution to the fashioning of the absolute state. Bodin's *Six Books of a Commonweal* has been constantly treated as though it were primarily about the concept of sovereignty, whereas it was an elaborate explanation of the principles which order a well-governed commonweal.[69] Although Bodin mixed empirical observation with abstract reasoning, these principles flowed from a profoundly metaphysical and moral view of the universe. A Neoplatonic and, at times, mystical conception of the harmony of the cosmos was fused with a Thomist belief that, beyond the provision of necessities and security, the purpose of government was to lead its citizens to 'divine contemplation of the fairest and most excellent object that can be thought or imagined'.[70] Like virtually all his contemporaries Bodin was sure that monarchy in general was the form of government that most corresponded to the natural order and that a 'just' monarchy of the French type was the best of all. Its harmonious regulation of contrary forces best mirrored and encouraged contemplation of the divinely ordered cosmos of which it was part. Thus, whilst kings were given an absolute authority to command, it was desirable, indeed imperative if disaster were not to befall, that power should be tempered by prudence, wisdom and justice. Rulers should change the law only with great caution, take wise counsel and maintain the Estates of the realm. 'The just monarchy', emphasised Bodin, 'hath not any more assured foundation or stay than the estates of the people, Communities, Corporations and Colleges.' A 'commonweal can no more sustain itself without a Senate than the body without a soul or a man without reason . . .'.[71] This analogy also makes clear that Bodin's apparently contradictory statements about royal authority and its limits were rooted in conventional chain-of-being imagery. Man, part mortal and part immortal, finds his natural place betwixt the beasts and the angels. Civil society itself is composed of the traditional three Estates each with their specific functions and qualities. Such a well-ordered commonweal reflected man's own nature with understanding holding 'the chief place, reason the next, the angry power desirous of revenge the third, and brutish lust and desire the last'.[72] Order is preserved by a carefully contrived balance of forces in which the extremes of each element of the universal chain of being are linked by intermediate degrees one to another.

It is of course possible to find in the multi-layered richness of Bodin's text elements which lend themselves to an authoritarian or absolutist interpretation. It was, however, equally possible to use Bodin to defend representative forms of government.[73] What is impossible, given Bodin's moral view of the purposes of civil society and government, is to use his thought to claim that the idea of legislative authority had pushed aside the notion of the king as Judge. Nor is it possible to get around this problem by appealing, as Richard Bonney has done, to those who followed in Bodin's philosophical footsteps, notably Cardin Le Bret.[74] A jurist of undoubted authoritarian bent who put his talents at the service of Richelieu, Le Bret has become celebrated for his Bodinesque aphorism that sovereignty, like the point in geometry, was indivisible. According to Bonney, Le Bret used the concept of sovereignty in order to sustain the monarch's right to dispense justice by revocable commissions, thus heralding a transformation in the nature of the regime. Legal positivism of this sort, however, does no more justice to Le Bret than to Bodin. Le Bret's observation about the indivisibility of sovereignty was made in the context of a series of injunctions about the need for restraint and justice in the introduction and interpretation of laws. Elsewhere, he stressed that the principal purpose of the power bequeathed by God to kings was to enable them to dispense justice to all, to maintain the peace, and to conserve the state in its splendour.[75] Although the king was under no obligation to consult the council or the sovereign courts in order to change the laws, it was nevertheless 'always becoming to a great king to have his laws approved by his *parlements* and other principal *officiers* of the Crown'.[76] Echoing Bodin, Le Bret declared that nothing was 'more *auguste* or more venerable than the *parlement* of Paris and all the others. . . . Nothing represents with more lustre or splendour the Majesty of Justice.'[77] Moreover, in distinction to tyrannical or seigneurial states, the presence and use of representative institutions can do nothing but good; for in them is to be found a close liaison between the Head and its members, the king and his subjects.[78] Those who did not follow these precepts risked sedition and disorder and thus the chastisement of God.[79]

Few, if any, of the political writers and jurists who shaped the ethos of Louis XIV's regime displayed any intellectual obligation to make the concept of legislative sovereignty the overriding hallmark of royal authority. Le Bret thought that of the marks of sovereignty the 'most noble and most important for the state was that of instituting officers'.[80] Domat listed royal prerogatives in a very conventional manner, with the right to make laws placed second after that of making war.[81] Bossuet barely mentioned sovereignty as such; when he did it was by referring to the 'sovereign authority to judge' which suggests that he was little concerned about any distinction between the two functions.[82] Even the ardent Romanist, de Ferrière, who more succinctly than anyone else used the idea that legislative power constituted the highest mark of sovereignty to reduce all the lesser courts, their *règlements* and customary law to a highly conditional status, buttressed his argument with the emphatic observation that kings held their power not of the people but from God.[83] In general the concept of legislative sovereignty was subsumed within an essentially traditional world view in which the role of the king was as much to dispense justice as to make the law.

The continuing attachment to the idea of the king as Judge was of critical importance in enabling contemporaries to distinguish between absolute power and tyranny. This distinction ran like a leitmotif through the works of all the writers who have been mentioned, from Bodin to Domat. The function of kings was to dispense justice and the purpose of justice, in de Ferrière's succinct formulation, was 'a constant and perpetual endeavour to render unto each what belonged to them'.[84] In the context of contemporary assumptions about the naturalness of inequality, this apparently simple idea carried with it deeper implications for the manner in which justice ought to be executed. Given that men were differentiated by capacity, status and function, justice had to be rendered, at least in part, by reference to these differences. Bodin, in keeping with his endeavour to unite contrary qualities, thought that the best form of justice was precisely one which combined an endeavour to preserve the proper distance between social orders with a limited injection of the principles of equity. He represented this in thoroughly neoplatonic fashion as a 'harmonic' fusion of geometric and arithmetic principles which, as in music, created harmony out of potential discord.[85] A century later de Ferrière himself harnessed some of these notions to the Aristotelian distinction between distributive and commutative justice. The former related to the distribution of public office and was accomplished by 'geometric proportion . . . in accordance with status and merit' whereas the latter dealt with private contracts and obligations and was based on the formal equality of the participating individuals.[86] It would be difficult to find a more ingenious legitimisation of the social, civil and legal inequalities inherent in the structures of the state over which the king presided.

At the same time such ideas offered a sophisticated rationale for the devolution of authority to those whose status entitled them to a share in it.[87] The great legists were quick to point out that the king delegated significant powers of justice to both royal and seigneurial jurisdictions and that, in some instances, there was no right of appeal from them. Moreover, it was a fundamental principle of French justice that litigants should appear before their natural judges. There were, of course, mechanisms at the disposition of the king which made it possible to remove cases from the purview of the lower courts, notably the *cas royaux*, which reserved certain types of case for the royal judges, and that of *prévention*, whereby a higher court could intervene in the proceedings of an inferior jurisdiction. Although the Criminal Code of 1670 extended the list of infractions which fell within its purview as *cas royaux*, the magistrates, led by the first president of the *parlement* of Paris, effectively resisted the goverment's desire to reinforce the capacity of the higher courts to exploit their right of *prévention*. Whilst President Lamoignon conceded that all justice ultimately depended on the king, he went on to insist that, equally surely, it was patrimonial in character and 'inseparably attached to landed estates'.[88] Such a view was clearly contrary to the principle that fief and justice had nothing in common which had been incorporated into many local customs in the sixteenth century. Not surprisingly, the effort to reconcile the two principles generated considerable confusion and some fine legal distinctions. In reality, the combination of venal and seigneurial officeholding helped sustain the belief that devolved powers of justice, administered by an autonomous judiciary, were an integral part of a 'just monarchy'.

Roman law, contrary to the claims of some historians, had very little relevance to these issues. Its utility for an understanding of French public law was dismissed out of hand, even by those who most admired it like Domat and de Ferrière. When French legists did turn to Roman law, it was not always to support royal authority. On the contrary, it could be used to reinforce the devolution of authority. Lamoignon, for instance, argued strenuously that in Roman law the right of *prévention* did not exist.[89] Nor were French experts at all certain that the transformation of the *imperium merum* into the idea of an indivisible sovereignty was really sustained by Roman texts or usage; for Rome had in fact bestowed the supreme right – that of the sword – on its magistrates.[90] According to some, Roman law was, in any event, fairly useless as an instrument of monarchical power; for the Prince of the Romans held his authority by virtue of the people who had bequeathed sovereignty on him whereas the French king held his by the power of God alone.[91]

The power of the French monarchs was thus legitimated within the framework of a highly traditional religious teleology. Rooted in an amalgam of Aristotelian, Thomist and Neoplatonic conceptions, it continued to bestow on the king both the power of supreme judge and the obligation to dispense justice. This meant that, although the king was answerable only to God and unrestrained by any institutional claims to share his power, he was still constrained by the dictates of divine and natural law. An absolute monarchy was a just monarchy not a tyranny. Amongst other things this required a proper devolution of power to those occupying a privileged position within the social and legal hierarchy. All of which conformed to the dispositions and will of God as well as the better bits of Roman practice.

Overwhelmingly, the body of ideas which fashioned the regime of Louis XIV looked backwards. They offer a particularly idealised representation of a regime which was struggling to adapt to pressures from both without and within. It remains to be seen how effectively it did so.

BUREAUCRACY AND PATRONAGE IN THE BODY POLITIC

By the reign of Louis XIV France was the most over-administered country in Europe. For more than a century the number of corporate bodies and the offices attached to them had proliferated. At the apex of the system the various subdivisions of the royal council were served by increasingly specialised bureaux. By 1700 the ministry of foreign affairs comprised fifty resident bureaucrats, and twelve specialised bureaus, directing at least twelve embassies abroad.[92] The business of the *contrôle-générale* was managed by a small number of *intendants des finances* – eight in 1708 when they were supplemented by six *intendants de commerce* – and a growing number of specialised bureaus. By 1726 those responsible to the receiver general had eighty-two employees. Some of their time began to be devoted to the collection and systematisation of the sort of data required by all bureaucracies. Prior to the reign of Louis XIV some limited calculations of the population had been undertaken. But in 1694, in preparation for the introduction of the *capitation*, Pontchartrain ordered a systematic analysis of population in all towns, burgs and villages.[93] By 1711 the ministry of foreign affairs had acquired

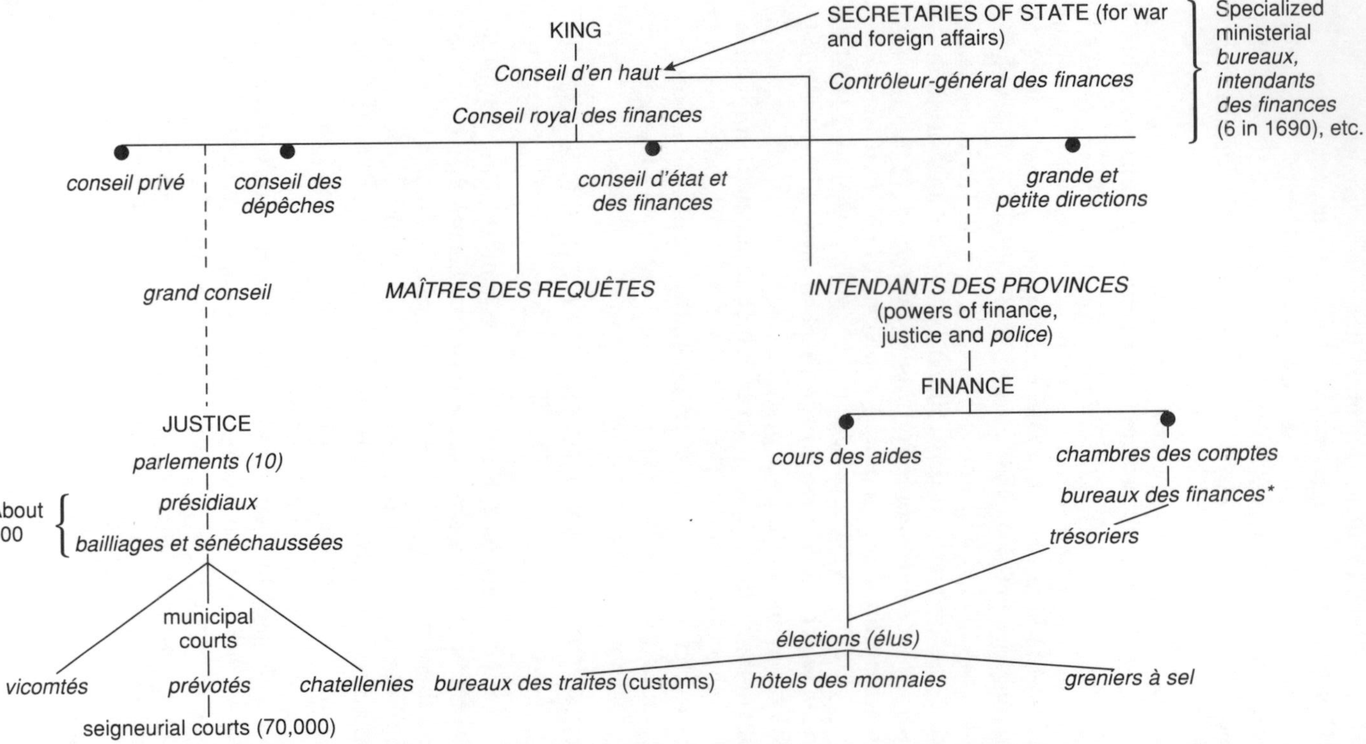

* There were *bureaux des finances* in each of the twenty-one *généralités* of the *pays d'élections*. The *pays d'états*, where provincial Estates functioned, and the newly conquered regions were organized differently.

Figure 6.1 Schematic diagram of the royal administration of the realm after 1661

Source: Parker 1989

its own *dépôt des archives* and archives were increasingly attached to such bodies as the *chambres des comptes* and municipalities.[94]

The domestic administration of the realm was theoretically divided into a hierarchy of courts responsible for the dispensation of justice and a hierarchy of corporate bodies concerned with the imposition and levying of the direct taxes. The ten *parlements* of France claimed the status of 'sovereign' courts and of these the most powerful and prestigious was that at Paris with its 200 judges. Those at Toulouse and Bordeaux were half the size, whilst the small *parlement* at Pau in the deep south-west boasted fifty magistrates. Beneath the *parlements* came 400 or so intermediate courts (*présidiaux, bailliages, sénéchaussées*) and below them a host of municipal and seigneurial jurisdictions. The hierarchy of fiscal bodies was equally extended. It was headed by about a dozen or so 'sovereign' courts of finance (*chambres des comptes, cour des aides*) and twenty or more *bureaux des finances*. Beneath them were 200 or so *élections*, on whose operations hinged the levying of the direct taxes, and many smaller *bureaux* responsible for the collection of customs, salt taxes and other impositions. From the 1640s the existing financial officials were subordinated to the tutelage of the intendants whose comprehensive powers of justice, finance and police made them the supreme representatives of royal authority in the provinces. Excluded entirely from this description and from the accompanying diagram (Figure 6.1) are the tax farmers who acquired the leases of all the major indirect taxes, principally the customs, *aides* and *gabelle*. They eventually spawned the Company of Farmers General, a consortium of forty major financiers, with its own elaborate administrative hierarchy. Also excluded are the inspectors general of manufacturers who numbered thirty-four by 1715 and the subordinate officials responsible for the enforcement of manufacturing regulations.

The French administration was beginning to acquire some of the features of a modern bureaucracy, notably a degree of specialisation, hierarchy and regulation. Yet it is all too easy to be misled by its size and complexity into an overestimation of its modernity. Even at the highest levels the functional subdivisions of the royal council were far from watertight, as the same people frequently sat in each of them on different days of the week and items were not always dealt with in conformity with the formal divisions of business. Its nominally distinct executive and judicial functions were extremely blurred.[95] In this respect the Royal Council reflected the character of the entire system. Domat observed that there were bodies which had mixed powers of *police* and justice (*parlements* and seigneurial courts), some which had judicial and legal powers (*élections*), and others with rights of justice only, but there were none with powers of *police* that did not also possess powers of justice.[96] The fact that financial bureaus also functioned as courts was a guarantee of bitter disputes over rights of jurisdiction. Functional specialisation was still in its infancy.

This situation was compounded by venality of office which precluded any possibility of separating office from officeholder and of the bureaucracy meeting the criterion of impersonality postulated by Weber's typology. Whilst it is true that the venal officeholders did produce distinguished families with a long tradition of state service, the cost was the consolidation of private interest at virtually every level of the administration. It was precisely the widespread unreliability, dishonesty and unproductive rivalry of the officeholders that explain the enormous array of responsibilities bestowed on the intendants. The fact that these held their posts by revocable commission and not by purchase has led to claims that they transformed the nature of the royal administration.

There were, however, only thirty or so *intendants des provinces*. Brittany did not have one at all until 1685. Common sense as well as empirical observation dictate that they were not going to escape dependence on others for assistance, expertise and local knowledge. In drawing up the celebrated memoirs of 1697–8 for the instruction of the Duke of Burgundy with their detailed descriptions of the economic, social and political topography of their *généralités*, the intendants turned to those who were most readily available; in one case this happened to be a local historian and in another an archivist. At Lyon a questionnaire was sent out to 734 priests.[97] Although some intendants made use of their own subordinate officials, the permanent assistance available to them was usually inadequate and remained so.[98] When the need for the intendants to have permanent assistance finally overcame official anxieties about creating new sources of local power, the problem was solved by the establishment of *subdélégués*. For a period, from 1704 to 1715, these became venal offices but even when they ceased to be so the positions were frequently filled by the local officeholders. As the *ancien régime* approached its end some of them had clearly become well and truly ensconced. In 1788 one of the *subdélégués* in Brittany was 77 years old. Doyen of the judges in the *bailliage royale et présidial* of Chaumont-en-Bassigny, he had held the post of *subdélégué* for forty years. At Chalons a similar official managed to see out a half-century in the post.[99]

The significance of these observations is reinforced by the extent to which the intendants themselves came from the world of the *officiers* and shared their background and culture. Drawn almost exclusively from the ranks of the *maîtres des requêtes*, they invariably returned on completion of their term of service to take up office in the magistracy or central government. Permanent careers were rarely made in the intendancies although there was a moment in the mid-eighteenth century when two-thirds of those in the post had received two separate commissions.[100] Intendants did receive stipends but complaints about their inadequacy were frequent. The language in which these were couched was also indicative of the aristocratic and unprofessional milieu which they inhabited: a memoir of 1738 noted that 'it was in the king's interest and those of his subjects that sufficient emoluments are attached to the position (*état*) of intendant to provide for all the expenses which this position demands'.[101] An intendancy was as much a means of social promotion as a step up a defined bureaucratic hierarchy. Success was as dependent on the right patronage as on the right qualifications. Etienne Jean Bouchu, who became intendant of Dauphiné in March 1686, was just 30 years old and had been a *maître des requêtes* for only a few months. He had, however, the advantage of being the son of a former intendant of Burgundy.[102] The multiple marriage ties of the intendants further reflected the powerful tendency to social endogamy characteristic of the *ancien régime*; Mousnier estimated that in the eighteenth century the intendancies were monopolised by 200, at most 300, families.[103]

The state remained overwhelmingly dependent on the quality of the officers thrown up by the patrimonial mechanisms of the legal world. This is nicely illustrated by reference to the 'curriculum vitae' of a certain Jean Baptiste Lemaître, son of an agent of the Duc d'Orléans. He was educated at Pontoise and Paris, where he obtained his *licence en droit* and became a barrister in the *parlement*. In 1681 he also combined the office of *bailli* of the seigneurial jurisdiction de l'isle Adam with several others. In 1686 he bought an office in a *grenier à sel*; when this was suppressed ten years later he bought a quite different office of *lieutenant criminel* in the *élection*. Subsequently he was appointed administrator of the hospital of the *pauvres renfermées* at Pontoise and obtained a more important position in the administration of the *gabelle*. In 1701 he became a *subdélégué* of the intendant of Paris at Pontoise. By 1717 he had secured the post of first *échevin* in this town which he had coveted for some time. His granddaughter married a *parlementaire*.[104]

It was on this sort of socially ambitious officeholder, educated in the classics and law, trained largely on the job, that the day-to-day functioning of the regime depended. But the effectiveness of officeholders in general was a chancy matter. At Metz in 1675 three presidents and 'the best part of the judges' rarely attended; in 1701 absenteeism by the thirty judges of the *présidial* de Valence had reached such proportions that barristers were called in to make up the numbers.[105] Career structures and professional training were haphazard. A magistrate in the sovereign courts required three years' study for a law degree but there is much evidence to suggest that this requirement was waived, partly waived or subverted. French law did not become a university subject until Louis XIV's reign and even after that the essential test for a new *parlementaire* was to give a short commentary on a Roman law text which he usually had had plenty of time to consider in advance. Whilst the system did produce some legists of integrity and learning, social standing still counted for much in the acquisition of office.

Those who came most to resemble modern bureaucrats were possibly the *premier commis* who staffed the central ministerial bureaus. Their offices were not venal, some attempt was made to relate salaries to seniority, and they had security of tenure. At first the *premiers commis* had not infrequently been related to ministers or had themselves acquired ministerial office but by the eighteenth century they were increasingly drawn from the lesser nobility and even commoners. A gap opened up between them and the ordinary *commis* from whose ranks they largely came. Yet recruitment was still conditioned by family connections and the ultimate objective of a *commis* was to buy an office.[106]

Effective government required the cooperation not only of the plethora of courts but also of older loci of authority. Amongst these were provincial Estates, municipalities and seigneurial jurisdictions. Although their autonomy had been reduced, these institutions remained vital to the orderly execution of policy and continued to play a positive administrative role. Improvements in road and water transport, urban development and agricultural innovation were as likely to stem from the initiatives of towns, merchants, or provincial Estates as from the intendants.[107] In Languedoc the Crown would have been hard pressed to increase the yield of taxation without the relatively sophisticated fiscal administration that still remained in the hands of the provincial Estates. It would also have been in severe difficulties over key projects, such as the building of the *canal du Midi* and the development of textile manufactures.[108]

Despite the sapping of their institutional autonomy, municipalities retained some significant functions particularly for the maintenance of order, poor relief, and the regulation of economic activity. The *capitouls* of Toulouse were responsible for more than a hundred municipal appointments ranging from councillors to street cleaners and lawyers to musicians, painters and soldiers. However, their sense of public obligation was frequently limited. Some of the *capitouls* of Toulouse at the end of the century had never even set foot in the city.[109] Moreover, the Crown's policy of turning elected positions into venal offices served to entrench the position of those judicial and financial officeholders who were on hand to buy them. Some towns strove to repurchase their posts. At St Quentin, where the municipality only had sufficient funds to buy back one of the two alternate mayorships, the position then alternated between an elected mayor and one who owned the office – hardly a recipe for efficient government.[110] The need to borrow significant funds for such purchases further perpetuated urban indebtedness and the consolidation of vested financial interest.[111] It was not surprising that when the government required a major organisational effort from the towns, the response was very mixed.

In the vastness of the French countryside where most people lived, seigneurial authority remained the most obvious source of day-to-day administration. The seigneurial *procureur fiscal* kept an eye on the *curé* as well as on blasphemers and those who behaved indecorously during the hours of holy service, on crossroads as well as schools, on public security as well as chimneys. Seigneurial agents in the north might regulate the price of meat and wheat, control the activities of 'foreign' merchants, regulate land usage, and watch over charivaris, masquerades and marriage celebrations.[112] General assizes, usually held in a public square or other convenient spot, continued in many localities down to the Revolution. These allowed the seigneur and his agents to assure themselves that their dependants had not been suborned by a rival jurisdiction, to fine those who absented themselves and to issue general orders for the maintenance of good conduct. Seigneurial courts, in keeping with the principle that litigants should be dealt with by their natural judges, also continued to play the critical role in matters relating to dues and obligations. It was generally felt that neither the definition of the *cas royaux* nor the right of *prévention* could be used to deprive seigneurs of their power over their dependants. Some legists determinedly defended the right of seigneurs to distrain the possessions of defaulting tenants without right of appeal. Similar ideas emerged in commentaries on Article 11 of the Civil Code of 1667 which dealt with the grounds for challenging the competence of judges. This could not be interpreted, emphasised de Ferrière, as a means of denying seigneurial judges the right to deal with all matters relating to their 'domains, dues, ordinary and casual revenues, whether of fiefs or non-noble land, including leases, sub-leases and other entitlements . . .'. De Ferrière felt there was nothing amiss in allowing seigneurs to be judges in such cases because it could be safely assumed that their 'subjects and tenants were refusing to fulfil their obligations' and 'it would be inconvenient to the seigneurs if they were obliged to pursue their claim for payment before other judges'![113]

In areas where seigneurial institutions were weaker, the responsibility for keeping order remained the collective responsibility of the village community. Although the intendants had the ultimate power to coerce rural communities into paying their taxes, they themselves were anxious to preserve communal responsibility because village representatives were better able to track down individuals. Expenses were also kept down.[114] In 1702 the government bestowed on village communities corporate responsibilities for tax collection, road maintenance, and the billeting of troops. For this purpose it created new offices of *maires et assesseurs perpétuels*.[115] In Burgundy the provincial Estates bought most of the offices and the resultant change in the pattern of rural administration was minimal. Local courts also continued to rule on business over which the intendant had been given formal jurisdiction. When the village of Agencourt wished to sell parts of its communal forest it obtained approval from the *bailliage*. The sale was subsequently overridden, but by the *maître des eaux et forêts*, not by the intendant.[116]

The intendancies were thus superimposed on a system of administration which they did little to alter, certainly not to modernise. Moreover, under Louis XIV, it became very clear that there was to be no repetition of the cavalier disregard for the legitimate authority of the officeholders suffered at the hands of Richelieu and Mazarin. Whilst asserting the supremacy of the royal council over the *parlement* of Paris, Louis was careful to confirm its judicial authority. All the chancellors, particularly those who held office between 1667 and 1714, showed a willingness to pursue a policy of reconciliation, consulting the magistrates about the formulation and implementation of legislation and defending the supervisory powers of the *parlement* over the lesser courts. Procedures were revised and adhered to whilst the *parlements* were given the opportunity to express their concerns and grievances.[117] This policy was reflected in the consistent and partially successful endeavour to reduce the number of requests made to the royal council for the annulment or suspension of parlementary decisions and in efforts to limit the use of *évocations*.[118] Colbert repeatedly enjoined the intendants not to infringe unnecessarily on the powers of established bodies; in 1676 they were explicitly instructed to allow the appropriate judges their authority in matters of taxation. The king, it was said in 1685, 'does not readily interfere with the jurisprudence established by the *parlements*, when it does not disturb the good of his service or that of his subjects and is not directly contrary to the Ordonnance' [of 1676].[119] Thus, whilst intendants retained the right to be present at the proceedings of the *présidiaux* they could not act as judge without a specific order to that effect.[120] Even in tax cases, where their intervention was required in order to speed things along, the intendants were urged to act with care. After Colbert died in 1683 de Harlay reported from Burgundy that he had few 'extraordinary affairs' to deal with; matters relating to the tax farms were being judged *in situ* as Colbert had insisted that things followed their normal course.[121]

Just as the government compromised over the judicial functions of the *parlements* it also did so over the material interests of the officeholders. Attempts to manipulate the *paulette*, bludgeon officeholders into forced loans or smother institutions in waves of new offices became things of the past. In 1693 when the government wished to create and sell nine new offices in the *parlement* of Provence, negotiations with the magistrates followed; they agreed to buy the lot for 440,000 *livres* with the freedom to allocate them as they wished to the various chambers.[122] It is true that at the outset of the reign there were some limited attempts to establish key posts such as those of *receveurs généraux des revenus casuels* as commissions but the effort was not sustained and, within a few years, they were converted into offices.[123] Abandoning his proclaimed intention of making inroads into venality, Colbert contented himself with reducing the value of magisterial offices, imposing minimum age requirements for office and renewing measures to prevent relatives sitting in the same court. Even these were frequently waived by the government itself in response to requests from influential families. Relationships inside the *parlements* of Toulouse and Rennes became so incestuous by the end of the century that it was decided that where several relations or allies were of the same opinion they should only have one vote between them.[124] Theoretically, to reach the key position of *maître des requêtes* it was necessary to be 30 years old and to have held office in a superior court for six years or in a *présidial* or *sénéchaussée* for six or to have practised at the bar for twenty. The average age of entrance under Louis XV was in fact 29, a figure concealing the presence of those whose family influence had secured them the position at a much younger age. Some passed through the courts in as little as six, five or even three months.[125]

Colbert's much-trumpeted attempt to tackle the vested interests in the financial world petered out in the same way. There was actually nothing innovatory about the *chambre de justice* which he established in order to investigate them; and in 1669, complaining of obstruction, some of which almost certainly came from people of the greatest status and influence, Colbert abandoned his investigations.[126] As on previous occasions, the collection of fines imposed on those found guilty of malversation was farmed out to a new consortium, one in which Colbert had confidence.[127] All that was achieved was the transfer of profits and influence from one group of financiers to another. After Louis' reign had drawn to its close another *chambre de justice* found itself dealing with exactly the same problems.[128] The French Crown thus confirmed the fact that the administrative system had become the property of the families, kin-groups and clienteles who had secured their positions within it during the period of rapid expansion prior to the mid-seventeenth century. It was lubricated by 'elaborate patterns of etiquette' involving exchanges of gifts, sometimes of a substantial nature which even ministers of the Crown thought it quite normal to accept.[129] By the reign of Louis XIV these decidedly unbureaucratic modes of operation were irreversible.

Such a conclusion may appear to sit uneasily with my earlier suggestions about the utility of the concept of absolutism. It is certainly clear that the prestige and power of the royal authority cannot be attributed in any simple way to the development of bureaucratic modes of administration. If anything, patrimonial mechanisms of government were more solidly entrenched than ever. Yet it was precisely these mechanisms which made the elevation of the king not only necessary but also possible: necessary, because without royal regulation and arbitration patrimonial rivalries constantly threatened to get out of hand; possible, because those at the centre were increasingly able to exploit these rivalries to their own advantage.

It has long been understood that Richelieu bolstered his position inside the government by developing relations with the secretaries of state which owed as much to their personal dependence as to his formal superiority. The First Minister augmented their incomes, facilitated advantageous marriages and provided offices and pensions for their own dependants.[130] More recently it has become clear how much the penetration of ministerial authority into the farthest regions of France owed to similar modes of operation. The power of both Richelieu and Mazarin turned on their ability to establish clienteles which outshone, outflanked or subordinated those of distant and troublesome provinces. Brittany and Provence stand out. In the former Richelieu made his brother Alphonse Archbishop of Aix and Abbot of Saint Victor at Marseille. A major client, Archbishop Sourdis of Bordeaux, became commander-in-chief of the naval forces whilst a nephew was appointed to lead the Mediterranean galleys. Of the fifteen provincial, naval and army intendants dispatched to the province, eight were personally dependent on him. In Brittany the story was much the same. Richelieu became governor of the province himself, installed a cousin as acting governor and *lieutenant général* who, in turn, appointed a relation to the governorship of Nantes. Yet another cousin presided over the Estates and was placed in the governorship at Brest. Also at Richelieu's disposition were the Bishops of Nantes, Rennes and Léon and, perhaps most importantly, the syndic and the treasurer of the provincial Estates. This enabled Richelieu to control payments to the unpredictable Breton nobility. Similar observations can be made about Mazarin. His most striking success was probably in Provence where the erstwhile *frondeur* and president of the *parlement* of Aix, Baron d'Oppède, came to terms. In return for the post of first president he utilised his wealth and connections to break down various centres of resistance. Friends and relatives secured office in the principal municipalities, d'Oppède's younger brother was appointed Bishop of Toulon, whilst cousins occupied sensitive positions in the Provençal assemblies.[131]

With power came unsurpassed riches. The colossal size of the fortunes accumulated by Richelieu and Mazarin and the crucial part played by state investments in their acquisition have already been mentioned.[132] Richelieu even turned his post of grandmaster and *surintendant* of commerce from a commission into an office. Thus whilst his activities in this capacity marked a significant stage in the extension of royal authority over the realm's maritime resources, the personal benefits for the cardinal were also considerable. Proceeds from shipwreck and flotsam rights, sailing permits, anchorage dues and the sale of admiralty offices all came Richelieu's way. His revenues from such resources rose from 96,000 *livres* in 1631 to 230,216 *livres* nine years later.[133] The naval council established in 1624 was made up of his clients, including his uncle who deputised for him. It met in a room in the *palais cardinal* known as the *salle de la marine*.[134] This ambiguous situation meant that many of the conflicts between centre and periphery, traditionally seen in institutional terms, should be placed in a significantly modified context. Richelieu's displacement of the Duc de Montmorency as grand admiral was an act both of state and of personal aggrandisement by Richelieu. It led directly to conflict with the *parlements* of both Bordeaux and Brittany which objected to the creation of admiralty courts and officials. The *parlement* of Bordeaux also came into conflict with the *fermiers* of the *convoi et comptablie*, an amalgamation of theoretically distinct customs and subsidies going back to the sixteenth century in which Richelieu acquired a major interest. What is not clear is whether the *parlementaires* appreciated precisely whose private interests lay behind the public operations of the tax farmers. One imagines not. For, when Richelieu, in similar fashion, had taken advantage of the extension of fiscal controls to the hinterland of La Rochelle in the aftermath of its defeat, he had been careful to buy up the newly created offices under another name.[135] Mazarin was even more rapacious, accumulating cash reserves greater than those of the Bank of Amsterdam. At the end of his life, having first indicated a willingness to leave all his wealth to the king, he took rapid steps to make sure it passed to his heirs; a full and public inventory, he claimed, would not be in the interests of the state.[136]

This view was shared by Colbert who had been Mazarin's personal intendant since 1651 and who alone had access to the cardinal's most confidential papers. Thanks to the revealing work of Daniel Dessert it is now appreciated that Colbert's unprincipled campaign to get rid of Fouquet on charges of malversation and treason had as much to do with concealing the truth about Mazarin's fortune as in cleansing the state of its predators. The evidence against Fouquet was thin and his wealth modest by comparison with that of Mazarin. His departure, however, also facilitated the replacement of his clientele by that of Colbert which was as extensive – particularly within the financial world – as that of his predecessors.[137] He did not of course forget his family. One brother was ambassador to England, another an army intendant, whilst his son succeeded him as minister of the navy; a first cousin became intendant of the navy at Brouage and a brother-in-law intendant at Soissons. The list could be extended.

Colbert's personal aggrandisement also helps to explain the relative decline in the influence of the Chancellor under Louis XIV which has traditionally been treated in institutional terms.[138] In 1672 the king announced that he had resolved to keep the seals and give audience himself, apparently on the grounds that there were abuses in the Chancellery which required rectification. But, as Olivier d'Ormesson observed, Colbert then took over,

> distributing all the jobs to the *maîtres des requêtes*, proposing on his own the people for all the vacant charges, giving them all to his relations, like that of first president of the *cour des aides* and of *lieutenant-civil* to M. le Camus; that of *procureur général* of the *cour des aides* to M. du Bois, son of a first *commis* of the treasury who was a relation; that of first president at Rouen to M. Palus who married a Camus . . .[139]

When Colbert died his son, the Marquis de Seignelay, became Secretary of State for the Navy but without a seat in the royal council. Le Peletier, who was a protégé of Le Tellier, replaced Colbert both there and at the *contrôle-générale*.[140] In 1690 Louis de Pontchartrain acquired both posts as well as that of Secretary of State for the *maison du Roi*.[141] When he moved to the chancellorship in 1699 his son Jérome retained the secretaryships of both navy and household. These were then used to undermine the authority of Chamillart who had secured the *contrôle-générale*. Although the *maison du Roi* was hardly at the centre of the administration, it gave its holder regular contact with the king which Pontchartrain exploited with devastating effect. There flowed from his office a stream of correspondence and instructions to all and sundry including fellow ministers. Clashes with Chamillart over their spheres of authority, particularly in relation to commercial and colonial policy, produced some vitriolic reactions. But nothing perhaps indicates better the nature of the system than the promise, extracted from Chamillart in 1701, that one of Pontchartrain's own vessels would be allowed to sail without the tax farmers being informed.[142]

If the progressive concentration of power, wealth and patronage in the hands of a few great families served the interests of the Crown it did not, as these examples illustrate, extinguish the rivalries between them. At every level of civil society the jostling for favour and advantage was intense, sometimes bitter. However, conflicts that once might have erupted into violence were now largely resolved by legal means. Indeed, the labyrinthian judicial system was to a large degree, particularly in its higher reaches, a mechanism for resolving the disputes between the families and clans that had bought their way into it. Members of the judicial profession or their relatives, allies and clients constantly appeared in court as litigants. Battles over successions and property together with rights of justice, conflicts of jurisdiction, and the possession of office raged for years and sometimes decades.

Although the incestuous nature of the system posed major problems for the effective and honest dispensation of justice, it was impossible to do more than limit the damage. The reiteration of legislation, stretching back at least to the Edict of Blois of 1576, designed to prevent immediate relations (fathers, uncles, brothers) from sitting in the same court, was a testimony to its lack of effect. As we have seen, it was frequently subverted by the Crown itself. The Edict of Blois is also instructive because of the way in which it outlawed *évocations de propre mouvement*, whereby the Crown through executive decision removed cases from the normal courts, whilst simultaneously leaving the door open to those who sought *évocations* on their own behalf. This was necessary in order to cope with the many instances in which members of the courts were closely related to the litigants.[143] The spate of *évocations* by the royal council which so enraged the *parlementaires* during the minority of Louis XIV were not mainly those of *propre mouvement*; they were those obtained by people with sufficient influence to profit from the prevalent 'confusion and disorder'. Such *évocations* and, indeed, many *cassations*, although formally executive acts of the sovereign, were the result of private lobbying by those seeking protection for their private affairs at the very highest level. Most vexatious were the *évocations générales* which assured the recipient that all their affairs, for a specified period of time, would be dealt with outside their natural jurisdiction. One of the most blatant cited by the magistrates was the *évocation générale* given to Turgot, himself a *maître des requêtes*, and to his domestics enabling them to transfer all their lawsuits pending in Normandy to the *parlement* of Rennes. Yet the *parlementaires* could do little more than complain about specific cases. For, as individuals who themselves were agents of powerful patrimonial interests, they were both participants in, and beneficiaries of, the system as a whole. All that was possible during Louis XIV's reign was a tidying up and a restatement of the legislation of the Edict of Blois, specifying the grounds for *évocations* and trying to limit manipulation of the system by the well placed.[144]

Most illustrative of the scale of the problem was the decision in 1701 to rearrange the procedure for *évocation* of cases from one *parlement* to another. Traditionally this had occurred on a reciprocal basis between two sovereign courts but it was discovered that well-placed *parlementaires* could find as much credit and favour from relations, allies and clients in one as in the other. It was therefore decided that, in future, cases evoked from Rouen should go to Brittany, from Brittany to Bordeaux, from Bordeaux to Toulouse and so on. Similar tensions even affected the proceedings of the royal council and those closest to it. For a time after 1669 *évocations* from the *grand conseil* appear to have been sent to the *parlement* of Paris; but from 1687 they went to the *conseil privé* to be dealt with on the report of the *maîtres des requêtes*. The *conseil privé* also acquired, at the expense of the *grand conseil*, the right to resolve cases of disputed jurisdiction amongst the judges of the sovereign courts and to arbitrate on the many disputes over competence and jurisdiction which affected the subordinate ones. However, the *grand conseil* continued to determine conflicts involving the *présidiaux*, even where these were with *parlements*.

These somewhat technical considerations further illuminate the king's role as supreme judge. When Louis, at the outset of his reign, made it clear to the *parlementaires* that there were limits to their powers, this was not just because they would otherwise infringe his sovereignty but also because they would destroy

> the subordinate position of the judges, constituted for different purposes throughout the entire realm, all in conformity with the supreme authority of the Council which His Majesty has established in order to keep an eye on the other jurisdictions, to regulate the differences that occur between them, to prevent subjects being constrained to take their cases before suspect judges, and to deal with those which for reasons of state ought not to be concluded elsewhere than in the said council . . .[145]

In other words, it was the responsibility of the royal council to act as the final arbiter, presiding over a system of devolved justice which itself required regulation.

The operation of the judicial system, however, also shows that the concentration of power at the centre was not simply an expression of the will of the king. Those engaged in the factional, patrimonial and corporate rivalries which provided its inner dynamic themselves required a mechanism for the mediation and resolution of their conflicts. Nothing illustrates this better than the system of *évocations* which institutionalised the interplay of patrimonial interests and allowed for the regulation by the supreme legal bodies of potentially destabilising conflicts. By the reign of Louis XIV the need for a ruler who was 'fully the master, the judge and the arbiter of all' was well understood.[146] An enormous amount of time and energy was thus devoted by those with power not to Affairs of State in the grandest sense, but to maintaining the equilibrium of the social system. Many of the cases snatched by decision of the royal council from the purview of the courts during Louis XIV's minority had little to do with *raison d'état*; but they had everything to do with the rivalries that beset the ruling class. Whilst the personal rule of Louis XIV brought stability it did not fundamentally change the way the system functioned. This is apparent not only from the activities of the *conseil privé* whose judicial character meant that it was preoccupied with the material interests of wealthy and influential litigants, but also from the decisions of the *conseil des dépêches*. Although this was nominally the executive branch of the royal council, its socio-political function was in some ways not very different from that of the *conseil privé*. It, too, spent a large amount of its time in extending the benefits of royal protection to those requesting a delay in paying their debts, protection from their creditors, or suspension of the seizure of their possessions and so on.[147]

None of this should be taken to mean a total absence of bureaucratic modes of behaviour and thought. In some ways bureaucratic developments were assisted by the patrimonial nature of the system. Venality of office, for all its manifest disadvantages, did allow the development of a tradition of state service and the accumulation of expertise by certain families. Kettering thinks that patron–client ties became gradually 'more pragmatic and political, less intensely personal and emotional', more like machine relationships and more compatible with other loyalties. The 'brisk businesslike tone' of Colbert's letters, she says, contrasts sharply with the personal and effusive tones of *officier* letters a century earlier.[148] The intendants, for all their patrimonial characteristics, were probably as effective as, if not more so than, their Russian and Prussian counterparts whose bureaucratic formation was more closely regulated and involved a much greater emphasis on technical expertise.[149] In the French case the boundary between patrimonial and bureaucratic forms of rule is not easily delineated. None the less, the success of the French monarchy in claiming to act on behalf of the country was secured more through its command of the levers of patronage than through bureaucratic efficiency.

Moreover, although the Crown and its ministers proved very adept at turning the patrimonial dynamics of the system to their own advantage, this meant that they could not push too hard against the interests of those who made it work. To do so, as the Fronde made clear, was to court political disaster. Whilst the officeholders came to appreciate the need for a ruler with sufficient prestige to regulate the system effectively, Louis XIV abandoned any ideas of radical structural reform. On the other hand, immense effort was put into the creation of a royal court and into the 'fabrication of Louis XIV' himself.[150]

THE COURT AND ITS CULTURE

As with the bureaucracy the Court cannot be reduced to a simple expression of the will of Louis XIV. Neither the physical character of Versailles, nor the court society and culture which it nurtured were the result of a preconceived blueprint. Versailles took fifty years to complete and many developments were hit and miss. Projects were abandoned mid-stream, whilst interiors and exteriors were frequently modified by a costly process of trial and error: the central area of the Trianon (1697) was pulled down at least three times.[151] The initial development of Versailles may owe as much to Louis' fondness for the countryside as anything else. Its subsequent evolution owed much to the demands of housing the very large royal family.[152] This included the queen, the king's brother and his brother's second wife, certain cousins, Louis' children, his mistresses, their children by him and eventually even his grandchildren, great-grandchildren and the spouses of all these. Nor, as with so many aspects of the reign of Louis XIV, was there anything particularly novel about the elements which went into the transformation of Versailles into a 'mammoth shrine to the Sun God'.[153] The association of French kings with the sun goes back to the fourteenth century. Louis XIII had been represented as the rising sun on the medal struck to commemorate the *lit de justice* of 1610 which transferred power to him so precipitously.[154] *Fête* and *divertissement* had been used as instruments of politics by the Valois. Richelieu had virtually articulated the strategy to be put into place by the Louis XIV when he urged his predecessor to ensure that the royal household was staffed by nobles; this would, he said, both enhance his dignity and increase their loyalty.[155] The process of concentrating cultural patronage in royal hands was also apparent at least from the time of Richelieu who not only established the *Académie Française* but also sought to undermine rival centres of patronage.[156]

All that said, it remains evident that the physical and social environment of the Court reflected the aspirations of Louis XIV and those around him. As early as 1662 Jean Chapelain, the poet and founder member of the *Académie Française,* wrote a long report for Colbert on the uses of the arts 'for preserving the splendour of the king's enterprises'. According to Peter Burke, it was this plan which was put into practice in the next decade with the foundation of the great cultural academies, most of whose members worked for the king and acted as patrons commissioning works which would glorify him.[157] The person of the king and his actions were represented in art and architecture, plays, ballets, and opera, in poems, sermons and speeches, and with medals and monuments galore. On paper, and in paint, bronze, stone and tapestry Louis was presented as Apollo, Mars, Hercules, Jupiter and Neptune; sometimes identified with Clovis and Charlemagne and more commonly St Louis (Louis IX), he was also associated with great heroes of the past: Alexander, Augustus, Constantine, Solomon and Theodosius. He was even represented as Christ.[158] In 1678 it was decided to replace the project for the *grande galerie* at Versailles, which was to have been devoted to the life and labours of Hercules, with a history of the king's actions.[159] In this Louis' determination to dispense with a First Minister, his independence of the papacy, his encouragement of commerce are all extolled with an abundant use of mythology and allegorical detail; the figures of France, Justice, Victory and Fame join Mercury, Mars, Minerva and the Muses in hailing Louis, the personification of France.

The cult of the king was sustained by the royal claim to be the source of all cultural patronage. The first major step in this direction came with the fall of Fouquet who, somewhat foolishly, had 'virtually replaced the king as the kingdom's leading patron'.[160] This eliminated his most conspicuous cultural rival and released a string of talented artists and writers. Amongst them were Corneille and Molière, the painter Le Brun, the architect Le Vau and the garden designer Le Nôtre. The last two were soon at work on the transformation of the small château of Versailles whilst Le Brun became the director of the Gobelins tapestry works, *premier peintre du Roi* and chancellor of the revived Academy of Painting. With these positions came the awesome responsibility of immortalising the heroic deeds of the monarch, an obligation which resulted in the extraordinary images which decorate the ceilings at Versailles.[161]

The foundation of the Royal Academies involved the elimination of the traditional *corps de métiers* such as those of the violinists, dancing masters and master painters.[162] A relatively small number of artists and writers – forty-two down to 1690 – were fortunate enough to secure royal pensions and amongst those the concentration of cultural power was immense.[163] Le Brun's dominance was enormous, if not quite undisputed, whilst Lully wrested control of the Academy of Music in 1672 from its founder Pierre Perrin whose hapless financial management left him languishing in prison. Lully acquired the right to produce for the public the pieces that he presented for the king; in addition he secured a total prohibition on all persons 'singing any piece entirely in music, either in French verse or other languages' without his permission on pain of a fine and confiscation of all theatre props and costumes.[164] Despite an appeal to the *parlement* by those who felt injured, the government moved rapidly to close down competing operatic productions; it further reinforced Lully's monopoly by declaring that no copies of his works should be made without agreement and if any were published it was to be under his close supervision.[165] Lully even succeeded in making his control of the Academy hereditary; on his death in 1678 it passed to his son-in-law.[166]

Cultural patronage was inseparable from questions of power and power relationships. When Colbert died in 1683 Louvois acquired the office of *surintendant des bâtiments* and with it control over the Academy of Painting and Sculpture. Le Brun lost influence and Perrault lost his position as a member of the *petite académie*. Le Nôtre was forced into retirement.[167] In this area as in others the king acted to maintain some sort of equilibrium. Above all, he asserted his right to be the sole provider and custodian of the *divertissements publics*. They were, he said, 'not so much his as those of his court and all the people' (Solnon 1987: 272). An observer of the royal entry into Paris on 26 August 1660 would undoubtedly have shared the sentiment. One of the most ostentatious parades in French history, it nevertheless allowed the city of Paris and its corporations to receive their king and for him to share his glory with his mother and Cardinal Mazarin. She made one appearance on an arch of triumph as the Goddess Minerva and on another in the guise of Juno and yet a third as a pelican – symbolising the mother who sacrifices herself for her children. The fact that gout prevented Mazarin from putting in a personal appearance was no barrier to his representation on another arch as Mercury and Atlas.[168] It was not long before the great and the good had another opportunity to share in the glory of their monarch. In June 1662 an extraordinary carousel was held at the Tuileries involving five teams of horsemen, supposedly Roman, Persian, Turkish, Indian and American. These were commanded variously by the king's brother and the great princes. Louis appeared on horseback as the 'Emperor of the Romans' with a shield decorated by a sun dissipating the clouds and the emblem 'as I saw I conquered'.[169]

Two years later, Versailles was chosen as the site for the celebrated *fête* of *les plaisirs de l'isle enchantée* which lasted three days before an audience of 600 courtiers. Based on the tale of the imprisonment of Knight Roger by a sorceress it again incorporated a carousel in which the Imperial theme was to the fore whilst the nobles revelled in the power of a victorious king. The Sun's chariot was surrounded by the four ages of Gold, Silver, Bronze and Iron – the latter a symbol of crushed revolts. There followed a musical spectacle-cum-ballet, orchestrated by Lully who was dressed as Orpheus. During this the controllers of the king's household, representing Abundance, Joy, Propriety and Good Cheer, brought in a laden table. The second day was given over to Molière's play *La Princesse d'Eliade* interspersed with recitations and ballets in which both king and courtiers acted out their roles.[170]

The great nobility were thus offered a dazzling opportunity to represent themselves to themselves. Traditional state ceremonials had been, as Giesey has observed, events which momentarily interrupted the rhythms of everyday life. With court ceremonials the distinction between normal and unreal time disappeared.[171] Transported to their imaginary island, participating in pastoral idylls, basking in the glory of a deified monarch, the nobility acted out a role in which illusion and reality, the imagined past and the active present, were thoroughly confused. With the definite installation of the Court at Versailles in 1682 the ephemeral decorations, motifs and themes which had gone into the *fêtes* and *entrées* were fixed in stone and plaster. As the cast of thousands settled down on the great stage, *Le Roi-Machine,* to use Apostolidès' effective metaphor, became the director and focal point of a continuous performance deemed necessary to maintain respect and order.

It was precisely this concern which meant that, at Court, rights and prerogatives were not guaranteed by either status or function but depended on the grace of the king. The princes of the blood, for instance, did not have entry to the *petit lever* nor automatic access to the king's retreat at Marly – one of the most coveted of royal favours.[172] Not surprisingly it provoked astonishment and some jealousy when Racine was offered the supreme accolade of a room there.[173] In some ways there was little new about the careful dispensation of royal favour. Anne and Mazarin had themselves insisted that the right to be received was a courtesy which they dispensed, not a courtesy expected. But, with Louis XIV, court etiquette was systematised and enforced as never before. The Prince of Condé was required to apologise for not descending from his coach to greet Louis when he encountered him coming the other way.[174] As Louis himself observed, the assertion of his pre-eminence was not merely a matter of mere ceremony as those unable to penetrate the mysteries of government might suppose.[175] It could be used to rein in potential troublemakers. Louis Armand de Bourbon, Prince de Conti, lost the privilege of the *grande entrée* for having gone off to fight in Hungary without leave.[176] The king's brother was refused the governorship of Languedoc with the admonition that 'the Princes of the Blood were never at ease in France other than at the Court'.[177] The days when malcontent grandees flounced out of Court were certainly over.

It would, however, be a mistake to interpret what Ranum has aptly described as 'tyrannising patterns of courtesy' as simply a manifestation of a royal conspiracy to put great nobles in their place. Louis XIII had once caught up with an unfortunate passer-by outside the Louvre to reprimand him for not raising his hat when passing the royal chambers.[178] Such obsession must also be placed in the context of the significant shifts in aristocratic attitudes which we have already encountered. So too should Louis XIV's suspicion of the motives of others. His advice to the Dauphin on how to distribute favours so that the jealousy of some would serve as a restraint on the ambition of others displays a perception of human nature epitomised by the famous Maxims of La Rochefoucauld.[179] Although not overtly intellectual, the king's view of the body politic was profoundly marked by contemporary conceptions of *amour-propre*.[180] Monarchy was the form of government most suited to the regulation and direction of self-interest in the common good. A wise king was in a position to pick trustworthy advisers but really trust no one, to stand above the fray and to motivate his subjects.[181] Princes in whom 'a brilliant birth and proper upbringing usually produce only noble and magnanimous sentiments' were much better able to govern than 'people of middling condition who govern aristocratic states'. The former were capable of putting aside their private interests, whereas the latter would be guided solely by personal considerations or by the immediate interests of the state.[182]

As this last observation suggests, Louis' rather gloomy view of human motivations was constrained by a sense of moral purpose. His imagery displayed a thoroughly conventional view of the need for hierarchy and order; he clearly saw himself as the divinely appointed head of the body politic, *parens patria*, and as the dispenser of Justice.[183] If his conception of Justice hinged on the desire to distribute rewards and punishments effectively, it was tempered by a concern to reward 'private individuals justly'.[184] His attitudes also reflected and sustained the widespread preoccupation with status and rank. Such distinctions, he felt, were 'virtually the first motive of all human actions'.[185] This conviction manifested itself in the elaborate etiquette and the highly refined distribution of honorific privileges at Versailles, the systematic regeneration of the great military Orders, and the careful selection of those suitable for elevation as *ducs et pairs*.

The evolution of Court society did not therefore represent the imposition of alien values on a hostile world. On the contrary, in asserting his position Louis drew on the ideological and cultural resources of the people around him. This is most plainly seen in the classical idiom in which his propagandists conveyed their message. Certainly, the emphasis on harmony and restraint which imbued both visual and literary art forms corresponded to the interests of the state. But their impact depended on an audience which enjoyed and understood the use of classical allegory and mythology. French classicism also gave expression to the recast noble ethos of the seventeenth century in which military values, though still highly esteemed, were tempered by civility and *bienséance*. The emotional appeal of the Baroque gave way to an appeal to the intellect. Passion was subordinated to reason, ambition and love to duty. Blood was banished from the artist's canvas and battles from the stage. Form was valued more than colour. A neoplatonic idealism was present in virtually every art form. Music, of course, had long been held to express the harmony of the cosmos and to constitute the most admirable medium for bringing order to society and instilling virtue in the soul. But painting, not held in the greatest esteem by Plato because it merely depicted immediate reality, was also used by the French classicists to make universal statements about human nature. Their stylised figures were not real people but representations of virtues, emotions and attitudes, the significance of which could be appreciated by those familiar with the principles of composition and classical mythology. Even landscapes were stylised representations of nature, not the identifiable locations so beloved of the Dutch who had invented the genre. Similarly, tragic operas and dramas explored, with a brilliance that has made so many of them timeless, the mainsprings of the human condition. Their characters were not just historical or contemporary figures in disguise, but vehicles through which the eternal conflicts between reason and passion, love and duty, self-interest and virtue, were utilised to make simultaneous observations about human nature and how men ought to conduct their affairs. Nothing symbolised more obviously the desire to bring human society into harmony with an idealised universal order than Louis' appropriation of Apollo. Chief of the Muses, God of Music, Ruler of the Planets, the Sun, God himself – Apollo was the quintessence of the harmony of the Cosmos. Self-evidently of value to those who sought to use the arts in the service of the state, French classicism also made a direct appeal to an aristocratic milieu in the process of coming to terms with the stresses and strains of a changing world.

Versailles, then, was much more than a product of the king's ego. It sustained and was sustained by an entire class. Most of the 3,000 or so nobles who were presented at Court each year and the select few who secured lodgings there did so because they wished to be there. Long before the days of Versailles military governors had begun to congegrate of their own free will in Paris. There they built fine houses, rode about in magnificent carriages, attended the Court, invested in offices, tax farms and state loans and were on hand to defend their patrimonial interests before the *parlement* or the *conseil privé*.[186] In the early 1670s the grandees, encouraged by the king, were already building hotels at Versailles.[187] After the permanent installation of the Court and government there in 1682 the competition for apartments was intense though most of them were cramped, cold and dirty. Versailles was, as Madame de Motteville observed, 'a great market'. Here courtiers arranged advantageous marriages, dealt in army commissions and obtained lucrative privileges. Consortia of *officiers* came into being to wheel and deal in newly created offices although this was forbidden.[188] Material incentives and access to government officials thus worked to reinforce the desire to participate in the rituals of Louis XIV's court.

The Court thus gave expression, both symbolic and real, to the social and cultural phenomena which have been encountered in this study. It was the aristocratic family residence *par excellence* with a household and retinue which outshone all others in size and colour. The king presided over his family with patriarchal severity but with a concern for his own blood and lineage which he sometimes placed above the interests of the state and his subjects. His public and private roles were almost indistinguishable, as was shown both by the design of the royal apartments and the daily rituals in which his courtiers could participate. Even the family hour which followed his evening meal was held with the doors of the cabinet flung wide open so that all could see.[189] The Court also gave expression to the attachment to rank and hierarchy which had become ever more intense; in doing so it compensated the grandees for the loss of their autonomy whilst preserving their privileges, status and influence. The intensity of the competition for all three was, however, mitigated by the dictates of *honnêteté* and *bienséance*. The Court was thus a well-constructed mechanism for managing the pursuit of place and favour. In this perspective, as home of both court and government, Versailles was the symbolic and real focal point of a state apparatus dedicated to the redistribution of the wealth squeezed out of the labouring population.

The Court rested on a carefully contrived equilibrium of its component elements. All were subject to pressure and change which cannot be fully captured by the model described here. It is in fact arguable that it captures only that fleeting moment when the social forces which have been analysed pushed absolutism towards its apogee. The days of royal and noble participation in court spectacles were in fact already passing before the king took up permanent residence at Versailles. It was in 1670 at Saint Germain, playing first Neptune and then Apollo, that he danced in his last ballet.[190] Without the royal sun the cast of courtiers lost their supporting role and the *ballet de cour* faded away. Dancing *chez le roi* continued but became steadily less improvised. Comic ballets disappeared on Molière's demise in 1673 and were replaced by operatic performances; they were mostly tragedies which the courtiers paid to watch.[191] Financial constraints subsequently made it difficult to sustain the expensive productions of the early years. Operas were sometimes converted into concerts and during the War of Spanish Succession disappeared completely from Versailles. It became necessary to go to Paris to see them.[192] However, the ninety-four singers of the Chapelle continued to perform daily, offering a variety of hymns, psalms and motets, supported by a small orchestra. On occasion, they provided an accompaniment at royal meal times. Members of the royal family, some of whom, like the Duc de Chartres, were gifted players, offered their own *appartements de soirées* preceded by operatic recitals.[193] The king withdrew more to his private chambers and visited less and less. It apparently became a discourtesy for those paying their respects 'to talk about almost anything except births, marriages, deaths, the king's health, the weather, French victories, literature, gardens, music, plays and the *faux pas* of others'.[194] The king's retreat, suggests Apostolidès, had the effect of 'exposing the political classes as a whole'.[195]

The changing social and cultural ambience of the Court reflected the fact that by the end of the 1680s, despite the liberation of additional funds, the years of greatness were over. Le Vau, Molière, Corneille, Lully were all dead. Le Brun died in 1690. The long years of war which followed made it more and more difficult to sustain the image of a great and glorious king. 'Twelve years of war', Burke observes, 'generated only twenty-four medals.'[196] Victories were few, the population increasingly debilitated. At Versailles life, it was claimed, carried on normally. In 1690 the official government journal noted that the *divertissements* had taken place as usual for, in Louis XIV's France, art and entertainment were not halted during war. Commenting on the carnival season of 1708 it maintained that money was plentiful, industry productive and that, in spite of all the military reverses, the balls given by the king, the Duchess of Burgundy and James of England were unusually extravagant. In truth the financial situation was little short of disastrous and specie in desperately short supply. The following year Louis XIV announced that he was sending all his gold service, plates, dishes and salt cellars to the Mint. It was his contribution to the relief of his starving subjects hit, amidst the long years of war, by the most bitter winter for fifteen years.[197] At that moment the symbolism of the great gallery of Versailles denuded of its glittering silver was perhaps more telling than the triumphant imagery which adorned it.

WARFARE, FINANCE AND THE REAL WORLD

It was entirely appropriate that Louis XIV should be portrayed as Mars as well as Apollo and that Le Brun's great gallery should lead from the *salon de paix* to the *salon de guerre*. Expenditure on war, averaged out over the entire reign, accounted for over half the total, soaring in bad years to well over 70 per cent.[198] There was nothing new about this. At some points during the 1630s the proportion had been even higher. By then the government was already spending an average of 38 million *livres* a year on war compared with a mere 5 million at the beginning of the century.[199] By 1688 the sum was 70 million, in 1701 virtually 100 million. It peaked at nearly 175 million in 1705.[200]

It would be inadequate to attribute the constant financial embarrassment of the French monarchy simply to the cost of war. Prior to 1636 the *taille* yielded about 10 million *livres* annually to the central treasury but within seven years it had risen to an astonishing 48 million *livres* – so astonishing that much of it was certainly never collected. Between 1645 and 1654 it fell back to a yearly average of 25 million. Albeit in less dramatic fashion, the income from the major revenue farms followed a similar course: 5 million at the beginning of the century, 10 million by 1636, reaching 23 million in 1643 before settling at the 10 million mark. As a result for most of the 1640s (1647 and 1648 excepted) the revenue from ordinary taxation was more than enough to meet the immediate costs of war even though the balance might have been insufficient to cope with the remaining ordinary expenses. The essential problem faced by the government was that there was no way of raising the huge sums required without surrendering the financial system to private interests. Once entrenched these not only drained the system of its reserves but became a formidable impediment to financial reform. It is conceivable that with a period of sufficiently prolonged peace this vicious circle and the grip of the financiers might have been broken.

The peaceful decades of 1600–10 and 1660–70 did see a reduction in the private obligations of the Crown but nowhere near sufficient to allow it to embark on wholesale reform. Although Sully managed to accumulate a reserve of 15 million, this was at the expense of a number of creditors on whose loans he simply defaulted. None the less, in 1607, he still spent between 11 and 11.5 million *livres* on servicing the debt – about 35 to 40 per cent of the revenues. The Crown's dependence on its own tax farmers for considerable sums was already clear. In that same year Antoine Feydeau, farmer of the *aides générales*, gave the king an advance of 200,000 *livres* as well as a loan of 1.5 million.[201] After 1610 the situation worsened steadily. According to an official estimate made as revenues collapsed during the Fronde, no less than 57 million *livres* – over one and half times the depleted tax yield – was required merely to service the debt.[202] To meet its extraordinary expenses the Crown required extraordinary revenues. It has been estimated that between 1620 and 1635 over a third of the revenues which arrived in the treasury came from the *parties casuelles* which largely comprised revenue from the sale and taxation of offices.[203] As the market in offices became saturated the emphasis switched decisively to loans. In 1634, 8 million *livres* were raised against the *taille* and 3 million on the *gabelle*. By 1640 the interest on such *rentes* cost about 20 million. But they were insignificant in comparison to the 90 million worth of loans contracted in the three years from 1639 to 1641 and likewise assigned to particular royal revenues. *Traités* with the tax farmers also multiplied. They made an estimated 172 million *livres* profit between 1620 and 1644.[204] By this time the Crown's extraordinary revenues constituted a full half of the total receipts of the central treasury. Between 1650 and 1654 the proportion rose to no less than 63 per cent. In striking contrast the *taille* at this moment accounted for just a fifth of treasury receipts.[205] Even that, however, was increasingly mortgaged to the financiers; by 1645 income from the *taille* had been anticipated as far ahead as 1647 and in the crisis year of 1648 loans were secured against the revenues for 1650 and 1651.[206]

These figures, whilst graphically depicting the deteriorating position of the central treasury as it struggled to maintain the flow of cash, certainly do not represent anything like the total picture. Considerable sums of money were spent locally. In 1620 the *généralité* of Caen sent forward 70 per cent of its revenues, that of Bordeaux a mere 23 per cent.[207] Thus the treasury accounts largely exclude the money used to pay the judiciary, the financial officers, most of the standing army, the mounted constabulary, some of the army and navy expenses (especially fortifications and *étapes*), and various other expenses. In Champagne in 1620, 55 per cent of the local taxes, excluding a special levy for the repair of local roads and bridges, went to the salaries of the local officers.[208] If this procedure had merely been an administrative device for the direct payment of basic costs it would have made sense. But the proliferation of venal offices, whilst channelling ever greater sums through the state machine, simultaneously created a gigantesque system of spoils. Not only did 35,000 fiscal officers and agents require salaries but they had invariably acquired a personal interest in the revenues from the transactions which they supervised or the taxes which they levied. Many doubled up as private financiers, lending the king his own money. Nor were the venal officeholders the only group to which local revenues were assigned, particularly in times of political instability. A random survey of the activity of the royal council in 1644 is revealing. In January, it granted the Maréchal de St Luc 18,000 *livres* from the general receipts of the *généralité* of Bordeaux in part payment of his emoluments as lieutenant-general of Guyenne. In March, the son of the Duc de Chaulnes, governor of Amiens, was granted continued payment of 8,000 *livres* to be drawn on the *élection* of Amiens for the duration of war. In May, the taxpayers of Languedoc were required to find 66,000 *livres* for the Duc d'Orléans, recently appointed governor of the province. In August, the seigneur de Barry, formerly governor of the southern port of Leucate, was confirmed in his annual pension of 3,000 *livres* to be drawn on the *gabelles*. The cost of rehabilitating the Duc de Bellegard, disgraced after his participation in the revolt of Orléans in 1631, was 675,000 *livres*. It was decided that he should receive 60,000 p.a. from the *cinq grosses fermes* and a tax imposed on the *draperie de Paris*.[209]

From time to time the Crown exerted pressure on its officers by demanding forced loans or simply defaulting on payments. It was general policy during the 1640s to pay *gages* and *droits* at three-quarters or a half or even three-eighths of face value. The treasurers at Bourges complained that they were paid nothing at all between 1640 and 1643.[210] More concerted efforts to claw back the ill-gotten gains of the financiers were made through the periodic *chambres de justice* or by declaring a bankruptcy. But the *chambres de justice*, as that instituted by Colbert showed clearly, were largely devices for fining those who had grown too rich. If they raised a modest amount of money this came from the farming out of the fines or from the compositions made by those who wished to secure exemption.[211] In no way did such investigations extricate the Crown from its dependence on the financiers, although some of these certainly came to grief. During the Fronde the threat to them seemed at first to be more serious. Under pressure from the *parlementaires*, incensed by the threat to their own interests as officeholders and *rentiers*, the government revoked between 80 and 120 million *livres* of loan contracts. Yet, although it was also obliged to dismiss the *surintendant*, Particelli d'Hemery, the threatened general investigation into the affairs of the financiers did not materialise. There was no general confiscation of assets. Instead, the *parlementaires* concentrated their attacks on those who had made loans to the government secured by cuts in the magistrates' own salaries. A number were involved in the pillaging of financiers' homes. But the *parlementaires* could not afford, any more than the government itself, to undermine a financial system of which they were so much a part. In the event the revoked loan contracts were not abolished but reassigned. 'The bankruptcy of 1648', concludes Bonney, 'paralysed the government without permanently removing the burden of debt.'[212]

This dire situation was compounded by the fact that most of those in receipt of royal largesse were also exempt from taxation. The problem had been recognised almost from the moment when the *taille* became a permanent royal tax. Back in 1445 Charles VII restricted exemption to those nobles who bore arms or had ceased to do so because of old age, students, the household servants of the Crown and the destitute.[213] Over the next two centuries the Crown engaged in a long and losing battle to reduce the extent of privilege. There was a flow of measures designed to prevent nobles claiming exemption on land secretly leased to others, to investigate fraudulent titles, to reduce the privileges claimed by the princes and princesses on behalf of their households and to limit the exemptions secured by the growing army of *officiers*.[214] Yet what the Crown took with one hand it subsequently gave away with the other. In September 1610 the officers of the royal households were denied exemption from the *taille* unless they were actually in military service; in December the following year the exemptions were maintained for the queen mother, her brother and sisters, the Prince de Condé, the Duchesse d'Angoulême, and the Duc d'Anjou and the Duchesse de Bar.[215] In similar fashion every creation and sale of the more prestigious offices continued to be accompanied by the inducement of tax exemption. In 1634, when the government endeavoured to ease the burden on the populace by granting a remission of the *taille* for one quarter of that year, it took the opportunity to define more closely those groups that would be exempt in the future. But the length of the list of those who remained exempt is in itself testimony to the fact that by this time the elite of the judicial and financial world, who in any event were best placed to benefit from the money passing through their hands, were also to remain untaxed. The *trésoriers de France* paid no *taille* or military levies, no *gabelle*, no river or road tolls and in general they were exempt from the charges imposed by municipal authorities. Evidently the treasurers constituted a particularly privileged group; but all the principal fiscal officeholders retained their exemption from the *taille* and associated levies.[216] In 1640, still expressing anxiety about the burdens of the *taille*, the Crown returned to the attack by revoking ennoblements of less than thirty years, including those given to officers of the royal household and the judicial and financial officers of the *généralités*, *bailliages*, *élections* and *greniers à sel*.[217] When the intendants were given general authority for the *taille* in 1643 one of their functions was to ensure that those whose exemptions were revoked by this act did indeed pay.[218]

Such decisions were, however, rendered academic by the near collapse of the fiscal system during the 1640s. From 1642 entire villages failed to draw up tax rolls. Rouergue and Gascony paid only a third of taxes from 1642 to 1644. Three parishes near Montargis in the Orléanais had not paid any *tailles* in four years. In the Lyonnais 'prisons were jammed with parish collectors'.[219] During the Fronde collection of taxes was brought to a halt in some part of every *élection* in the realm. Recovery of the arrears proved impossible. Throughout the 1650s much of the southwest remained in a state of tension with repeated attacks on the brigades sent to enforce payment. Further north in the *généralité* of Alençon twenty-five parishes in a single *élection* refused to appoint any collectors of the *taille* from 1647 to 1659.[220]

By the time of Colbert's administration it was clear that 'tax relief . . . was a necessary condition for the restoration of royal authority and power'.[221] Louis expressed the view that by dint of economies and without recourse to loans or extraordinary measures he could not only balance his budget but also reduce the tax burdens on the population.[222] During the peaceful years of the 1660s this did not seem as over-optimistic as later developments were to prove. Guéry estimates that expenditure in 1661, whether measured in money of account or in silver equivalent, was less than half its 1656 level.[223] Most dramatic was the success in reducing the charges on the revenue from the *pays d'élections*; these came down from around twenty-five million *livres* to eleven or twelve million. Some reduction in the costs of the tax farms was also achieved. Their reorganisation and consolidation contributed to a threefold rise in revenue from them between 1660 and 1690. Additional sums were also wrung out of the *pays d'états*. Even though they were still contributing a mere 2 per cent of ordinary revenues, by the end of the century their share of total receipts had risen, albeit with sharp fluctuations, to between 20 and 30 per cent. During the period 1662–83 the extraordinary expenditure of the Crown was also pegged back to just over a fifth of the total compared with the two-thirds reached during the previous two decades.[224]

However, even in the years of relative financial comfort, Colbert was unable to free the government from dependence on the *traitants* whose help was required in order to recover the sums due on repurchased *rentes*, offices and *droits*, from the investigations into the nobility and, above all, from the proceeds of the *chambres de justice*.[225] By 1681 expenditure had again risen to its 1656 level and with it the charges incurred by renewed borrowing and sales of office. In the 1690s a deteriorating economic situation led to a collapse of revenue from the tax farms.[226] By

1703 some were in such difficulty that the government took over their direct management.[227] The shortage of specie also became acute.[228] In 1693 the government did not even have the funds necessary to purchase the old coins which it wished to refont.[229] Without a major overhaul of the system there seemed no way of bringing the budget deficit, now around 72.5 million *livres*, under control. If dependence on the financiers never quite reached the heights of the 1630s and 1640s, the Crown none the less raised 758 million *livres* from them between 1689 and 1715 on which 174 million was payable in interest charges.[230]

The nub of the problem faced by the French monarchy had long been understood in the highest circles. Isaac Loppin, *secrétaire du Roi*, had many years earlier dedicated a splendid pamphlet to Richelieu attacking both the burden of taxation and the cost of the fiscal apparatus. The innumerable legal proceedings undertaken in the council and *parlements* by a host of *officiers*, tax farmers and their agents, he believed, were almost as onerous as the tax burden itself. The remedy required not only the abolition of venality, which had been suggested many times, but also the ending of tax privileges and the introduction of a single tax to replace all the existing ones.[231] But it was not until 1695 when, faced with looming financial disaster, the government finally made any significant challenge to the tax exemptions of the privileged by introducing the *capitation*. For this purpose the entire population except those too poor to contribute were divided into twenty-two 'classes' which bore some relationship to ability to pay.[232]

Despite the social significance of the *capitation* it was not, as Boisguilbert pointed out, a truly just tax; this, he felt, would have required a sliding scale so that the rich paid proportionately more of their assets than the poor.[233] Whilst the *capitation* did represent an effort to overcome the arbitrariness associated with the territorial repartition of the *taille*, the tariff proved to be both excessively rigid and open to circumvention. Substantial variations resulted in the amounts levied from members of the same classes depending on the *généralité* in which they were taxed. In the Lyonnais the tariff was largely abandoned in the interests of raising the required revenues.[234] Even so, they proved insufficient.[235]

Expenditure continued to rise, reaching an unprecedented 258 million in 1707. The following year the debt was an estimated 651.5 million.[236] The country at large was once again denuded of specie and the government was again unable to pay its suppliers.[237] Two years later, in the aftermath of the bitter winter and subsistence crisis of 1709–10, the government launched the *dixième*. This was a tax of 10 per cent on all forms of income whether from land, office or commerce. It was to be evaluated by self-assessment and validated by the intendants with the assistance of controllers and directors. Although the *dixième* did raise

95 million *livres* over four years this was far short of the potential yield. For there was no way that the privileged classes were going to entertain the detailed scrutiny of their family affairs that was required, even if the expertise was available to carry it out. In some parts of the country the nobility procrastinated or simply refused to make the necessary declarations. Bonney suggests that the average degree of underassessment was as much as 80 per cent. The *subdélégués*, whose offices at that time were venal, were accused of partiality whilst the determination of the intendants to execute the scheme varied considerably. In the *généralités* of Bordeaux and in Languedoc the tax was transformed into an adjunct to the *taille*. Most of the *pays d'états* negotiated *abonnements* in lieu of the tax, thus subverting its progressive intent. The intensity of upper-class opposition to the *dixième* was sufficient to secure its revocation in the aristocratic reaction which followed the death of Louis XIV.[238]

One of the partial successes in relation to the *dixième* was that overheads were kept to below 10 per cent.[239] This was in striking contrast to the generally soaring costs of servicing the state debt. According to Malet (whose successful financial career ultimately led him to the *Académie Française* and distinction as a *chevalier de l'ordre de St-Michel* and on whose personal archives historians have been dependent ever since), the *rentes* payable on royal revenues, which had been reduced by Colbert to a mere 7 million *livres*, rose to no less than 42 million in 1715. The salary bill had also risen from 16.4 million in 1683 to 37.6 million. Malet, like Loppin and others, believed that it was not the increase in expenditure which had created difficulties for the state but the payment of *gages* and *rentes* on ordinary revenues.[240] It is also striking that during the War of Spanish Succession military expenses peaked in 1706, levelling off thereafter, whilst extraordinary expenditure continued to rise. At the outset of the war the ratio of the latter to the former was approximately 1:4; by the end it was 4:5 (see Figure 6.2). This shifting balance is certainly another manifestation, unfortunately unquantifiable in absolute terms, of the rising costs of servicing the debt.

One of the motivations for the introduction of the *dixième* had been the French government's perception of the advantages gained by the English as result of the land tax introduced in 1692.[241] The founding of the Bank of England two years later caused even deeper reflection. For dependence on private financiers was a costly business. It not only kept interest rates high but offered no way of sustaining a paper money which might have helped resolve the almost perpetual crisis of liquidity. From 1706 recourse was had to paper transactions with *billets de monnaie* in order to overcome the shortage of coinage. Not surprisingly, these served to encourage inflation and diminish confidence.[242] The possibility of establishing a bank was considered by the royal council in 1702, possibly at the behest of John Law, but met with such resistance from within

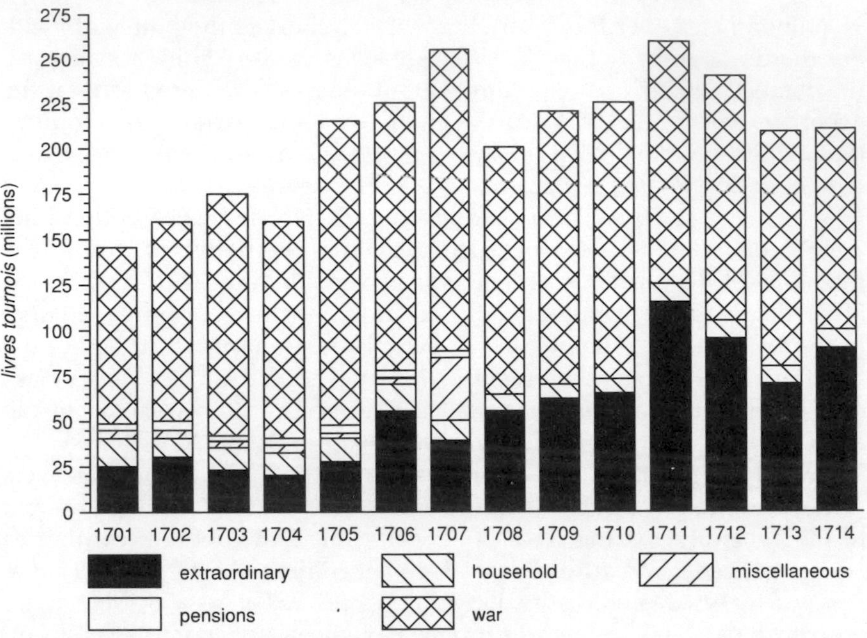

Figure 6.2 French royal expenditure during the War of Spanish Succession, 1701–14

Source: Bonney 1993

and without that all that resulted was an issue of interest-bearing *rentes*.[243] Subsequent proposals were more concerned with raising money for the king than establishing a public bank.[244] In 1708, when Samuel Bernard suggested the establishment of a bank which would take deposits and issue paper money he met with considerable hostility. Objections came, predictably enough, from the receivers general, but also from deputies to the council of commerce. Amongst the arguments deployed was a concern that the bank would not be able to make cash repayments and that, anyway, such a project was not suited to monarchical forms of government.[245] Bernard's project was abandoned in favour of short-term credit operations. In the autumn of 1715 a further plan was offered by John Law; this involved the minting of two million new pieces, many different coins and an equal number of paper pieces. The issuing bank would offer opportunities for investment as well.[246] Amongst those who opposed this plan was Samuel Bernard who brought forward precisely the same objections with which his own proposal had been met.

Lack of confidence in the government, vested interest, sectarian rivalries and mental blockages thus conspired to prevent radical reform of the financial machinery and the fiscal system on which it rested. Structural weaknesses in the French economy also combined with social constraints to limit the Crown's room for manoeuvre. On the one hand, the resistance of the landed classes to investigations of their wealth placed limits on the prospects for a further expansion of direct taxation. On the other hand, the excessive burdens on the labouring population compounded all the structural weaknesses in the French economy, inhibiting both investment and consumption. Yet without economic growth a significant extension of the tax base was not possible. Given the constraints, the French state was actually extraordinarily successful in raising the tax yield to unprecedented heights. It was, however, achieved at great cost to the real economy on which its long-term prospects depended. Towards the end of Louis' interminable reign government legislation continued to reflect the old concerns about tax exemption and the way in which the burden of the *taille* debilitated the populace at large.[247]

There are those who argue that the French state, simply by virtue of the scale of the financial transactions which it stimulated and regulated, was *ipso facto* capitalist. This view is unconvincing not only because of the way in which state fiscalism drained the economy of resources and imposed a punitive level of taxation on the labouring population but also because the money raised was rarely transformed into productive capital. Only a tiny handful of the 534 major financiers investigated by Daniel Dessert in his penetrating investigation of their murky world displayed entrepreneurial interests or abilities. Financiers certainly deployed a proportion of the royal revenues passing through their hands in investments across a range of agricultural, manufacturing and commercial interests. Yet they were governed by essentially speculative and short-term considerations and such investment could all too easily disappear when they over-extended themselves or suffered a political mishap.[248] It did little to bring together capital and skill in a permanent way. The use of finance capital for the construction of the *canal du Midi* stands out as an exceptional success with the huge loans – raised largely from local sources – being repaid by 1712.[249] The metallurgical industries of Dauphiné also appeared to have benefited from a supply of finance capital but it was slow to produce results.[250] On the other hand, it is difficult see what other pattern of development was possible. The huge upward movement of money via the fisc and the constant movement of entrepreneurial capital into *rentier* capital meant that all too often financiers were the only ones who could either lay their hands on sufficient reserves or be induced to invest them.

THE ABSOLUTE STATE IN PERSPECTIVE

The French state was not simply an instrument for repressing the lower classes. However, its capacity to meet both the strains of war and the greed of those who had bought themselves a share of the fiscal system certainly depended on its continuing ability to plunder the productive classes. The fiscal apparatus was at one and the same time a military machine and a spoils system sustained at the expense of the vast majority of the people. Popular unrest cannot, therefore, be gutted of its class or social content because of its primarily anti-fiscal character; it in fact pinpoints with great precision the antagonism between the exploiters and the exploited, between those with influence and those who were powerless. Moreover, although the ruling classes were saved by the limited ideological dimensions of popular unrest from the fate that awaited them in 1789, its impact was certainly a factor in persuading them of the advantages of settling their own differences. Conflict between sectional interests rooted in lineage, clan, corps, community and faction had destabilised the country for a century or more. The great achievement – if it can be described as such – of French absolutism was the accommodation of the sectarian divisions amongst the upper classes within a comparatively stable regime which still continued to serve their interests. They now fought out their frequently interminable and inconclusive disputes over successions and property, money and office within a judicial system so complex that it was not always understood by the lawyers let alone the litigants. Moreover, like the fiscal apparatus, it was thoroughly venal and patrimonial in character, the property of those who controlled it. At the apex of the system the king, through his council, both reflected and maintained the irredeemable confusion of public and private interest by combining the functions of supreme judge, bureaucrat and ultimate dispenser of all patronage. Often it was impossible to distinguish the exercise of one from the other.

Central to all this was the elevation of the person of the king. In part his increased authority was an illusion, disguising the compromise made in the post-Fronde years with the powerful forces that had so rocked the kingdom. Yet, inasmuch as the illusion was indispensable to the stabilisation and legitimisation of the regime, it was real enough. The myth so carefully created by the royal image-makers became part of the fabric of French absolutism without which it would have certainly been different and infinitely more vulnerable. Although there remained sections of the nobility who yearned for a return to more representative and consultative modes of monarchical government, on the whole the French upper classes came to terms with the changing world. In part this was because, as the experience of the Fronde made clear, they no longer had the military capacity to plunge the kingdom back into the chaos of the sixteenth century. Nobles also discovered that they could benefit from the enhanced prestige of their king. However, to conceive of the changing relationship between king and nobility simply in terms of a power relationship, of domination and obedience, is to miss the significance of the vital shifts in noble culture which made absolutism possible and gave the regime a resilience without which it is difficult to explain how it survived for so long. As valour gave way to a certain discretion and the heroic yielded to the stoic, the nobility developed a modified aristocratic mode of behaviour and a set of values perfectly in tune with the requirements of the political regime. In the process, potentially subversive ideas, whereby virtue was related to merit and education, were confronted, transformed and incorporated within a restructured conception of nobility. Significantly, this hegemonic counter-offensive was aided and abetted by middle-class writers who revealed the general inability of their own milieu to shake off the prevailing noble ethos. Although the inherited religious and Aristotelian cosmology was undoubtedly under strain and there were indications of emergent bourgeois ideas, these were far too limited and fragmented to constitute a coherent alternative to the dominant ideology."

The old idea that Justice and Religion were the mainstays of the monarchy demonstrated an impressive resilience. Whilst the concept of enlightened self-interest had entered philosophical discussion, it was not yet perceived how this could be the driving force of human society and made compatible with the general good. Such a conclusion was precluded partly by the pervasiveness of Augustinian convictions about the inherent sinfulness of men but perhaps most of all by the remarkable resilience of the traditional cosmology with its concomitant assumptions about natural inequality, rank and order. As long as rights pertained to these and liberties were equated with privileges it was impossible to imagine, let alone construct, a bourgeois world of formally equal individuals. And, as has been seen, a critical element in the formation of absolutism was precisely a renewed emphasis on rank and degree; at first a reaction to the disturbing upward social mobility (both real and perceived) of the sixteenth century it was consolidated by the increasing sclerosis of the social arteries after 1650.

Versailles was the ultimate expression of the absolutist regime and of the social pressures which made it. It was both court and government where the public and private were inseparable. By the same token it was a society in which, notwithstanding the snootiness of some courtiers, the material interests and social comportment of robe and sword were drawn even closer together. It was also the home of the very large royal family, sustained by the largest domestic household in France, whose concern over lineage and blood exemplified that of every noble line. In its preoccupation with rank, order and etiquette, underpinned by an elaborate system of patronage, Versailles embodied some of the most deep-seated pressures in French society. Together with the legal system the Court was the most important vector of relationships between king and ruling class. The concentration of patronage in royal hands combined with an extraordinarily systematic use of the arts for political purposes also meant that, although cultural activity was to be found outside Versailles, the culture of France was overwhelmingly a court culture, reflecting and consolidating, largely through the classical idiom, a pervasive aristocratic ethos. At the same time the Court was flexible enough to welcome a reprobate like Molière into its fold.

Versailles symbolised the regime's failure as well as its success. There was no more eloquent testimony to the 'unmediated cohabitation' of power, wealth and status in the *ancien régime*, nor of the gulf which had opened up between rulers and ruled, between rich and poor, between those with influence and those without.[251] Its creation at a time of economic stagnation (despite the admonitions of Colbert), as well as its detached physical isolation, reveals how ill-equipped the regime was to grapple with those issues on which its future success and stability would depend: administrative efficiency, healthy finances, mercantile strength and the prosperity of its people. Although all of these issues were addressed by the most far-sighted of government advisers and agents, they were not themes that inspired the royal image-makers or sat easily with the aristocratic virtues incarnated at Versailles. At best Louis was represented as the bringer of Order and Abundance; but on those increasingly rare occasions when he visited the capital city the poor were kept from sight as he advanced. Whilst absolute monarchy brought a period of stability and even magnificence to the *ancien régime* it was beyond its powers to transform the socio-economic order on which it depended and in whose image it was created. Despite its natural wealth and human resources, its long coastlines and great ports, France's defeat in the War of Spanish Succession made it apparent, as the long reign of Louis XIV drew to a close, that the realm was ill-equipped to sustain the long struggle for world supremacy which was to dominate the following decades.

In this struggle France was to meet defeat at the hands of a country a third of its size, which prior to 1650 had been of little military account and was renowned for its political instability. It was a blow from which the *ancien régime* never recovered and a victory for capitalism as momentous as that of 1989; as such, it was also the denouement of the qualitatively different paths of development followed by the two great powers, increasingly divergent in their state structures, political culture and economic organisation. The contrast between France and England provides the ultimate demonstration that absolutism had far more to do with restoring an old order than creating a new one.

7

FRANCE, ENGLAND AND THE CAPITALIST ROAD

ENGLAND'S ECONOMIC SUPREMACY

The historical development of England and France, as François Crouzet has recently reminded us, has had much in common.[1] Early examples of nation states, both subject to violent internal revolutions and sharing a common pool of political ideas, they were also leading imperial powers blessed with a comparatively high degree of prosperity. Yet their interlocking evolutions have aroused as much suspicion as amity on both sides of the Channel and no one familiar with both cultures can doubt that the divergences are often more striking than the similarities. The English experience of living in large cities and working in large factories has produced rhythms of work and patterns of behaviour far removed from the culture of a country which into the twentieth century remained a nation of peasants and artisans. Even today this social terminology has a usage and resonance in French life and politics whilst it means nothing in the British context. Similarly, the long endeavour to impose centralised forms of government on a highly disparate amalgam of provinces has nurtured both a fondness for and an antipathy to bureaucratic solutions whilst the relative homogeneity of English society fostered (until the Thatcherite onslaught on the autonomy of civil institutions) a much less tense relationship between national and local government, the central state and its subordinate elements. Significant differences in social and political evolution have been further compounded by divergent religious traditions which have left their mark on a range of phenomena such as attitudes to work, the family, education and the relationship between church and state. Above all, the wealth generated by industry and empire made possible a degree of domestic comfort and provision of public services in Britain that the French state was, until the rapid transformations of the last thirty years, either unable or unwilling to sustain.

Such reflections on the differences between the two countries have a long historical pedigree. Awareness of them, particularly in relation to questions of government, taxation and general prosperity, can be detected from the end of the Middle Ages. In the seventeenth and eighteenth centuries they entered the consciousness not only of enquiring tourists but also of politicians, philosophers and economists. Some no doubt, like those English parliamentarians who feared they would share the fate of the Estates-General, exaggerated for political effect. But many Frenchmen were also sure that the English regime was of a very different sort from that to which they were accustomed. The ambassador to the court of Charles II wondered what Aristotle would have made of a monarchy which despite its appearance was very far from being one.[2] Montesquieu, Voltaire, Rousseau and the physiocrats all found inspiration in the English experience which in their several ways they perceived to be different from their own. Nothing conveys this more vividly than Voltaire's *Lettres Philosophiques*.[3] In these Voltaire presented with journalistic flair those facets of English politics and culture which provided the most striking contrasts with his native land: the parliamentary system of government, an aristocracy with virtually no privileges but a willingness to engage in commerce, religious toleration and diversity, and, last and by no means least, a culture of scientific enquiry.

In recent years it has become fashionable either to ignore or to devalue the admittedly impressionistic but voluminous observations of contemporaries about the distinctiveness of English developments. The effect of this approach is to take away the most obvious explanation of how it came about that England, which, prior to the late seventeenth century, was a second-rate power beset by political instability, proved able to outpace and outfight the world's most powerful country. That explanation lies in the fact that on the verge of industrialisation, England had become Europe's most prosperous country with a revamped and exceptionally effective fiscal machine which enabled its government to mobilise unprecedented sums. This itself was made possible by a precocious development of capitalism and the concomitant creation of a state apparatus and government in which England's capitalists had confidence. These developments provide not only a major part of the explanation for the crisis which finally overwhelmed the *ancien régime* but a comparative perspective within which to further assess the structural weaknesses in the French economy.

For some, the attempt to minimise the differences between France and England is a continuation of the long-standing endeavour to deny the revolutionary nature of the economic and political developments of the seventeenth century which prepared the way for England's ascendancy. Hence Jonathan Clark's extreme contention that the term *ancien régime* is an appropriate description of eighteenth-century English society.[4] His analysis, which might be thought to reveal a limited grasp of European realities, has gained some credence because of distinct but pertinent work by those economic historians who have challenged the traditional conception of England's industrial revolution. Such has been their emphasis on the slow pace of technical progress and of social change that the industrialisation of England has come close to losing its revolutionary character.[5] In recent years a number of economic historians have pushed the argument even further with an attempt to show that French economic growth in the eighteenth century was virtually as rapid as that of England. According to some, this growth was so rapid that, by the eve of the Revolution, per capita production and income were as high, if not higher, in France – a view which challenges every common-sense deduction about her relative position. Markovitch's exhaustive study of French textiles led him to conclude that France was the world's leading industrial power.[6] A less controversial way of demoting Britain's industrial supremacy is to adopt the now common view that economic modernisation was achieved by a variety of routes, all of which had something to contribute to the net result and none of which was inherently superior or more advanced.[7] Ironically, one of the consequences of the attempt to place French economic growth on a par with that of England in the eighteenth century is to rehabilitate the traditional notion that the way was prepared for the French Revolution by the maturation of a bourgeoisie within the framework of the *ancien régime*. As a result of the endeavour to minimise the progress of capitalism in England, the French bourgeoisie, virtually excluded from the field of play by some Marxists, as well as by revisionist historians, looks as though it might reappear in the first division.

There is little doubt that from about 1720 France did show renewed economic buoyancy. Subsistence crises became less frequent and less acute; grain prices, though far from stable, oscillated less wildly. Mortality rates improved, resulting in a steady, if not dramatic, annual increase in the population of about 0.3 per cent which, in the absence of significant urbanisation, was largely sustained by the countryside itself. Although more impressionistic, there is clear evidence of a quickening of domestic trade. In 1678, for instance, the number of boats on the Loire at Orléans was 400; a century later 1,600 left Digoin.[8] The ducal owner of the road tolls at Vienne saw his revenue increase by 614 per cent between 1726 and 1788.[9] Foreign trade, which had already displayed a degree of immunity from the economic malaise of Louis XIV's reign, developed with élan. There seems little reason to dispute the claim that it quadrupled between 1716 and 1788, growing at an aggregate rate of 3.1 per cent per annum which exceeded that of England's overseas trade. On the eve of the Revolution French foreign trade was valued at 1062 million *livres* compared to England's £775 million.[10] According to Crouzet, even the export of British manufactures increased no faster than that of the French.[11] Perhaps the most visible sign of economic vitality in France was the doubling in size of its two great

Atlantic ports, Bordeaux and Nantes. Bordeaux grew from 45,000 in 1700 to 110,000 on the eve of the Revolution, reflecting a prodigous tenfold increase in France's colonial trade.[12] The figures for industry and manufacturing, although less dramatic and more treacherous, point in the same direction. According to Léon, coal output increased by 700 to 800 per cent and iron production by 468 per cent between 1720 and 1790 compared with a mere doubling of output in England. The production of Rouen cottons rose by over 100 per cent and the number of silk looms in Lyon, by 185 per cent.[13] Cloth production at Sedan increased by an estimated 1.4 per cent per annum between 1731 and 1785.[14] All in all, Crouzet thinks that industrial production in France and England grew at much the same rate of around 1.1 per cent annually down to 1790; Butel offers a figure of 1.5, and Léon an even higher one.[15] Given the almost insuperable problems involved in calculating eighteenth-century growth rates with this sort of precision, the most rational course of action is probably to split the difference.

It is, in any event, clear that the presentation of these figures requires considerable qualification. Some of them, most obviously for coal, simply reflect a very low starting point; despite its rapid growth French output was never within sight of matching that of England even in global terms. France also produced less non-ferrous metals, ships and cotton products. Moreover, the whole comparison looks very different if it is extended by one or two decades. English iron production, stymied until mid-century by the technical bottleneck created by the shortage of wood, suddenly took off. Between 1757 and 1788 production grew by 40 per cent each decade; between 1788 and 1806 it doubled again.[16] Much of the growth in French textiles also came in the first half of the century after which there were signs of renewed stagnation in many of the major textile centres, notably Amiens, Beauvais and Rouen. With the ending of the protective regime in Languedoc the production of quality cloth proved unable to survive the pressures of English competition in the markets of the Middle East.[17]

More seriously, the extreme revisions of output and income have been established using figures now widely considered to be unreliable. This is particularly true of Toutain's exaggerated view of a 65 per cent increase in grain output between 1700–10 and 1780–90 which temporarily misled people into a search for a revolution in French agriculture.[18] There now seems to be something of a consensus on Le Roy Ladurie's estimate of a 40 per cent increase between 1715 and 1789. Even this modification does not cope with the problem created by using aggregate figures which have not always been deflated to take account of either price or population figures. Riley's reworking of the figures on this basis led him to conclude that the per capita annual growth in agricultural output was 0.4 per cent, just exceeding that of the population, 0.33 in wool cloth production and between 1 and 1.7 in foreign trade.[19] Such figures undoubtedly lend credence to Crouzet's contention, steadfastly maintained amidst the conflicting estimates, that whilst rhythms of growth in the two countries may have been similar there was no question of France catching up in per capita output or income.[20]

It is a conclusion amply justified both by contemporary observations about England's greater prosperity, and by more objective economic criteria. Even the most revisionist of quantitative historians accept that in the 1780s real wages may have been as much as a third higher in England.[21] Moreover, this was in the context of a massive surge in population. In 1715 the total population of England, Scotland and Wales was just over seven million; by 1765 it had topped the eight million mark before taking off with abandon to surpass ten million by the end of the century. The French population was an estimated 22,000,000 in 1700, 24,600,000 in 1740 and 28,600,000 by 1790. The modesty of this growth is brought home by Dupâquier's estimate that from constituting 18 per cent of the European total, the French population dropped to just under 16 per cent. What is more, the proportion of France's urban population barely changed over the course of the eighteenth century.[22] In 1789 those living in cities of over 10,000 accounted for 9 per cent of the population, more or less what the figure had been at the beginning of the century. Using the same criteria England's urban population rose from just over a tenth of its total to 17.5 per cent between 1670 and 1750 and to almost a quarter in 1800. Over half the total urban growth in Europe during this period occurred in England, a country with less than 8 per cent of Europe's population.[23]

At this point the contrasting fortunes of France and England become sharpest. For urban expansion could not and did not take place without a significant increase in agricultural output and, indeed, in productivity. This appears to have come in the late seventeenth and early eighteenth century when French output was stagnating. Between 1670 and 1750 the number of people supported by 100 members of the agricultural workforce rose from an estimated 165 to 219. By the mid-eighteenth century it is possible that a majority of the English population were engaged in non-agricultural work.[24] Wrigley estimated that the 'rural agricultural' population fell from around 70 per cent of the total in 1600 to 55 per cent by 1700 and to 36.25 per cent in 1800. On the basis of these figures, and allowing for net exports or imports of foodstuffs, Chartres concludes that there was a doubling of labour productivity in farming over the period.[25]

Despite the improved prospects for some parts of the peasantry French agriculture proved unable either to match the progress of England or to provide sufficient dynamism to overcome the obstacles to self-sustained growth. True, an expansion of the area of cultivated land, better distribution of grain, an easing of the tax burden, stable monetary conditions and less competition from urban purchasers of the land made it possible to sustain the modest rise in population. But productivity stagnated.[26] Grain yields of between 5:1 and 8:1 remained the norm throughout large areas of the country. Even in the fertile plain of the Tarn and Garonne they did not exceed this. Significantly better results were obtained in the Beauvaisis and Picardy where soil and climate resembled those of England. Yet, even here, it did not prove possible to match English wheat yields which were greater by an estimated 28 per cent. In general, yields were an estimated 40 to 50 per cent higher in England.[27] An increase in agricultural experimentation can be detected in some French regions, particularly after 1760, but its impact was limited. Continuous rotation was practised in Artois and Flanders, specialised beef production in the Charolais, and by 1778 the potato crop in Alsace was matching that of grain.[28] The diffusion of the potato, however, was a century behind that achieved not only in England but also in Ireland.[29] Measures to limit communal grazing rights and make possible some enclosing of the land, at least to protect clovers and fodder crops, were tardy and hesitant. In 1766 the intendants of Languedoc authorised proprietors to enclose a fifth of their holdings in each parish provided that they were artificial grassland.[30] The same year the *procureur* of the *parlement* of Rouen suggested the extension to other parts of France of the usage established in Normandy whereby 'it suffices for the proprietor or tenant of a property to plant in one or two places only a few branches with strings of straw to indicate his intention of forbidding access'.[31] Progress towards a more intensive agriculture was slow. As late as 1840 as much as 27 per cent of arable land may still have been under fallow.[32]

For most of the peasantry economic prospects changed little. Genuinely independent peasants with a marketable surplus were certainly in a position to benefit from rising prices. It is reasonable to assume that these contributed to a growing demand from the better-off peasantry for manufactured articles; but most peasants remained on the margins of such activity.[33] Moreover, whilst agricultural prices rose by about two-thirds to three-quarters between the 1730s and 1780s, rents doubled. So even those tenants with commercial leases were left at a disadvantage.[34] Income from tithes and feudal dues was also maximised. In 1741 the cathedral chapter of Rouen collected a quarter of its revenues in tithe; by 1789 this had risen to 54 per cent. In the Seine Maritime the Marquisate of Granville in 1711 received 12 per cent of its revenue in seigneurial dues; by 1777 this proportion had almost doubled.[35] The impoverishment and expropriation of the peasantry thus continued, albeit at a generally slower pace, but much faster in the north than the south. On the eve of the Revolution, in parts of Anjou nearly 90 per cent of peasant proprietors owned less than one *hectare*. Around Laon three-quarters of them held less than one and a half. About a quarter of the peasantry of the Beauce and Gâtinais were non-proprietors; at Versailles over half. In such cases possession of a cottage and garden, possibly a few cows and sheep and access to grazing land, prevented total expropriation.[36]

The continuing inability of the economy to absorb this potential labour force was also manifest. Despite a degree of proto-industrialisation, in 1786 it was estimated that there were over four million people (nearly 15 per cent of the population) whose subsistence was not ensured for one month.[37] Two years later the structural weaknesses of the French economy reasserted themselves in a major subsistence crisis which sent grain prices soaring with traumatic consequences for the textile industry and those dependent on it.[38] A large part of France's population were still locked into social structures which continued to prevent them, as it had done for two centuries, from contributing to economic development either as producers or consumers.

Nor, despite vigorous growth, was France's commercial sector powerful enough to transform the situation. Significant foreign trade was confined to a handful of centres. Between them Bordeaux and Marseille accounted for virtually half the value of the country's exports and imports.[39] The colonial trade was concentrated almost entirely in four ports (Bordeaux, Marseille, Nantes and Havre-Rouen), making it highly vulnerable during the Seven Years War.[40] With the exception of Paris and Lyon the role of the inland towns and regions in France's export trade was diminutive. In 1787 the nine inland *généralités* provided less than 3 per cent.[41] Moreover, despite a significant rise in the quantity and value of manufactured exports, the part played by them in France's export trade remained constant. Whilst the commercial activity of Bordeaux provided a stimulus to the manufacturers of its hinterland, commerce and industry together sustained only 600,000 to 700,000 of the five million inhabitants of south-western France.[42] In 1787 industrial exports accounted for just 40 per cent of France's colonial trade compared with two-thirds of that of England.[43] On the other hand, the relative importance of colonial re-exports doubled between 1716 and 1787 by when they accounted for a third of all exports. The most important single commodity was sugar which alone constituted three-quarters of French colonial trade.[44] Bordeaux re-exported 87 per cent of sugar, 95 per cent of its coffee and 76 per cent of its indigo.[45] Furthermore, much of the trade with northern Europe was still not in French hands. Every one of 273 boats arriving in Amsterdam in 1786 from France was Dutch.[46]

It may well be that dependence on foreigners was more damaging to French commerce than the dependence on a limited range of commodities. For had not London built its commercial prosperity in the last half of the seventeenth century on the exchange of a narrow range of colonial goods? By 1700 40 per cent of its exports were re-exports and for a significant period after 1660 – as with France a century later – the sugar islands were the most valuable source of imports.[47] Not until the 1720s did the diversifying power of colonial markets begin to make itself felt. By this time England had already established a lead in the value of her trade per capita which France never overcame.[48] As Brenner has stressed, the critical factor was that practically from the moment when the English set out to challenge first the Portuguese and Spanish and then the Dutch, the import trade was controlled by English traders and shippers.[49]

French industry, whilst displaying areas of significant growth, also failed to transform the basic character of the economy. Cloth and linen manufacture, despite a discernible concentration of capital and control in fewer hands, remained hugely dependent on dispersed labour, much of which constituted a secondary activity for an overwhelmingly agricultural workforce.[50] The production of cottons and *indiennes* lent itself to greater physical concentration of plant and workforce and this was evident from the 1770s.[51] Yet even here it was a question of degree. The nineteen *fabriques* of Mulhouse, whose output of *indiennes* soared between 1758 and 1784, had an average of fifty-three printing tables. But throughout Alsace cotton spinning remained dependent for several decades to come on small-scale domestic activity.[52] The labour-intensive character of French manufactures, made possible by the availability of a large pool of cheap labour, partly explains the slowness with which mechanisation occurred. By 1790 there were only an estimated 1,000 spinning jennies in France compared with 20,000 in England; at the Revolution only eight establishments appear to have been using Arkwright's waterframe compared with 200 in England.[53] Exceptions to the general picture were provided by one or two major industrial enterprises. Le Creusot, founded in 1782 with royal help and the involvement of Wilkinson, boasted 4,000 investors, four high furnaces, two large forges and several steam engines. The Anzin Coal Company, of which the Duc de Croy was a director, employed 4,000 workers and ran twelve steam engines at the Revolution.[54]

As these figures suggest, the diffusion of technical innovations was slow and demonstrably much slower than in England. This was most obvious perhaps in the application of fuel coal technology which, with the exception of wrought iron, had been 'achieved throughout British industry' by 1710.[55] In part, this contrast reflected the poor quality of France's own coal and the increasingly heavy duties imposed on English imports.[56] Given that coal-fired furnaces required two and half times to three times as much capital as wood-burning ones, such additional costs were hardly conducive to experimentation. Shortly after 1700 some attempts were made to copy English practices by making dark brown or black bottles in coal-burning furnaces; but there were only four furnaces of this type in existence in 1720. It is also apparent that there were technical obstacles to a more general substitution of coal for wood by the glass-making industry. For, although the problem of preventing coal-smoke discolouring glass had been overcome in England in 1612 by using covered crucibles, these were not found in France before 1740 and not to any significant degree until after the Revolution. The Plate Glass Company used wood right up to the Revolution.[57]

Despite similar problems and hesitations in relation to the development of appropriate furnaces, coal seems to have been somewhat more readily used for iron production. All the anchor-producing forges of the Nivernais were using it, for instance, in 1694. Yet, as the eighteenth century wore on, the technological gap between France and England widened to enormous proportions, particularly after the – initially hesitant – diffusion of Darby's discovery of coke. A commission was sent to England in 1756 to investigate uses of coke technology and subsequently to Germany and Scandinavia. But the first industrial application of coke to smelting did not take place (at Le Creusot) until fifty years after its discovery.[58] Even then, notwithstanding the help of William Wilkinson, the transfer of technology was barely successful. Le Creusot coke-pig was apparently of very poor quality; at the cannon foundry of Indret-sur-Loire, it was dearer than English pig-iron despite the active involvement of Wilkinson. In the early revolutionary period Le Creusot resorted to making bronze guns, importing charcoal iron for guns and using cast iron only for shot and ballast.[59] The arms crisis was further compounded by the poor quality of French 'natural' steel which was derived from pig iron. Yet the process of cementation, which was critical for the manufacture of fine steel, had been imported from Germany into England as early as 1613. Increasingly concerned, the French government dispatched official commissions and industrial spies to the steel-making centres of England; but in 1788, the French *bureau de commerce* was still bewailing the inability to produce steel to English standards. Similar problems were encountered in the transplanting of English technology for the production of non-ferrous alloys, rolled silver plate, and gilded manufactures. Even when established the resulting products could not compete with English ones in terms of price.[60]

According to John Harris, from whom these examples have been drawn, the essential problem was that the French were trying to accomplish in decades 'the quiet and unsung changes which had taken Britain on an increasingly divergent technological path for well over a century'.[61] The broad band of techniques and associated craft skills which had been built up simply could not be replicated on demand. For 'craft knowledge is untidy, compounded of visual judgments and manual knacks'. This was why England had such a minute technological literature.[62] In

France, by contrast, a *dirigiste* state struggled to provide by direction and exhortation what spontaneity failed to provide. At the forefront of this endeavour was a prolonged and systematic investigation by the Academy of Sciences of a remarkable array of machines and devices from clocks to canal locks and candle makers to steam engines.[63] Yet the Academy's concept of utility was narrow and largely divorced from the world of practising craftsmen. Some of the most prominent experimental scientists were also excluded from its ranks whilst its pre-eminence had a damaging effect on other centres of activity.[64] Even the members of the officially sponsored, but short-lived, Académie de Caen found the problems of coping with their patrons and the Parisian Academy demoralising.[65] Attitudes had not improved much by the 1730s when the Academy destroyed the rival *société des arts* which did intend to admit artisans and devote itself to inventions.[66] Not surprisingly, the most important technological advance of Louis XIV's reign – that for rolling molten glass – was made by a trade professional with no scientific background.[67] Persistent and pointed criticisms about the detached and intellectual approach of the academicians were still being heard in the early years of the Revolution.[68]

The divide that separated theoretician from craftsman was not simply the result of academic elitism. It also reflected the general attachment to guild organisation and a strict demarcation between crafts. Artisans were particularly anxious to preserve trade secrets. In the vital area of instrument manufacture it proved necessary, as late as 1774, to create a special corps of instrument makers so that different skills could be brought together.[69] Once again, the contrast with England, whence came much of the inspiration for a Royal Academy, is telling. For there, a Royal Academician like Hooke was able to divide his time between investigating balance wheels for watches, improving pumps, and the inverse square law.

Of course the slow assimilation and diffusion of new technologies were not the sole cause of France's failure to keep pace with England. They do, however, provide a measure of the differences in the quality and pace of economic development. By 1700 England had already seized a lead in trade, a commanding colonial position, and superiority in the manufacture of textiles and in agricultural productivity. Her per capita output and income were already greater. France's problem in the eighteenth century was to catch up whereas England had reached a point at which further growth was unlikely to be made without a technological breakthrough.[70] Much of the pressure for innovation can be attributed to the demands of England's growing home market combined with a shortage of labour in some sectors of the economy. On the eve of industrialisation Braudel thinks that British domestic trade was of perhaps four or five times the volume of foreign trade and recent estimations are that four-fifths of industrial output was consumed at home.[71] By contrast, the vast reservoir of cheap labour in France both imposed severe limits on home demand and diminished the incentive to introduce new technologies. Breaking out of this vicious circle was to be a protracted business. The French worker, Frederick Le Play observed in 1846, suffered not only from the greater cost of his tools compared with the English worker 'who buys excellent tools very cheaply' but also from the loss of time resulting from his defective equipment.[72]

It is crucial to remember in the midst of this negative assessment of France's economic fortunes that her aggregate output and colonial interests made her a wealthy country. The economy undoubtedly grew in the eighteenth century. There was also a significant advance, particularly from mid-century, in bourgeois culture; it may be discerned in the reduction in the size of upper-class households and changing concepts of the family, in the rise of the novel, in the reception of Lockian conceptions of government and, above all, in physiocratic political economy which all served to undermine the ideological hegemony of the absolutist regime. It did not, of course, do this without arousing the deepest anxiety and resistance. But it is possible that had the economy been able – in some hypothetical way – to develop free from the pressure of competition with England its progress would have certainly been less troubled and more rapid. Unfortunately this was not an option. Whatever utility there may be in recognising the validity of different routes to modernity, its historical benchmark in the eighteenth century was provided by England. French politicians, soldiers, economists and intellectuals had little choice but to measure their country's performance against that of her major rival. In competing with England for global supremacy the structural weaknesses of the *ancien régime* became unmanageable. The Revolution and Revolutionary wars which followed may have removed the legal and institutional impediments to the operation of the free market but they certainly deepened and prolonged the economic crisis in most sectors of the economy. In addition, by contributing to the survival of a large but none too prosperous peasantry the Revolution precluded a rapid development of capitalism; the already remote chance of matching England's performance was gone.[73]

THE MODERNISATION OF THE ENGLISH STATE

Perhaps the ultimate demonstration of the fact that the English population was indeed generating a greater level of wealth per capita was the ability of the English state to mobilise unprecedented resources in order to pursue its global ambitions.

From the end of the seventeenth century the English state acquired with great rapidity a fiscal bureaucratic apparatus which, like that of its rival, was geared to continuous and large-scale warfare. In 1688 there were an estimated 10,000 officeholders and public servants; by the 1720s 12,000 and 16,000 forty years later.[74] Central to this expansion was the even more marked increase in fiscal officials. Numbering only 1,200 in 1660 – itself an increase on pre-Civil War days – there were already 2,500 by 1688. In the following hundred years the excise administration grew fourfold, becoming larger by the 1720s than all the other revenue departments together. By the American War the Excise alone was as big as the entire fiscal bureaucracy had been in 1688.[75]

Even though this rapid expansion of the fiscal system did not bring the weight of the British bureaucracy up the level of the French one, it more than matched French efforts to raise the tax yield. Revenue doubled between 1688 and 1697 and went up by a further 75 per cent between 1702 and 1714.[76] According to O'Brien, taxation took 3.4 per cent of national income in 1665, 8.8 in 1700 and 10.8 by 1720.[77] This massive increase – considerably higher than that achieved by either the French or the Dutch during the same period and in excess of the underlying economic growth – set the pattern for the next century. Down to 1789 the English taxpayer paid about twice as much as his French counterpart; the difference was to become even greater during the Napoleonic wars. Moreover, the real tax burden, measured as a proportion of either per capita income or aggregate commodity output, whilst rising in England, probably fell in France after 1735.[78] By the period of the Napoleonic wars Britain was, for the first time, raising more revenue in absolute terms, thus putting the comparative trends beyond all doubt.[79]

Between 1692 and 1713 the most important contribution to the English government's revenues was made by the land tax; at one point it accounted for an impressive 40 per cent of the total. Thereafter, until the wars against Napoleon once again demanded a sacrifice from the landed classes, the excise brought in between 40 and 50 per cent, and the customs and land tax around 20 per cent each.[80] The weight of Britain's rising tax burden was therefore borne by domestic industry and services. Despite an attempt to minimise the incidence of taxation on basic necessities, notably food and plain clothing, and the inclusion of upper-class luxuries, the excise tax was a fundamentally regressive tax. It fell on articles of daily consumption, many of which were indispensable: salt, beer, candles, coal, soap, leather, glass, and bricks. By and large the effort was sustained by the middling ranks of British society.[81] That it was accomplished without generating significant unrest reflects not only the careful calibration of the burdens falling on different commodities and social groups but also a widening tax base, the increasingly rapid circulation of goods and their comparatively low real costs. In France by contrast, despite a 90 per cent increase in income from the General Farm between 1726 and 1774, the contributions of indirect and direct taxes were roughly equal. Moreover, 70 per cent of the yield from indirect taxes came from impositions on wine, salt and tobacco; in 1750 a quarter of the General Farm revenues came from the *gabelle* alone.[82]

The inescapable conclusion is that England possessed a much more diversified and prosperous home market, generating a level of demand capable of responding to the unprecedented fiscal demands. The economic and social physiognomy of France, on the other hand, imposed severe limitations on the room for fiscal manoeuvre. Constrained by the narrowness of the tax base as far as indirect taxes were concerned, the possibility of raising much more from direct taxes was also limited by the hostility of the privileged classes to any effective investigation of their wealth.[83] In the aftermath of the War of Spanish Succession the French government temporarily solved the problem of its massive debt of 2,600 million *livres* level by writing off a substantial proportion and bringing down interest rates. This achievement was completely ruined by the demands of the Seven Years War during which the *parlement* of Paris vigorously reasserted its right to register fiscal edicts. After the war, despite widespread demands for fiscal reform, the fear that the proposed national survey of land holdings would amount to an assault on liberty left the upper classes in a state of paralysis. When Turgot assumed office as *contrôleur-général* in 1774 he warned the king that without retrenchment 'the first gunshot will drive the state to bankruptcy'. Just before his fall two years later he opposed the intervention in America on the grounds that the cost would defeat all hope of financial reform without damaging Great Britain. 'On both counts,' Doyle comments, 'time proved him right.'[84]

Of course, neither England nor France relied directly on tax revenues to fund their wars. In the four wars undertaken by England between 1702 and 1783 three-quarters of the additional amounts that were required came from loans.[85] The governments of both countries borrowed on the strength of deferred taxation. By 1788 debt service in England, as in France, consumed about 60 per cent of tax revenues.[86] Most striking, given these similarities, was the fact that the ratio of debt to GNP in England was possibly twice that of France. French observers found it difficult to understand how England could sustain a debt of such size.[87] Yet the unsuccessful endeavours to found a bank in France along the lines of the Bank of England suggest that some, at least, appreciated very quickly the significance of this new institution. Confidence in it was such that within a few months of its establishment it was able to advance the not inconsiderable sum of 1.2 million pounds, partly in cash and partly in notes.[88] Whilst the French system of credit was virtually paralysed by masses of *billets de monnaie* circulating at debilitating discounts, the successful development of exchequer bills also produced stability in the short-term credit market.[89] English interest rates, which were at 10–14 per cent in the 1690s, were down to 5–6 per cent by the early 1700s.[90]

What really distinguished the funding of the English national debt, both from French practice and from that adopted previously by Parliament, was its permanent character. When Parliament had passed the first act to raise money by long-term lending in 1693 it still undertook to repay part of capital with the interest; in other words the debt would eventually be liquidated. With the establishment of the Bank of England the bulk of the national debt acquired a perpetual character and lenders received only their interest funded by taxation. Such was the security offered by this system that, during the American revolutionary war, the British government was able to borrow at 3 per cent, making the annual repayments entirely manageable. The French government, on the other hand, moved in the opposite direction, largely abandoning perpetual *rentes* in favour of short-term and life contingent loans. The first five loans floated in the Seven Years War for a total of 168 million *livres* were all repaid by life annuities. Moreover, a lack of actuarial expertise, reflective of the comparative immaturity of French financial practices, led the government to offer excessive rates of return; interest rates were twice as high as those paid by the British government. Although these annuities were abandoned in 1770, at least 30 per cent of the debt service in 1788 was for the amortisation of debts incurred during the Seven Years War. This sort of borrowing, which, not surprisingly, proved to be highly popular, was also politically sensitive because it made it difficult to write off the debt by defaulting in the traditional manner. After 1780, whilst the confidence of those on whom the French government had depended ebbed away, the British fiscal system went from strength to strength with the establishment of the Sinking Fund, the Consolidated Revenue Fund and improved public accounts.[91]

By French standards England's fiscal bureaucracy was reliable, efficient and non-venal. The move away from private contracting of finance began in 1671 when the customs farm was cancelled and put in Commission; the excise farm went the same way in 1683 and the hearth tax the following year. The system of administration through publicly accountable commissioners was cemented in 1691 with the establishment of a group of members of the Commons as Commissioners of Public Accounts. The right of the Commons to investigate extraordinary expenditures was soon extended to all expenses with the exception of the civil list; the Treasury also became accountable to the Commons. The separation of public and private interest was further guaranteed and symbolised by the exclusion from the Commons of the land tax collectors, salt tax commissioners and the commissioners for customs and excise.[92] As two visiting French officials noted with some surprise in 1713, 'here everything is in commission (*régie*)'.[93] Not until the 1760s did the French government take the first tentative steps towards the reduction of venality in the fiscal administration. The Revolution was about to break when Necker and Lomenie de Brienne finally took measures to sweep away the host of venal treasurers and create a central Treasury commission responsible for the control of all receipts and expenditure.[94]

Nothing illustrates better the different quality of the relationship between private and public interest in the two countries than the establishment of the Bank of England. Not only were its investors guaranteed interest from additional customs and excise duties but the Bank was empowered by statute to borrow money on the security of parliamentary revenue. Such a 'modern' articulation of private interest and investment with public utility and control could not be replicated within the structures of *ancien régime* France. Significantly, one of the things the Bank could not do was to lend money to the king, although he could subscribe like everyone else. Through Parliament the Bank remained firmly under the control of the same class whence its major investments came, yet clearly in the 'public' arena.

A significant consequence of Britain's administrative arrangements was the growth of a tradition of public service. Whilst this was certainly not free from abuse or the power of patronage, or, indeed, the ability of certain families to attach themselves to particular offices, it offered an increasingly stable and professional administrative environment. Its most striking manifestation was the emergence of the professional administrator with a career ladder and graded appointments. As early as 1713 more than half the government offices offered employees a pension scheme.[95] According to O'Brien the excises, which were critical to the performance of the entire system, were 'administered by one of the most professional and efficient bureaucracies available to any government in Europe' which 'anticipated most of the best features of the Victorian civil service'. A certain level of education was required for entry to the service which then provided training. Promotion was on merit and rewarded with 'good salaries, a secure position, bonuses and pensions'.[96]

Whilst these developments within the excise service may have been exceptional, they are indicative of the increasingly autonomous character of public administration. Thus the purges of the excise and other officers which occurred in 1694–5 and in 1715–17 were not repeated. Careers were not ruined by the Jacobite plot of 1723 nor the rebellion of 1745.[97] It seems that even JPs, who continued to administer the shires in a largely voluntary way and were as much beset by absenteeism as any corporation of provincial France, participated in the growing professionalism. Their commissions increased in size whilst the declining attendance of the upper gentry was compensated for by the presence of their lesser brethren. These gave their time in order to oversee the administration of highways, bridges and the policing of rural England. Because they met for such purposes, which were vital for the maintenance of both the communications infrastructure and of good order, in petty rather than general sessions, their proceedings were largely free from disabling political rivalries.[98] The contrast with the persistent confusion of private and public interest which continued to debilitate the French monarchy hardly needs spelling out.

Political stability and confidence were at the heart of the remarkable and rapid development of the British state. Here the contrast is not only with the pre-Revolutionary situation in France where, once again, the monarchy forfeited the confidence of the ruling class in general and its financial backers in particular; it is also with the earlier history of England and the fatal crises engendered by the repeated endeavours of the Stuarts to overcome the constraints on effective monarchical rule. In 1640 Charles I had found it impossible to raise the relatively small sums that would have freed him from parliamentary control; to make matters worse he was pushed around by the citizens of London who effectively made financial assistance conditional on his relinquishing control of the Irish army and on the execution of Strafford.[99] But, by the early eighteenth century, the mercantile elite of London and the Home Counties had become the prime and willing source of public finance. The assets of the landed classes were mobilised as never before for the war against France.[100] France, struggling with a deepening financial morass, obliged to fight both a continental and a maritime war but unable or unwilling to put enough resources into the creation of a navy, found that it was faced with a power which had 'secured its Irish flank, strengthened its financial institutions and rebuilt its army and navy'.[101]

None of this would have been possible had the prolonged conflicts of the previous century failed to resolve themselves in a stable system of government in which the upper classes as a whole could find confidence. That is exactly what the revolutionary moments of 1649 and 1688 were about. For they were the outcome of a collision between two contrary conceptions of government. One was similar to that which prevailed in France; it rested on the simple proposition that authority was divinely bestowed and that the body politic was best regulated by a single person. The other was rooted in the belief that power had its source in the community; it produced a parliamentary system of government, resting on a quite different mode of mediating between public power and private interest. The misfortunes of the Stuarts were a clear demonstration of the fact that the English state was already well launched on a path of development qualitatively different from that which led to Louis XIV.

THE MAKING OF A HOME MARKET

Neither England's modernised state nor the economic order on which it rested were the fortuitous consequence of short-term events and circumstances. There are indeed those who argue that England always had been exceptionally – almost naturally – prosperous and enterprising. Its beneficent climate, Kerridge stresses, was ideal for corn and sheep husbandry and the sale of its unrivalled wool had long ensured a constant supply of good coinage.[102] For Alan Macfarlane a thriving market economy, dominated by independent and individualistic small farmers, in which both land and labour had already become commodities, had existed from at least the thirteenth century (Macfarlane, 1978, *passim*). If such views are not without merit, it would none the less be foolish to claim that England's ultimate economic triumph was in any sense inevitable. Natural resources, as the French experience clearly showed, could easily be plundered and entrepreneurial attitudes inhibited.

There were, indeed, indications that England might run into the sort of blockages that afflicted France. In the middle years of the sixteenth century the country struggled to cope with the distress of the landless and unemployed. This was exacerbated by war against France, military excursions against the Scots, monetary instability and a series of bad harvests. Prices of essential foodstuffs, textiles and fuel rose by 91 per cent between 1508 and 1545.[103] Another period of acute difficulty followed in the 1590s. There were harvest failures of national proportions in 1586, 1594–9, 1623–4 and 1630 with localised difficulties in 1608 and 1614. In the 1620s England showed a vulnerability to subsistence crises 'not known for three centuries' whilst manufacturing was badly affected by the dislocation of home and foreign markets.[104] During these critical decades England also experienced an upward movement of rents, ostensibly as threatening as those recorded across the Channel.[105] There is also evidence to suggest that, as in France, there was a tendency to respond to the pressure on the land by the cultivation of poorer soils. 'A veritable explosion of small holdings' occurred in moorland and upland areas from Lakeland to Devon.[106] A shortage of grazing land in some areas contributed to a rise in the number of smallholders who were left denuded of cattle.[107] Overall, two-thirds of English labourers and cottagers possessed only their houses and garden plots. The proportion of the population classified as indigent was not very different from that in France; at moments of crisis it could rise to include half the members of a community.[108]

Plague was far from unknown. In London a quarter of the population died of it in 1563; it hit again in 1593, 1603, 1625, and in 1665 when between a fifth and eight of the population was lost. Norwich had six major epidemics between 1579 and 1665; Bristol lost a sixth of its

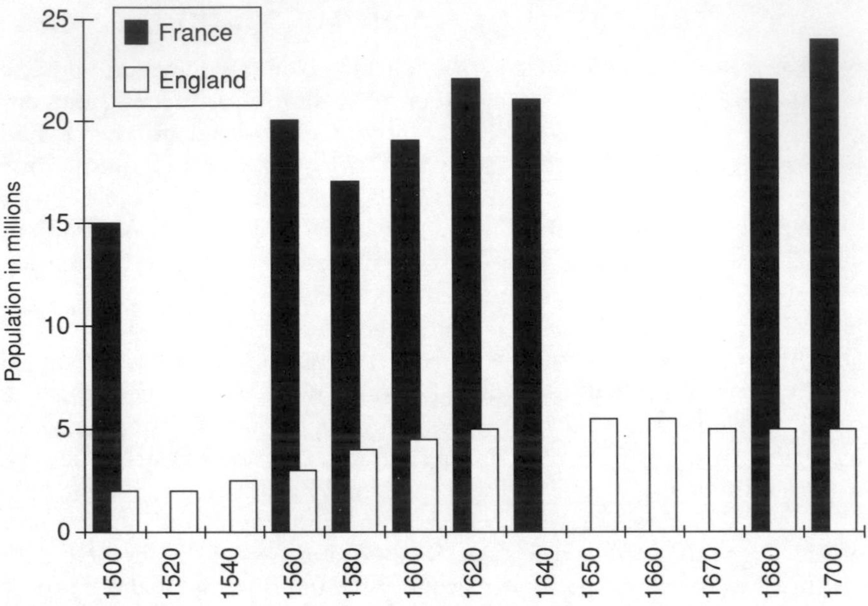

Figure 7.1 Population trends in France and England 1500–1700

population on three occasions prior to 1603. In the worst epidemics a population loss of 30 per cent was recorded and in Colchester in 1665–6 as much as a half. Given the undoubted economic, social and demographic turbulence suggested by these observations it is not surprising to find that the English were as attached as their Continental cousins to the wisdom of late marriage.[109] This appears to be the explanation for the hiatus between 1660 and 1690 in the otherwise impressive growth of the English population.[110]

Yet the more such similarities are emphasised the more striking becomes the transformation of the situation in England. By the mid-seventeenth century, despite the occasional dislocation of the harvest, the worst of the difficulties were over. The subsistence crisis of 1623 proved to be the last one of major proportions and that was confined to Cumbria, the Lancashire uplands, Northumberland and Yorkshire.[111] Despite a sequence of bad harvests in the 1640s there was no repetition.[112] With the advantage of hindsight it is possible to see that the ensuing period of demographic stagnation was no more than a modest blip in the upward movement of the population, a slightly sunken plateau, which provided the launch pad for a second phase of rapid increase. From 2.5 million in 1520 England's population had grown to perhaps 4 million at the beginning of the seventeenth century and by a further million by 1650. Between 1560 and 1650 the English population expanded at a much faster rate than the French and the relative position was not significantly altered in the following decades. Furthermore, whereas only 4 per cent of the population had lived in towns in 1520, this had risen to about 11 per cent by 1650; London alone accounted for a prodigious 8 per cent. Although the tripling of its population during the seventeenth century exceeded by far that of the provincial towns, the biggest of them were also subject to impressive growth. Thus the total urban population of East Anglia grew by 50 per cent between 1603 and 1670 but that of Norwich more than doubled by 1695. Bristol grew even faster.[113] If England was no more urbanised than France towards the end of the seventeenth century she was now setting the pace.[114]

The French actually produced more children than the English but they lost a lot more – a pattern which, as noted earlier, was particularly marked in the towns.[115] Moreover, the higher birthrate was probably a consequence of the greater mortality rate because the curtailment of breast feeding produces a reduction of the intervals between births. The significance of England's better infant mortality rate is then very clear; the obvious inference is that, despite all the uncertainties, the English people benefited from a higher standard of living.[116] Survival rates for the adult population of France were also worse. It is striking that, whilst the high marriage age in England seems to have prepared the way for the renewed demographic growth of the eighteenth century by bringing the population into equilibrium with available resources, in France its effects were much less helpful. They continued to be offset by mortality rates which, although beginning to decline, did not begin to approach those of England until the nineteenth century. Not surprisingly the age of marriage remained persistently high, possibly rising after 1750.[117]

A major factor in these contrasting demographic evolutions was diet. Eric Kerridge has claimed that, by the mid-seventeenth century, English agricultural labourers, at least in the advanced regions, were eating wheat instead of rye or barley and would consume each week bacon, ¼lb cheese, some butter, milk and fish, a little fruit, spice, salt and hops and oatmeal and they would also have at times peas, beans, carrots, turnips.[118] Clearly, such a diet could not have been universal but anything even approaching these standards stood in marked contrast to the situation in France where, outside favoured areas such as Brittany, the staple diet of soup and bread has been noted. It is possible that French dietary standards had deteriorated since the end of the Middle Ages.[119] Visitors to England, on the other hand, continued to comment, as they had long done, on the plentiful cattle and sheep and the meat-eating capacities of the people.[120] One contemporary suggested that nearly three million people ate meat once a week towards the end of the century and over half of them on two days. The demand was such that the substantial increase in imports of cattle from Ireland (until banned in 1667) was absorbed without any lowering of prices. There was also a growing demand for specialised dairy produce and for fruit and vegetables; these occupied a fifth of the cultivated land and accounted for 9 per cent of total agricultural output.[121] The French being short of grazing land, under remorseless pressure to cultivate grain, and frequently to sell such dairy produce and fruit as was produced, the diet of the French populace improved not at all.

A further difference between the two countries lay in the fact that, despite the widening gap between rich and poor, economic growth in England was sufficient to absorb the growing labour force and thus to generate a definite improvement in material conditions. Joan Thirsk emphasises the success of pastoral areas in overcoming their characteristic tendency to underemployment. Sucking in surplus population from the arable regions, they offered employment in new and specialised activities, notably livestock husbandry and dairying. The former employed more labour than traditional extensive pasture grazing, which characterised the uplands of France, whilst the latter increased the number of smallholdings.[122] Their proliferation was not analogous to the process of *morcellement* and impoverishment seen in France. At the same time a 'wider geographical dispersal' of burgeoning industrial by-employments 'wrought a qualitative change in the content of the pastoral economy'.[123] Concern about the excessive number of people, evident at the beginning of the century in exhortations to seek a better life in Virginia, faded away. By 1674 it was possible for observers like Carew Reynel to suggest that a million more people would not come amiss.[124]

It was not, however, the most advanced arable regions that required them. For it appears that, with the exception of specialised crops such as vegetables, saffron and hops, the growth in output required to sustain the country at large was achieved without an increase in the agricultural workforce.[125] This lends credence, as does the entire economic situation, to Kerridge's view of an early agricultural revolution which he propounded nearly three decades ago. For it drew attention to techniques which, despite disagreement about the speed of their advance, made possible a reduction in unit costs and a substantial increase in yields. Foremost was the introduction of up and down husbandry which involved the periodic conversion of grassland into tillage and vice versa, thus ending the usual permanence of both and improving the quality of both pasture and arable. This innovation was invariably associated with enclosure but the extent to which it spread outside the advanced Midland regions has been contentious. Other major advances were made in the floating of water meadows which, as well as improving the quality of pasture, provided an early crop of hay. Well established by 1620, they rapidly became an integral part of husbandry along the southern half of the Welsh border and throughout much of Dorset, Wiltshire and Hampshire.[126] These developments were accompanied by a significant growth in the production of fodder crops and experimentation with special grasses. According to Clay these were the 'greatest single source of increased productivity . . . before modern times'.[127] For they made possible an expansion in livestock husbandry which, in turn, provided the manure which permitted the reduction or abolition of the fallow. Although the acreages involved may have been small it seems agreed that a minority of farmers had introduced turnips, clover and other artificial grasses in most parts of the country by 1700.

If Kerridge overestimated the speed with which these innovations were diffused it has also become clear that there has been an underestimation of the degree to which progress was being made on traditional open fields, without recourse to the large capital outlay required for land reclamation and water meadows. Improvements in manuring, liming, the introduction of new crops and even a measure of convertible husbandry could be undertaken on holdings of any size. Despite the frequent lack of records, careful scrutiny of inventories left by the sheep-and-corn farmers in Sussex and those of open-field Oxfordshire has revealed significant improvements made with grass leys, a concern with increasing livestock to give more manure and the introduction of clovers and pulses in a longer rotation to reduce fallowing and increase wheat production. Rye grasses, clover, trefoil and lucerne and, above all, sainfoin were all incorporated into the rotation systems of Oxfordshire even if this required the temporary fencing off of parts of the open fields. In Leicestershire by 1700 grass leys frequently covered up to a quarter or a third of the acreage of unenclosed villages. Similar developments have been observed in large parts of Northamptonshire, Bedfordshire and Buckinghamshire.[128] Kerridge himself has returned to the subject by emphasising the variation and high degree of tolerance in the choice of crops and rotation cycles which could be found in open field systems. Cultivators might, for instance, choose between wheat, rye and maslin for the winter corn field and between barley, peas, oats and dredge for the spring field. It was even possible to grow flax, hemp or saffron, even though the latter stood several years in the same field. Such flexibility, combined with the ancient technique of folding sheep on the tillage, enabled a degree of permanent cultivation which eluded the French. It also encouraged an expansion in the numbers of sheep at a time when flocks were diminishing in France.[129] Thus, through a combination of measures to improve the quality of both arable and grassland and by assiduous attention to fodder crops, it was possible for small farmers to achieve the same objectives as the larger landlords secured by engrossing and enclosing. It is worth considering whether it was the small English farmers who by example and endeavour prepared the way for the larger landlords rather than the reverse.

What is clear, despite the obvious difficulties of making precise quantitative assessments, is that by 1650 agricultural productivity was considerably higher in England than France. Even if Kerridge's belief that the most progressive farmers were obtaining up to five times the yield of their medieval forebears is thought to be ill founded, significant increases were undoubtedly achieved. Clay reckons it is safe to assume a doubling of yields for the country as a whole between 1500 and 1700 which implies considerably more in the most advanced areas. Such progress, reinforced by an expansion of the area under cultivation of about a quarter (including much fertile fenland), the deployment of more intensive crop rotation systems and a greater variety of crops, makes it possible to explain how England sustained her rising population. As most of this demographic expansion took place before 1650 the picture of an early agricultural revolution remains credible.[130]

A major corollary of rising agricultural productivity was a reduction in costs. This contributed directly to increased consumption. Tentatively from 1620, positively by mid-century as grain prices fell, the real value of wages began to rise for the first time since the fifteenth century.[131] Although by European standards nominal wages remained low, the declining cost of living meant that they went farther. Kerridge (typically pushing the argument to its limits) thinks that 'the most important cause of English industrial success was an ample and unimpeded supply of inexpensive food and drink stuff'.[132] It is certainly true that the English population in general was not only better fed than that of France but better clothed and housed. By the end of the century the labouring classes in the pastoral/manufacturing regions were finding spare cash for consumer goods – brass cooking pots, iron frying pans, earthenware dishes, knitted stockings – that had found no place in their budgets in 1550.[133] Husbandmen and wage labourers bought cottons, woollens, linens and silks, crockery, buckles, buttons and pins in significant amounts. Particularly notable was the increase in linen goods revealed by inventories from Shropshire, Warwickshire and the farming regions of Cambridgeshire. A steady rise in the number of sheets per bed, and in the presence of tablecloths, bed and window curtains, wall cloths or tapestries, together with a greater variety of clothes, are all testimony to a remarkable improvement in material comfort. In Cambridgeshire the wealth of poor households rose by an estimated 85 per cent between 1580 and 1680 but the value of their linen by no less than 271 per cent; linen accounted for between 10 and 17 per cent of the value of household goods regardless of wealth or status. Such improvements in domestic comfort are difficult to imagine without an improvement in the quality of houses themselves. By the end of the century the chances of living in a three-bedroom cottage with glass windows had almost certainly risen, once again confirming the contrast with the situation of the mass of the French peasantry and artisans.[134] The inventories of the husbandmen of the Forest of Pendle in Lancashire, for instance, show that nearly half of them were worth £50 or more.[135] At the century's end this was probably the equivalent of five or more years' wages, revealing a capacity for saving infinitely higher than that of a French *manouvrier* or most artisans. Yeomen, of course, had long lived in well-furnished houses with fine shows of pewter and silver; they wore clothes of good quality and had cash to spare.[136]

It is almost impossible to calculate the stimulus provided to textile manufacturing by the growth in disposable income. According to Thirsk the home demand for knitted stockings was sufficient to employ one knitter from 13 per cent of all labouring poor households, a figure which rises to only 15.3 per cent if foreign demand is included.[137] Spufford has calculated that 2,559 licensed chapmen in 1687–8 were alone carrying goods to the tune of £100,000 including a million yards of cloth.[138] The beginnings of a ready-to-wear market has been detected in some parts of the south.[139] Such observations are testimony to the way in which textile manufacturers had adapted to the saturation of the traditional overseas markets for heavy broadcloths.[140] With the exception of Gloucestershire, which retained the lion's share of what was left of the market for heavy woollens, English producers turned to the manufacture of lighter and cheaper cloths. A seemingly endless variety of cloths with exotic trade names was the result: damazines, damazellas, virgenatoes, callimancoes, nockadoes, bombazines. More prosaically Essex and Suffolk became known for their mixed woollen and worsted fabrics known as bays and says, the West Riding for its kerseys and dozens, Norwich for its 'light, bright and attractive' stuffs and Devonshire for its serges and perpetuannas. There were between 40,000 and 50,000 people producing bays and says in Essex by 1629. The proportion of Norwich's booming population engaged in textile production rose from 23 to 58 per cent over the course of the century.[141] Whilst some of the new products, above all the better-quality serges, made a major contribution to Britain's trade balance, the relative importance of the export market actually diminished. By 1700 domestic outlets consumed the bulk of the textile output in volume and at least half in value. No more than a quarter of Norwich says were destined for the foreign market and most of the West Riding's products went into the homes of the less well-to-do. Moreover, with the notable exception of the invention of the knitting frame, the expansion of the English textile industry was achieved with minimal technological change.[142] Its success derived from a seemingly optimum combination of expanding home demand and comparatively cheap labour costs.

Growing prosperity, regional specialisation and urbanisation brought into being a home market of exceptional resilience and dynamism. Regional and national markets were increasingly integrated. Worcester with thrice-weekly markets and four annual fairs had a hinterland of its own as well as constituting a link between the north and south-west, between Bristol and the upper Severn valley. King's Lynn linked both coastal and international trade with an extensive system of navigable rivers which happily posed far fewer problems than many French ones.[143] Recent work, it is worth emphasising, has shown that improvements to the road system were probably achieving a reduction in transport costs even before Parliament assumed responsibility for its general oversight in 1689. Increasing volumes of traffic and reduced unit costs almost certainly explain why English producers and traders were then able to take the arrival of substantial road tolls in their stride.[144]

London dominated the entire economy. Through it came the greatest proportion of the imports of colonial goods which tumbled in price as they became articles of mass consumption: sugar, tobacco, calicoes. The capital was, however, not only the major entrepôt for foreign trade but also the power house and principal distributive centre for the domestic market. By the early seventeenth century almost every town in the country was linked by weekly or fortnightly carrier departures for London, even those as far off as York, Manchester and Plymouth.[145] Its pull was felt by the sheep farmers of the Welsh marshes, the coal producers of Newcastle and the metalworkers of Sheffield. During the seventeenth century sixteen new markets were established in the suburbs of the capital and there were no less than eighteen quays specialising in various branches of provincial traffic.[146] Out of 140 London aldermen in the early Stuart period about half were engaged in domestic trade and in the late seventeenth century the majority of great merchants whose estates were registered in the court of orphans were not primarily export merchants.[147] As the eighteenth century dawned, London shops were heralding the arrival of a consumer society. Displays of merchandise, protected, as one French visitor observed, by their clear glass windows, offered 'a fine sight from every direction'.[148]

It would, however, be misleading to conclude discussion about the home market on this note. For it is clear that England's urban population – still no larger proportionately than that of France – could not account for the 80 per cent of the country's significantly enlarged output that was sold at home. Signs of rising demand had been evident before the huge London market really became dominant and even then its growth is insufficient to explain the burgeoning network of provincial roads.[149] The increasing prosperity of the rural world was as much a stimulant to urban growth as the reverse; English towns did not simply take in their own washing.[150] In order to generate significant change, as the French experience shows, cities had to be more than reservoirs of poverty with only a small elite of prosperous merchants and office-holders sustained by a privileged group of artisans. England's economic progress rested on a seemingly optimal distribution of wealth in which the prosperity of the gentry, yeomanry and many husbandmen, the commercial activity of the towns and the wage-earning capacity of large numbers of the relatively poor all contributed to the achievement of self-sustained growth. In this fashion England overcame the essential problem which so bedevilled French economic development: the creation of a dynamic and self-sustaining market.

CAPITALISM'S AGRARIAN ROOTS

It is not possible to imagine England's buoyant home market independently of its distinctive system of agrarian relations. The distance that had opened up between the performance of English and French agriculture was not simply a quantitative one. Nor can it be reduced to, or explained in terms of, the greater provision of cattle and manure as Le Roy Ladurie implies, crucial though this was.[151] Indeed, if the difference between the *laboureurs* and the independent farmers of England resided only in the former's technological tardiness this would be difficult to explain. It only begins to make sense in the context of the immense contrast between the slow but evident decline of the independent peasantry in France and the social weight and dynamism of a broad stratum of English farmers.

Some historians, as already observed, believe that English rural prosperity was the product of a long-established commercially oriented individualism. Macfarlane has further linked this to England's centralised system of law in which, he claims, collective and family rights associated with peasant cultures were subordinated to those of the individual. Although the thrust of Macfarlane's argument carries a great deal of weight he undoubtedly oversimplifies the uncertainties and hesitations which accompanied the commercialisation of English society. The remarkable economic growth of the twelfth and thirteenth centuries, though of benefit to landowners and wealthy townsmen, did not lead directly to the dissolution of serfdom. Primogeniture, despite its pre-eminence in common law, was not universal; partible inheritance and customs with similarities to those of northern France endured in some localities and towns into the seventeenth century.[152] The emancipation of the individual from the demands of community was, as Britnell has recently emphasised, a protracted development. Labour legislation in the aftermath of the Black Death was decidedly restrictive whilst statutory regulation of the market by urban authorities also increased from 1330. Attachment to the concept of a harmonious and organic community remained evident in the character of popular festivities.[153] In striking similarity to French developments, the formal stratification of upper-class society also became more marked. Five different grades of peerage were invented, mostly before 1400, by which time the distinctions between knights, esquires and gentlemen had also crystallised. 'The commercialised society of the later middle ages,' says Britnell, 'passed on this uncompromisingly hierarchic ideal' to the even more commercialised period that followed.[154] The religious teleology and chain-of-being imagery of Elizabethan and indeed Stuart writers would certainly have made immediate sense to their French counterparts. It is of course true that, as in France, the increased stress on rank and degree was a response to the dislocation of the social order.[155]

Where Macfarlane appears to be absolutely right is in suggesting that the English system of law provided a congenial framework for the development of a market economy. For the common law, by inserting itself between the king's tenants in chief and their dependants, had the effect of bestowing on small farmers a remarkable degree of security. The idea that all free tenants were the king's tenants may be traced back to 1086 and was incorporated into the crystallising legal system of the following century. All affairs concerning freemen and free tenures became the business of the royal courts.[156] In Europe royal courts were not accessible to freemen in the twelfth century.[157] The principle of primogeniture subsequently made it possible for an inheritance to be secured even though the feudal 'relief' had not been paid. By the *Quia emptores* of 1290 any freeman was also able to alienate his fee and sell freely; moreover, if he did so, the purchaser of the tenure held it not from him but from the grantor's lord, thus abolishing the practice of sub-infeudation.[158] The initial effect of these developments was to confirm the inferior status of customary tenants, particularly tenants-at-will, who were denied the benefits of access to the royal courts. It appears, however, that by the end of the thirteenth century manorial courts were adopting the procedures of common law and the royal courts even where such tenants were concerned. The careful codification of manorial custom, though no doubt undertaken with the lord's interest uppermost, also had the effect of confirming the fact of customary tenure as well as the conditions attached. Arbitrary treatment of ordinary villagers, both unfree and free, became less common; many impositions that had once been arbitrary were moderated or fixed.[159] It also became possible for manorial copyholders of inheritance to alienate their holdings in the style of freemen. The Statute of Wills of 1540 further consolidated the property rights of copyholders by providing for the free disposal of tenures by will or by gift *inter vivos*, thus nullifying the significance of holding them 'at the will' of the lord.[160] Distinctions between the unfree and free had also become extremely blurred, with many freeman holding customary tenures; the exclusion of copyholders – by far the largest category of tenants – from the royal courts thus disappeared.[161] By the end of the sixteenth century it was possible for copyholders to seek the recovery of their lands through the royal courts.[162]

The contrast with France at this point is critical. Despite the tendency of historians to treat the French peasantry as though they were owners of their land, they were overwhelmingly customary tenants if not also sharecropppers and, in practice, immensely constrained in their use of it. In part, as has been seen, this was a question of economics rather than the law. But it was also a manifestation of the enduring power of the seigneurial regime and the absence of a sense of absolute property rights. Although tenants could normally expect their heirs to succeed them, this was achieved by the strict application of customary law which also deprived the tenant of any freedom of choice as to the best course of action. A departure from the rules of inheritance or any alienation of the land without the lord's consent could result in the invocation of the *retrait féodale* or *lignager*. In any event the capacity to alienate land was impeded not only by the need for seigneurial permission, but by the payment of dues required on any change whether by sale or gift and also by the concomitant obligation to retain the seigneurial perquisites. Failure in these respects could result in the seizure of the land or its fruits. Although appeals to the royal courts were theoretically possible, the capacity of individual peasants to appeal was limited both by cost and by the determination of the legists to preserve the power of seigneurs over their dependants.

The persistence in France of the idea that everyone should be judged by their natural judge was in fundamental opposition to the common law principle that no man should answer in any court for his freehold unless commanded to do so by the king's writ. This led quite rapidly to the erosion of the belief that it was primarily the duty of the king to hold a court for his tenants-in-chief and not to usurp their functions by meddling with the disputes of the lesser tenants. Simpson observes that had this not occurred there could have been no common law as we know it.[163] The result was the early development of a system of public law unusually suited to the representation and mediation of the interests of all property owners. This almost symbiotic relationship between public authority and private interests was precluded in France by the formal separation of public and private law. Royal power was in the former domain whilst private law remained rooted in custom and, as far as small holders were concerned, in the hands of the seigneurs.

The relative legal security of the English peasantry was reinforced by the comparatively high level of monetarisation of the economy. By 1400 most rents, customary fines and wages were paid almost entirely in cash.[164] This both reflected and sustained a degree of economic independence which the cash-starved peasantry of France could not match. Of course – and this is the major flaw in those interpretations which emphasise the ancient foundations of England's wealth – there was absolutely no guarantee that this state of affairs would endure. In Eastern Europe the shortage of manpower in the late Middle Ages proved to be the point of departure for the transformation of free peasants into serfs. In England, however, it proved possible for the peasantry to combine both political and economic pressure not only to defeat the pressure for greater rents, taxes and exactions but effectively to get rid of the last traces of serfdom. By flight, resistance and legal pressure the peasantry won considerable concessions from landlords whose greatest need was to find capable and willing tenants. In order to retain them many customary leases became hereditary ones or were converted into non-customary ones. Very long leases, for as many as sixty or even eighty years, were not uncommon. Even small cottagers found it possible to obtain mortgages for improvements or to tide them over some bad harvests. Although restrictive clauses – such as that forbidding sowing in the last two years – could be found, their resemblance to the prescriptive nature of French leases is limited. On the contrary, they give a clear impression of an entrepreneurial rather than a *rentier* approach to the resolution of their economic difficulties, the success of which depended on a degree of cooperation between landlord and tenant. Quite substantial farmers took on customary leases. In France the less buoyant situation of the peasantry and the levers at the command of the seigneurs encouraged a search for *rentier* solutions which ultimately had the effect of squeezing out the middle-ranking peasants.[165]

Even when the balance of forces shifted back towards the lords in the sixteenth century the gains made by the English peasantry were not lost. Of course, many small copyholders who had escaped custom fell into difficulties as prices rose and the lords recovered their position. These joined the growing ranks of the poor and dispossessed. The very long leases of the fifteenth century gave way to much shorter ones with twenty-one years tending to become a maximum although leases for lifetimes remained widespread. In any event, such leases remained substantially longer than those which became the norm in France, certainly long enough to encourage purposeful borrowing and offer incentives to improvement. Larger farms were rarely let on short leases and substantial tenants were in a position to benefit from rising prices. Some of these were often lessors and lessees at the same time and engaged in subletting within an entirely commercial framework. Frequently the prime agents of engrossing and enclosure, a growing number of farmers were thus able to share in the rising profits of the sixteenth century. Of course they could not – and did not – do this without undermining the hold of the less well-placed on the land.[166] The process of differentiation within the ranks of the English peasantry, which can be traced back to at least the thirteenth century, thus continued.

The thrust of this argument runs contrary to Brenner's belief that manorial lords were the prime agents of expropriation and the transformation of agrarian relations. This was achieved, he suggests, by effectively turning copyholds into leaseholds at the market rates; legal judgments, reflecting the terms on which land was held throughout large parts of the country, offered little protection to the tenant.[167] Each of these assumptions is open to doubt. It is, of course, possible to find attempts by the lords to turn copyholds into leaseholds but there appears to have been no sustained move in this direction. In the early sixteenth century there was little incentive to do so and later on such moves were likely to provoke resistance from tenants whose holdings had become increasingly profitable. Even raising fines could be problematic. So lords increasingly resorted to offering confirmations of custom as the only way of extracting some profit from the situation, particularly when the tenants were supported by the courts. Sir John Talbot, lord of the manor of Ford in Shropshire, attempted to raise the level of fines during the 1590s but in 1608 conceded defeat and sold confirmation to the tenants for £1,880.[168] Not far away at Myddle, leases for years were being converted to leases for lifetimes; by 1602 only three tenants held for years.[169] Leasehold was also being converted into freeholds as tenants took advantage of the fluid market in land which lasted down to 1650. Hoyle even presents an example of an entire manor being bought and parcelled out, a development which corresponds to Lawrence Stone's general picture of the decline in desmesne farming by the peerage who for a time adopted a *rentier* style of existence.[170] If, within the space of fifty years, England's aristocrats found it necessary to become improving landlords in order to survive in a competitive world, it was not essentially they who created it.

The tenor of these observations has been strikingly borne out by a recent and close examination of the evolution of customary tenure on the Scottish border and notably in Cumberland to which Brenner alludes as an area of particular insecurity.[171] In fact, two-thirds of the land was still held by customary leases at the end of the eighteenth century.[172] Whilst the sixteenth century saw a massive increase in fines there were few attempts to break the custom and impose leasehold.[173] Properly managed customary leases could be profitable and, in any event, the courts were likely to find in the tenants' favour. From the 1580s resistance by tenants was helped by the common law ruling that all arbitrary fines on customary estates had to be reasonable. In 1625 the Star Chamber found in favour of tenants in the Barony of Kendal who, when threatened with the conversion of their tenures into leasehold, asserted rights of inheritance. The Earl of Northumberland also failed to coerce his tenants into becoming leaseholders at triple the old rent and resorted to pushing up entry fines. Between 1620 and 1670 they rose twentyfold. When the dispute went to court in 1678 the court found for the tenants and ordered that the fines should be reasonable. A number of lords also lost their claim to a share of the harvest (so common in France) and in the next century they were still struggling with only marginal success to deprive tenants of customary rights in the woodland.[174] What finally brought an end to the traditional agrarian structures of the north was growing industrialisation and changing attitudes to property. Joan Thirsk has observed that, generally speaking, it was not until the eighteenth century that small men and commoners were really put to the test.[175]

Until that moment the net result of these processes was a range of holdings with a significant proportion in the middle range using some wage labour and producing for the market.[176] At the upper end the yeomanry represented a class of prosperous capitalist farmers unique in Europe. Constituting perhaps 3 or 4 per cent of the rural population, farming between fifty and seventy acres, they constituted the biggest single group renting desmesne land.[177] They were a larger group than the armigerous gentry into which many of them rose, thus contributing directly to the remarkable increase in the presence of the latter in English villages by the mid-seventeenth century. Whilst it is not possible to quantify the contribution of the yeomanry to economic developments, it is clear that as employers of the growing pool of labour, as consumers and as entrepreneurs their presence could only have brought weight and stability. It may well have been crucial in sustaining economic progress through the difficult years of the late sixteenth century when their prosperity and purchasing power were already evident.[178] Little distinguishable from the yeomanry was a substantial stratum of comfortably off modest farmers. Over half of those from the forest of Pendle, not the richest area of England, left estates worth more than £100.[179] The presence of these groups made possible a degree of cooperation between landlord and tenant which the depressed French peasant was less and less able to sustain; the medium-length leases also encouraged both parties to invest in improvements.[180]

The growth of a market-oriented, prosperous and independent class of farmers – some 150,000 according to Clay – was critical to the raising of agricultural productivity and the creation of the broad home market which prepared the way for industrialisation.[181] Accounting for perhaps 12 to 15 per cent of the population, such farmers and their families had a socio-economic weight which was not equalled even by the *laboureurs* of the Ile de France and certainly not by the village notables of the poorer provinces.[182] The capacity of England's farmers to take up and use the growing pool of wage labour was one of the obvious differences between the two countries. However, this process was significantly eased by the diversification of the economy; by mid-century only half the workforce was employed full time in agriculture.[183] This contributed to a considerable degree of personal mobility. Adolescents seem to have moved easily from one position to another; most children did not settle and marry in the parishes of their birth, making a striking contrast with the evidence from rural France.[184] Much of this movement may be classified as 'betterment' migration as opposed to the flight from poverty which generated the influx into French cities.[185]

Paradoxically, the development of capitalism in England was facilitated by the growth and presence during the critical decades of a thriving class of small farmers. Of course, to emphasise the point once more, this went hand in hand with the expropriation of a large part of the rural population; indeed, these were two facets of the same process and fed off each other. Yet as the French experience shows, the simple process of proletarianisation, albeit a general precondition of capitalist development, was not a sufficient one. A peasant population which was largely impoverished by the demands of landlords and state was a major impediment to the creation of the self-sustaining market without which capitalism had no future. It should also now be clear that the emphasis on the home market which is fundamental to this entire analysis does not require the displacement of class struggle as an explanatory factor. Indeed, the two were inextricably linked as the growth of the English home market was in part the fruit of the success of the small farmers in England in preserving and increasing their independence. Conversely, the inability of the French peasantry to resist the remorseless pressures to which they were subject was to have a profoundly negative effect on the whole of French economic development. Thus, if Brenner is right to insist on the centrality of class struggle to economic development, he completely inverts the developments taking place on the two sides of the Channel.

If the comparative buoyancy of the farmers of England needs any further demonstration it can be seen in the fact that they were not dominated by a parasitic urban bourgeoisie; and certainly not by venal officeholders of the French type with their symbiotic, if ambivalent, relationship to the central state. This is not to suggest that English towns did not spawn enclosed oligarchies. There existed the same tendency for power to concentrate in self-perpetuating elites and for a tiny handful of exceptionally rich taxpayers to dominate as occurred in France.[186] A similar desire to diversify investment and to acquire social standing can also be seen. Merchant capital flowed into houses, furnishings and land. Here, however, differences start to outweigh the similarities. For money invested in land in England did not forsake its commercial character for a *rentier* one. The progress of capitalist agriculture made possible a fusion between landed, commercial and industrial interests. In the process it effectively blunted the antagonism between commercial activity and social status which for so long inhibited the emergence of capitalist values elsewhere. Moreover, although English towns sought charters of incorporation, introduced measures of economic protectionism and controlled the guilds, and although merchant elites endeavoured to shut out retailers from the great trading companies, there was never any general prescription on economic activity, no formal prohibition on trade. Of more than 8,000 apprentices bound to the London companies in 1576–1646 an eighth were sons of knights, esquires and gents, the rest being drawn from the middling ranks of urban and rural society.[187] By 1660 half of the freemen of the drapers' company of Shrewsbury were of gentry stock.[188]

Despite their growth English towns were on the whole much smaller than French ones and they housed many fewer non-productive elements: officers, ecclesiastics or the masses of immigrant poor. Until the eighteenth century England was predominantly a country of market and county towns. Even in the five provincial capitals – Bristol, York, Exeter, Newcastle and London – trade was basic. At Newcastle some of the wealthiest citizens were the butchers who were also graziers – an inconceivable situation in any of the front-rank French towns.[189] Membership of the Common Council of Bristol required considerable wealth and was consequently dominated by members of the Merchant Adventurers; none the less manufacturers, retailers and innkeepers (an increasingly prosperous profession) found their way on to it. The seventy-five mayors of Norwich between 1620 and 1690 accounted for no less than fifteen different trades.[190] The more exclusive government of London was nevertheless in the hands of the merchants of the East India and Levant Companies. Municipal government thus remained in the hands of the bourgeoisie properly speaking and was not top-heavy with venal officers.[191] Whilst leading urban officials acted as JPs, assumed responsibility for the maintenance of the king's peace, and were empowered to raise money for local need, they could not deflect taxes on to the rural population.

These observations bring into focus the diminutive nature of the state bureaucracy and the limited demands which it imposed on the economy. Much to the benefit of the rural world, the fiscal demands of the English state were neither onerous nor borne disproportionately by its productive classes. Indeed, for more or less a century from 1550 they were barely taxed at all, a factor of inestimable significance in helping to explain how the economic difficulties of the sixteenth century were endured and surmounted, and finally gave way to rising prosperity. But what was good for the long-term economic health of the nation turned out to be very damaging to that of its monarchs. For they were left struggling to tap the resources of an increasingly prosperous realm without any effective means of doing so.

'A LIMITED POWER TO GOVERN'[192]

The Stuarts never possessed the fullness of power of French monarchs. Paradoxically, the early unification and political homogeneity of England bequeathed to them a slender machinery of government which proved unable to cope with the mounting fiscal pressures of the early seventeenth century. On the eve of the Civil War the Exchequer consisted of no more than 200 personnel; outside London there were as few as thirty receivers of Crown revenues.[193] Overwhelmingly, the Crown was dependent on the good offices of the JPs, together with the Lord-Lieutenants of the Shires, sheriffs and the principal officers of the towns. Yeomen were also thought by some to be amongst those who governed the nation through their virtual monopoly of key parish positions such as churchwarden, bailiff, constables and feoffees of charities.[194] The small size and homogeneity of England's ruling class stretching across land, commerce, law and the church made possible a degree of cohesive self-government precluded in France by the power of sectarian divisions which the Crown then turned to its advantage. It did this, as we have seen, by the deployment of a massive system of patronage. Yet it was precisely this that the early Stuarts lacked as they strove to enhance their resources and authority. Gerald Aylmer has listed those agencies – apart from the Royal Household itself – in which the Crown had offices at its disposition and they were comparatively few.[195] The multiplication and sale of office on the French scale would almost certainly have run into political opposition and it is doubtful whether they would have been taken up. For the reluctance of many of those with requisite status and wealth to take on even the most prestigious municipal positions was in marked contrast to the French pursuit of office.[196] Whilst English officeholders did improve their chances of social promotion, the economic benefits were in most cases limited; income from land far outweighed that from office. In any event, as the French experience showed, the benefits of sale of office for the Crown were ambiguous and the idea seems not to have appealed to Charles I.[197]

The problems posed by the monarchy's institutional weaknesses were compounded by the development of agrarian capitalism; for this shifted the distribution of wealth and power away from the monarchy and the aristocracy. As a result it became ever more difficult for the Crown to secure its base in the countryside. As in France the presence there of the great aristocracy diminished as they drifted to the capital and the Court; but, in contrast to the French situation, this development was not welcomed by the monarchy. On the contrary, the early Stuarts made repeated enjoinders to the 'principal gentlemen' to depart from Court, reside in their home areas, carry out their public duties, keep hospitality, maintain good order and curtail the flow of both poor and rich into the cities. Between 1580 and 1590 Lord Burghley had kept lists of the names of men in each county who were either JPs and deputy lieutenants or influential figures suitable for elevation to office.[198] However, the Crown was never able to replicate the achievement of the French Crown in meeting an essentially similar problem through the creation of its own clienteles linking provincial elites to the Court and government. The significance of this failure was considerable given that the number of villages with resident gentry, many of whom emerged from the ranks of the yeomanry, was steadily rising.[199] The gulf between the Court, increasingly staffed by 'men of little knowledge', and the country grew wider.[200] Charles made a determined effort to improve communications. However, this went hand in hand during the period of personal rule with a more vigorous imposition of policy by the Privy Council and was often resented.

The Stuarts also suffered from the fact that most of England's wars had been fought on the territory of others and that for a century or so she had been almost a non-participant in the great Continental conflicts. This deprived the Crown of the leverage required to overcome the limits on its tax-raising powers. The argument from necessity, which had enabled the French monarchy to transform its extraordinary taxes (the *taille*, *gabelle* and *aides*) into ordinary ones from the end of the fifteenth century, had little purchase on an English population confident in its security.[201] The yield from the tenths and fifteenths imposed on movable property was meagre by comparison.[202] Crown lands had been sold to the point of exhaustion. Loans were raised from the City of London, the East India Company and Levant Companies but the willingness to make them was dependent on royal support for the great merchant interests. During the reign of James I the government substantially reduced and rationalised levies on trade to make them more acceptable to the merchant companies.[203]

The best prospects for additional revenues lay in the Customs for they were farmed out in French fashion and could be used to secure loans from the farmers.[204] Unfortunately for the king the idea that extraordinary taxation required parliamentary consent was well embedded in the English consciousness by the early seventeenth century and was to become even more so as a result of the Stuarts' attempts to deny this. The Crown had succeeded on several occasions since the celebrated Bates case of 1606 in asserting its right to raise customs without parliamentary approval. But by 1628–9 this policy provoked a major confrontation with the king's financial backers in the City of London. After the seizure of large quantities of currants by customs officials both the big companies turned down royal requests for assistance.[205] Moreover, thirty well-heeled and connected London merchants broke into the custom-house and removed a large part of the confiscated merchandise. In January 1629 the Levant Company rejected the Privy Council's demand that it should order its members to pay customs dues. Parliament was thus recalled in the midst of a merchant revolt in order to resolve the issue.[206] Its failure to do so led directly to the king's decision to rule without it.

Although, as Russell has insisted, the king continued to collect tonnage and poundage by means widely regarded as arbitrary, the cost was an attempt to rule without the support of the political nation. This proved impossible once the pressures of war mounted again. As the crisis engendered by the Scots War in 1638 deepened, Ship Money sheriffs complained that they could not rely on the cooperation of their constables, and deputy lieutenants faced reluctant, even riotous, recruits.[207] Charles was obliged to turn once again to the only institution which offered any hope of mobilising the support of the nation.

There was no institution in France or throughout Europe which was comparable to the English Parliament. Despite its claims to have inherited the functions of the dormant Estates-General, the *parlement* of Paris was neither a representative nor a national body. It proved quite unable to bestow any sense of direction or unity on the divided, conservative and sectarian movements of opposition to the government. Moreover, the recall of the English Parliament in 1640 after eleven years of personal rule makes a telling contrast with the ability of the French monarchy to dispense with the Estates-General, crisis or no crisis. It had been dismissed contemptuously in 1615 without even receiving a reply to its *cahiers* of grievance and, even during the Fronde, with the Spanish pressing at the door, Mazarin was able to avoid implementing promises to summon it. True, it is possible to point to the continuing activity of important provincial Estates in France, the fact that they possessed permanent commissions and in some instances also controlled the tax-raising machinery.[208] This was also true of the Cortes of Castille, although it did not prevent their demise after 1665.[209] Those of Catalonia, supreme in their role as guardian and maker of her laws and liberties, were powerful enough to resist the Spanish monarchy in all-out struggle, thus prolonging Catalonian autonomy for another half-century.[210] Yet such institutions, for all their frequently underestimated successes, cannot be compared with the English Parliament which represented a unified political nation and did so in a markedly different way. Its bicameral nature, resulting from the separate representation of the clergy in convocation, was almost unique whilst its structures and procedures substantially reduced the capacity of the Crown to exploit differences between the houses. Majority voting encouraged meaningful debates in contrast to the manipulation of deputies required in the Catalan Cortes where a single *dissentiment* could bring proceedings to a halt.[211] This went hand in hand with the plenary authority of Parliament; unlike in the Cortes of Castille or the Estates-General of the United

Provinces decisions could be taken without local approval. Parliament also had the capacity to intimidate and remove royal ministers in a way not open to Continental institutions. The impeachment of Lord Treasurer Cranfield in 1624, of Laud and Strafford in 1640 and twelve bishops the following year was an old device used to devastating effect.

Most importantly, the electorate itself was overwhelmingly and uniquely determined by a property franchise. The economic buoyancy of the rural world meant that by the seventeenth century the forty-shilling freeholder qualification was attained by a wide range of the population. In many parts of the country a holding of four to five acres would yield the requisite income; in 1621 it was felt necessary to introduce a bill to exclude cottagers.[212] Urban oligarchies were also increasingly obliged to yield to pressure for a widening of the franchise so that 'by 1630 the majority of parliamentary boroughs had large electorates' which could not be ignored.[213] Overall, 200,000 plus of the electors could vote – about a quarter of the male adult population.[214] The Commons which, on the whole, favoured wider urban franchises also successfully asserted its claim to be the sole judge of the validity of elections.[215] The contrast with the ability of the French government to manipulate the elections to the Estates-General of 1614–15 is unavoidable.

English parliamentary structures provided, under the impact of the issues which began to divide the country in the 1620s and 1630s, not simply an increase in the number of contested elections but also the conditions for the emergence of embryonic political parties. Hirst reckoned that there were at least forty contests in 1624, sixty in the spring of 1641 and eighty in the autumn.[216] At one election or another, nearly all the counties had some sort of contest, even though in many cases they were largely a matter of ritual and many of those eligible certainly did not vote.[217] Revisionist scepticism about the precise number of contests and the attempts to reduce conflict to a simple factionalism cannot obscure the distinctive development of England's political culture. By 1614 elections were already providing an occasion for attacks on papists, courtiers, and most tellingly 'royalists'. In the years that followed, all the obvious grievances to do with taxation, religion, the billeting of troops, and the Scottish campaign surfaced as issues in parliamentary elections. So did the existence of Parliament itself.[218] Specifically political activity undertaken by people who may legitimately be described as politicians was creating a new and different culture.[219] The electors of Cheshire in 1624 were encouraged to guard against 'busie headed working Politicians'.[220] Elsewhere they were subjected to a victory parade by a victorious parliamentary candidate, an event which is unimaginable in the French context.[221]

The king was thus not alone in 1640 and 1641 in looking to Parliament for some resolution of his problems. If it was still formally a royal institution, by the end of 1628 – if not earlier – it had also become the principal agency through which the fears and aspirations of the population were expressed. The contrast between the taxpayers of London crying for a Parliament and those of Paris with their shouts of 'vive le roi sans gabelle' is more than symbolic. So is that between the particularist appeal to ancient Norman liberties made by the Nu-Pieds of 1639 and the widespread 'bell and bonfires' which greeted Charles I's reluctant acceptance of the Petition of Right.[222] Basic grievances over taxation and arbitrary government, little different from those which moved the French to revolt, achieved a national expression and resonance precluded by the fragmented nature of French institutions and society. Despite revisionist insistence on the paramountcy of local issues in England and the frequently alleged indifference of communities to national ones, the fusion of the local and national was, in seventeenth-century terms, exceptional. Most obvious perhaps was the conflict over the level and nature of taxation which in France, apart from a fleeting moment during the Fronde, was rooted in countless different local situations. Thus Bristol's merchant elite, frustrated and angry at the constant harassment by royal commissioners in search of men, money and ships, felt it was worthwhile to insert a complete record of the parliamentary debates over the Petition of Right into the municipal registers.[223] Similar records undoubtedly found their way into many individual and municipal archives and the Bristolians were far from alone in their attention to the details of parliamentary debate. A developing commercial market in political newsletters and 'separates', offering accounts of parliamentary proceedings and other events, is testimony to a burgeoning public opinion. Private diaries written by people who rarely travelled beyond their locality suggest a close following of national events and an awareness of the broad issues which lay behind them.[224] Conversely, the need to satisfy the 'country' and the electors permeated the debates of the 1620s.[225] Members of Parliament sustained a steady flow of information to their constituents whom they often met and to whom they distributed copies of speeches and petitions.[226] The practice of appealing to the country may be traced back to the disputes over monopolies which had vexed the last Parliaments of Elizabeth; by the 1640s it was filled with subversive implications.[227] The Protestation of Loyalty to Parliament which was sent down to the country in January 1642 to be taken by all adult males was 'an open invitation to the populace to involve itself in the doings of Parliament'. It reduced the issues to their emotive kernel.[228] Those taking it swore to maintain 'His Majesty's royal person and estate' and to defend 'the power and privilege of Parliaments, the lawful rights and liberties of the subjects' and to preserve the true reformed Protestant religion.[229]

In 1641 and 1642 the 'country' also came to Westminster with its own petitions. That from London secured 10,000 signatures, despite lacking the approval of the merchant oligarchy; it expressed opposition to Ship Money, impositions, monopolies, religious innovations, the war with Scotland and the summoning and dismissing of Parliament without redress of grievances.[230] London was far from alone. Of the forty English counties only two had not presented a petition to Parliament by August 1642. The number of signatures was impressive and in some cases suggestive of a high level of organisation. The Somerset petition in defence of episcopacy, presented in December 1641, claimed over 14,000 signatures and there were similar documents from Dorset and Wiltshire. These provoked a series of counter-petitions.[231] Some of the petitions were particular and some general, touching amongst other things on Ireland, Scotland, the Triennial Act, Ship Money and innovations in the church. They were, observes Fletcher, intended for public consumption and shared a sense of the destiny of Parliament.[232]

All this is not to deny that there were many local issues which remained just that. Yet, if that is all there had been, the abolition of the monarchy would have been inconceivable. Nothing reveals the limits of factionalism and localism better than the Fronde. It should not, however, be concluded that the institution of Parliament alone explains the difficulties of the early Stuarts or that the absence of such an institution in France fully explains the disarray of the Frondeurs. The dramatic and unexpected emergence of the National Assembly in 1789 serves as a reminder of how readily the institutional vacuum was to be filled in a different political climate. What made it possible for the English Parliament first to challenge the legality of acts taken under the royal prerogative and subsequently to arrogate supreme authority for itself was not its formal constitutional position or its institutional character. It was the fact that by 1600 it enjoyed in Russell's words 'a hold on public and patriotic sentiment that many European estates could not enjoy', the fact that it had acquired a 'fixed place in English thought'.[233] This observation (barely compatible with his claim that Parliament was an event rather than an institution) points the way to that rich matrix of political, legal and religious ideas which legitimised the authority of Parliament and provided the conviction necessary for the public execution of a king who was alleged to have exceeded his powers and waged war on the people whom Parliament represented.

It is not necessary to believe that the English Civil War or the execution of Charles were inevitable in order to recognise that the ideological ammunition for such a moment had long been lying around. The view that there was a fundamental difference between English and French government can be traced back at least as far as Sir John Fortescue in the 1460s. He thought that whereas the king of England might not make laws or impose taxes without the assent of the people, the French monarchy rested on a right of conquest.[234] Even if it were to be agreed that Fortescue's main object was 'to score points off the national enemy' his understanding of the situation was not totally misconceived.[235] Chauvinistic he may have been, but he was not imagining things when he said that the French king compelled people to buy salt even though they did not need it.[236] Moreover, if Fortescue was in error it was an error which came to be shared by innumerable Englishmen; by the seventeenth century it was widely assumed, as Underdown observes, that there was only one mode of assisting the Crown and that was in 'a parliamentary way'.[237] Furthermore, unparliamentary taxation came to represent, as Linda Popofsky has so well shown, not only unpopular taxes but a threat to the liberties of the subject which raised profound constitutional issues.[238] These can be discerned in the judgment given by one of the Exchequer judges in the Bates case when he cast doubt on Parliament's right to regulate customs duties by statute. Two years later the Lord Treasurer extended impositions to cover a broad range of commodities. These were opposed in Parliament by reference to fundamental liberties and immemorial rights. Hakewill warned that if Parliament conceded a power of emergency taxation, there would be no way of deciding whether circumstances justified such taxes or not.[239] The Commons was also urged not to be too generous over the Great Contract – which was indeed rejected – otherwise the king would be able to rule by proclamation. This had happened in France where 'by power of edicts' parliaments were never called.[240] Similar fears surfaced in the 1614 Parliament and again in 1625 after the Solicitor General had attempted to use the Jacobean Act of Tonnage and Poundage as statutory authority for impositions and for the pretermitted custom. The 1626 Parliament ended with Commons declaring that tonnage and poundage could not be collected without its assent and the Privy Council insisting, to the contrary, that the king could indeed do so.

By the time of the 1628 Parliament the issue had been further inflamed by the government's determination, under the fiscal pressures created by its brief wars with Spain and France, to collect unauthorised dues and to pursue those merchants who refused to pay. The Commons was insistent that the levying of tonnage and poundage was 'a breach of the fundamental liberties of this kingdom' and contrary to the principles embodied in the Petition of Right. The king declared that he intended to continue to raise it by prerogative right.[241] When the Commons summoned the customs officials who continued to pursue the rebellious London merchants to answer charges of contempt, Charles backed off, saying he had not asserted prerogative right but only demonstrated necessity. None the less the pursuit of the merchants continued, with the government standing four square behind its officials. The king finally dissolved Parliament, declaring that the Commons had violated the constitutional balance between the liberties of subjects and his royal prerogatives. Reasserting that tonnage and poundage were his of right, he withdrew his earlier disclaimer of prerogative. The issue was rejoined in the Long Parliament; the Grand Remonstrance of 1640 renewed the charge that tonnage and poundage had been illegally collected.

The conflict over taxation thus became inseparable from a highly conscious and explicit public debate about the nature of royal power and its limitations.[242] Some appealed to the distinction established by Fortescue when he claimed that whereas France was a *dominium tantum regale* (a merely regal monarchy) England was a *dominium politicum et regale*. This meant that the political powers which the English king exercised in Parliament and the activity of his common law judges ought to be subject to the law. Inevitably, the problem of explaining the relationship between the king's regal and his political persona led to the drawing of some fine distinctions; so too did that of determining to which persona the power of taxation pertained. Nevertheless, the duality of this whole line of thought was diametrically opposed to the Bodinian insistence on the indivisibility of sovereignty.[243] It also helped perpetuate the distinct but related concept of the King's Two Bodies. Obliterated in France by the all-encompassing *majesté du roi*, the distinction between the royal office and person could be deployed in England in partial justification of Parliament's usurpation of executive authority. A crucial moment came in the aftermath of the king's departure for Scotland in 1641 when Parliament issued its first ordinances without his personal presence but with the fictitious participation of his office. Condemned at the Restoration for its subversive implications, the idea of the Two Bodies passed into Whig political thought.[244]

The willingness to accept the idea of mixed forms of government was as much the result of the practical role played by Parliament as of abstract political theory. Pocock traces it back to the medieval position of 'parliament as the great council of the kingdom which could guard the Crown against even the king himself' and specifically against evil counsellors.[245] However, there was no reason why the notion of a restraining power in itself should have led to the assertion of parliamentary sovereignty. As has been seen, the *parlement* of Paris baulked at drawing such a conclusion from its undoubted capacity to restrain, whilst the pursuit of evil counsellors was the stock in trade of rebels everywhere. Something more was required in order to overcome the conviction that the king was the ultimate source of authority.

What bestowed on the English Parliament an unusual degree of political leverage, cemented the notion of mixed government and provided the springboard for an assertion of parliamentary sovereignty was the development, from the end of the fifteenth century, of statute law. This marked the English Parliament off from virtually all its Continental counterparts which remained bodies of petition. Some 677 statutes were passed in the reign of Henry VIII. If Parliament was subsequently much less active, this was not sufficient to undermine the conviction which led many to assume with Sir Thomas Smith in 1565 that the 'most high and absolute power in the realm of England consisteth in the parliament'.[246] Selden told the Commons in 1628: 'an act of Parliament may alter any part of Magna Carta'.[247] It was of course true that, as yet, the idea of the superiority of Parliament had not led to any explicit denial of the powers of the king to exempt subjects from legislation.[248] But there was, as Sommerville notes, a widespread conviction that he could not set aside whole statutes nor create them. Without recognising the presence of these convictions it is impossible to explain the revolutionary decision of May 1642 when it invoked the coronation oath to deny the king a veto in law-making; in November the two houses declared that the king was obliged to assent to bills that were approved by both.[249]

There were those who thought that the common law of England, tried and tested in the courts, should constitute the foundations of government. A certain tension therefore existed between this view and that which emphasised the superior power of Parliament. Throughout the reigns of Elizabeth, James I and Charles I, government frequently operated by letters patent, and acts of the Privy Council, subject only to tests in the courts of law. Parliament itself in 1614 and 1621 passed no laws.[250] However, the common lawyers certainly regarded the law as a constraint on royal power and not as an instrument of the royal prerogative. The common law, explained Sir John Davies, attorney-general for Ireland in 1615, acquired its force 'by usage accepted and found appropriate' whereas the edicts of a sovereign were 'imposed upon the Subject before any trial or probation made, whether the same be fit and agreeable to the nature and disposition of the people'.[251] Lord Chief Justice Coke not only denied the king's right to interpret the law or stop common law proceedings but was sweeping in his certitude that: 'the king hath no prerogative but that which the law of the land allows him'.[252] Only in a state of war were the laws generally recognised to be silent. Yet, even then, it was Parliament which ought to determine what was and was not a state of war. Emergency powers could not be at the discretion of the king.[253] The contrast with France, where the appeal to necessity flowered, under Richelieu, into an authoritarian *raison d'état*, was complete.[254] Even without this there was no dubiety that royal edicts could modify or overrule French custom.

Despite the potential disjunction between the claims of the common law and the law-making capacities of Parliament, in practice they came together in their opposition to an unfettered royal prerogative. Indeed, the symbiotic nature of their relationship added to the resilience of Parliament.[255] Whereas in France magisterial resistance to the claims of royal authority was impeded by the separation of French law into its private and public components, in England the defence of the public authority of Parliament fused with a defence of the rights – particularly the property rights – of every individual. 'The preserving of those fundamental liberties which concern the freedom of our persons, and propriety of our goods and estates,' the Commons told the king in 1628, 'is an essential means to establish the true glory of a monarchy.'[256] The idea of the inviolability of property was, of course, far from absent in French thinking. However, French public law assumed an uneven distribution of office, privilege and patrimony and hinged on the notion that rights were attached to corporate identity or social rank; determined and protected by customary law they also required a monarchical dispensation of privilege. By contrast in England the defence of corporate liberties, privileges and immunities was transformed into a defence of individual rights.[257] Individuals, and not just communities, declared John Floyd in 1620, had inalienable rights.[258] Ironically, this development, of enormous significance not only for its political consequences but for the whole of English culture, was in part made possible by the way in which the royal judges had long inserted themselves between lords and tenants. All these tendencies, reinforced by Parliament's unitary position, the national character of English politics and an individual property-based franchise, made possible the claim that it – Parliament – represented the ancient liberties of all Englishmen.

ROYAL AUTHORITY SUBVERTED

The increasing inability of the Stuarts to rule effectively either with or without Parliament was thus a measure of two closely related problems: their lack of the practical means to do so and their growing isolation from the political nation. Underscoring both was the rapid erosion of the ideological foundations of monarchical rule.

This may in part be attributed to the growth of a vigorous home market and the development of agrarian capitalism. Their effects were perhaps most clearly seen in the emergence of *laissez-faire* attitudes and of opposition to the Crown's paternalistic and regulatory role. Most famously, the parliamentary attack on monopolies was eventually rewarded with the statute of 1624 making illegal 'all monopolies, commissions, grants, licences, charters and patents for the sole buying, making, working or using of any commodities within the realm'.[259] The privileges of the Merchant Adventurers' Company were also severely dented, although the Crown restored its rights in 1634.[260] Rather more significant was the fading of the restrictions on manufacturing and domestic trade which in any event had never been incorporated into a system of centralised inspection and control in the way prescribed by Colbert's regulations. Indeed, the general system of regulation embodied in charters and Elizabethan legislation was undermined by contrary decisions of the courts and the Privy Council. As early as 1599 a test case determined that the confiscation and forfeiture of goods during a search were illegal. An ordinance forbidding a freeman of the Merchant Tailors to sub-contract work to foreigners was also declared to have no binding force. The controls on the movement and employment of labour embodied in the Statute of Artificers were less and less enforced as employers and labourers alike sought to benefit from the expanding market and adapt to the changes in its structure. In 1614 the courts decided that it was possible for apprentices who had completed seven years in apprenticeship in one trade to freely abandon it for another. The London Common Council was not even consistent in its opposition to non-freeman engaging in business.[261] Although some guilds clung to their privileges well into the eighteenth century, the erosion of their economic functions eventually left only a certain social exclusivity. The espousal of market forces is even more strikingly illustrated by the fading restrictions on the production and sale of bread and grain, which had been as characteristic of sixteenth-century England as they continued to be of France. Hoarding was actually encouraged by an act of 1663 in order to reward those who invested in the improvement of wastelands.[262]

The political implications of changing economic attitudes became apparent, as Joyce Appleby has demonstrated, in the debate aroused by the monetary shortage of the 1620s. The problem lay not in the inadequacies of fiscal controls, said Thomas Mun, but in the balance of trade. In sustaining this view he argued that the system of exchange was regulated only by impersonal economic mechanisms.[263] 'Let Princes oppress, lawyers extort, Usurers bite, Prodigals waste . . . so much treasure will only be brought in or carried out of the Commonwealth as the Forraign trade doth over or under balance in value.'[264] Thomas Missenden, a pamphleteering Hackney merchant, tackled head-on the conventional notion that the shortage of coins was the result of profiteering by unscrupulous merchants and that the remedy therefore lay in the more vigorous application of regalian rights. Exchange, insisted Missenden, was intended to be profitable and would only take place when it was advantageous. Evidently merchants were better placed to judge this than the king. Moreover, the charge that such activities were contrary to the public interest was misconceived for was 'not the public involved in the private, and the private in the public? What else makes a Commonwealth but private wealth . . .?'.[265] It was to be the middle of the eighteenth century before such notions, reinforced by the impact of English ideas and experience, began to exert an influence in France.

It should not, however, be imagined that England's cultural transformation was the work of a new or revolutionary class brought into being by the forces of capitalism – at least in any simple sense. On the contrary, many of the ideas and assumptions to which reference has been made had slowly become those of the ruling class. This applied not just to matters economic but to the much more abstract and potent questions of royal prerogative and the law. Throughout the century the Stuarts were to find that those on whom they depended did not share their own view of the body politic. The most dramatic illustration is provided by Lord Chief Justice Coke, who was dismissed in 1616 and committed to the Tower in 1621; his house was ransacked for manuscripts as he lay dying in 1634 in a desperate attempt to suppress his views. Recovered in 1641 on the orders of the Long Parliament, Coke's *Reports* and *Institutes* subsequently became part of conventional legal wisdom.[266]

A significant manifestation of the ideological crisis that faced the monarchy was a marked decline in deference. As Peter Lake has pertinently observed, sixteenth-century rulers had seemingly been able to change the nation's religion but James I was not even able to marry his son to the infanta without arousing a storm of protest.[267] Charles was confronted at the very outset of his reign by the parliamentary onslaught on Buckingham. Such episodes were enough in themselves to try the patience of any self-respecting monarch. They can, however, be placed in the context of a much wider loss of respect for those with status and authority without which the attack on king, lords and bishops would have been impossible. The loss of deference is a vast subject. Let us merely note that from the beginning of the century dramatists were assuming the corruption of courts and courtiers. More significant, perhaps, was the pejorative use of the term 'royalist' to describe court candidates in the elections of 1624–5.[268] The stereotypical image of the Cavalier was also 'derived from the impression that Charles I was surrounded by irresponsible, swaggering soldiers, intent on destroying English liberties . . .'. By 1642 the terms 'papist', 'malignant' and 'Cavalier' had become virtually interchangeable.[269] 'Virtue', on the other hand, tended to become an opposition prerogative, frequently associated with the Puritan concept of the Godly;[270] it could be employed to justify a career open to the talents or even to attack the social and political order. Christopher Hill points to the character in *The Gentleman Usher* (1602) who declared:

> Had all been virtuous men
> There never had been princes upon earth,
> And so no subject; all men had been princes.
> A virtuous man is subject to no prince,
> But to his soul and honour.[271]

Whilst similar sentiments about the nature of virtue could be found amongst the French libertines, and in some Jansenist quarters, they tended, as has been observed, to lead to a retreat from the world and political engagement. Criticism was largely philosophical and introspective, unable in the end to resist the renewed insistence on hierarchy, order and obedience which underpinned the regime of Louis XIV. In England disillusion with the high and mighty overflowed into trenchant displays of public disrespect. 'Write on', declared a Dorset parson in 1626 when he noted a member of the congregation taking notes of his denunciation of injustice and corruption: 'I . . . would speak so much though the king were in presence.'[272] Like hundreds, if not thousands, of equally bold individuals this preacher almost certainly found the courage of his convictions in the notion that a papist plot was afoot to destroy the liberties of true-born Englishmen and perhaps in the millenarian notion that the Second Coming was to hand. It was a conviction far more impelling, far more scornful of conventional social values than the notion of a conspiracy of financiers which brought magisterial passions to simmering point in France.

The doctrine of predestination itself, by dividing humanity into the Godly and Ungodly, also 'undercut existing hierarchies of political office, birth or property'.[273] Whether or not we follow Underdown in his view that Puritan sobriety and discipline took greatest root in pastoral regions where commercial pressures were destroying traditional communal solidarities, the close relationship between Puritanism and the rhythms and values of an increasingly commercialised culture has been firmly established. The social and political value of the theory of the Elect to 'the sober sort of men of the middle rank that will hear reason' is beyond dispute.[274] So too was its appeal to the independent craftsmen and yeomen whose religious enthusiasm was crucial in generating the force and conviction necessary to defeat the king.

In every way the political and ideological terrain of England was much less propitious for the sort of assertion of royal prerogative and divine right that was so effective across the Channel. Charles, it has been said, was convinced that there was 'a deep-seated conspiracy against monarchical authority'.[275] If so, this was an oversimplified view but an understandable reaction. For as he and his advisers struggled to engage the hearts and minds of the people, it became apparent that their ideological offensive was ineffective and counter-productive. A series of tracts and sermons published between 1626 and 1628 endeavoured to place the royal prerogative in the context of a broader view of royal authority as the guarantor of social harmony, buttressed by conventional analogies of the king as father of the people. However, the associated demand for obedience, which enabled opponents to be castigated as rebels and supporters of resistance theory, simply eroded the middle ground.[276]

So too did the Arminian or Laudian religious offensive. The central insistence on the importance of 'outward ceremony, public prayer and the sacraments to the life of the church' required the restoration of religious practices – genuflection, the raising of altar rails, the taking of private confession before communion – which had long faded and were inevitably perceived as popery.[277] From these preoccupations flowed an effort, very marked from 1630, to enhance the role and status of the clergy, notably in the cathedral towns. At Chester and York, the municipal corporations were ordered to attend cathedral services in full regalia on Sunday mornings in order to set a good example and 'reduce competition between pulpits'.[278] It became a serious offence if a minister failed to bow at the name of Jesus, did not give communion at the altar rails or gave greater weight to sermons than to catechisms and homilies.[279] So was a failure to read the Book of Sports. Nothing expresses better the fears of the establishment about the subversion of the social order than this blatant exhortation to the people to abandon the Godly discipline of the Puritan Sunday in favour of diverting and reinvigorating traditional pastimes.

The inseparability of religious and political objectives was made unmistakably clear by the way in which assertions of royal divinity were used to justify the king's right to levy taxes. The very first of the revised and highly contentious canons of 1640 was explicit. 'Tribute and custom, and aid and subsidy and all manner of necessary support be respectively due to kings from their subjects by the law of God, nature and nations, for the public defence, care and protection of them.'[280] It is no wonder that a recurrent theme of the petitions of 1642 was the attribution of all the troubles of the realm to the 'popish Lords and bishops'.[281] If sovereignty were simply of divine origin and above all human consent, said the industrious pamphleteer, Henry Parker, then all men are slaves and Englishmen would suffer the same fate as the 'asinine peasants of France . . . whose wooden shoes and canvas breeches sufficiently proclaim what a blessedness it is to be born under a mere divine prerogative'.[282] The strategy adopted by the royal entourage served only to reinforce such connections in the minds of their opponents and to fuel the fears that would drive the country to open conflict.

The deliberate efforts of Charles to 'establish government and order' at court which 'from thence may spread with more order throughout all parts of our kingdoms' also failed to have the desired effect.[283] His insistence on courtly decorum and order with a strict respect for rank and protocol had nothing like the political and cultural resonance achieved through such means by Louis XIV.[284] In part this may be explained by Charles' failure to communicate with his subjects. He did so mainly by proclamation and there was no systematic image-building. Even his coronation was a private affair; ordering the removal of the arches prepared for his entry into London, he proceeded to Westminster by water.[285] Royal progresses, once exploited by Elizabeth with a canny blend of magnificence and accessibility, became hunting trips around the royal parks and residences of southern England. Charles made no entries into London until 1638 when the arrival of his mother-in-law, the Queen Dowager of France, made it unavoidable.[286] The habit of touching for the king's evil was also firmly limited to Easter and Michaelmas with repeated proclamations made to prevent people coming to court for that purpose. Only after 1639 as the political situation worsened did Charles become more assiduous in this regard.[287]

More was at work, however, than a technical failure to communicate with the country. Louis XIV, after all, retreated from Paris to Versailles with his court and government, venturing forth less and less as the years passed. What the Stuarts lacked was the social basis for a pervasive court culture. Charles simply did not have the wherewithal, even if he had felt the inclination, to make the Court the pivot of a vast system of patronage on the French model. Despite his fondness for acting in court masques which, in England as in France, were an excellent vehicle for the portrayal of royal virtues, there was no way Charles could emulate the French Court. 'The most splendid pageant' of his entire reign was in fact the Triumph of Peace mounted by the Inns of Court in 1634.[288] The £20,000 that it cost was well beyond the means of the king who was also anxious for some demonstration of loyalty from the legal profession at a time when it seemed none too assured. In this instance he was rewarded with a tale of the return to earth of Peace, Law and Justice who honoured Charles and Henrietta Maria as their true parents.

Yet Court and Country were moving apart. The gentry distanced themselves from the Court and its culture, ceasing to build houses with long galleries in which they could receive the king and his entourage. Their homes were far more functional in conception.[289] They certainly did not festoon them with the sort of Baroque iconography which was employed, most famously in Rubens' series of commemorative paintings of the reign of James I on the ceiling of the Banqueting House at Whitehall. Probably commissioned by Charles I in 1629–30 and completed in 1634, they exalted the achievement of a divine and all-powerful monarch in bringing unity, peace, plenty, religion, justice and wisdom to his people.[290] However, such legitimacy as might have been found in this extravagant message rapidly diminished. For the culture of Charles' court was far more inward-looking than that of his father, whose openness had enabled Shakespeare, Jonson, Bacon and Donne to bestow on it a sense of intellectual dynamism. It had possessed, according to Graham Parry, a certain role as 'a forum of national activity'. Now as 'innovation was replaced by cultivation' the gap between image and reality became unbridgeable.[291] It may also be that the royal retreat into privacy and away from conspicuous consumption reflected a general change in upper-class comportment.[292] Be that as it may – whether the king is perceived to be following the dictates of French fashion or the predilections of his own upper classes or both – the Court as the vector and focal point of an entire social system was almost finished. Understood as a question of values, the much criticised antithesis between 'Court' and 'Country' makes great sense. Indeed, it reflects the way these terms were used by contemporaries.[293] There were, of course, those in France who disliked and despised the life at Louis XIV's court. But the prestige and effectiveness of his regime were indubitably bound up with the triumph of a court culture in which it was advisable for the ambitious to participate. In England it failed to engender a common sense of purpose even amongst those closest to the king.[294]

The suppression of Court and monarchy, together with the House of Lords and the church, all proved insufficient to settle the political and ideological tensions which led to their demise. The execution of the king was pushed through by a minority in Parliament, in alliance with army radicals and the most militant citizens of London.[295] Thereafter, finding a broad enough social basis for the republican government proved impossible. In some ways parliamentary rule proved to be as oppressive as the old regime and the experience of Godly rule taught many that they did not really like it. Popular attachment to dancing, plays, feastings, wakes and ales was not easily broken.[296]

On the other hand, as Christopher Hill has long emphasised, the old order did not come back in its entirety. The prerogative courts disappeared, the King's Bench succeeded to most of the Star Chamber's jurisdiction and in conjunction with Parliament jointly supervised the legal processes which the Privy Council had previously exercised. In addition, the country had twenty years' experience of parliamentary rule when administration by committees responsible to Parliament had become the norm. Between 1661 and 1678 the Commons finally established their right to initiate money bills and appropriate supplies whilst denying the Lords the power to amend them.[297] It was clearer than ever that the king should not raise taxes without consent and the possibility of creating an independent royal bureaucracy of the type required to bypass Parliament receded.

In this situation any assertion of the royal prerogative was a high-risk policy. Charles II none the less ignored the revamped triennial act which required a fresh Parliament every three years and levied taxes illegally. Under James the royal army reached unprecedented size, troops were once again billeted on the populace, local authorities and universities were manipulated, intimidated and purged on a considerable scale. Louis XIV lurked in the background. All this was accompanied by a barrage of patriarchal language and an ever greater manipulation of traditional festivities in the interests of political conformity.[298] But, if the later Stuarts could browbeat their subjects, they were unable to recover for the monarchy the ideological hegemony required to achieve assent to their acts. As the French experience makes clear, even absolutism was a form of government which depended on the assent of the upper classes.

It has been suggested by some that the monarchy had already lost its ideological grip in June 1642 when Charles I replied to the Nineteen Propositions. For in doing so he accepted the definition of the three Estates as King, Lords and Commons, thus abandoning the traditional conception of the king as head of the body politic.[299] What this episode certainly showed was the extent to which his advisers themselves were already under the influence of ideas which undermined the position of the monarchy. Royalists, notably Henry Spelman, realising the damage that had been done, immediately went on the counter-attack with expositions of monarchical sovereignty.[300] None the less, in 1660 the principle of mixed government 'by kings, lords and commons' was written into the convention Parliament's proceedings with the assent of both houses. The cavalier Parliament of the following year, whilst explicitly safeguarding the king's role in law-making, did no more than that. In the years that followed the idea of a mixed monarchy, variously interpreted, 'took firm hold of the national imagination'.[301] In an endeavour to recover the initiative the government, apart from censoring what it held to be seditious doctrines, revised the Book of Common Prayer to eliminate any impression that the king was only one of three Estates in Parliament. The enacting clauses of parliamentary statutes were also given the fixed form they have retained to the present, making it clear that legislation was enacted by the king with the advice and consent of the Lords temporal and spiritual and of the Commons.[302] All of this was but further testimony to the ground that had been lost. The notion of 'mixed monarchy' was indeed a more accurate reflection of political realities than the classic defence of divinely ordained monarchical authority which Charles had delivered at his trial and on the scaffold.

This became clear in 1673 when his successor effectively made an open appeal to the House of Lords after the Commons had denied him the power to dispense with the ecclesiastical penal laws. Rebuffed even by the Lords, the king was compelled to withdraw the Declaration of Indulgence and within a month the first Test Act was also law. It is not necessary to concur with the view that this amounted to the 'most striking surrender ever made by the Stuart kings' in order to recognise the acute isolation of the monarchy.[303] James II was obliged to issue his two Declarations of Indulgence in 1687 and 1688 by proclamation. There were, of course, still those, including some judges, who found this procedure perfectly acceptable. Speck notes that whilst James may have strained his prerogative to the limit he never went beyond it.[304]

Such legal niceties, however, are only effective as long as they fulfil wider purposes which command general assent. By the time of the popish plot of 1678 this was hardly forthcoming as fears grew that the 1640s were about to repeat themselves. The attempt to prevent a Catholic succession by debarring James from the throne precipitated a major political crisis, a renewal of appeals to the public and a dramatic intensification of political debate. Within a few months of loyally promoting the Declaration of Indulgence, the Chancellor, the Earl of Shaftesbury, at odds with the king over the francophile and Catholic orientation of royal policy, fell from office. By 1675 he was leading opposition to the attempts to impose on the clergy, officeholders and members of Parliament an oath declaring illegal any armed resistance to the king and any attempt to change the constitution of the church.[305] His determination to prevent James succeeding to the throne cost him several months in the Tower of London. He was released by a London jury and died in exile. It was in these circumstances, after hope of preventing the succession of James had faded, that Shaftesbury's protégé, Locke, who was also dangerously immersed in Whig political agitation, probably wrote his Second Treatise.[306] It was the most enduring result of the exclusion crisis and, amongst other things, a barely veiled justification for resistance.

Locke got round the problem of the royal prerogative by observing that where it was employed for the benefit of the community it was not questioned; in England it had always been 'largest in the hands of our wisest and best princes'. If misused, the people will seek to limit it. In any event the supreme power in a commonweal was the legislative power which was itself held in trust on behalf of the people whilst the executive was the essential but mere executor of the public law.

> When he quits this representation, this publick will and acts by his own private will, he degrades himself, and is but a single Person without power, and without Will, that has any right to obedience; the members owing no obedience but to the publick Will of the Society.[307]

The publick will was manifest in the civil law instituted by the people as they moved from a state of nature into society. It was the rule of law which ensured the preservation of life, liberty and property; any government which abandoned this principle thereby lost its legitimacy.[308] Absolute monarchy, far from being, as some would have it, the only government in the world, was 'no form of civil government at all' because the monarch was exempted from the rule of the publick law which distinguished civil society from a state of nature.[309] In 1681 such ideas were unpublishable and Locke was soon to flee to Holland. But when the *Treatises* were finally published (though still anonymously) in 1689 it was the simplest thing in the world to adjust the text to the circumstances of James' departure. The abandonment of office by the executive power,

Locke now added, has the effect of dissolving the government which the people are then at liberty to reconstitute.[310] In doing so he virtually replicated the wording of parliamentary resolutions to this effect and lent weight to the view that 'William in assenting to the Bill of Rights recognised the consensual or contractual limits of his power'.[311]

Others exploited the circumstances of the royal departure to claim that nothing much had happened; for them the convention Parliament of 1688 was a normal Parliament. Without assenting to this instant rewriting of history, it is possible to see the events of 1688 as a rather anti-climactic denouement of struggles stretching back almost a century, the ultimate failure of the monarchy to recover the allegiance of its subjects. The continuity of issues from beginning to end of the century is unmistakable and the manner of James' departure in 1688 testified to his total isolation. A man of proven military capacities simply capitulated before a far from perfectly executed invasion of 14,000 men. 'Wracked by guilt that the Dutch invasion was God's punishment for a sinful life and convinced that Providence had deserted him', isolated by the utter collapse of all his political, religious and military calculations, reduced to a state of panic as parts of his army deserted, the king fled without a word of justification.[312] Few came to his aid and few defended him. The hundred or so tracts justifying resistance that appeared between the autumn of 1688 and 1694 outnumbered those espousing ideas of non-resistance or passive resistance.[313]

In a different perspective the events of 1688 may be seen as the decisive settlement of the question of sovereignty and the critical turning point in the wider history of monarchy as a form of government. The Declaration of Rights declared the use of the dispensing and suspending powers to be illegal, recognised Parliament's right to dispose of the Crown, and placed the peace-time army under its authority. William and Mary undertook in a revised version of the coronation oath 'to govern the people of this kingdom of England . . . according to the statutes in Parliament agreed on, and the laws and customs of the same'.[314] The powers retained by the new monarchs in 1688 – to make war and peace, to summon and dissolve Parliament, to appoint and dismiss ministers – were all eroded in the years that followed as Parliament took advantage of the need for it to meet every year to provide supply. William vetoed five bills before 1690 but they all subsequently became law and after that he did not use the veto. Anne's veto of 1708 was the last in English history.[315] Eighteenth-century ministers were invariably Privy Councillors and responsible to Parliament whose support became essential for the effective tenure of office. The financial independence of the Crown was reduced to what the civil list would sustain and the threat of an independent royal army receded for ever. So too did the threat to the autonomy of the English towns. The right to appoint judges at pleasure was not exercised by William and Mary and disappeared with the accession of George I. They were placed under parliamentary control in 1701. As Speck has so aptly concluded, what triumphed was 'a version of the rule of law which saw the king as beneath not above it'.[316] This monarchy now had virtually nothing in common with the regime of Louis XIV. It was entirely appropriate that Queen Anne should graciously decline to accept the appellation of monarch by divine right.[317]

The entrenchment of parliamentary government was accompanied by a new surge in the size of the electorate which, comprising some 4.6 per cent of the population, was as least as 'representative' as it was to be after the 1832 Reform Act.[318] This was yet a further indication of a political system whose principles and mode of operation were light years away from those of *ancien régime* France. Whatever its shortcomings by modern criteria, the representative system in England enabled contemporaries to discern through the behaviour of the electorate the 'sense of the nation'. Perhaps the most effective testimony to the significance of the electorate is the ample scope that it has offered in recent years for historical research; it would not, however, be much use embarking on a study of the French electorate before 1788. Of course, it is true that the social changes of the eighteenth century gradually diminished the capacity of the British system to reflect the 'sense of the nation' and led to demands for major reforms. But this was a problem of an entirely different order from that facing France. Here the *sine qua non* of any attempt to introduce a constitution which might adequately represent the nation was the demolition of the absolutist regime and all the assumptions on which it rested. In 1789 Louis XVI was confronted, as Charles I had been, with demands for reform that required an abandonment of his conception of the natural order, the body politic and his place in it. The French kings, however, showed rather more ideological resolution. As late as 1795 Louis XVIII was still declaring his intention to bring back the three Orders if he were restored to throne.[319]

Charles, as has been seen, was felt to have abandoned the traditional conception of the body politic far too readily. Yet it is doubtful whether the initiative was any more recoverable for the English monarchy in 1642 than it was for the French one in 1789. It is supremely ironic and further indicative of the erosion of the ideological foundations of the old order that Hobbes was amongst those who criticised the royal advisers for their failure in this regard.[320] For the conception of the social and political order depicted in his *Leviathan* owes nothing to the conventional world view. Although the assertion of the need for an all-powerful sovereign power makes it tempting to treat Hobbes as a lineal successor to Bodin, the break with Bodin's mode of thinking was complete. Whereas Bodin deduced the need for a sovereign authority in traditional teleological fashion and made the pursuit of the *summum bonum* its *raison d'être*, Hobbes deduced the need for a state from his view of the appetitive nature of human beings. He dismissed the old moral philosophers out of hand. Where Bodin assumed natural inequality and a society of corporate hierarchies, Hobbes assumed both natural equality and equality before the law; intermediate bodies between state and subject, including the family, were insignificant in the Hobbesian world of competing individuals. Bodin had anchored his conception of the law to traditional moral and teleological conceptions about the purpose of government; but for Hobbes law was only the contracts made by men to ensure their own security and self-interest. 'Injustice' he defined simply as a failure to abide by them. Whereas Hobbes' world view still retains a capacity to appeal to the modern mind, Bodin's metaphysical universe belongs to an age which has gone.[321] Locke's modernity is even more self-evident. His remarkable synthesis of well-established ideas about the obligations and limited powers of monarchs with a clear exposition of the supremacy of the law which he derived from the natural rights of the people has exerted an influence on real politics ever since.

The political cultures of France and England thus moved farther and farther apart. Locke's world view from which he deduced the nature and purpose of government bore no relationship to that which sustained Louis XIV. His conception of natural rights and equality meant that it also had very little in common with the aristocratic constitutional thinkers in the entourage of Louis XIV's grandson. Their views, however irksome to authority, did not break the bounds of the inherited world view on which royal power rested. In England, of course, there were those who espoused views identical to those of the apologists for Louis XIV. Filmer's deduction of the patriarchal and unchallengeable power of kings from the power bestowed on Adam by God has a close affinity to some passages of Bossuet.[322] Locke's *First Treatise* tore Filmer's biblical exegesis to shreds. The *Second Treatise* provided a totally different way of looking at the natural order, civil society and therefore the foundations and purpose of government. It is no misuse of words to say that by 1688 two diametrically opposed ideologies were in confrontation both across the English Channel and inside England itself.

This may also be seen in the commonplace association of tyranny, absolutism and wooden shoes. The fear and loathing of the French regime which was repeatedly expressed down the century reflected a widespread belief that absolutism was not a form of government which could ensure either prosperity or property rights. During the exclusion crisis the point was hammered home by writer after writer. William Petyt put it succinctly: 'We have a particular advantage over France in the nature of our government; under which liberty and property are by law, and public constitutions secured, which must be a vast encouragement to trade and traders.'[323] In more abstract vein, Locke contended that, whilst absolute monarchy might be, as Filmer believed, a possible form of government in primitive times, it was quite inappropriate in economically advanced societies where the function of government was to preserve property. Here Locke's thought met up with the widespread view, particularly associated with Harrington, that it was a shift in the distribution of landed property which explained and justified a shift in political power.[324] The idea that commercial activity was not best suited to monarchies, however, was not the exclusive property of English radicals. It was widely voiced by the defenders of aristocratic, monarchical regimes themselves, particularly by those who felt threatened by the progress of trade. If, explained one French pamphleteer in 1754, nobles were allowed to trade freely, 'in a short space of time one would see the disappearance of this warrior spirit which has always distinguished the French nobility'. Another posed the equally weary rhetorical question about why it was that states in which commerce have flourished have been republican. Because, came the reply, 'the spirit of commerce is that of equality . . . when the national spirit is that of commerce the form of government always leads to the diminishing of the great . . .'.[325]

Nothing brings home more sharply the integrated character of economic, political and ideological perspectives than the French debate over the freeing of the grain trade. Herbert in his famous essay *The General Police of Grain* (1753), which he described as a contribution to the happiness of the people, invoked the patronage of both Locke and Newton. 'It is', he wrote, 'the destiny of humanity to be highly motivated only by personal interests'. He continued, 'needs and interest govern the Universe . . . unite these wellsprings and men by a natural instinct will direct themselves in concert towards the objectives of their needs and country'.[326]

For some, such sentiments amounted to nothing less than a frontal assault on the entire social and political order. The *parlement* of Rouen, which in 1763–4 lent its support to the freeing of the grain trade, retracted five years later as grain shortages loomed. It now argued that private interests would violate the natural order which it was supposed to guarantee and that to establish self-interest, 'this violent passion', as the general law would be 'to cast us into the state of nature'.

> Suppress all Regulations, leaving only an unlimited liberty, the balance wheel of society will be destroyed; the Peoples will be [indiscriminately] blended; the Sovereign will be nothing more than a magnate distinguished by some sort of mark but without any power to be useful; thus this system which appears to lay the foundation for everything in fact tends to shake and destroy everything.

'Unlimited liberty', said the *parlementaires,* is not only 'contrary to the happiness of your subjects' but also 'an Alteration to the French Constitution'.[327]

As the political and intellectual climate of France became more open to the assimilation of the assumptions which had gone into the making of Locke's thought so the dissolution of the *ancien régime* moved a step nearer. The idea that society was an aggregate of individuals, best regulated by the equitable operation of the law with its source in the community rather than in God, was to subvert the Bourbon dynasty as it had that of the Stuarts. That it had become possible for Hobbes, Locke and others to perceive society in this way reflected, as MacPherson argued many years ago, the steady disintegration of traditional hierarchies under the impact of market forces.[328] But the Lockian synthesis, which went well beyond Hobbes, was also a product of the peculiarities of the English system of representative government, the power of the common law and the ideological climate which sustained both. It was these which both precipitated and cut short the absolutist aspirations of the Stuarts. Had the political institutions and culture of England been like those of France, the conditions for economic development, as many contemporaries themselves understood, would have been nothing like as favourable.

8

EMPIRICAL RÉSUMÉ AND THEORETICAL AFTERTHOUGHTS

There is, as Philip Abrams pointed out, no obvious reason why the transition from feudalism to capitalism should involve a passage through the absolute state.[1] French absolutism does, indeed, appear to have very little to do with capitalism. Inasmuch as the French state pursued policies which were of interest to the mercantile and industrial bourgeoisie, this reflected its own perceptions of the threat posed by the Dutch and the English rather than a response to the demands of its own merchants. On the contrary, merchant communities were frequently ambivalent or hostile towards government policies. It was not until 1700 that the resuscitated Council of Commerce gave them any permanent place at the centre of the French state. This late arrival was a fair reflection of the regime's priorities and of the limited numbers and social weight of merchants and manufacturers of substance. Their position does not appear to have been much improved by Colbert's interventionist policies, the impact of which was variable and which probably had only a marginal effect on France's overall economic development. The comparative buoyancy of the commercial sector of France's economy had much more to do with the power of the Atlantic economy than protectionism. This is brought home by the fact that the lucrative trade in sugar, which had undoubtedly benefited from the watchful eye of Colbert, rapidly became an area of free trade. In fact, the resources and power of the French state were never directed towards the protection and aggrandisement of commercial interests with the same determination as England displayed from the mid-seventeenth century. To the extent that the government bolstered the position of the larger merchants through its dispensation of privilege it also made life more difficult for the retailers and craftsmen who far outnumbered them. Entrepreneurial activity became less important than an ability to manage the system. Guild organisation placed restraints on economic activity and probably impeded technical progress. Anyway, the general attachment to guild organisation was attributable neither to the will of the government nor to the progress of capitalism; artisans and merchants saw guilds as essential means of protecting their share of an inflexible, possibly shrinking, domestic market. Colbert's overwhelming concern with the production of high-quality cloth for the export markets did little to overcome this problem; there is evidence to suggest that it may well have compounded it by drawing resources away from the manufacture of cheaper textiles. In England the shift away from the manufacture of heavy broadcloths to lighter products for the domestic market owed little to government intervention.

It is, in any event, probably mistaken to measure the development of capitalism in France by the progress of overseas trade or industry. Even the rapid commercial growth of the eighteenth century could not compensate for the stagnant home market nor induce the social transformations required for its development. Commercial activity may even have compounded the problem by its tendency to depress the position of the small producers. Despite the consolidation of some colossal commercial fortunes, the drift of commercial capital into *rentier* investments in land and office continued throughout the *ancien régime*. Even in the great port of Bordeaux the merchants were outnumbered by officials, professional people, *rentiers* and property owners. At Rouen the proportion was three to one.[2] The comparison with England confirms the force of these observations. It is hardly possible to exaggerate the significance of agricultural developments for her economic development. They laid the basis for a resilient home market, made possible a rapid expansion of the urban population and eroded the antithesis between status based on land and commercial activity. Of course, like their French counterparts English merchants sought status through the purchase of land. But the commercial nature of agriculture meant that such investments continued to work in a capitalist way. However snooty the eighteenth-century county set were to become about the monied men, there was absolutely no equivalent to the custom of *dérogeance* which had such an inhibiting effect on the French nobility. Family connections and economic investments linked many of the gentry directly to the world of commerce. Politically, the English revolution was in part made by an alliance of gentry and London's colonial merchants. So too was the aggressive commercial policy that developed in the years that followed.

Whilst French officials became increasingly aware of the need to generate greater prosperity in the countryside, this aspiration was completely nullified by the economic and fiscal orientation of the regime. Such considerations were in practice subordinated to the short-term interests of a ruling class which was very far from capitalist. Embracing sword, robe, the upper clergy and municipal elites, it derived its wealth from a capacity to appropriate through a combination of rents, feudal perquisites and fiscal devices the 'surplus' wealth generated by the peasantry. Its domination was ensured partly by the pattern of land distribution. This gave members of the ruling class by far the largest share around the major cities and towns, as well as a disproportionate hold on valuable meadowland and woods. An extensive range of coercive mechanisms for the extraction of the wealth of their estates removed any necessity to become capitalist entrepreneurs. This situation was not changed by the development of *fermage*, the allegedly modern leases of northern France. In practice the distinction between these and *rentier*/feudal modes of exploitation was thoroughly blurred and did nothing to alter the economic dynamics of the system. Everywhere, shorter and highly prescriptive leases were used to force up rents to unsustainable levels. Even when sizable estates were consolidated – frequently by resort to the *retrait féodale* – the *rentier* mentality persisted. Indeed, the revenue from feudal dues and perquisites seems to have been more significant the larger the estate. If the decision of the Roncherolles of St Pierre du Pont in 1585 to withdraw entirely from farming and live off their seigneurial rights was an extreme case it was none the less indicative of a wider trend and a pervasive *rentier* mentality. By the eighteenth century, concludes Jones, seigneurialism was 'adapting to the role it performed best: surplus extraction', the seigneurs having 'long since sacrificed the coherence of their desmesne land in an effort to stay solvent'.[3] Le Roy Ladurie's view that the seigneury provided a vehicle for the development of capitalism is no better founded than Brenner's stress on the pioneering role of England's feudal landlords.

Chaunu's suggestion that the fiscal operations of the French state *ipso facto* rendered it capitalist is also unconvincing.[4] The money flowing through the state apparatus went either directly into the costs of war or into usurious or *rentier* investments. It is of course possible to find some financiers (more, perhaps, as the eighteenth century advanced) who invested in commercial enterprises. The military needs of the state also played a large part in stimulating iron production. Yet, as Dessert's meticulous analysis has shown, the overwhelming majority of the principal financiers were not entrepreneurs, whilst the perilous nature of their activities meant that dependence on them for investment was likely to bring as many difficulties as opportunities. Not surprisingly, they were also a major obstacle to the development of a banking system to match that of England. The central role played by private financiers reflected the extent to which merchants and entrepreneurs were displaced at nearly every level of government, including municipal administrations, by *rentier* officeholders. Many of these, of course, particularly prior to 1650, came from mercantile backgrounds which they had abandoned and often tried to hide. English towns, by contrast, were dominated by merchants, numbers of whom even refused to hold municipal office. It is impossible to calculate the damage done to France's economic development by the proliferation of venal officeholding which, apart from draining the countryside of its wealth, remained a permanent inducement to the abandonment of trade.

Venal officeholding reinforced the economic dominance of the landowners by giving them direct control of the bureaucracy. At every level, beyond the most humble, financial and judicial office became the property of landowning families. They were, as Jacquart has said of the *parlementaires*, part of a hierarchy which was both feudal and *étatique*.[5] Even the great nobility of the sword, despite their overt disdain for money and the upstarts whose rise it had facilitated, surreptitiously purchased offices and a large share of the spoils. Whatever had been the case in the later Middle Ages, by the early modern period the notion that the state existed as an independent competitor of the nobility for the revenues of the peasantry will not stand scrutiny. It was itself the property of landowners who were thus able to divert by legal, quasi-legal and sometimes illegal means an inestimable proportion of the tax proceeds into their own pockets. This was the reason why the immensely swollen ordinary revenues of the Crown, which should have been sufficient to finance its wars, never could. Peasant antipathy to the *gabeleur*, far from revealing a lack of class consciousness, thus pinpointed with great accuracy the divide between exploiters and exploited. For in addition to paying for the king's wars, the populace was shouldering the burden of his obligations to the ruling class as well. The peasants' view that both they and the king were being fleeced by those in a position to manipulate the system was an accurate representation of its operation. Those on whom their wrath fell were frequently either royal or municipal officers whose position enabled them to alleviate the burdens on their own tenants at the expense of the rest of the community.

Government dissatisfaction with the performance of the financial officials resulted in a significant extension of the supervisory and executive powers of the intendants. However, given their own roots in the officeholding world, it would have been surprising had this sufficed to overcome the utter confusion of public and private interest which governed the dynamics of the absolutist state. Although proposals for the reduction or even abolition of venality were constantly mooted, the Fronde brought home the impossibility of any fundamental attack on it. Louis XIV subsequently bought the political acquiescence of the great officeholders, notably the *parlementaires*, in exchange for a tacit recognition of their material and judicial interests which were, in fact, inseparable. The intendants, although re-established after the Fronde, were enjoined not to interfere with legal procedures. Colbert's determination to purge the financial system faded rapidly in face of obstruction, his own need for clients and the pressing fiscal problems of the Crown. Indeed, Colbert, who installed his family and dependants in every part of the state machine, confirmed rather than subverted its patrimonial nature.

It is therefore entirely possible to analyse French absolutism in terms of the now rather *passé* vulgar Marxist notion that the state does not simply serve ruling-class interests but is actually an instrument in the hands of the ruling class. It would in fact be difficult to find a clearer example of the 'unmediated cohabitation' of power and wealth.[6] Paradoxically, in England a state was in the process of creation which ultimately proved to be a more resilient and effective servant of the ruling class precisely because it offered a formally distinct 'public' arena for the mediation of sectional interests.

In the short term the French state fulfilled its class function with devastating effect, draining the countryside of its not inconsiderable wealth to the benefit of a privileged minority who accumulated colossal fortunes. Nothing exemplifies this better than the desperate shortage – frequently total absence – of useful coinage in the homes of the poor whilst the liquid assets of the rich grew in proportion to their location in the state hierarchy. Class differences further expressed themselves, as they do today, in houses, furniture, dress, diet and mortality rates. Whether used loosely in this way or in a more precise structural way France was a class society and the state was an integral part of it. Class antagonism and conflict, albeit often lacking a larger ideological dimension, were real enough. What is more, despite Bercé's claim that the upper classes really had things under control, they were naturally frightened when their town halls were invaded, their houses burnt down and their goods pillaged. Concessions were required to restore order. The long years of popular unrest undoubtedly predisposed the upper classes to settle their own differences and come to terms with the king.

Despite the very direct part played by the absolute state in surplus extraction and class oppression, its functions cannot be reduced to this. Moreover, to do so risks confusing its functional operation with the causes of its rise. Such confusion may be seen not only in Porshnev's 'class against class' explanation of absolutism but also in Anderson's description of absolutism as a compensation for the landlords' loss of local powers of 'politico-legal coercion'. Whilst this view of the exploitative character of absolutism makes partial sense of its class function it is unconvincing as an explanation of its rise. Empirical investigation shows that the higher echelons of the absolute state did not act as Anderson's view requires. On the contrary, they displayed a firm disinclination to appropriate the jurisdiction of the seigneurial courts over their tenants; remaining strongly attached to the principle that all should be judged by their natural judges, the members of the sovereign courts were prime defenders of the patrimonial nature of the legal system.

Given the symbiotic relationship between the state and landowning class this was hardly surprising. Much more surprising is the way the legal system of England developed a mode of operation sufficiently autonomous for it to insert itself between landlords and their customary tenants; the latter acquired a degree of legal protection not available to the vast majority of French peasants.

The centralisation of political power in seventeenth-century France had its genesis in two inseparable phenomena: first, as the chronology and character of institutional change make clear, in the demands of large-scale warfare; second, in the intense competition for place, influence and profit which was fuelled by the channelling of unprecedented riches through the growing state apparatus. The antagonism between robe and sword was but one expression of the pressures which pitted centre against periphery, clientele against clientele, family against family, one corporation against the next and, indeed, officer against officer. Fissures in the social fabric ran in all directions. The result was the Fronde, in which the multiple sources of opposition to Mazarin, despite a common conviction that he had stolen the government and wealth of France, could not unite long enough to dispose of him. However, Mazarin also survived precisely because the wealth and powers of patronage now at the disposition of the central government made it increasingly possible to subvert or outflank rival clienteles. Simultaneously and somewhat paradoxically, the upward movement of power was given a further boost by the growing realisation of the need for a ruler who could rise above the fray. Much of the literature of opposition during the Fronde demanded that the king do precisely that. Louis' decision to rule without a First Minister was a response to these pressures, not simply an expression of his ego. The elevation of the king was essential to the stabilisation of the regime.

There was, of course, a degree of illusion in this process. The administrative machinery over which Louis XIV presided remained the property of families who worked assiduously from one generation to the next to increase their economic assets, social standing and influence. Consequently the ruling class was riven with tensions. However, they were now resolved – or sometimes never resolved – within the framework of that machinery itself, with the king as ultimate arbiter. Thus the royal courts, right up to the level of the Privy Council, far from passing most of their time imposing the political will of the king, were occupied with successions, debts, privileges and the possession of office itself. To a quite startling extent the legal machinery was a device for either regulating itself or coping with conflicts involving its own officers. Almost byzantine procedures were developed, notably that of *évocation* which allowed litigants to obtain the transfer of proceedings elsewhere if they were disadvantaged on home territory by the presence of rival clans and clienteles. In parallel fashion, the fiscal machinery was a system for moving usurious money around and managing the relationships of all those who, either openly or covertly, had a finger in the pie. In other words, the state apparatus was as much an arena for the regulation of conflicts inside the ruling class as an instrument of class domination, although the two functions were indissolubly linked. The 'great market' of Versailles worked to the same end. At the apex of the system the king combined the often indistinguishable functions of supreme judge and fount of all patronage. The ceaseless jockeying for position and royal favour also helps to explain the ever more intense concern with rank and status. Forged in conflict, the elaborate hierarchy of the absolute state was a manifestation of the deep tensions which continued to trouble the body politic. It did, however, bring both political stability and a greater sense of cohesion to the ruling class.

Such an analysis makes possible a coherent synthesis of the functions of French absolutism and the processes by which it arose and which endowed it with some of its particularly distinctive features. Yet to let the argument rest here would still be inadequate. Much more is required to explain what prevented the precarious equilibrium underpinning French absolutism from collapsing into the factional strife typical of earlier decades. It is also necessary to reflect on why the widespread resistance to monarchical centralisation did not open up a different path of development, particularly since France, like England, had inherited a body of constitutional ideas which at the end of the wars of religion were still influential. Moreover, there existed a widespread feeling that the entire natural order was under threat. Religious division, massive popular unrest, and the long years of violent conflict all conspired to induce a sense of social decay and self-doubt.

As it turned out, the monarchy was well served by these gloomy perceptions. For they encouraged both a renewal of neoplatonic idealism and a retreat into self. The former was epitomised by Bodin's belief, formulated amidst the turmoil of the religious wars, that a commonweal should reflect and sustain the harmony of a metaphysical and moral universe. Religion and Justice were its principal mainstays. This contributed as much to the intellectual tone of the next century as his emphasis on legislative sovereignty. The long years of strife and misery also bequeathed a pervasive pessimism about the sinfulness and inadequacy of human beings whose only salvation lay in God. Whilst this could lead to varying degrees of austerity and genuine piety, unsettling to those with worldly responsibilities, it also served to reinforce the need for obedience and humility before the powers ordained of God. So too did the conviction, graphically confirmed by experience, that diversity of religion struck at very foundations of Monarchy and good Order. By mid-century the conflicts between Protestant and Catholic, Ultramontane and Catholic, had resolved themselves in a gallicanised counter-Reformation bringing together divine right theories and an intense Catholic piety in a powerful legitimation of the regime. This also affected the organisation of public assistance and charity, and in the means adopted for the disciplining of the *menu peuple* which served the interests of both the secular and the ecclesiastical authorities. The uncanny affinities between reforming Catholicism and Puritan godliness have even led to the former being described as a bourgeois religion.[7] Had a rapid development of French capitalism been in prospect maybe it would have played a similar role to Puritanism in transforming attitudes to work. As it was, the austere and repressive morality of France's municipal patriciates served only to offer future salvation in return for humility and submission. A similar message was increasingly conveyed to the tattered remnants of France's Protestant congregations by their own leaders.

The crucial agent in the renewal of the social fabric was the nobility itself. Emerging from the wars of religion with diminished self- and public esteem, many nobles were acutely aware that their social pre-eminence if not their very *raison d'être* was being destroyed by factional strife, the power of money, the swollen ranks of state officials and by new conceptions of merit and virtue. It was in response to these pressures, frequently through an appeal to a highly idealised past, that the nobility redefined itself. Helped by the distinct slowing down of upward social mobility after 1650, they succeeded in elevating birth, blood and ancient stock as the essential preconditions for honour and virtue. Both these concepts were themselves subtly but significantly altered. Losing their exclusively military connotations, they now embraced a recognition of the need for a degree of education and civilised behaviour. Frequently vacillating between a Corneillian assertion of the will, bouts of intense piety and a libertine existence, the nobility painfully came to terms with the need for greater self-control. In the classical idiom and ethos of French culture many of them found a vehicle for the reconciliation of the need for external order and their preoccupation with self. Conflict was internalised and removed from the realm of the temporal in the abstractions of the great classical tragedies; ancient mythology restored a fading sense of identity, whilst *fêtes* and *divertissements* enabled the nobility to reassert their position as the principal pillars of a revitalised monarchy.

The real triumph of the recast conception of nobility was its success in determining the terrain on which the battle of ideas was fought. Writers of middle-class origin contributed magnificently to the reinvigoration of the heroic and stoic, as well as to the elaboration of the concept of *honnêteté* through which courtly behaviour was sustained. Potentially subversive notions of virtue, based on merit and education, were incorporated into aristocratic views of the relationship between good breeding and proper upbringing. New perceptions of social worth were assimilated into established categories of thought. Loyseau thus rejigged the rungs of the social hierarchy in order to place the principal magistrates on a par with the great magnates but did so entirely within a conventional chain of being. Some writers, it is true, did move away from such imagery, finding that Descartes' mechanical universe, with its swirling whirlpools of matter, offered a more faithful reflection of the social dynamics of French society. The widespread preoccupation with *amour-propre* appeared to open up the possibility of a Hobbesian view of social behaviour. In fact it proved unable to break the grip of hierarchical and corporate conceptions of the social order or prevailing religious views about the need to love God and one's neighbour. Nor was majority opinion yet prepared to believe that merchants could safely be left to pursue their devices without wounding the general good. French individualism thus remained a speculative concept, largely locked up in the bosoms of philosophers and libertines, who were certainly much more interested in observing the world than in changing it. The development of individualism was also constrained by prevailing conceptions of hierarchy, lineage, family and property whose development owed as much to magistrates and lawyers as to grandees of ancient stock. An assertion of patrimonial interests is not in all circumstances inherently anti-capitalist; but it was certainly deployed at this time in defence of the privileged orders and the hierarchical society on which they depended. Nor, as Anderson believed, did the revival of Roman law engender a clear sense of absolute property rights. On the contrary, even the romanised south was penetrated by the customary and feudal notions of the north. Magistrates continued to expound on the complexities of the fief at enormous length. The French nobility, ably supported by those aspiring to that status, thus succeeded in recreating a culture in which everybody knew their place and in renewing their own sense of purpose and identity. This enabled the upper ranks of the nobility to rebuild their ties with the monarchy, partly through the elaboration of an increasingly refined system of courtly behaviour. Louis XIV adeptly manipulated the rewards and punishments at his disposition.

It is thus not surprising that the currents of constitutional thought so apparent in the sixteenth century lost ground without ever being completely vanquished. Indeed, at the end of the century the peers of the realm were insisting on their right, as heirs to the ancient feudal barons, to counsel the king whilst Fénélon was getting into trouble on account of his views about the need to restore a monarchy tempered by conciliar government, traditional governorships, and representative institutions. By this time, however, the appeal to the ancient liberties of an idealised past had much less resonance than in England. This was because no one knew what to do if the king declined to observe them. The idea that tyrannical kings could be called to account by the people or even the better part of the people became untenable. The conviction that all power was ordained of God and that kings were responsible only to God disarmed every movement of opposition in the seventeenth century. Of none was this more strikingly true than the French Protestants who, having disavowed their earlier radicalism, left themselves defenceless against the ideological onslaught which accompanied the destruction of their allegedly 'republican' organisation by Louis XIII. The Protestants, as such, played no part in the Frondes. By the 1680s many of them believed that their fate was a sign of divine displeasure. Equally significantly, the most articulate constitutional theorist of the Fronde, Claude Joly, despite a presentation of contract theory that would have been well appreciated by the English regicides, could not translate his ideas into the conviction that resistance was justified.

In England the decline of deference, fuelled by religious conviction, made it possible to cross this barrier. Contractual theories of monarchy and the distinction between the person of the king and his offices, which was gradually obliterated in France, retained their credibility. More profoundly, perhaps, the cultural, religious and political hegemony of the monarchy had been severely eroded by a powerful individualism. Whereas French constitutionalism rested on a defence of traditional liberties of Estates, towns, provinces and corporate bodies, the appeal in England was to the fundamental rights of freeborn Englishmen and to a system of representative government which they believed guaranteed them. By the beginning of the seventeenth century the common law had moved a long way towards establishing a sense of equality before its dispositions and inviolable property rights. This meant that many of those responsible for running England's diminutive state apparatus, including a Parliament which was still formally a royal institution, subscribed to a set of essentially bourgeois ideas. The gentry who sat in the Commons became vociferous defenders of commercial freedom against the wishes of the Crown. Hierarchy was simultaneously challenged by the progress of Puritan attitudes and practices. Conventional chain-of-being imagery made less and less sense of England's social and political structures whilst scientific progress added to the doubt. 'Prince, Subject, Father, Sonne are things forgot', wrote John Donne in 1611. By 1651 when Hobbes responded to the collapse of monarchical authority it was not by resurrecting such analogies, which find no place in the *Leviathan*; his starting point was the isolated and 'appetitive' individual.

In this perspective it is not difficult to see why the attempt by Charles I to restore the integrity of the monarchical regime was so counterproductive. The English Parliament may still have been at his disposition to summon and dismiss; but his inability to rule through it was testimony to the narrowing political and ideological basis of his government. More powerful and prestigious than any other representative institution in Europe, Parliament had become the symbol and bulwark of English liberties. The attempt by the early Stuarts to recover the political and ideological initiative turned into a disaster. The use of the prerogative, particularly when justified by an assertion of the divine source of authority to override so-called fundamental rights, simply divided the nation. The Arminian endeavour to renew a sense of obedience and humility before the powers ordained by God aroused fears of popery. To the extent that Charles' advisers accepted the widespread assumption that England's government was a form of mixed monarchy, the royal response was also confused and hesitant. The post-Restoration attempt to reassert the royal prerogative made little headway. The result, under James II, was the endeavour to produce an amenable Parliament through a combination of arbitrary rule and concessions to Catholics. It completely misjudged the public mood. Whereas Charles I at least had a royalist party to fight for him, James was abandoned by virtually the entire ruling class. The political crises of the 1680s also generated a further and decisive radicalisation of political attitudes. By harnessing the idea of natural equality to the notion that civil society was established for the preservation of private property and to the widespread assumption that the royal prerogative was not unlimited, Locke forged a coherent view of the nature of political authority which was utterly incompatible with those of the Stuarts, the Bourbons or any of their apologists.

His explicit denial of the legitimacy of absolute monarchy was perfectly in tune with English anxieties which were constantly fuelled by perceptions of European developments. Although the commonplace association of tyranny with popery and wooden shoes was crude, insular and arrogant, it was not, it should be said, totally misconceived. There undoubtedly was a connection between the consolidation of the monarchical and aristocratic regime in France and the fate of the French peasantry on whose labour it rested. The impoverishment of the French population at the hands of landowners, urban patriciates and fiscal agents (often the same people) undermined any possibility for the rapid development of a buoyant home market. Small farmers lacked the incentive and means to improve their holdings; the dispossessed were more likely to join the swollen ranks of the dependent poor than become generators of demand. Whilst this process of proletarianisation was a precondition for the ultimate development of capitalism, it simultaneously set severe limits to the expansion of the market which capitalism required. The economic trajectory followed by England meant that for a crucial period, roughly from the mid-sixteenth to the late seventeenth century, small and medium-sized farmers played a vital part as producers, consumers and employers of labour in preparing the way for the transition towards the classical three-tier agrarian structures of the eighteenth century: large-scale capitalist landlords, tenant farmers and wage labour. The buoyancy of English agriculture, of course, had little to do with altruism. Smaller farmers were increasingly at the mercy of market mechanisms. The easing of the restrictions on enclosure made clear the limits of upper-class paternalism. On the other hand, the degree of cooperation between landlords and tenants and the commercial good sense embodied in the length and terms of leases betoken a very different attitude from that of French landlords who drained the rural world of its wealth and vitality. The result was a much greater ability and willingness to innovate, even in open field systems. Although advanced techniques were not unknown in France the French peasantry were constrained by their poverty, lack of security and prescribed systems of cultivation. The numerous examples of protection offered by English courts against the unreasonable raising of fines might also suggest a degree of comprehension about the negative consequences of placing excessive burdens on the productive classes. Whilst the French succeeded in stabilising the monarchical order through the operation of a gigantic system of spoils, it was undoubtedly at the expense of its economic future.

That such a populous and wealthy country was outpaced by England over the course of the seventeenth century is a major indictment of the *ancien régime*. 'Early industrialism and an extended market economy', it has been observed, were 'relatively modest in their infrastructural and technological requirements.'[8] Had the advice of the most far-sighted French ministers, officials and commentators been implemented, greater economic progress would surely have followed. Unfortunately the abolition of venality and a restructuring of the fiscal system were merely contemplated for two centuries. Failure to do more than tinker with these problems may in part be attributed to the sheer greed of those who made fortunes as well as careers out of the system. But ruling classes do not make history in conditions of their own choosing any more than anyone else. The restoration of political stability which was the immediate task facing the rulers of France could only be achieved with the material and ideological resources to hand. The result was that the short-term brilliance of Louis XIV's regime was achieved at the cost of its future health. In the eighteenth century, despite some significant indications of economic growth, the French regime proved unable either to mobilise sufficient resources to sustain the military contest with England or, in the end, to feed its people.

France's rival, on the other hand, as she headed towards industrialisation, had enlarged her state apparatus and become a front-rank military power. Parliament, having successfully denied the Stuarts access to the resources of the realm, now mobilised them in the pursuit of global supremacy. What became clearer as the contest unfolded was that those who felt that the governments and societies of England and France were qualitatively different were right. Their rivalry was not

> simply a conflict between colonial rivals, but between two different models of political and social organisation, generating fundamentally different ideologies. Not only did England contribute to the demise of the *Ancien Régime* by exhausting it in a colonial competition for which its resources were inadequate, but by furnishing much of the philosophical ammunition with which to undermine the ideological assumptions on which it rested.[9]

Despite the determined efforts of revisionist historians to dispense with revolutionary processes of all kinds and to emasculate the differences between the political and economic evolution of France and England, this conclusion remains as tenable now as it did more than twenty years ago, even if some parts of the picture are significantly different.

In this study I have suggested that it is possible to combine a structural definition of state and class with a non-reductionist explanation of their evolution in a specific historical context. One of the reasons why this is possible is that, in the context of an essentially empirical investigation, the theoretical dichotomy, emphasised by cultural Marxists, between class as structure and class as agency fades away.

It is perfectly possible to analyse French society in a good old-fashioned way, defining class by relationship to the means of production. Classes defined this way certainly existed and they direct one quite well to some of the key divisions and to the exploitative character of the state. It is also apparent that there existed a much higher degree of class feeling amongst the peasantry than is frequently allowed. On the other hand, it had clear limits and did not overflow into a sense of class unity. Artisans and peasants certainly did not challenge conventional wisdom about the social order, still less France's political arrangements. Some historians have mistaken this lack of political consciousness for an absence of class consciousness; but they are not the same thing. The latter can in fact be highly conservative and politically limited, which is the form it took. The privileged orders were equally conservative but, despite their acute divisions, displayed a high level of awareness about perceived threats to their dominant position and a growing sense of their own identity. Insistence on rank and status was in part a mechanism for the defence of class interests and cannot be used to prove that classes did not exist. Whilst perceptions of status and economic position may not have matched perfectly, they were much closer than is frequently alleged and far from antithetical. As Hobsbawm has noted, empirical observation leads to the fairly common-sense conclusion that there are varying degrees of classness.[10] It may have been relatively low in pre-capitalist societies but it certainly existed.

The notion of the transition from feudalism to capitalism also retains its value as a description of the shift from one sort of class society to another. However, the mechanisms by which this process took place have lost much of their revolutionary simplicity. This is partly because it is possible to see feudalism as the matrix of capitalism as well as its opposite. Under certain conditions feudalism was clearly capable of releasing considerable economic potential and, as Anderson suggested, of preparing the ground for the development of absolute property rights. Engels clearly had some sense of a revolutionary process when he described the gradual breaking of the fetters of feudalism in England but the helpfulness of this approach has all too often been lost in an emphasis on a revolutionary rupture in the 1640s.[11] Still, the basic contention that capitalist development hinged on English developments remains as defensible today as it did when Marx penned the historical bits of *Capital*.

The view that absolute monarchy marked a stage on the capitalist road, on the other hand, has always been more problematic. The general contradictions which propelled France in an absolutist direction were those characteristic of feudal society: tensions between dispersed *loci* of power, the constant need for conquest which might approximate to capitalism's constant need to maximise profits, the ever-deepening antagonism between the demands of warfare and inelastic economies, the indispensability of religious uniformity to unstable but hierarchic societies, and the conflicts between the papacy and incipient nation states as they emerged from medieval Christendom. To these it is possible to add the tensions generated by the intrusion of some forms of capitalism in the sixteenth century, and the widening gap between rich and poor generated by inflation, urbanisation and dispossession. But the seventeenth century proved to be a much less dynamic century: merchants became *rentiers* and officeholders, population stagnated; by the reign of Louis XIV, despite an easing of various pressures on the populace, the domestic market had taken a battering from which it would recover only slowly and hesitantly. The process of primitive accumulation, the development of capitalist relations, the expansion of the productive forces advanced slowly if at all. What took over in the seventeenth century as the force which determined the final contours of the absolute state was the need to find, as structural functionalists like Eisenstadt and Elias almost suggested, means of regulating the disputes between sections of the upper classes.

The motor of capitalist development in England may be located in a combination of two factors which are sometimes – quite unnecessarily – counterposed: class struggle and the development of the productive forces. The virtually continuous development of the productive forces from at least the end of the fifteenth century was a tangible demonstration of the fact that 'agricultural systems were inherently capable of modest growth'.[12] But a major reason for this was the struggle of the peasantry, in the advantageous conditions of the fifteenth and early sixteenth centuries, to emancipate themselves and enlarge their freedom of economic action. 'The collapse of serfdom', observes Britnell, 'was the most important thing that happened between 1330 and 1500.'[13] Many small farmers continued to extract concessions from the landlords well into the seventeenth century. Of course, others succumbed to the very market forces which they had encouraged. However, it was precisely the differentiation within the ranks of the peasantry which produced the buoyant home market, giving a further boost to the productive forces and putting England in a different economic league from France. Substantial peasants, particularly if they became yeomen, and above all the many yeomen who contributed to the expanding ranks of the gentry, not only bought things but also employed others. It is true that the process was far from straightforward. From the mid-sixteenth century to the early seventeenth it seemed that the poverty of the dispossessed might get the upper hand. There was also an incipient tendency for the peerage to adopt the posture of their French counterparts, resort to rack renting and become *rentier* – indeed, absentee – landlords. Theoretically England might have fallen into the same downward spiral that gripped the peasantry of France.

A key factor in preventing this, which positively contributed to the development of the productive forces, was the absence of a burdensome state machine. During the difficult decades the people of England were barely taxed. Those farmers, big or small, with a marketable surplus took a share of the profits from rising grain prices. In sharp contrast to the French situation, specie was not drained from the countryside, thus preserving the already highly monetarised character of the English economy. Whereas the lightweight English state did not impede the inherent capacity for agricultural growth, the bloated French bureaucracy did incalculable damage. Moreover, the absence of a large state apparatus, the limited opportunities for military endeavour and the diminishing benefits of royal patronage meant that, in the long term, the remaining elements of the 'feudal' aristocracy could only survive by becoming improving landlords and equipping themselves for government. From the mid-seventeenth century they did this with consummate success, re-establishing their social dominance within the framework of a capitalist mode of production and a system of parliamentary government.

These observations all sit within the broad framework of the base–superstructure model of classical Marxism. For it is possible to use this model to arrange empirical data in a meaningful way without descending into either economic determinism or an unstructured form of social history. The dangers of the former were nowhere better illustrated than by Porshnev's class versus class model of French absolutism; but similar tendencies can also be seen in the focus of both Brenner and Comminel on the determining effect of the mechanisms of surplus extraction and even in Anderson's view of absolutism as a consequence of the ending of serfdom. All these approaches precluded a clear recognition of the reciprocal relation of base and superstructure, of the specifically political dynamics of the absolute state and the impact which it had on the pace and character of social and economic development. The French state was instrumental in moulding the shape and character of key social strata through sale of office, the creation of Versailles, and the systematic projection of carefully elaborated cultural values. In England the appeal to ancient liberties acquired a radical and forward-looking character not simply because the development of a market economy provided a solid anchor for concepts of individual rights but because the structures of the state, the nature of the common law, and political struggle itself made that possible. The state was indeed an area of struggle in its own right. The formation and character of both the French and the English states by the end of the seventeenth century clearly owed as much to the way in which conflicts within the ruling class were resolved as they did to conflicts between classes. It is equally clear that much of the pressure on them was caused directly or indirectly by war.

Faced with the evident reciprocity of base and superstructure, some have been tempted to simply abandon the model in favour of an unstructured mishmash of interacting elements or to refine it so that it becomes theoretically watertight.[14] It has even been claimed that when Marx described the state and law as superstructures he was referring to a 'bewitched world of appearances', the ideological but illusory expression of the social relations of capitalism which manifested themselves in the form of ostensibly independent economic and non-economic spheres.[15] Suffice it to say that these spheres may not have been independent but they did exist, even in pre-capitalist society, as this discussion of French developments has shown. Without some such conceptualisation, common-sense empirical investigation of the interaction of political and economic developments would run into the ground. Moreover, an empirical approach, assisted by a few ideas from the Marxist classics, together with a little Gramsci and E.P. Thompson, makes it quite possible to employ the base–superstructure model in a flexible but still recognisably Marxist manner.

The first, fairly banal but useful notion from the classics is that all ideas have a material basis and that the ruling ideas in every epoch are those of the ruling class.[16] A second, which qualifies this starting point, is that these ideas are not just a passive reflection of class defined by relationship to the means of production. Class is an agency as well as a structure and its collective consciousness reflects its whole social being. The French nobility thus contributed directly to the stabilisation of the regime by redefining itself. At the same time it successfully incorporated into its redefinition ideas emanating from its critics and made them its own. The English gentry, on the other hand, eventually cut the ground from beneath the monarchy by espousing a range of political, cultural and economic attitudes which subverted the world view on which it depended. In neither case would these ideological and intellectual developments have been possible if there had been no material base for them but, as with Thompson's working class, the French and English ruling classes were present at their own making.[17] Their attitudes played an integral part in determining the conditions under which economic activity was to take place; as Gellner has observed, the development of the market required an appropriate 'political and cultural framework'.[18]

The third helpful notion which allows flexibility to be combined with structure is that of the relative autonomy of the superstructure. Much abstract blood has been spilt over this concept. But in the context of this study the relative autonomy of French political and ideological superstructures can be fairly well delineated by the unsuccessful attempts of the state to go beyond the limits of the social and economic structure of which it was part. It proved unable to restructure French society in order to compete with the capitalist countries to the north. Nobles, on the whole, refused to become commercial entrepreneurs, despite the progressive dismantling of the restrictions on economic activity; plans to modernise the nation's finances, to create a bank that could match the Bank of England, foundered for lack of public confidence and in face of the entrenched interests of the great financiers. Nor could the state detach itself from the interests of a highly traditional ruling class. Religion was placed higher in the scale of values than economic common sense. Foreign policy continued to reflect dynastic and territorial ambitions, relegating to second place for long periods the development of an aggressive colonial policy. Whilst the French state was the principal motor of seventeenth-century developments it could not overcome its own origins sufficiently to transform the productive forces or the basic character of property relations.

The relative autonomy of the English state appears to have been greater, its 'separation out' from society more advanced. This was partly because the French state was still constrained by the hierarchical and patrimonial devolution of power and privilege. As a result neither the fiscal nor the legal system was able to constitute a clearly defined public arena. By contrast, in England both the fiscal and the legal machinery acquired a measure of autonomy. They were formally detached not only from the monarchy but also from the political parties and politicians who, logically enough, made their appearance at the same time. The confusion of private interest and public authority was further diminished by a growing separation of powers and the emergence of a professional civil service. All this confirms the old notion that the modern state with its ostensibly 'public' character went hand in hand with the 'atomisation' of society which was itself induced by the development of market forces. The recognition and acceptance of individual private interest made necessary a spectrum of public and political mechanisms for the mediation of conflict in the interest of the ruling class as a whole. Those Frenchmen who feared that the legitimisation of 'private' interest would subvert the foundations of the French monarchy were probably right. Unfortunately the resistance to change perpetuated an inextricable confusion of patrimonial and public interests which in the end proved just as debilitating.

This approach makes it possible to recognise the instrumental role played by warfare in the formation of the state without making it the determinant of specific forms. It is important to acknowledge that warfare was not an 'external' or 'exogenous' factor intruding in some way on the real processes of history. For the prolonged civil, territorial and dynastic strife of the sixteenth and seventeenth centuries was an integral part of the dynamics of feudalism. Brought into being by the tension between dispersed *loci* of power, the supreme 'national' dynasties which emerged from the fray had a deep sense of the need to sustain their 'reputation'.[19] Moreover, within the context of relatively inflexible economies the drive to war became self-reinforcing as it could only be sustained through the acquisition of additional land and resources. The slide from this type of warfare into a more capitalist mode, in which the competition for markets became central, was at some points almost imperceptible. England's ultimate victory over France, of course, opened up new markets for her producers and traders.

However, the impact of war was mediated through specific social and political structures in particular historical circumstances. Absolutism and bureaucratic centralisation were not the only possible response to the demands of large-scale warfare, even in countries whose social and political structures were still feudal in complexion.[20] Similarly, it is not possible to use 'external' pressures in order to explain the outcome of the political crises which pushed England along the road to parliamentary government. Every Parliament in the 1620s, Russell remarks, was called because of war or the rumour of war.[21] Precisely; in England that is what was likely to happen in such circumstances. Moreover, the problems created for Charles I by the relatively footling wars with Spain and France and then, more seriously, with Scotland and Ireland produced in each case a further weakening of royal authority. So, too, did the Dutch invasion of 1688. Finally, in the years after 1688, as the country began to experience the pressures of involvement in large-scale and continuous warfare, William sacrificed most of what was left of old-style monarchical authority. The rapidly developing bureaucracy was firmly under parliamentary control. In France, by contrast, each threat and crisis had exactly the contrary effect, pushing it a little further down the absolutist road. This is not to diminish the significance of the pressures thus created nor to suggest that they did not influence the direction of events. In Bohemia the traumas of the 1620s threw a whole social system into reverse together with its religious and political traditions.[22] Had the English monarchy come under real pressure during the sixteenth century things might have turned out very differently. Yet even this observation confirms the point that 'external' pressures are inevitably mediated by the general conjuncture.

In the process of making these observations the conception of bourgeois revolution derived from the *Communist Manifesto* is significantly modified. This postulated a growth of capitalism inside the womb of feudalism and the birth of a bourgeois class which then seized power from its feudal masters. For some time the purchase of this approach on Marxist interpretations of the English Revolution has been much less evident than in the case of the French Revolution. This is ironic because it is more difficult to identify a bourgeois class in late eighteenth-century France than in mid-seventeenth-century England where a class of capitalist landlords certainly existed. It might, however, be suggested that it was the progress of bourgeois ideas which ultimately determined the pace of change and the fortunes of both monarchies. The ruling classes of both countries were first subverted and then divided by conceptions of the social and political order which challenged the assumptions on which absolute monarchy depended. By 1688 the isolation of the monarchy in England was complete. The same happened in late eighteenth-century France when many nobles, officeholders, merchants and clergy alike espoused a set of assumptions, largely derived from England, which were fundamentally bourgeois. In such circumstances, there was no prospect of repeating the ideological triumph of the previous century or of coping with the deep structural problems which that very triumph had left embedded in the heart of the *ancien régime*.

NOTES

INTRODUCTION (pp. 1–5)

1 Lublinskaya, 1968: 329.
2 Le Roy Ladurie 1994: 155; see below pp. 15, 58, 236.
3 Russell, 1979; see below p. 241.
4 Clark, 1986: *passim*.
5 Doyle, 1989: 401.
6 Marx and Engels, 1845–6: 37.
7 K. Thomas, *New York Review of Books*, vol. 22, no. 6 (April 1975)

CHAPTER 1 APPROACHES TO FRENCH ABSOLUTISM (pp. 6–27)

1 Mettam, 1988: *passim*; Morrill, 1978: 29; Henshall, 1992: *passim*.
2 Guenée, 1985: 5–6, 22, 207–8.
3 Rule, 1976: 262.
4 Shennan, 1974: 112–13.
5 Mousnier, 1979 and 1984: vol. 1: 108.
6 Kettering, 1986a: 142.
7 ibid.: 204–5.
8 ibid.: 207–37
9 Mousnier, 1979 and 1984: vol. 1: 640–2.
10 Bonney, 1989: 62.
11 Bonney, 1978: 441–2.
12 Dyson, 1980: 113.
13 Lagarde, 1951: 247–9.
14 Dyson, 1980: 136; Skinner, 1978: vol. 2: 264.
15 Skinner, vol. 2: 264; cf. Dupont-Ferrier, 1923: 393.
16 Shennan, 1986: 42.
17 ibid.: 50.
18 ibid.: 125.
19 Bonney, 1989: 108, 118.
20 Skinner, 1978: vol. 2: 131.
21 ibid.: 129–30.
22 Tipps, 1973: 204; Abrams, 1984: *passim* esp. 18–23.
23 Gusfield, 1967: 358.
24 Eisenstadt, 1963: 11.
25 cf. Abrams, 1984: 183ff.

26 ibid.: 183.
27 Eisenstadt, 1963: 120, 140–3, 270.
28 ibid.: 153–4, 353–60.
29 Elias, 1983: 70–1.
30 ibid.: 127.
31 ibid.: 137.
32 ibid.: 180.
33 ibid.: 152, 290.
34 ibid.: 167.
35 ibid.: 149.
36 ibid.: 181.
37 ibid.: 186.
38 ibid.: 114.
39 Eisenstadt, 1963: 115ff.
40 Shennan, 1974: 112.
41 ibid.: 112–13.
42 Shennan, 1986: *passim*.
43 Mousnier, 1979 and 1984: vol. 2: xix.
44 Braudel, 1972–3: vol. 2: 681.
45 ibid.: vol. 1: 449–51.
46 Marx, 1843: 166.
47 Corrigan and Sayer, 1986: 185.
48 cf. Guenée, 1964: 333.
49 Engels, 1884: 271.
50 Cited in Draper, 1977: vol. 1: 480.
51 Marx, 1871: 328.
52 Marx, 1847: 333.
53 Marx and Engels, 1845–6: 90.
54 Cited in Draper, 1977: 476.
55 cf. Engels, 1844: 271.
56 Kiernan, 1980: 103.
57 cf. Brenner, 1989: 272–303.
58 Engels, 1892: 289.
59 Marx, 1867: 791–2, 828.
60 Marx, 1894: 444.
61 ibid.: 449.
62 Dobb, 1946: 121.
63 Hobsbawm, 1956; Parker, 1980: esp. ch. 3.
64 Wallerstein, 1974: vol. 1: 247.
65 ibid.: vol. 1: 92.
66 Brenner, 1977: 57.
67 ibid.: *passim*.
68 Wallerstein, 1974: vol. 1: 106–7.
69 ibid.: vol. 1: 268–9.
70 ibid.: vol. 1: p. 295.
71 ibid.: vol. 1: 133, 138, 269, 284, 269, 355.
72 Braudel, 1981–4: vol. 1: 512.
73 ibid.: vol. 2: 89–385.
74 ibid.: vol. 1: 528.
75 ibid.: vol. 3: 288, 297.
76 ibid.: vol. 3: 277.
77 ibid.: vol. 3: 541.
78 ibid.: vol. 3: 295, 296.

79 ibid.: vol. 2: 250ff.
80 ibid.: vol. 2: 283; vol. 3: 561–3.
81 ibid.: vol. 2: 282.
82 ibid.: vol. 3: 324.
83 ibid.: vol. 3: 336.
84 ibid.: vol. 3: 51; vol. 1: 527.
85 ibid.: vol. 2: 550–1.
86 ibid.: vol. 2: 551.
87 Lublinskaya, 1968: 331.
88 Parker, 1971: 67–89.
89 ibid.: 67–89; 1980: *passim*.
90 Lublinskaya, 1972: 71; 1973: 359.
91 Porshnev, 1963: 294.
92 ibid.: 579.
93 ibid.: 568.
94 Beik, 1985: 579.
95 ibid.: 339.
96 ibid.: 29, 335–6.
97 ibid.: 336.
98 ibid.: 325.
99 Anderson, 1974: 403.
100 ibid.: 197.
101 ibid.: 19.
102 ibid.: 18.
103 ibid.: 17.
104 Porshnev, 1963: 529.
105 Beik, 1985: 25.
106 ibid.: 26–7.
107 ibid.: 339.
108 Anderson, 1974: 39, 41.
109 ibid.: 41.
110 ibid.: 422.
111 ibid.: 25, 27.
112 ibid.: 28.
113 ibid.: 425.
114 ibid.: 420.
115 ibid.: 429.
116 ibid.: 103.
117 ibid.: 94.
118 ibid.: 103.
119 ibid.: 108.
120 Brenner, 1985a: 56ff.
121 ibid.: 58.
122 Brenner, 1985b: 289, 262–4.
123 Comminel, 1987: 194.
124 ibid.: 195.
125 ibid.: 196.
126 ibid.: 170.
127 Mousnier, 1958: 90–106; 1962: 34.
128 ibid.: 34–5.
129 Mousnier, 1959: 346.
130 ibid.: 364.
131 ibid.: 362–3, 365, 367.

132 Mousnier, 1963: 228–9.
133 ibid.: 230.
134 Mousnier *et al.*, 1965: 15.
135 ibid.: 16.
136 ibid.: 18.
137 ibid.: 47.
138 Mousnier, 1979 and 1984: vol. 1: 66.
139 ibid.: vol. 1: 24–6.
140 ibid.: vol. 1: 549.
141 Mousnier, 1972: 292.
142 Ariazza, 1980: 42 n. 15; Kettering, 1986a: 244 n. 65.
143 Mousnier, 1979 and 1984: vol. 1: 253, cf. 3–16.
144 ibid.: vol. 1: 161, 202ff.
145 ibid.: vol. 1: 100.
146 Kettering, 1986a: 38.
147 ibid.: 19–20.
148 ibid.: 191.
149 Mousnier, 1979 and 1984: vol. 1: 40.
150 cf. Chaussinand-Nogaret, 1991: 186–201.

CHAPTER 2 THE FRENCH ECONOMY: A CASE OF ARRESTED DEVELOPMENT (pp. 28–74)

1 Parker, 1983: 73–81, 127–30.
2 ibid.: 176–8.
3 Temple, 1966: 19–22.
4 Parker, 1980: 48–9.
5 Duby, 1981: vol. 3: 179.
6 Gascon, 1971: vol. 1: 370–80, 410–12; Duby, 1981: vol. 3: 163.
7 Isambert *et al.*, 1822–33: vol. 19, no. 1464: 158–64; Temple, 1966: 25–9; Parker, 1980: 48–9.
8 Thomson, 1982: 126; Beik, 1985: 288.
9 Parker, 1971: 82–3.
10 Bosher, 1964: 28.
11 Schaeper, 1983: 73–5.
12 Cole, 1939: vol. 1: 496–501, 505.
13 Bosher, 1964: 32–4.
14 ibid.: 35; Schaeper, 1983; 204–8; Gille, 1947: 38–40.
15 Schaeper, 1983: 89–91, 95–6.
16 ibid.: 202–3; Bosher, 1964: 29–31.
17 ibid.: 14–23, 156.
18 Romano, 1978: 165–225.
19 Thomson, 1982: 138–9; Butel, 1993: 32.
20 Clark, 1981: 26–7, 155; Parker, 1980: 63–95; Delafosse, 1949: 240–4.
21 Delumeau, 1966: 99.
22 ibid.: 97–8; Clark, 1981: 26–7, 155; Boutruche, 1966: 476.
23 Delumeau, 1966: 172–6; Duby, 1981: vol. 3: 81; Boutruche, 1966: 457.
24 Léon, 1967: 41–2; Braudel, 1988: vol. 2: 565–76.
25 Butel, 1993: 29–30.
26 Delumeau, 1966: 99.
27 Cole, 1939: 55; Parker, 1980: 85; Clark, 1981: 162–3.
28 Schaeper, 1983: 108–34.

29 Boutruche, 1966: 472.
30 Meyer, 1984: vol. 1: 68–9.
31 Gascon, 1971: vol. 1: 203–8.
32 Frêche, 1975: 796.
33 Braudel, 1972–3: vol. 1: 220–1.
34 Frêche, 1975: 799.
35 Parker, 1980: 62.
36 Delafosse, 1963: 666–7.
37 Baehrel, 1961: 50–1 and *Graphiques* iii; Frêche, 1975: 689–92; Goubert, 1960: 493–504; Le Roy Ladurie, 1966: 512–14; Jacquart, 1974: 192.
38 Chevet, 1993: *passim*.
39 Dupâquier, 1989: vol. 2: 198–9, 203.
40 Frêche, 1975: 682.
41 ibid.: 101.
42 Baehrel, 1961: 50–7, 70–1, 92, 304, 622 and *Graphiques* ii and iii; Le Roy Ladurie, 1966: 585–92.
43 Croix, 1985: 152–3, 219, 282, 308.
44 Frêche, 1975: 2; Le Roy Ladurie, 1966: 211–13.
45 Croix, 1985: vol. 1: 150.
46 Le Goff, 1981: 7; Butel, 1993: 33; Lespagnol, 1991: 427–30.
47 Caillard *et al*., 1963: 15–20.
48 Goubert, 1960: 115–18.
49 ibid.: 90.
50 ibid.: 89–91.
51 Léon, 1967: 41.
52 Frêche, 1975: 639–53.
53 Gascon, 1971: vol. 1: 191.
54 Frêche, 1975: 598; cf. G. Durand, 1979: 109; Gascon, 1971: vol. 1: 183.
55 Thibaut, 1979: 149–50.
56 Scoville, 1950: 61.
57 Braudel, 1988: vol 1: 212–15.
58 Gascon, 1971: vol. 1: 189–90.
59 Le Goff, 1981: 9.
60 Pocquet de Livonnière, 1729: 621.
61 Goubert, 1960: 87–8.
62 Deyon, 1967: 90–4.
63 ibid.: 90.
64 Scoville, 1950: 61.
65 Braudel, 1981–4: vol. 3: 290–2; Bosher, 1964: 13–22.
66 ibid.: 20.
67 Clark, 1981: 177.
68 Bosher, 1964: 21.
69 Poussou, 1983: 265–6.
70 Croix, 1985: vol. 1: 40–5.
71 Thomson, 1982: 66–7.
72 Plaisse, 1961: 405–7.
73 G. Durand, 1979: 94–7, 126–8, 498ff.
74 Goubert, 1959: 30.
75 ibid.: 70–2.
76 Goubert, 1954: 8–20; Goubert, 1960: 340–1.
77 Thomson, 1982: 56–8, 65.
78 Trocmé, 1950: 109.
79 El Kordi, 1970: 61–2.

80 Goubert, 1960: 312–13.
81 Le Goff, 1981: 32–4.
82 Deyon, 1967: 546–7.
83 Coste, 1970: vol. 2: 381.
84 Clark, 1981: 68.
85 ibid.: 79.
86 Deyon, 1967: 295.
87 Clark, 1981: 43.
88 Goubert, 1960: 142–3, 146, 309.
89 Deyon, 1967: 229–31.
90 Markovitch, 1976: 18, 149–51.
91 Thomson, 1982: 301–11.
92 Deyon, 1967: 172–3, 339, 346–7, graph 34.
93 ibid.: 230.
94 ibid.: 227; Goubert, 1960: 317.
95 ibid.: 128; Deyon, 1967: 207.
96 Deyon, 1966: 60; Duby, 1981: vol. 3: 85.
97 Dornic, 1956: 40.
98 Gille, 1947: 145–54.
99 Scoville, 1950: 153–5.
100 Markovitch, 1976: 20–1, 91, 94, 104–5, 121–3; Braudel, 1988: vol. 2: 515–19; Thomson, 1982: 172–248; Poussou, 1983: 229.
101 Gille, 1947: 186–9.
102 Scoville, 1950: 30, 32, 40–1, 73, 99–104, 114, 143.
103 Thomson, 1982: 374ff.
104 Gille, 1947: 31.
105 ibid.: 46–7.
106 Scoville, 1950: 108–12.
107 Benedict, 1981: 15.
108 Trocmé, 1950: 26–8.
109 Clark, 1981: 15.
110 Gascon, 1971: vol. 2: 680, 720.
111 Deyon, 1967: 218.
112 ibid.: 224; Markovitch, 1976: 174–5.
113 Goubert, 1960: 274; Gascon, 1971: vol. 2: 680–1; cf. Ranum, 1984: 174–9.
114 Deyon, 1967: 97.
115 ibid.: 233.
116 Gascon, 1971: vol. 2: 675–731.
117 Scoville, 1960: 386–7.
118 Markovitch, 1971: 312.
119 Markovitch, 1976: 141.
120 ibid.: 272.
121 ibid.: 351.
122 ibid.: 321.
123 ibid.: 209–10, 233–5.
124 ibid.: 19–23.
125 ibid.: 351.
126 ibid.: 484.
127 ibid.: 483.
128 ibid.: 457.
129 Thomson, 1982: 214, 227, 232; cf. Deyon, 1967: 169–70.
130 Tilly, 1986: 166.
131 Markovitch, 1976: 243.

132 Parker, 1983: 140.
133 Deyon, 1967: 241, 258–62, 540–1.
134 Boutruche, 1966: 484; cf. Doyle, 1974: 52ff.
135 Farr, 1988: 80–1; Farr, 1989: 148, 169.
136 Goubert, 1960: 287–8.
137 Farr, 1988: 79; cf. Roupnel, 1955: 135.
138 Fairchilds, 1976: 75; Gutton, 1971: 53; Schneider, 1989a: 32; Frêche, 1975: 340; Sumner, 1995: 49ff.; Norberg, 1985: 190.
139 Gascon, 1971: vol. 1: 402.
140 Farr, 1988: 109–12.
141 ibid.: 105–9; Gallet, 1983: 582; Goubert, 1960: 297, 548–51; Deyon, 1967: 516–19; Braudel and Labrousse, 1970–7: vol. 2: 668–9; G. Durand, 1979: 180; Constant, 1972: 200–1.
142 Delumeau, 1966: 124; Deyon, 1967: 109.
143 Goubert, 1960: 140–1.
144 Deyon, 1967: 341; Saive-Lever, 1979: 53–6; Labatut, 1958: 67.
145 Farr, 1988: 116.
146 Dupâquier, 1989: vol. 2: 305, 222–3, 370–3, 421–2; Duby, 1981: vol. 3: 53; Benedict, 1989: 13–15.
147 Jacquart, 1974: 687, 693.
148 Le Roy Ladurie, 1966: 511–37.
149 Slicher Van Bath, 1960: 130–53.
150 Le Roy Ladurie, 1987: 107–9.
151 Molinier, 1985: 177.
152 Jacquart, 1974: 291–5; Venard, 1957: 84.
153 Frêche, 1975: 230, 275; Goubert, 1960: 93–5; Le Roy Ladurie, 1966: 223–4.
154 Baerhel, 1961: 115–16.
155 Charbonnier, 1980: vol. 2: 830–62, 919.
156 Merle, 1958: 114.
157 Neveux, 1981: 271; Dewald, 1987: 84.
158 Le Roy Ladurie, 1987: 108–16.
159 Jacquart, 1974: 291–5.
160 Fontenay, 1957: 212–13.
161 Lease of 1679 cited by Dewald, 1987: 79; cf. Jacquart, 1974: 192.
162 Merle, 1958: 126–7; Venard, 1957: 84; Fontenay, 1957: 212–13; Molinier, 1985: 177–86; Castang, 1967: 123.
163 Le Roy Ladurie, 1987: 51.
164 Neveux, 1981: 187–93.
165 ibid.: 218–19.
166 Le Roy Ladurie, 1987: 52.
167 Jacquart, 1974: 328–9.
168 Dewald, 1987: 86–7.
169 Merle, 1958: 136.
170 Frêche, 1975: 213–24.
171 Castang, 1967: 74; Isambert *et al.*, 1822–33: vol. 20: 201–2.
172 Cited by Merle, 1958: 137.
173 Le Roy Ladurie, 1966: 240–51; cf. Frêche, 1975: 187–90.
174 Neveux, 1981: 242–3.
175 Molinier, 1985: 158.
176 Sabatier, 1966: 48, 131.
177 Baerhel, 1961: 417, *Graphiques* 31; Gallet, 1983: 345–72; Charbonnier, 1980: vol. 2: 1027; Cabourdin, 1977: vol. 2: 605.
178 Molinier, 1985: 159; cf. Le Roy Ladurie, 1966: 239–59.

179 Hamon, 1959: 17–21.
180 Goubert, 1986: 26; Braudel and Labrousse, 1970–7: vol. 2: 476.
181 Molinier, 1985: 147, 157–8; Sabatier, 1966: 131.
182 Baerhel, 1961: 397–9.
183 Frêche, 1975: 135–7.
184 Baerhel, 1961: 399.
185 Goubert, 1960: 154–8.
186 Frêche, 1975: 154, 157.
187 ibid.: 155.
188 ibid.: 160.
189 ibid.: 463–4.
190 Boutruche, 1947: 313ff; Hoffman, 1986: 38–9.
191 Venard, 1957: 25–6.
192 Frêche, 1975: 160.
193 Venard, 1957: 27–9.
194 Jacquart, 1974: 724.
195 Gascon, 1971: vol. 2: 818; G. Durand, 1979: 406–48; Cabourdin, 1977: vol. 2: 530–5, 543–60.
196 Venard, 1957: 26.
197 Fontenay, 1957: 187–8.
198 Frêche, 1975: 165–6.
199 Jacquart, 1974: 340–1.
200 Frêche, 1975: 161.
201 ibid.: 165–6.
202 Fontenay, 1957: 191.
203 ibid.: 186. See glossary for note on the size of an *arpent*.
204 Roupnel, 1955: 275.
205 See the Ordonnance of Orléans (1563) in Isambert *et al.*, 1822–33: vol. 14: 94.
206 Gascon, 1971: 862–7; cf. Deyon, 1975: 26–8; Hoffman, 1986: 44.
207 Archives Municipales de Toulouse BB 1880 fos. 269, 276, 293.
208 Goubert, 1960: 330; Neveux, 1981: 319–23.
209 Garnault, 1899: 6.
210 Hoffman, 1986: 43.
211 Fontenay, 1957: 187.
212 Constant, 1972: 165–9.
213 Saint-Jacob, 1960: 52–3; Merle, 1958: 106.
214 Shaffer, 1982: 49–51.
215 Le Roy Ladurie, 1966: 254–6.
216 Klimrath, 1843: 139–42; Blondeau and Gueret, 1723: 878–88: Thaumas de la Thaumassière, 1691: 549–50.
217 Hamon, 1959: 20.
218 Gallet, 1983: 339; Collomp, 1983: 282–4; Dontenwill, 1973: 144–62.
219 Merle, 1958: 53–8; cf. Peret, 1976: 18, 75.
220 Boutruche, 1947: 333–43; Forster, 1963: 685.
221 Forster, 1960: 52–3.
222 Catellan, 1703: vol. 2: 473–84, for a long discussion of the *retrait lignager* and *féodale*, cf. Ourliac, 1952: 329–32.
223 Thaumas de la Thaumassière, 1691: 392.
224 Goubert, 1960: 174–6, 206–7.
225 Venard, 1957: 103.
226 Devèze, 1960: 100–4.
227 Dontenwill, 1973: 94–5.

228 Fontenay, 1957: 247–50.
229 Goubert, 1960: 174.
230 Fontenay, 1957: 254–5.
231 Venard, 1957: 81, 94, 111–12; Goubert, 1960: 172–5; Jacquart, 1974: 234–5.
232 Dontenwill, 1973: 100.
233 Constant, 1972: 165–202.
234 Peret, 1976: 148–50; Dontenwill, 1973: 178–81; Jacquart, 1974: 341.
235 Le Roy Ladurie, 1994: 155.
236 Dewald, 1987: 72–3.
237 Goubert, 1960: 173.
238 Brenner, 1985a: 28.
239 Dewald, 1987: 76.
240 Le Roy Ladurie, 1987: 418; Le Roy Ladurie, 1974: 12–21.
241 Plaisse, 1961: 389–400.
242 Archives Départementales de Tarn et Garonne 1E 21, 23, 85, 86.
243 Forster, 1963: 687; cf. Julien-Labruyère, 1983: vol. 1: 56–8; Gallet, 1983: 456.
244 Dewald, 1987: 199.
245 Neveux, 1981: 328.
246 Forster, 1963: 686–7.
247 Dewald, 1987: 80–1.
248 Neveux, 1981: 191–2.
249 Fontenay, 1957: 206–8.
250 Venard, 1957: 52–4
251 Fontenay, 1957: 206.
252 Bois, 1976: 223–4.
253 Jacquart, 1974: 349.
254 Gallet, 1983: 105.
255 Dewald, 1980: 199.
256 Dontenwill, 1973: 45–50; cf. Julien-Labruyère, 1983: vol. 1: 218–19; Le Roy Ladurie, 1975: vol. 1: 408–13.
257 Shaffer, 1982: 70, 113–21.
258 Merle, 1958: 55–6; Dewald, 1980: 212–13.
259 Venard, 1957: 68; Hoffman, 1986: 44.
260 G. Durand, 1979: 481–2; Garnier, 1982: 340–56.
261 Frêche, 1975: 247; Le Goff, 1981: 51–5.
262 Bois, 1976: 219; Venard, 1957: 117; Merle, 1958: 178–80; Cabourdin, 1977: vol. 2: 599; Frêche, 1975: 248, G. Sicard, 1956: 24–5; Jacquart, 1974: 335; Garnier, 1982: 344–5; Julien-Labruyère, 1983: vol. 1: 73; Meyer, 1985: vol. 2: 1670–1.
263 G. Durand, 1979: 481–2.
264 Bourcier, 1960: 89–91.
265 ibid.: 126.
266 Merle, 1958: 172–4.
267 Molinier, 1985: 162.
268 Shaffer, 1982: 49–51; Charbonnier, 1980: vol. 1: 225.
269 G. Sicard, 1956: 31.
270 Merle, 1958: 178–80.
271 Jacquart, 1974: 348; Venard, 1957: 81–2.
272 Jacquart, 1974: 348; Merle, 1958: 116–17, 172–4; Shaffer, 1982: 125; G. Sicard, 1956: 44; Sauzet, 1897: 42.
273 Shaffer, 1982: 175; cf. Merle, 1958: 91–2.
274 G. Sicard, 1956: 24.
275 ibid.: 30.

276 Bourcier. 1960: 104–5; cf. Collomp, 1983: 243–4; Dontenwill, 1973: 86.
277 Ch. Guyot, 1889: 8; Bourcier, 1960: 45–6.
278 Shaffer, 1982: 182.
279 Jacquart, 1974: 343; Dewald, 1987: 231, 241.
280 Venard, 1957: 83.
281 Fontenay, 1957: 206; Jacquart, 1974: 54.
282 Deyon, 1967: 139–40.
283 Fontenay, 1957: 206, 234–4; Goubert, 1960: 140–1.
284 Merle, 1958: 100; cf. Meyer, 1985: 658, 669.
285 Venard, 1957: 96–103.
286 Merle, 1958: 183.
287 Bacquet, 1688: 869.
288 Pocquet de Livonnière, 1729: 535–6.
289 Julien-Labruyère, 1983: 66; Peret, 1976: 112; Garnier, 1982: 322–3; Pocquet de Livonnière, 1729: 535–6.
290 Le Goff, 1981: 158–61; Meyer, 1985: 720–55.
291 Julien-Labruyère, 1983: vol. 2: 651–2.
292 Duby, 1981: vol. 3: 73; Le Roy Ladurie, 1987: 175.
293 Cabourdin, 1977: vol. 2: 260–2; Goubert, 1976: 51; Dewald, 1987: 102–3.
294 Baerhel, 1961: 347–8.
295 Le Roy Ladurie, 1987: 175.
296 Peret, 1976: 119; Constant, 1972: 196–8.
297 Dewald, 1987: 102–3; Meyer, 1985: 652–3.
298 Fontenay, 1957: 176–9.
299 Molinier, 1985: 153.
300 Baerhel, 1961: 347.
301 G. Durand, 1979: 89–90.
302 Pocquet de Livonnière, 1729: 265–6.
303 Peret, 1976: 94–6.
304 Gallet, 1983: 495–6.
305 Ramière de Fortanier, 1932: 64.
306 Goubert, 1960: 212–13.
307 Dewald, 1987: 98–9.
308 ibid.: 241.
309 ibid.: 35–6.
310 Plaisse, 1961: 389–400.
311 Dewald, 1987: 249–50.
312 ibid.: 267, 285–6.
313 ibid.: 227–8.
314 ibid.: 219; cf. Plaisse, 1961: 619–20; Gallet, 1983: 397.
315 Dewald, 1987: 227–8, 267.
316 Gallet, 1983: 389–90.
317 Gascon, 1971, vol. 2: 831; cf. Neveux, 1981: 328.
318 Cabourdin, 1977: vol. 1: 374.
319 Bois, 1976: 228–9.
320 Jacquart, 1974: 46–7, 618.
321 Le Roy Ladurie, 1966: 465–6.
322 Duby, 1981: vol. 3: 73–6; cf. Baerhel, 1961: 363.
323 Braudel and Labrousse, 1970–7: vol. 1: 978–80; Spooner, 1972: 305–15; Cooper, 1985: 184: cf. Hinckner, 1971: 43 and Duby, 1981: vol. 3: 72–7.
324 Guéry, 1978: 227; Tilly, 1981: 120; cf. Le Roy Ladurie, 1987: 17–19.
325 Baerhel, 1961: 311–13.
326 Devèze, 1959: 112–13.

327 Molinier, 1985: 247–50.
328 Baerhel, 1961: 315.
329 Roupnel, 1955: 250–80.
330 Dontenwill, 1973: 249 and Gallet, 1983: 359–63 for two contrasting situations. cf. Goubert, 1960: 516–32.
331 ibid.: 180–2; Goubert, 1956: 66–7; Le Roy Ladurie, 1966: 586–92; Jacquart, 1974: 203, 630–6; Roupnel, 1955: 257ff.
332 Deyon, 1967: 313; Le Roy Ladurie, 1987: 348ff.
333 Cited by Church, 1969: 97–100.
334 Braudel, 1988, vol. 2: 590–2.
335 ibid.: vol. 2: 599.
336 Guichard, 1966: 176; cf. Goubert, 1960: 146.
337 Molinier, 1985: 147; Frêche, 1975: 340; Jacquart, 1974: 140–6.
338 Frêche, 1975: 390; Fontenay, 1957: 241–2; Goubert: 1986: *passim*.
339 Dontenwill, 1973: 94–6.
340 Gallet, 1983: 578–80.
341 Frêche, 1975: 224; Molinier, 1985: 262–77; Castang, 1967: 19; Goubert, 1956: 86–9.
342 Frêche, 1975: 391.
343 Le Roy Ladurie, 1966: 265–7.
344 Dupâquier, 1989: vol. 2: 223.
345 Croix, 1985: vol. 1: 198; Dupâquier, 1989: vol. 2: 237–8.
346 ibid.: vol. 2: 422–9.
347 ibid.: vol. 2: 305.
348 Croix, 1985: vol. 1: 191–6.
349 Dupâquier, 1989: vol. 2: 305.
350 Baerhel, 1961: 305.
351 Dupâquier, 1989: vol. 2: 431.
352 Gallet, 1983: 397–8; Dewald, 1987: 285–6.

CHAPTER 3 THE ROOTS OF CONFLICT (pp. 75–110)

1 Moote, 1989: 112.
2 Elliott, 1984: 146–7.
3 Bonney, 1982: 822–3; Kettering, 1986a: 25.
4 Dégarne, 1962: 4–5.
5 Beik, 1974b: 243–62.
6 Coquelle, 1908: 76.
7 Cited by Jouanna, 1989: 270.
8 ibid.: 274–7.
9 Salmon, 1984: 267–92.
10 Bernard, 1975: 137–56; Borzeix *et al.*, 1982: 251–7; Garlan and Nières, 1975: *passim*.
11 Pillorget, 1975a: 388–9.
12 Borzeix *et* al., 1982: 119–267. These include all incidents, riots and rebellions limited to a single community but involving a spontaneous act of resistance and *mouvements* lasting for more than a day which embraced more than one community.
13 Goubert, 1986: 205.
14 Bonney, 1978: 224ff.
15 See above p. 7.
16 The account which follows is based on Pillorget, 1975a: 316–53; Kettering,

1978: esp. 150–81. Briggs, 1989: 120–4 also provides an account based on the same works.
17 This paragraph is drawn from Kettering, 1978: 111–19.
18 Parker, 1980: 47.
19 Porshnev, 1963: 143.
20 Mousnier, 1967: 52.
21 Beik, 1987: 37.
22 Gallet, 1975: 148.
23 Germain, 1839: 586.
24 Coquelle, 1908: 76.
25 Sully to Séguier 16 July 1645 in Porshnev, 1963: 648.
26 Logie, 1951: 49; Foisil, 1970: 117; Caillard *et al.*, 1963: 36.
27 ibid.: 106–18.
28 Briggs, 1989: 155.
29 Pillorget, 1975a: 504.
30 ibid.: 830ff.; Kettering, 1978: 298–328.
31 Caillard *et al.*, 1963: 124–5.
32 Pillorget, 1975a: 414.
33 Bercé, 1974: vol. 1: 42.
34 Beik, 1987: 38–40.
35 Bercé, 1974: vol. 1: 69; Beik, 1985: 142–4; Kettering, 1978: 57; Foisil, 1970: 62; Caillard *et al.*, 1963: 132; Bonney, 1991: 205–6, 231–3.
36 Beik, 1985: 141; Beik, 1987: 39.
37 Caillard *et al.*, 1963: 102.
38 Bercé, 1974: vol. 1: 73–4.
39 Y. Durand, 1971: 57; Bonney, 1981: 313.
40 Beik, 1987: 57.
41 Bercé, 1974: vol. 2: 403–4.
42 Gallet, 1975: 143.
43 Porshnev, 1963: 311ff.; Briggs, 1989: 143ff.; Caillard *et al.*, 1963: 58–9.
44 Salmon, 1984: 268.
45 Beik, 1974b: 245.
46 Bernard, 1975: 166ff.
47 Tilly, 1986: 18.
48 Beik, 1974b: 247.
49 Briggs, 1989: 150–1.
50 Garlan and Nières, 1975: 153–4.
51 ibid.: 152.
52 Salmon, 1984: 271–2, 381–2, 288.
53 ibid.: 277.
54 Parker, 1983: 68–72.
55 Cited by Salmon, 1984: 276.
56 Foisil, 1970: 190.
57 Garlan and Nières, 1975: 101–4.
58 Pillorget, 1975a: 286–94.
59 ibid.: 43.
60 ibid.: 106.
61 Bercé, 1974: vol. 2: 368.
62 ibid.: vol. 2: 370.
63 Mousnier, 1971a: 199.
64 ibid.: 200.
65 Kettering, 1978: 61.
66 ibid.: 190–215.

67 Bercé, 1974: vol. 1: 182–3.
68 ibid.: vol. 1: 133.
69 ibid.: vol. 1: 140–2.
70 Salmon, 1984: *passim*.
71 Bercé, 1974: vol. 1: 146.
72 ibid.: vol. 1: 363.
73 Davis, 1975: 119.
74 Kettering, 1978: 213.
75 Beik, 1990: 5.
76 Bercé, 1974: vol. 2: 633.
77 ibid.: vol. 2: 645.
78 ibid.: vol. 1: 181.
79 ibid.: vol. 1: 184, vol. 2: 628.
80 Bercé, 1987: 115.
81 Beik, 1985: 117–27, 232–3.
82 Kettering, 1978: 59–71; Major, 1980: 92–3, 431–2; Pillorget, 1975a: 100–6.
83 Parker, 1980: 178–9, 48–9.
84 Roques, 1908: 12; R. Sicard, 1953: 10–12.
85 Archives Municipales de Toulouse AA 211 fos. 298v–303r.
86 ibid.: fo. 303.
87 Pillorget, 1975a: 508–9.
88 Gallet, 1975: 137–41.
89 Tilly, 1986: 137–42.
90 Aguesseau to Séguier 20 May 1635, in Porshnev, 1963: 386–7.
91 Verthamont to Séguier, 26 June 1635 in Porshnev, 1963: 589–90.
92 ibid.: 216.
93 ibid.: 133, 272; Bercé, 1974: vol. 2: 314; Bernard, 1975: 165; Tilly, 1986: 19.
94 Parker, 1980: 41.
95 Pillorget, 1975a: 388–9.
96 Porshnev, 1963: 137, 169.
97 ibid.: 352.
98 Bernard, 1975: 170.
99 Garlan and Nières, 1975: 87.
100 St Géran to Séguier, Moulins 21 July 1640 in Porshnev, 1963: 606–7.
101 Briggs, 1989: 136.
102 Mousnier, 1949: 74; Briggs, 1989: 148.
103 Gallet, 1975: 149.
104 Verthamont to Séguier from Périgueux 18 June 1635 in *Bulletin de la Société historique et archéologique du Périgord*, vol. 10 (1883), 380; see also Verthamont to Séguier 26 June 1635 in Porshnev, 1963: 589–93.
105 Coquelle, 1908, 70–2. cf. Tilly, 1986: 138–9.
106 Bercé, 1974: vol. 1: 411.
107 ibid.: vol. 1: 147–9, 455.
108 ibid.: vol. 1: 147–9, 411, 455; cf. Bernard, 1975: 161–3.
109 Cited by Briggs, 1989: 147.
110 Bercé, 1974: vol. 1: 430.
111 Briggs, 1989: 147.
112 Laissaigne, 1962: 15ff.
113 Delevaud, 1891: 267ff.
114 Bercé, 1974: vol. 1: 147.
115 Cabrol, 1910: 23–4.
116 Tilly, 1986: 151.
117 Briggs, 1989: 150; Porshnev, 1963: 355.

118 Westrich, 1972: 60.
119 ibid.: 46.
120 Rohan, 1646: 229.
121 Golden, 1981: 56; Salmon, 1969: 94–101.
122 Golden, 1981: 18–68.
123 Tilly, 1986: 80–1.
124 Cubells, 1967, 193–7; Mousnier, 1949: 61–2.
125 ibid.:; 51.
126 'Décisions prises par l'assemblée du Tiers Etat du Périgord, portant sommation aux villes de libérer les prisonniers pour fait de taille et convocation dans la forêt d'Abzac' (4 April 1594), in Bercé, 1974: vol. 2: 704.
127 'Lettre de la Saigne aux consuls de Domme . . .' (12 April 1594), in ibid: vol. 2: 706.
128 'Manifeste des paysans d'Angoumois' (summer 1636), in ibid.: vol. 2: 739.
129 'Mémoire adressé par Simon Estacheau, juge seigneurial dans la châtellenie de Brossac, au Cardinal Richelieu pour la réforme des tailles' (Sept. 1636), in ibid.: vol. 2: 746–7.
130 'Plaintes et revendications contre les impôts présentées par les députés des châtellenies d'Angoumois au comte de Brassac, gouverneur de la province et à l'intendant Villemontée' (Aug. 1636), in ibid.: vol. 2: 744.
131 ibid.: vol. 1: 331–3.
132 Foisil, 1970: 194–202.
133 ibid.: 197, 201–2; Caillard *et al.*, 1963: 93.
134 Germain, 1839: 584–5.
135 Bercé, 1974: vol. 1: 333–4.
136 Tilly, 1986: 102.
137 Bernard, 1975: 166–9.
138 Westrich, 1972: 49.
139 Pillorget, 1975b: 15.
140 'Plaintes et revendications contre les impôts présentées . . .', in Bercé, 1974: vol. 2: 744.
141 Jouanna, 1977: 8–9, 16ff.
142 ibid.: 192.
143 ibid.: 196.
144 'Remonstrance de la noblesse du bailliage de Troyes' (1649), clause 45, in Mousnier *et al.*, 1965: 146.
145 Robillard de Beaurepaire, 1876–8: vol. 1: 60 art. 21; Gutton, 1975: 112.
146 Robillard de Beaurepaire, 1876–8: vol. 2: 33 art. 11, 41 art. 23, 44 art. 29; Gutton, 1975: 114.
147 'Remonstrances de la noblesse de la bailliage de Troyes' (1649), in Mousnier *et al.*, 1965: 153.
148 Major, 1986: 408–9; 'Cahier des remonstrances de la noblesse d'Angoumois' (1649), clause 13 in Mousnier *et al.*, 1965: 86; Lassaigne, 1962: 15ff.
149 Y. Durand, 1966: 213, 277; 'Cahier des remonstrances de la noblesse d'Angoumois', clause 15 in Mousnier *et al.*, 1965: 87; 'Cahier des remonstrances de la noblesse du bailliage de Troyes' (1649), clause 37 in ibid.: 145; Lassaigne, 1962: 117; Gutton, 1975: 116.
150 ibid.: 18.
151 Jouanna, 1989: 267–8.
152 Parker, 1980: 121.
153 Beik, 1987: 47.
154 Foisil, 1981: 158–61, 164–5, 167–8.

155 Mousnier, 1972: 210–13.
156 ibid.: 410.
157 Bercé, 1974: vol. 2: 175.
158 Archives Municipales de Toulouse AA 24 fo. 415, 4 Nov. 1640.
159 Archives Municipales de Toulouse FF 484, 23 and 31 Oct. 1641.
160 Archives Municipales de Toulouse BB 250, 2 July 1641.
161 Archives Municipales de Toulouse BB 1880, fos. 269, 276.
162 Beik, 1985: 205.
163 Archives Départementales de Haute Garonne B 1880 fos. 27ff., fo. 116; Beik 1990: 139.
164 Mousnier, 1959: 301–33.
165 Bercé, 1974: vol. 1: 166.
166 Kettering, 1978: 220.
167 Bercé, 1974: vol. 1: 309–10.
168 Beik, 1987: 42–3.
169 ibid.: 44–54.
170 Kettering, 1986b: 422.
171 Lozières to Séguier, 25 August 1644 in Porshnev, 1963: 635.
172 Bosquet to M. de la Vrillière, Montpellier, 1. Aug 1645, in ibid.: 651.
173 Verthamont to Séguier, Périgueux 26 June 1635, in ibid.: 589.
174 See above p. 97n100.
175 Bernard, 1975: 169.
176 Gutton, 1981: 137–8.
177 Archives Nationales U 987, 4 Dec 1609, April 1624, July 1676 amongst others.
178 Kaplan, 1979: 26.
179 Hoffman, 1984: 95.
180 ibid.: *passim*; Briggs, 1989: 181ff.; Muchembled, 1985: *passim*; Duby, 1981, vol. 3: 191–5.
181 Berger, 1978: 101–27.
182 ibid.: 111.

CHAPTER 4 ORDER AND CLASSES (pp. 111–35)

1 Marx, 1852: 187.
2 Mousnier, 1979 and 1984: vol. 1: 225.
3 Mousnier, 1971a: 414–15.
4 Benedict, 1989: 29.
5 Irvine, 1989: 112–14.
6 Beik, 1985: 265.
7 Collins, 1988: 126.
8 ibid.: 113.
9 ibid.: 135–6.
10 ibid.: 111.
11 ibid.: 141.
12 Bonney, 1981: 165.
13 Farr, 1988: 79, 91, 201–2.
14 Duby, 1980: 98 and ch. 13 esp. 273–84.
15 Perroy, 1962: 29–31.
16 Mohl, 1933: 34–95.
17 Clouatre, 1984: 236.
18 Loyseau, 1610: 4, 95, 101; Jouanna, 1968: 614.

19 Domat, 1722: vol. 2: 426.
20 Jouanna, 1968: 610.
21 Jouanna, 1977: 60.
22 Seyssel, 1519: 16.
23 Loyseau, 1610: 1–2.
24 ibid.: 101–3.
25 Goubert, 1976: 292.
26 Cited by Lis and Soly, 1979: 109.
27 Labatut, 1958: 69.
28 Farr, 1988: 115–16.
29 Saive-Lever, 1979: 59.
30 Gallet, 1983: 579.
31 Labatut, 1958: 67–70.
32 Gutton, 1981: 8, 174.
33 ibid.: 194–7; Fairchilds, 1976: 74.
34 Gutton, 1981: 199; Deyon, 1967: 547.
35 ibid.: 261, 341.
36 ibid.: 245–6, 547.
37 Collomp, 1983: 265, 302, 311, 316.
38 Jacquart, 1974: 521.
39 Drawn from Deyon, 1967: 259, 262, 267; Labatut, 1958: 60; Labatut, 1972: 262–70; Kettering, 1978: 231–2; Beik, 1985: 79; Bergin, 1985: 248, 311; Roche, 1967: 217–43.
40 Benedict, 1981: 27–31; Goubert, 1960: 265; Schneider, 1989a: 23–6; Fairchilds, 1976: 13; cf. Deyon, 1967: 247–52; Gascon, 1971: vol. 1: 435–43; Farr, 1988: 83–6.
41 Croix, 1985: vol. 1: 342–3.
42 Mousnier, 1979 and 1984: vol. 1: 708.
43 Gutton, 1981: 172.
44 Saive-Lever, 1979: 57–8.
45 Sabean, 1976: 101; Cabourdin, 1977: vol. 1: 340; Collomp, 1983: 213–14; Couturier, 1969: 139–41; G. Durand, 1979: 356.
46 Mousnier, 1979 and 1984: vol. 2: 329.
47 Cabourdin, 1977; vol. 1: 340. cf. G. Durand, 1979: 356.
48 Le Roy Ladurie, 1982: 141–51; Goody, 1976: 15–17; G. Durand, 1979: 353.
49 Farr, 1988: 136.
50 ibid.: 136–7.
51 Sturdy, 1986: *passim*.
52 Dessert, 1987: 17–85.
53 Hanley, 1989: 10–11.
54 Richet, 1977: 49; Harding, 1978: 143; Collomp, 1983: 217–20; Mentzer, 1994: 84–5, 102–3.
55 Ourliac and Malafosse, 1968: vol. 3: 266; Petot and Vandenbossche, 1962: 247–5; de Ferrière, 1677: 527–52.
56 Ourliac and Malafosse, 1968: vol. 3: 137.
57 Collins, 1989: 436–70; Kettering, 1989: 817–26; Neuschel, 1989: 78–9; Farr, 1988: 105, 142–3.
58 Flandrin, 1979: 14.
59 Kettering, 1989: 826–37.
60 Bodin, 1576: 8.
61 Cited by Flandrin, 1979: 8.
62 ibid.: 4–10.
63 Gutton, 1981: 18–19.

64 ibid.: 27–8.
65 ibid.: 41–7.
66 Collomp, 1983: 117–25.
67 Farr, 1988: 127–9.
68 Mousnier, 1979 and 1984: vol. 1: ch. 2.
69 ibid.: vol. 1: 401–4; cf. Thaumas de la Thaumassière, 1691: 550–6.
70 Mousnier, 1979 and 1984: vol. 1: 67–9, 78; Ourliac, 1952: 328–55; Ourliac and Malafosse, 1968: vol. 3: 490–1.
71 Farr, 1988: 125.
72 ibid.: 128–33.
73 Mousnier, 1979 and 1984, vol. 1: 215.
74 Lougee, 1976: 170.
75 ibid.: 151–62.
76 Kettering, 1978: 216–17;
77 Bohanan, 1991: 57, 59; Bohanan, 1993: 7, 79.
78 Dewald, 1993: 2; Dewald, 1980: 102–3.
79 Mousnier, 1970: 25.
80 ibid.: 57.
81 ibid.: 59.
82 ibid.: 60.
83 ibid.: 26.
84 Labatut, 1972: 187. Mettam, 1988: 88, treats these marriages as the result of Louis XIV's willingness to abandon his usual hostility towards *mésalliances* in order to knit together the greatest families of the land. This may explain Louis XIV's motives but, in doing so, it also confirms the objective realities with which Louis had to deal.
85 Jouanna, 1989: 19; Lougee, 1976: 110.
86 Kettering, 1978: 216–17; cf. Dewald, 1980: 187 n. 51.
87 Wood, 1980: 77, 91–4.
88 Constant, 1974: 565; Deyon, 1975: 34.
89 Irvine, 1989: 125.
90 Chagniot, 1979: 43.
91 Corvisier, 1959: 41–2.
92 Labatut, 1980: 277.
93 Ranum, 1963: 35.
94 Labatut, 1963: 18, 25, 31, 33.
95 Mousnier, 1970: 138–9.
96 ibid.: 96–8.
97 ibid.: 270–1.
98 ibid.: 121.
99 For example, Chaussinand-Nogaret, 1991: 170–7.
100 Roche, 1967: 242.
101 Labatut, 1972: 274; Dewald, 1993: 162.
102 Dessert, 1984: 359, ch. 15.
103 Bergin, 1985: app. 1, table 4.
104 Beik, 1985: 271–3.

CHAPTER 5 THE NOBILITY: A HEGEMONIC *TOUR DE FORCE* (pp. 136–57)

1 Devyver, 1973: 267; Mousnier, 1951–2: 199–206; Ellis, 1988: 26–8.
2 Dessert, 1984: 82–109; cf. Bayard, 1988: 438.

3 Jouanna, 1989: 22–3, 28; Huppert, 1977: 7–8; Constant, 1979, 10–12; Chaussinand-Nogaret, 1991: 33–4, 42–3.
4 Farr, 1988: 79.
5 Deyon, 1967: 272–3.
6 Dewald, 1980: 29.
7 ibid.: 174.
8 Jouanna, 1989: 26–7; Orlea, 1980: 50–1.
9 Chaussinand-Nogaret, 1991: 154.
10 ibid.: 157.
11 Wood, 1980: 45.
12 This calculation is based on a coefficient of 4.5 and Dupâquier's estimation of a total population of between 18.9 and 21.8 million. Dupâquier, 1989: vol. 2: 68; cf. Chaunu and Gascon, 1977: vol. 1: 194.
13 Roupnel, 1955: 133–4.
14 Mousnier, 1971a: 127.
15 ibid.: 635–6.
16 Smith, 1993: 399–405.
17 Schalk, 1986: 106.
18 Jouanna, 1977: 148–50.
19 Mousnier, 1955: 1–20.
20 Lougee, 1976: 37, *passim* esp. ch. 3.
21 Jouanna, 1977: 69–71; Devyver, 1973: 80–3.
22 Cubells, 1970: 235–6.
23 Richard, 1960: 18; Devyver, 1973: 7.
24 Jouanna, 1977: 43–4.
25 Devyver, 1973: 34–5.
26 ibid.: 94 and n. 134.
27 Jouanna, 1977: 168–9.
28 ibid.: 23.
29 ibid.: 27–8.
30 Orlea, 1980: 51.
31 Bourde de la Rogerie, 1922: 237–312; Meyer, 1966: vol. 1: 52–36, 71; Devyver, 1973: 267; Sturdy, 1976: 549–72; Cubells, 1970: 238–9.
32 Devyver, 1973: 267.
33 Ellis, 1988: 121–36; Labatut, 1972: 372ff.
34 Jackson, 1971: 43–4.
35 Deyon, 1967: 218.
36 Thomson, 1982: 304.
37 Cole, 1939: vol. 2: 446–7.
38 Farr, 1988: 96, 98–103, 106–8, 139–40; cf. Couturier, 1969: 272–9.
39 Collomp, 1983: 222.
40 Irvine, 1989: 116–17, 125–7; Couturier, 1969: 227–8.
41 Mousnier, 1971a: 186.
42 Jouanna, 1977: 98–100.
43 Dewald, 1980: 76–8, 116.
44 Mousnier, 1979 and 1984: vol. 2: 329.
45 Constant, 1979: 9.
46 Wood, 1980: 45–55.
47 Cubells, 1970: 281–3.
48 Levantal, 1987: 23; Shennan, 1968: 117–21.
49 Jouanna, 1989: 26–8.
50 Chaussinand-Nogaret, 1991: 158.
51 Bluche and Durye, 1962: vol. 2: 23–5.

52 See below p. 192. Labatut, 1972: 98–108.
53 Jouanna, 1989: 104–8.
54 Krailsheimer, 1962: 79.
55 ibid.: 63.
56 Salmon, 1969: 378–9.
57 La Rochefoucauld, *Maxims*, 1959: 26–7.
58 Maland, 1970: 266; cf. Adam, 1974: 231–2.
59 Jocasta in *The Thebaid*, Racine's first play written in 1664. Racine, 1967: 17.
60 Cited by Devyver, 1973: 218.
61 ibid.: 220.
62 Schalk, 1986: 84.
63 Cited by ibid.: 75.
64 Jouanna, 1977: 154.
65 Schalk, 1986: 85.
66 Cited by Devyver, 1973: 92.
67 ibid.: 98.
68 ibid.: 98; Nadal, 1948: 296–7.
69 Devyver, 1973: 98–9.
70 Jouanna, 1977: 22.
71 Devyver, 1973: 228–30; Bitton, 1969: 46–52.
72 Jouanna, 1977: 26–30.
73 ibid.: 154.
74 ibid.: 61.
75 Cited by Jouanna, 1968: 605.
76 Cited by Schalk, 1986: 81.
77 Motley, 1991: 94–5; Brockliss, 1992: 264–5.
78 Motley, 1991: 125–7.
79 ibid.: 123.
80 ibid.: 177–8.
81 Brockliss, 1992: 240–5, 269–70.
82 Motley, 1991: 102–4.
83 ibid.: 118–19; cf. Lloyd, 1987: *passim*.
84 Motley, 1991: 94–5.
85 ibid.: 91.
86 Cited by Schalk, 1986: 131–2.
87 Cited by Motley, 1991: 72.
88 ibid.: 89.
89 ibid.: 93.
90 Cited in Lougee, 1976: 54.
91 Magendie, 1925: vol. 1: 355.
92 ibid.: vol. 1: 358; Dewald, 1993: 7.
93 ibid.: vol. 1: 345–6.
94 ibid.: vol. 2: 762–3, 768.
95 ibid.: vol. 1: 367, 389, vol. 2: 787.
96 Cited by Moriarty, 1988: 114.
97 ibid.: 122–3.
98 Lough, 1957: 70.
99 ibid.: 153.
100 Moriarty, 1988: 84; Motley, 1991: 63–5.
101 Lough, 1978: 141–2.
102 Cited by Rothkrug, 1965: 52.
103 Dewald, 1993: 2, 15ff., 70–9, 126–9.
104 *L'Astrée* appeared in successive volumes totalling 3,000 pages from 1607 to

1627; it remained popular, particularly amongst the nobility, down into the eighteenth century. It is a pastoral tale – or many tales – set within the frame of a principal story about three shepherdesses and their lovers. This provides a vehicle for endless debates about love. An unreal pastoral world, a world of courtly love, is the focal point whilst the real world of the fifth century is left in the background, save when violence intrudes.

105 Harth, 1985: 121–2.
106 ibid.: 123.
107 ibid.: 180–309.
108 Apostolidès, 1981: 116ff.
109 Ranum, 1980a: 315.
110 Bossuet, 1990: *passim*.
111 Dewald, 1993: 10.
112 Harth, 1985: 19–20; also 23, 29, 44–5, 60–1, 116, 140 for Harth's overestimation of the formation of the bourgeoisie.
113 ibid.: 51.
114 Magendie, 1925: vol. 1: 367.
115 Harth, 1985: 124–5.
116 ibid.: 66.
117 Dewald, 1993: 167–8.
118 Rothkrug, 1965: 227–8.
119 Keohane, 1980: 350–7; cf. Rothkrug, 1965: 356–64.
120 Schaeper, 1983: 169–72.
121 ibid.: 214.
122 Grassby, 1960–1: 29; Schaeper, 1980: 204–5.
123 Bastier, 1974: 253–73; Cambolas, 1659: 725–42; Galland, 1637: *passim*.
124 Caseneuve, 1633: 63.
125 ibid.: 94.
126 Thaumas de la Thaumassière, 1667: 12–14.
127 Keohane, 1980: 83.
128 ibid.: 195.
129 ibid.: 342.
130 Silhon, 1665: pt. 2, 111–13.
131 Charron, 1602: 205.
132 Cited by Keohane, 1980: 142.
133 Dewald, 1993: 44.
134 ibid.: 43.
135 Charron, 1602: 161–75.
136 Silhon, 1665: pt. 2, 217–18.
137 Domat, 1722: vol. 1: ii.
138 ibid.: vol. 2: 269–70, 274, 277, 298, 422.
139 ibid.: vol. 2: 470.
140 ibid.: vol. 2: 276–7.
141 Skinner, 1966: 153–67; cf. Rothkrug, 1965: 315–28.
142 Domat, 1828–30: vol. 4: 33.
143 Domat, 1722: vol. 2: 297.
144 Devyver, 1973: 267; Mousnier, 1951–2: 199–206; Ellis, 1988: 62–3, 73ff.
145 See above p. 139.
146 Jouanna, 1989: 287–8, 398–9.

CHAPTER 6 POWER, IDEOLOGY AND THE FRENCH STATE (pp. 158–206)

1 Mousnier, 1971a: 131; Charmeil, 1964: 13, 16, 420–1; Braudel and Labrousse 1970–7: vol. 1: 194.
2 Bonney, 1978: 150.
3 ibid.: 44–5.
4 Parker, 1983: 72–3.
5 Boislisle, 1874–97: *passim*.
6 Hayden, 1974: 160–1.
7 Mousnier, 1979 and 1984: vol. 1: 610.
8 Hamscher, 1976: 130–1, 144–5.
9 Parker, 1989: 57.
10 Hamscher, 1987: 85; Hamscher, 1991: 195.
11 Béranger, 1981: 14–19; Mousnier, 1970: 148–71, 6–10; Mousnier, 1946–7: 126–7; Antoine, 1970: 183, 191.
12 Henshall, 1992: 144.
13 Cited by Sommerville, 1986: 9–108.
14 *Maximes morales et chrétiennes pour le repos des consciences dans les affaires présentes pour servir d'instruction aux curés, aux prédicateurs et aux confesseurs ...* (Paris, 1649): 7; see also *De la puissance qu'ont les Roys sur les peuples et du pouvoir des peuples sur les Roys* (n.p., 1650): 17 in Carrier, 1982: vol. 1: no. 15.
15 Joly, 1653: 134–5
16 Salmon, 1975. 201.
17 Coquille, 1607: 39.
18 Cited by Jouanna, 1989: 326.
19 Giesey, 1985: 73–4ff.
20 Jouanna, 1989: 304–8; also 290–1, 315–17.
21 Coquille, 1607: 6.
22 *Les véritables maximes du gouvernement de la France justifiées par l'Ordre des temps depuis l'establissement de la monarchie jusques à present servant de réponse au prétendu arrêt du cassation du conseil du janvier 1652* (Paris, 1652) (B.L. 1492 m 17).
23 'Observations véritables et désintéressées sur un écrit imprimé au Louvre ...' (1652): 85, in *Mazarinades*, vol. 1.
24 Soule, 1966: 96; cf. Salmon, 1975: 220–1.
25 Villers, 1964: 125–6.
26 *De la puissance qu'ont les Roys sur les peuples et du pouvoir des peuples sur les Roys* (n.p., 1650): 19.
27 Joly, 1653: 150.
28 ibid.: 182–3.
29 ibid.: 399; cf. *Les raisons ou les motifs véritables de la défense du Parlement et des habitants de Paris contre les pertabateurs du repos public et les ennemis du Roy et l'Estat* (Paris, 1649): 6.
30 Joly, 1653: 363; also 321, 337.
31 ibid.: 434, 460.
32 Baricave, 1614: 505; Church, 1972: 35.
33 Parker, 1980: 157–9.
34 ibid.: 159–60.
35 Cited in ibid.: 163–4.
36 *Lettre et déclaration de l'assemblée nouvellement tenue en la ville de Niort en Poitou avec la permission du Roi par MM. de la R.P.R., envoyée aux habitants de La Rochelle sur les affaires de ce temps* (Paris, 1621): 10.

37 Giesey, 1985: 73–4.
38 Hanley, 1983: 255–7.
39 ibid.: 178–80; Giesey, 1985: 43–4.
40 ibid.: 61–6.
41 Hanley, 1983: 246–52.
42 ibid.: 263.
43 Giesey, 1985: 68ff.
44 ibid.: 76; Walton, 1986: 115–18.
45 Giesey, 1985: 75.
46 ibid.: 77–9.
47 Apostolidès, 1981: 131.
48 See below pp. 239–48.
49 Parker, 1980: ch. 6.
50 Kretzer, 1977: 66; Parker, 1980: 169–70.
51 Parker, 1978: 17.
52 Garrisson, 1985: 103.
53 ibid.: 163.
54 Cited by Prestwich, 1985: 330.
55 Moote, 1971: 124.
56 ibid.: 329ff.
57 Joly, 1653: 537.
58 ibid.: 135.
59 Shennan, 1968: 268.
60 'Avis d'estat à la Reyne sur le gouvernement de sa régence' (1649): 29, in *Collection of Mazarinades*, viii no. 10; for further Mazarinades which hinge on the distinction between monarchy and tyranny see Carrier, 1982: vol. 1 pieces nos. 25–8. Unfortunately they are misinterpreted by Carrier as 'utterly and violently antimonarchical', p. 11. This view is effectively criticised by Jouhaud, 1985: 157.
61 Church, 1972, esp. 415ff: Keohane, 1980: 175ff.
62 Parker, 1980: 165.
63 Cited by Parker, 1980: 161.
64 Bossuet, 1709: 191, 259.
65 Domat, 1722: vol. 2: 301.
66 ibid.: vol. 2: 304.
67 Brisson, 1609: 46.
68 See above pp. 8–9.
69 Parker, 1981: 253–85 for a fuller analysis.
70 Bodin, 1962: 7.
71 ibid.: 256, 383.
72 ibid.: 791.
73 'Observations véritables et désintéressées sur un écrit imprimé au Louvre . . .' (1652): 86 in *Mazarinades* vol. i.
74 See above p. 7.
75 Le Bret, 1632: 64–5.
76 ibid.: 71.
77 ibid.: 156.
78 ibid.: 644.
79 ibid.: 65, 515.
80 ibid.: 141.
81 Domat, 1722: vol. 2: 304–5.
82 Bossuet, 1709: 83.
83 de Ferrière, 1687: vol. 1: 15–17.

84 de Ferrière, 1677: vol. 2: 2.
85 Parker, 1981: 276–9.
86 de Ferrière, 1677: vol. 1: 2.
87 For the following paragraphs see Parker, 1990: 50–4.
88 *Procès-verbal des conférences tenues par l'ordre du Roi entre les commissaires du Conseil et MM, les députés du Parlement de Paris pour l'examen des articles de l'ordonnance criminelle* (Paris, 1776): 15.
89 ibid.: 13.
90 Gilmore, 1941: 73–4, 87.
91 L'Hommeau, 1605: bk i, v.
92 Rule, 1976: 261–73.
93 Dupâquier, 1989: vol. 2: 11–37.
94 Mousnier, 1979 and 1984, vol. 2: 174; Boislisle, 1874–97: vol. 1: xiv–xvi.
95 Parker, 1989: 68–70; Hamscher, 1987: 6–8.
96 Domat, 1722: vol. 2: 557–8.
97 Trénard, 1975: 25–6.
98 Emmanuelli, 1981: 45.
99 Ardascheff, 1903: 31.
100 Emmanuelli, 1981: 65–6, 69.
101 Cited by Antoine, 1970: 236.
102 Esmonin, 1923: 73.
103 Mousnier, 1979 and 1984: vol. 2: 554.
104 Bataillon, 1942: 62–3.
105 Lebigre, 1988: 70.
106 Mousnier, 1979 and 1984: vol. 2: 174–8.
107 Emmanuelli, 1981: 120–3.
108 Font-Reaulx Blaquière, 1967: 66; Frêche, 1975: 591; Thomson, 1982: 164–70, 215–16, 226–7.
109 Schneider, 1989b: 197, 211.
110 Benedict, 1989: 35.
111 Temple, 1966: 26–30; Schneider, 1989b: 210–13.
112 Achard, 1929: 172; Bataillon, 1942: 103–14.
113 Bacquet, 1688: 13.
114 Root, 1986: 33, 42.
115 ibid.: 51–2; Isambert *et al.*, 1822–33: vol. 20: 408, no. 1797; 418, no. 1823.
116 Root, 1986: 54.
117 Hamscher 1991: 194–5.
118 Hamscher, 1987: 29–31, 91–2, 105–6, 123; Hamscher, 1991: 190–1.
119 Cited by Lebigre, 1988: 97; cf. Hamscher, 1976: 138.
120 Beaucorps, 1978: 272.
121 Boislisle, 1874–97, vol. 1: 1–2.
122 Pillorget, 1975a: 887.
123 Mousnier, 1979 and 1984: vol. 2: 206–7.
124 Lebigre, 1988: 70.
125 Antoine, 1970: 232; cf. Hamscher, 1976: 25–9.
126 Collins, 1988: 85–6; cf. Dessert, 1984: 268–71.
127 ibid.: ch. 11, 330–4.
128 ibid.: 242–57.
129 Schaeper, 1983: 86–7.
130 Ranum, 1963: 77ff.
131 Bergin, 1985: 89–91; Kettering, 1986a: 86–8; Dunckley, 1980: 1–12.
132 See above p. 132.
133 Bergin, 1985: 96–7.

134 ibid.: 53–4.
135 Bercé, 1964: 48–66; Parker, 1980: 91–2. Bercé makes no allusion to Richelieu's interest in the *convoi et comptablie*. This information is provided by Bergin, 1985: 105–6.
136 Dessert, 1987: 217–29.
137 ibid.: 149–64; Dessert, 1984: ch. 13, 325–35.
138 Bluche, 1990: 96.
139 Cited by Antoine, 1970: 51–2.
140 Pagès, 1936: 291.
141 Frostin, 1979: 117–40.
142 Frostin, 1980: 201–6, 210, 218.
143 Isambert *et al.*, 1822–33: vol. 14: 405 art. 97, 410–11, arts. 117–21.
144 The material for this paragraph and the following one is drawn from Parker, 1989: 54–65.
145 *Extrait des registres du Conseil d'Etat le 8 juillet 1661* Arch. Nat. AD II IA.
146 Abbé Duguet, *Traité des qualités, des vertus et des devoirs d'un souverain* (London, 1739), cited by Bérenger, 1974: 189. This work was composed in 1699.
147 Parker, 1989: 69–70.
148 Kettering, 1986a: 209–10, 214.
149 Armstrong, 1972a: 21–40; Armstrong, 1972b: 2–29.
150 Burke, 1992.
151 Walton, 1986: 152–3.
152 ibid.: 182.
153 Isherwood, 1973: 166.
154 Hanley, 1983: 251.
155 Ranum, 1980b: 435 n. 18.
156 Solnon, 1987: 242.
157 Burke, 1992: 50–1.
158 ibid.: 16–31.
159 ibid.: 86–7.
160 ibid.: 49–50.
161 Solnon, 1987: 242.
162 Apostolidès, 1981: 35; Isherwood, 1973: 154–5.
163 Solnon, 1987: 399.
164 Cited by Isherwood, 1973: 183.
165 ibid.: 184–5.
166 ibid.: 202.
167 Burke, 1992: 91–2.
168 ibid.: 44.
169 Apostolidès, 1981: 42.
170 Solnon, 1987: 270, 276–7; Walton, 1986: 36.
171 Giesey, 1985: 77–9.
172 Solnon, 1987: 322, 364.
173 ibid.: 364.
174 Ranum, 1980b: 444.
175 Sonnino, 1970: 151.
176 Solnon, 1987: 352–3.
177 ibid.: 346.
178 Ranum, 1980b: 432.
179 Sonnino, 1970: 239.
180 ibid.: 262–3.
181 ibid.: 31–8.

182 ibid.: 196.
183 ibid.: 84.
184 ibid.: 223.
185 ibid.: 80.
186 Harding, 1978: 171–7.
187 Solnon, 1987: 270, 276–7.
188 Levron, 1968: 78–80; Levron, 1960: 103–4.
189 Walton, 1986: 39.
190 Isherwood, 1973: 148 states that it was *Les amants magnifiques*; Apostolidès, 1981: 115 identifies *Le ballet de flore*.
191 ibid.: 63–4; Benoit, 1971: 72–3.
192 Solnon, 1987: 416–17.
193 ibid.: 409–10.
194 Ranum, 1980b: 449.
195 Apostolidès, 1981: 154.
196 Burke, 1992: 111.
197 Bluche, 1990: 534.
198 Bonney, 1993: 413, figs 1, 2.
199 Calculated from Bonney, 1981: 307.
200 Bonney, 1993: 413–14, figs 2, 3.
201 Collins, 1988: 70–3.
202 Bonney, 1981: 320, table IX B.
203 ibid.: 142–3, 312–13; Mousnier, 1971a: 421–2.
204 Bonney, 1981: 165–6, 186, 189.
205 ibid.: 313.
206 ibid.: 197–8.
207 Collins, 1988: 116.
208 ibid.: 120–1.
209 Le Pesant, 1976: nos. 140, 178, 184, 185, 207.
210 Collins, 1988: 144.
211 Bonney, 1981: 117–19.
212 ibid.: 205, 227.
213 Brisson, 1609: 356–7.
214 Laurière, 1720: vol. 1: Edicts of May 1583 666–9, Jan. 1598 694–5, Mar. 1600 708–14, Sept. 1610 741; see also Deyon, 1975.
215 Laurière, 1720: vol. 1: 741; Girard and Joly, 1638, 1645: vol. 1: 822.
216 Laurière, 1720: vol. 1: 854.
217 ibid.: vol. 1: 912.
218 ibid.: vol. 2: 674, clause 7.
219 Collins, 1988: 103.
220 Bonney, 1978: 227, 229–31.
221 Collins, 1988: 209.
222 ibid.: 110.
223 Guéry, 1978: 224; Bonney, 1991: 202, 228 chart 2.
224 ibid.: 204, 221–2 graphs 8, 9; Bayard, 1988: 19–20; Bonney, 1993: 413 fig. 1.
225 Dessert, 1984: 163.
226 ibid.: 161.
227 ibid.: 185.
228 ibid.: 173–6.
229 ibid.: 185.
230 Bonney, 1981: 316 table VIIB.
231 Loppin, n.d.: 11–22.

232 Guéry, 1988: 1041–60. cf. Bluche and Solnon, 1983: *passim*.
233 Gross, 1993: 84.
234 Bonney, 1993: 384.
235 Bonney, 1991: 208.
236 ibid.: 194.
237 Dessert, 1984: 211ff.
238 Bonney, 1993: 384–412; Bonney, 1991: 196.
239 ibid.: 405.
240 ibid.: 188–90.
241 Bonney, 1993: 391.
242 Dessert, 1984: 213–15.
243 Harsin, 1933: 15–36.
244 ibid.: 37–40.
245 ibid.: 45.
246 ibid.: 49–53.
247 Laurière, 1720: vol. 2: 480–6, 2 Oct. 1713.
248 Dessert, 1984: 91, 202, 383–94, 399–400. cf. Thomson, 1982: 147, 162–3.
249 Frêche, 1975: 589–90.
250 Léon, 1953: vol. 1: 69–73.
251 Bergin, 1985: 5.

CHAPTER 7 FRANCE, ENGLAND AND THE CAPITALIST ROAD (pp. 207–61)

1 Crouzet, 1990: 6.
2 Hill, 1967: 107.
3 Voltaire, 1965.
4 Clark, 1986: *passim*.
5 For the debate on English industrialisation see Hayek, 1954; Mcloskey, 1981; Coleman, 1977; Coleman, 1992; Berg and Hudson, 1992: 24–50.
6 Markovitch, 1976: 257.
7 For example Goodman and Honeyman, 1988.
8 Braudel and Labrousse, 1970–7, vol. 2: 182.
9 ibid.: vol. 2: 509.
10 Crouzet, 1966: 262; Butel, 1993: 81.
11 Crouzet, 1990: 33.
12 Dupâquier, 1989: vol. 2: 92; Lewis, 1993: 9.
13 Léon, 1960: 179.
14 Butel, 1993: 66.
15 Crouzet, 1966: 265; Crouzet, 1990: 45–52; Butel, 1993: 66; Braudel and Labrousse, 1970–7: 527; cf. Lewis, 1993: 58.
16 Chaunu, 1971: 349; Léon, 1960: 179.
17 Crouzet, 1966: 269, 279; Braudel and Labrousse, 1970–7: vol. 2: 545–54; Thomson, 1982: 367ff; Lewis, 1993: 59.
18 Toutain, 1961: 1–216; Le Roy Ladurie, 1979: 173–91; Crouzet, 1990: 52–4.
19 Riley, 1986: 16–22.
20 cf. Kennedy, 1988: 79–80; Braudel, 1981–4: vol. 3: 382–5.
21 O'Brien and Keyder, 1978: 62, 70 table 3.7.
22 Dupâquier, 1989: vol. 2: 87–8.
23 Wrigley, 1987: 176–80; Corfield, 1982: 176 table II; Braudel, 1988: vol. 2: 444–7; Goubert, 1969–70: vol. 1: 191.
24 Brewer, 1989: 181.

25 Chartres, 1991: 144; cf. O'Brien, 1977: 166–81.
26 Jones, 1988: 7; Butel, 1993: 165–99; G. Durand, 1979: 425–8.
27 Castang, 1967: 21–3; Frêche, 1975: 297–301; Morineau, 1971: 63–8, 73, 76–9, 82, 84.
28 Le Roy Ladurie, 1986: 408–9: Molinier, 1985: 209ff.; Butel, 1993: 189.
29 Chaunu, 1971: 332.
30 Bloch, 1930: 355–6.
31 Cited by Dewald, 1987: 88.
32 Butel, 1993: 176.
33 Poussou, 1983: 265–6.
34 Braudel and Labrousse, 1970–7: vol. 2: 399–460.
35 Lemarchand, 1969: 83–4.
36 Jones, 1988: 9; Davies, 1964: 29.
37 ibid.: 29.
38 Labrousse, 1990 remains the classic description. Also Braudel and Labrousse, 1970–7: vol. 2; cf. Butel, 1993: 234–9.
39 ibid.: 85.
40 Braudel and Labrousse, 1970–7: vol. 2: 195; Butel, 1993: 85–7.
41 ibid.: 85.
42 Poussou, 1983: 259; Etienne, 1990: 168.
43 Crouzet, 1966: 264; Butel, 1993: 86–7.
44 ibid.: 87.
45 Braudel, 1988: vol. 2: 580–1.
46 Braudel, 1981–4: vol. 3: 238.
47 Davis, 1962: 257–60; Fisher, 1950: 154; Farnie, 1902: 209.
48 Butel, 1993: 81; Crouzet, 1990: 23.
49 Brenner, 1993: 15.
50 For two contrasting examples see Dornic, 1956: 40; Ligou, 1955: 107.
51 Butel, 1993: 228–34.
52 Braudel and Labrousse, 1970–7: vol. 259; Lewis, 1993: 58; cf. Levy-Leboyer, 1968: 292–3.
53 Braudel and Labrousse, 1970–7: vol. 2: 249; Taylor, 1964: 494–5.
54 Richard, 1974: 139–40, 171, 249.
55 Harris, 1988: 23–4.
56 Gille, 1947: 12, 76; Scoville, 1950: 62–3, 69.
57 ibid.: 11–12, 42–3, 61 n. 119.
58 Gille, 1947: 79–83.
59 Harris, 1988: 34–6; note, however, that charcoal iron was not inferior for most purposes other than castings, 39–40.
60 ibid.: 31–3.
61 ibid.: 44.
62 ibid.: 24–5.
63 Briggs, 1991: 66–74, 87–8.
64 Brown, 1934: 117.
65 Lux, 1989: 125–31, 148–54, 174–9.
66 Briggs, 1991: 66 n. 111.
67 ibid.: 55–6.
68 ibid.: 77; Brown, 1934: 68, 121.
69 Chaplin, 1968: 382–3.
70 Crouzet, 1990: 16–17, 41.
71 Braudel, 1988: vol. 2: 551; Braudel, 1981–4: vol. 2: 403; Clay, 1984: vol. 2: 22.
72 Cited by Briggs, 1991: 79.

73 Lewis, 1993: 76–9; Jones, 1988: 253–8.
74 Corrigan and Sayer, 1986: 90.
75 Brewer, 1989: 67–8.
76 Dickson and Spurling, 1970: 286.
77 O'Brien, 1988: 3.
78 Mathias and O'Brien, 1976: 604–11; Brewer, 1989: 95.
79 Kennedy, 1988: 79–80.
80 O'Brien, 1988: 14; Brewer, 1989: 98.
81 O'Brien, 1988: 17, 27.
82 Mathias and O'Brien, 1976: 53–4; Butel, 1993: 250–3; Y. Durand, 1971: 57.
83 For different estimates of the tax obligations of the French nobility see Behrens, 1962–3: 450–75; Cavanaugh, 1974: 681–92; Bonney, 1993: 413.
84 Doyle, 1989: 66.
85 Mathias and O'Brien, 1976: 623.
86 Butel, 1993: 248 gives a figure of 70 per cent for 1782.
87 Braudel, 1981–4: vol. 3: 176.
88 Clarkson, 1971: 190.
89 Dickson and Spurling, 1970: 289–315.
90 ibid.: 314.
91 Riley, 1986: 157, 166–76, 230; Weir, 1989: 95–124; Kennedy, 1988: 80–6.
92 Brewer, 1989: 77–8.
93 Cited by Braudel, 1981–4: vol. 2: 526.
94 Bosher, 1965: 587.
95 Brewer, 1989: 79–80.
96 O'Brien, 1988: 28.
97 Brewer, 1989: 74–5.
98 Rosenheim, 1989: 108–9, 116–19.
99 Brenner, 1993: 330–40.
100 Dickson, 1967: 260–85.
101 Kennedy, 1988: 103.
102 Kerridge, 1992: 126.
103 Thirsk, 1978: 159ff.
104 Wrightson, 1982: 143–4.
105 ibid.: 131–2.
106 ibid.: 9.
107 Outhwaite, 1986: 14–15.
108 Wrightson, 1982: 141; Clark and Slack, 1976: 112–13; Clarkson, 1971: 234; Beier, 1989: 231–3.
109 Wrightson, 1982: 68, 146; Flinn, 1981: 28–9.
110 Wrigley and Schofield, 1981: 208–9 tables 7–8.
111 Wrightson, 1982: 144–5.
112 Clay, 1984: vol. 1: 19, 103–4.
113 Clark and Slack, 1976: 83; Corfield, 1976: 217, 223, 229; Clay, 1984: vol. 1: 19–20.
114 The comparison between the two countries at the end of the seventeenth century is fraught with difficulties as the estimates which are necessarily involved are complicated by the different criteria of urbanisation employed. Using a base of 1,500 Dupâquier estimates that the urban population of France rose from 14.4 to 17.4 per cent over the course of the century. Clark and Slack with a baseline of 1,000 for England arrive at 20 per cent. They stress the growth of towns of 5,000 plus which they suggest accounted for 15 per cent of the population by 1700. However, two-thirds of this was accounted for by London. In France, on the other hand, Paris accounted

for much less – just over 2 per cent of the population – whilst there were many other big cities: six of more than 60,000, about ten between 30,000 and 40,000, and another forty or more with around 10–15,000. Excluding the capital cities, the proportion of the population living in French towns of over 10,000 was probably higher than the proportion living in English towns of over 5,000. Moreover, outside London the rate of growth of the urban population was not very different. England in 1700 had eight towns of over 10,000 compared with France's sixty or so. See Dupâquier, 1989: vol. 2: 87–8; Clark and Slack, 1976: 11; Clay, 1984: vol. 1: 169–70.

115 Wrightson, 1982: 105, 130; Flinn, 1981: 31–2, 130; Goubert, 1976: 195–203; cf. Beier, 1989: 230–1.
116 Wrightson, 1982: 145.
117 Dupâquier, 1989: vol. 2: 6; Weir, 1984: 33–5.
118 Kerridge, 1967: 332–5.
119 See above pp. 71–2.
120 Macfarlane, 1978: 171–2, 178–80.
121 Thirsk, 1978: 178; Clay, 1984: vol. 1: 139.
122 Thirsk, 1978: 165–8.
123 ibid.: 167.
124 ibid.: 179–80.
125 ibid.: 162–3; Thirsk, 1967–: vol. 4: 598, vol. 5: pt 2 511–12.
126 Kerridge, 1967: *passim*; Clay, 1984: vol. 1: 128–9.
127 ibid.: 133
128 Cornwall, 1954: 58; Havinden, 1961: 66–79; Clay, 1984: vol. 1: 134–5.
129 Kerridge, 1992: 68–71, 101–28; Havinden, 1961: 73–5.
130 Clay, 1984: vol. 1: 137–8
131 ibid.: 217–18.
132 Kerridge, 1985: 236.
133 Thirsk, 1978: 175.
134 Spufford, 1981: 2–3, 5, 108, 115–17.
135 Wrightson, 1982: 33.
136 ibid.: 136.
137 Thirsk, 1978: 167.
138 Spufford, 1981: 145.
139 ibid.: 121–2.
140 Clay, 1984: vol. 2: 16–21; Kerridge, 1985: 231; Brenner, 1993: 46ff.
141 Clay, 1984: vol. 2: 18; Wrightson, 1982: 138.
142 Kerridge, 1985: 169–72.
143 Wrightson, 1982: 129.
144 Braudel, 1981–4: vol. 3: 292; Chartres, 1977: 73–94; Pawson, 1977: 21–46.
145 Clay, 1984: vol. 1: 181.
146 Clark and Slack, 1976: 66–7; Fisher, 1948: 74–93; Chartres, 1977.
147 Clark and Slack, 1976: 66.
148 Cited by Braudel, 1981–4: vol. 2: 69–70.
149 Clay, 1984: vol. 2: 21–2; Chartres, 1977: 78–9.
150 Hoskins, 1965: 94–6; Pound, 1966: 55–8.
151 Le Roy Ladurie, 1994: 155.
152 Houlbrooke, 1984: 43, 242; Clay, 1984: vol. 1: 93–4.
153 Britnell, 1993: 172–4, 217.
154 ibid.: 211–12.
155 Stone, 1965: 27ff.
156 Simpson, 1964: 25.

157 Van Caenegam, 1988: 89–90.
158 Simpson, 1964: 47–8, 51; cf. Pocock, 1957: 65–9.
159 Britnell, 1993: 142–4.
160 Macfarlane, 1978: 82–4; cf. Mate, 1993: 49; Houlbrooke, 1984: 230–1.
161 Simpson, 1964: 145–9; Britnell, 1993: 222.
162 Simpson, 1964: 152–4.
163 ibid.: 24.
164 Dyer, 1968: 12.
165 Mate, 1993: 54ff.; Du Boulay, 1964–5: 448–9; Dyer, 1968: 11–33; Britnell, 1993: 221–2; Hoyle, 1990: 1–20.
166 Croote and Parker, 1985: 87; Underdown, 1987: 24–5; Thirsk, 1967–: vol. 4: 200–45; Spufford, 1974: 76–85; Clay, 1984: vol. 1: 86–7, 120.
167 Brenner, 1985b: 295. Brenner relies on Kerridge for this observation which is unfortunate given that the thrust of Kerridge's argument was to revise Tawney's view of the overriding power of the lords and to insist on the importance of security of tenure for economic development. Kerridge, 1969: 66–93.
168 Hoyle, 1990: 13.
169 Hirst, 1975: 35.
170 Hoyle, 1990: 14–16; Stone, 1965: 295–303.
171 Brenner, 1985b: 295.
172 Searle, 1986: 109–10.
173 Hoyle, 1987: 42, 47.
174 Searle, 1986: 112, 115, 121–2, 125–31.
175 Thirsk, 1992: 191–2.
176 Clarkson, 1971: 66; Thirsk, 1967–: vol. 4: 30, 32; Spufford, 1974: 69, 100, 138–9.
177 Clay, 1984: vol. 1: 58.
178 Spufford, 1981: 117.
179 Wrightson, 1982: 33.
180 Clay, 1984: vol. 1: 120–1.
181 ibid.: vol. 1: 24.
182 See above pp. 56–8.
183 Clay, 1984: vol. 1: 102.
184 Wrightson, 1982: 42.
185 Clark and Slack, 1976: 42.
186 ibid.: 56, 128–9; Evans, 1974: 48.
187 Wrightson, 1982: 28.
188 Clay, 1984: vol. 1: 120–1.
189 Clark and Slack, 1976: 49–50.
190 Evans, 1974: 74.
191 Sacks, 1986: 89–91.
192 'The Sentence of the High Court of Justice Upon the King', 27 January 1648–9.
193 Aylmer, 1961: 477.
194 Wrightson, 1982: 36.
195 Aylmer, 1961: 470–87.
196 See for example Lang, 1974: 42–3.
197 Aylmer, 1959: 333; Aylmer, 1961: 234–7.
198 Sharpe, 1986: 333; Larkin and Hughes, 1973: 21–2; Larkin, 1983: 350–3.
199 Clay, 1984: vol. 1: 156; Underdown, 1985: 20–1.
200 Sharpe, 1986: 337.
201 Russell, 1982: 218.
202 Clay, 1984: vol. 2: 266–7.
203 Brenner, 1993: 208–10.

204 Popofsky, 1990: 53.
205 ibid.: 230–1.
206 ibid.: 45; Brenner, 1993: 230–1.
207 Sharpe, 1986: 346.
208 Russell, 1982: 206.
209 I.A.A. Thompson, 1982: 29–45; Jago, 1981.
210 Elliott, 1963: *passim* esp. 218ff.
211 ibid.: 220–1.
212 Hirst, 1975: 31.
213 Clark and Slack, 1976: 135.
214 Hirst, 1975: 22, 49–50, 96, 105.
215 ibid.: 8–11.
216 ibid.: 11.
217 ibid.: 112.
218 ibid.: 146–52.
219 Cust, 1986: 72.
220 Hirst, 1975: 144.
221 Underdown, 1985: 124–5.
222 ibid.: 121.
223 Sacks, 1986: 97.
224 Cust, 1986: 63–4.
225 Hirst, 1978: 59; Hirst, 1975: 171.
226 ibid.: 179.
227 ibid.: 8.
228 ibid.: 186.
229 Cited by Underdown, 1985: 144–5.
230 Brenner, 1993: 311–13.
231 Underdown, 1985: 139.
232 Fletcher, 1981: 194–200; cf. Hughes, 1989: 138.
233 Russell, 1982: 216, 217.
234 Hinton, 1960: 411.
235 Henshall, 1992: 201.
236 Hinton, 1960: 415.
237 Underdown, 1985: 126.
238 Popofsky, 1990: 45.
239 ibid.: 44–5.
240 Sommerville, 1986: 179.
241 Popofsky, 1990: 58.
242 Sommerville, 1986: 154, 161–2.
243 Mendle, 1993: 102–8.
244 Schwoerer, 1993: 248; Weston and Greenburg, 1981: 51.
245 Pocock, 1993: 389, 390–1.
246 Cited by Sommerville, 1986: 88; Hinton, 1960: 420.
247 Cited by Sommerville, 1986: 80.
248 ibid.: 75–6.
249 Weston and Greenburg, 1981: 36.
250 Hinton, 1960: 423–4.
251 Cited by Pocock, 1957: 33.
252 Cited by Hill, 1965: 246; Sommerville, 1986: 100.
253 ibid.: 102–3.
254 See above pp. 163–4.
255 cf. Pocock, 1957: 170–5.
256 Cited by Sommerville, 1986: 135.

257 Sacks, 1986: 100.
258 Sommerville, 1986: 70 n. 34.
259 Clarkson, 1971: 197.
260 Brenner, 1993: 207, 213–18.
261 Kellet, 1958: 382–4.
262 E.L. Jones, 1970: 65.
263 Appleby, 1978: 41.
264 Cited in ibid.: 51.
265 Cited in ibid.: 45–6.
266 Hill, 1965: 243–5.
267 Lake, 1989: 87.
268 Hill, 1986: 49–50.
269 Underdown, 1985: 142–3.
270 Hill, 1965: 266–7.
271 ibid.: 267.
272 Cited by Underdown, 1985: 120.
273 Lake, 1989: 85.
274 Hill, 1964: 251.
275 Cust and Hughes, 1989: 18.
276 Cust, 1986: 79.
277 Tyacke, 1973: 130.
278 Cited by Foster, 1989: 208.
279 ibid.: 213.
280 Cited by Tyacke, 1987: 239; cf. Sommerville, 1989: 50–1.
281 Underdown, 1985: 141.
282 Cited by Sommerville, 1989: 54.
283 Cited by Sharpe, 1987: 258.
284 Richards, 1986: 78.
285 ibid.: 82–3.
286 Smuts, 1989: 77–8, 82, 91–2.
287 Richards, 1986: 88–93.
288 Parry, 1985: 192–3.
289 Mercer, 1954: 11–31.
290 Parry, 1985: 192–3.
291 ibid.: 264–5.
292 Smuts, 1989: 87–9.
293 Cust, 1986: 75–9.
294 Starkey, 1987: 24.
295 Brenner, 1993: 541–2.
296 Hirst, 1991: 33–66; Underdown, 1985: 282–8.
297 Hill, 1961: 223.
298 Underdown, 1985: 283.
299 Weston and Greenburg, 1981: *passim* esp. 41–52.
300 ibid.: 108–9.
301 Weston, 1960: 430–1, 437.
302 Weston and Greenburg, 1981: 154–9.
303 ibid.: 170–3.
304 Speck, 1989: 153.
305 Locke, 1993: Intro.: 19.
306 I am here following Wootton's view that the Second Treatise was written in the second half of 1681, that is, after the First Treatise and not before it in the winter of 1679–80 as Laslett has argued. Not only does Wootton's internal evidence for this dating seem convincing but it renders the devel-

opment of Locke's political views more coherent. Locke, 1993: Intro.: 73–89; cf. Ashcraft, 1980: 44–7.

307 Locke, 1993: 339.
308 ibid.: 328.
309 ibid.: 305–6.
310 Locke, 1988: 114–15, 410–11.
311 Tully, 1993: 259; cf. Schwoerer, 1993: 245–6.
312 Childs, 1988: 418, 423.
313 Schwoerer, 1993: 233–4.
314 Cited by Speck, 1989: 165.
315 Hill, 1961: 277.
316 Speck, 1989: 164–5.
317 I am grateful to Professor Speck for this information.
318 Holmes, 1986: 1–33.
319 Doyle, 1989: 106–7, 296–7.
320 Weston, 1960: 430–1, 437.
321 For this argument see Parker, 1981: 283–5. It owes much to Preston King, 1974.
322 Bossuet, 1709: 41–2, 46–7, 62ff.; Filmer, 1680: 60–1, 85.
323 Cited by Ashcraft, 1980: 183.
324 ibid.: 61–4; MacPherson, 1962: 162–74.
325 Cited by Levy-Bruhl, 1933: 220, 223; cf. Richard, 1974: 54–61.
326 Cited by Kaplan, 1976: vol. 1: 102–3.
327 Cited in ibid.: vol. 2: 422.
328 MacPherson, 1962: *passim* esp. 46ff.

CHAPTER 8 EMPIRICAL RÉSUMÉ AND THEORETICAL AFTERTHOUGHTS (pp. 262–80)

1 Abrams, 1982: 150.
2 Taylor, 1964: 486.
3 Jones, 1988: 44, 53.
4 Chaunu and Gascon, 1977: vol. 1: pt 1, 195–6, 212 in Brundel and Labrouse, 1970–7.
5 Jacquart, 1974: 78.
6 Bergin, 1985: 5.
7 Briggs, 1989: 370.
8 Gellner, 1988: 187.
9 Parker, 1973: 15.
10 Hobsbawm, 1971: 10–11.
11 Notably, Engels, 1892: 277–302.
12 Goodman and Honeyman, 1988: 27.
13 Britnell, 1993: 223.
14 For example Cohen, 1978; see Parker, 1990: 287–301.
15 Sayer, 1987: 94, 111.
16 Marx and Engels, 1845–6: 59.
17 E.P. Thompson, 1964: 9.
18 Gellner, 1988: 187.
19 Elliot, 1984: 41, 85, 105–6.
20 For example I.A.A. Thompson, 1976.
21 Russell, 1979: 72.
22 Polisensky, 1971: 245–6; Evans, 1979: 197ff.

SELECT BIBLIOGRAPHY

This bibliography contains only works cited in the notes section of the book. It is divided into four sections, each arranged alphabetically: printed sources; works on France; works on England (including Anglo-French comparisons); theoretical and miscellaneous. References to manuscripts, individual Mazarinades, specific memoirs and letters are given in the notes.

PRINTED SOURCES

Bacquet, M.J. (1688) *Les œuvres de M.J. Bacquet*, ed. C. de Ferrière, Paris.

Baricave, M.I. (1614) *La défence de la monarchie françoise et autres monarchies contre les détestables et exécrables maximes d'Etat des ministres Calvinistes . . .*, Toulouse.

Bignon, J. (1610) *De l'excellence des roys et du royaume de France*, Paris.

Blondeau, C. and Gueret, G. (1723) *Journal du palais ou recueil des principales décisions de tous les parlements et cours souveraines de France sur les questions les plus importantes de droit*, Paris, 3rd edn.

Bodin, J. (1576) *The Six Books of a Commonweal*, trans. R. Knolles, ed. K.D. McCrae, Cambridge, MA: Harvard University Press, 1962.

Boislisle, A. de (ed.) (1874–97) *Correspondance des contrôleurs-généraux des finances avec les intendants des provinces*, 3 vols, Paris: imprimerie nationale.

Bossuet, J.B. (1709) *Politics Drawn from the Very Words of Holy Scripture*, ed. P. Riley, Cambridge: CUP, 1990.

Brisson, B. (1609) *Code du Roy Henri III*, n.p.

Cabrol, U. (ed.) (1910) *Documents sur le soulèvement des paysans du Bas-Rouergue dits Croquants au commencement du règne de Louis XIV*, Rodez.

Cambolas, J. de (1659) *Décisions notables sur diverse questions en droit jugées par plusiers arrêts de la Cour du Parlement de Toulouse*, Toulouse.

Carrier, H. (ed.) (1982) *La Fronde: contestation démocratique et misère paysanne, 52 Mazarinades*, 2 vols, Paris: EDHIS.

Caseneuve, P. de (1633) *Le franc-aleu de Languedoc*, Toulouse.

Catellan, J. de (1703) *Arrêts remarquables du Parlement de Toulouse recueillies par Jean de Catellan augmentées par François et Jacques de Catellan*, 2 vols, Toulouse.

Charron, P. (1602) *De la Sagesse*, Paris: 1656 edn.

Coquelle, P. (ed.) (1908) 'Documents sur la sédition de Montpellier en 1645', *Annales du Midi*, vol. 20.

Coquille, G. (1607) *Les institutions du droit des Français*, Paris: 1630 edn.

Domat, J. (1722) *The Civil Laws in Their Natural Order: together with the Publick law*, 2 vols, trans. W. Strahan, London.

—— (1828–30) *Œuvres complètes*, 4 vols, ed. J. Remy, Paris.
Durand, Y. (1966) *Cahiers des doléances des paroisses du bailliage de Troyes pour les Etats-Généraux de 1614*, Paris: PUF.
de Ferrière, C. (1677) *La jurisprudence du Digeste de Justinien conferée avec les ordonnances royaux, les coutumes de France et les décisions des cours souveraines*, n.p.
—— (1687) *Institutions du droit français*, 2 vols, Paris.
Filleau, J. (1630–1) *Recueil général des édits, arrêts et règlements notables*, 2 vols, Paris.
Filmer, R. (1680) *Patriarcha and Other Political Works*, ed. P. Laslett, Oxford: Blackwell, 1949.
Font-Reaulx Blaquière, H. and A. de (1967) *Documents sur le canal des deux mers et la politique de Colbert en Languedoc*, Toulouse: Centre régional de documentation pédagogique.
Galland, A. (1637) *Du franc-alleu et origine des droits seigneuriaux*, Paris.
Girard, E. and Joly, J. (1638, 1645) *Trois livres des offices de France*, 2 vols, Paris.
Isambert, F.A. *et al.* (1822–33) *Recueil général des anciennes lois françaises depuis l'an 420 jusqu'à la révolution de 1789*, 29 vols, Paris: Belin-le Prieur.
Joly, C. (1653) *Recueil des maximes véritables et importantes pour l'institution du roy contre la fausse et pernicieuse politique du Cardinal Mazarin prétendu surintendant de l'Education de Sa Majesté*, Paris.
Larkin, J.F. (ed.) (1983) *Stuart Royal Proclamations*, vol. 2, Oxford: Clarendon Press.
Larkin, J.F. and Hughes, P.H. (ed.) (1973) *Stuart Royal Proclamations*, vol. 1, Oxford: Clarendon Press.
La Rochefoucauld, Fr. de (1665) *Maxims*, trans. L.W. Tancock, Baltimore: Penguin Books, 1959.
Laurière, E.J. de (1699) *Bibliothèque des coutumes*, n.p.
—— (1720) *Recueil des édits et ordonnances royaux*, 2 vols, Paris.
Le Bret, C. (1632) *De la souveraintété du Roy*, Paris.
Le Pesant, M. (ed.) (1976) *Arrêts du Conseil du Roi. Règne de Louis XIV*, Paris: Archives Nationales.
L'Hommeau, P. de (1605) *Maximes générales du droit français*, Paris, 1665 edn.
Locke, J. (1988) *Two Treatises of Government*, ed. P. Laslett, Cambridge: CUP, 1988.
—— (1993) *Political Writings*, ed. D. Wootton, London: Penguin Books, 1993.
Loppin, I. (n.d.) *Les mines gallicanes ou le trésor du royaume de France*, n.p.
Loyseau, C. (1610) *Traité des Ordres et simples dignités*, Paris.
Moreau, C. (ed.) (1853) *Choix de Mazarinades*, 2 vols, Paris: Soc. de l'hist. de France, Renouard et Cie.
Mousnier, R. (ed.) (1964) *Lettres et mémoires adressées au Chancelier Séguier*, Paris: PUF.
Mousnier, R., Labatut, J.-P. and Durand, Y. (eds) (1965) *Deux cahiers de la noblesse pour les états-généraux*, Paris: PUF.
Pocquet de Livonnière, C. de (1729) *Traité des fiefs*, Paris.
Racine, J. (1967) *Andromache and Other Plays*, trans. and introduction by J. Cairncross, Harmondsworth: Penguin Books.
Robillard de Beaurepaire, Ch. de (ed.) (1876–8) *Cahier des Etats de Normandie sous le règne de Louis XIII et Louis XIV*, 3 vols, n.p.
Rohan, H. de (1646) *Mémoires*, Amsterdam.
Seyssel, C. de (1519) *La grande monarchie de France*, Paris: Gollot de Pre, edn n.d.
Silhon, J. de (1665) *Le ministre d'état*, Paris.
Sonnino, P. (ed.) (1970) *Memoirs for the Instruction of the Dauphin*, London: Collier-Macmillan.
Thaumas de la Thaumassière, G. (1667) *Le franc alleu de la province de Berry ou traité de la liberté des personnes et des héritages du Berry*, Bourges.

—— (1691) *Questions et réponses sur les coutumes de Berry*, n.p.
Theveneau, A. (1647) *Commentaire sur les ordonnances contenant les difficultés mueus entre les docteurs*, Paris: Rigaud.
Vigier, J. (1650) *Les coustumes du pais et duché d'Angoumois, Aunis et gouvernement de la Rochelle*, Paris.
Voltaire, F. de Arouet de (1734) *Lettres philosophiques*, Oxford: Blackwell, 1965.
Anon. *Mazarinades*, 27 vols (np. nd.), Brit. Lib. 180 a, 181 a.
Anon. (1776) *Procès-verbal des conférences tenues par l'ordre du Roi entre les commissaires du Conseil et MM les députés du Parlement de Paris pour l'examen des articles l'ordonnance criminelle*, Paris.

WORKS ON FRANCE

Achard, A.J. (1929) *Une ancienne justice seigneuriale en Auvergne. Surgères et ses habitants*, Clermont Ferrand: Imprimerie Générale.
Adam, A. (1974) *Grandeur and Illusion: French Literature and Society 1600–1715*, Harmondsworth: Penguin Books.
Antoine, M. (1970) *Le Conseil du Roi sous le règne de Louis XV*, Paris and Geneva: Droz.
Apostolidès, J.-M. (1981) *Le Roi-machine; spectacle et politique au temps de Louis XIV*, Paris: Minuit.
Ardascheff, P. (1903) 'Les intendants de Province', *Revue d'histoire moderne et contemporaine*, vol. 5.
Baerhrel, R. (1961) *Une croissance: la Basse-Provence rurale*, Paris: SEVPEN.
Bastier, J. (1974) 'Une résistance fiscale du Languedoc sous Louis XIII: la querelle du franc-alleu', *Annales du Midi*, vol. 86.
Bataillon, J.H. (1942) 'Les justices seigneuriales du bailliage de Pontoise à la fin de l'ancien régime', Thèse Droit, Paris.
Bayard, F. (1988) *Le monde des financiers au XVII siècle*, Paris: Fayard.
Beaucorps, Ch. de (1978) *L'Administration des intendants d'Orléans de 1686 à 1713*, Geneva: Megariotis.
Behrens, B. (1962–3) 'Nobles and taxes in France at the end of the Ancien Régime', *Economic History Review*, ser. 2, vol. 15.
Beik, W. (1974a) 'Magistrates and popular uprisings before the Fronde: the case of Toulouse', J.M.H., vol. 46.
—— (1974b) 'Two intendants face a popular revolt: social unrest and the structure of absolutism', *Canadian Journal of History*, vol. 9.
—— (1985) *Absolutism and Society in Seventeenth-Century France: State Power and Provincial Aristocracy in Languedoc*, Cambridge: CUP.
—— (1987) 'Urban factions and the social order during the minority of Louis XIV', *French Historical Studies*, vol. 15.
—— (1990) 'The culture of protest in seventeenth-century French towns', *Social History*, vol. 15.
—— (1991) 'The Parlement of Toulouse and the Fronde', in M.P. Holt (ed.) *Society and Institutions in Early Modern France*, London: Humanities Press International.
Benedict, P. (1981) *Rouen during the Wars of Religion*, Cambridge: CUP.
—— (1989) 'French cities from the sixteenth century to the Revolution', in P. Benedict (ed.) *Cities and Social Change in Early Modern France*, London: Unwin Hyman.
Benoit, M. (1971) *Versailles et les musiciens du Roi. Etude institutionnelle et sociale*, Paris: Picard.

Bercé, Y.-M. (1964) 'La bourgeoisie bordelaise et le fisc sous Louis XIII', *Revue historique de Bordeaux et du département de la Gironde*, vol. 13.
—— (1974) *Histoire des croquants*, 2 vols, Geneva, Droz.
—— (1987) *Revolts and Revolutions in Early Modern Europe: An Essay on the History of Political Violence*, trans. J. Bergin, Manchester: MUP.
Bérenger, J. (1974) 'Pour une enquête européenne: le problème du Ministériat au XVII siècle', *Annales E.S.C.*, vol. 29.
—— (1981) 'Noblesse et absolutisme de François I à Louis XIV', in B. Kopeczi and E.H. Balazs (eds) *Noblesse française, noblesse hongroise XVI–XIX siècles*, Paris: CNRS, Budapest: Akademiai Kiado.
Berger, P. (1978) 'French administration in the famine of 1693', *European Studies Review*, ser. 2, vol. 8.
Bergin, J. (1985) *Cardinal Richelieu: Power and the Pursuit of Wealth*, London: Yale University Press.
Bernard, L. (1975) 'French society and popular uprisings under Louis XIV', in R.F. Kierstead (ed.) *State and Society in Seventeenth-Century France*, New York: Franklin Watts.
Bitton, D. (1969) *French Nobility in Crisis*, Stanford, CA: Stanford University Press.
Bloch, M. (1930) 'La lutte pour l'individualisme agraire dans la France du XVIII siècle', *Annales E.S.C.*, vol. 2.
Bluche, F. (1990) *Louis XIV*, trans. M. Greengrass, Oxford: Blackwell.
Bluche, F. and Durye, P. (1962) *L'Annoblissement par charges avant 1789*, Paris: Les Claires Nobles.
Bluche, F. and Solnon, J.F. (1983) *La Véritable hiérarchie de l'ancienne France. Le tarif de la première capitation*, Geneva: Droz.
Bohanan, D. (1991) 'The sword in the robe: seventeenth-century Provence and Brittany', in M.P. Holt (ed.) *Society and Institutions in Early Modern France*, London: Humanities Press International.
—— (1993) *Old and New Nobility in Aix-en-Provence: Portrait of an Urban Elite*, Los Angeles: Baton Rouge.
Bois, G. (1976) *La crise du féodalisme*, Paris: Presses de la Fondation nationale de sciences politiques.
Bonney, R. (1978) *Political Change in France under Richelieu and Mazarin*, Oxford: OUP.
—— (1981) *The King's Debts*, Oxford: Clarendon Press.
—— (1982) 'Cardinal Mazarin and the Great Nobility during the Fronde', *English Historical Review*, vol. 96
—— (1989) *L'Absolutisme*, Paris: PUF.
—— (1991) 'Jean Rolan Malet: historian of the finances of the French monarchy', *French History*, vol. 5.
—— (1993) '"Le secret de leurs familles": the fiscal and social limits of Louis XIV's dixième', *French History*, vol. 7.
Borzeix, D., Portal, R. and Serbat, J. (1982) *Révoltes populaires en Occitanie. Moyen âge et ancien régime*, Treignac: Les Monedières, Diffusion Alternative.
Bosher, J.F. (1964) *The Single Duty Project: A Study of the Movement for a French Customs Union in the Eighteenth Century*, London: Athlone Press.
—— (1965) 'French administration and finances in their European setting', *New Cambridge Modern History*, vol. 8.
Bourcier, J. (1960) *Le métayage dans la région d'Aix aux XVIII siècle*, Aix-en-Provence: La Pensée universitaire.
Bourde de la Rogerie, H. (1922) 'Étude sur la réformation de la noblesse en Bretagne', *Mémoires de la Société d'Histoire et d'Archéologie de Bretagne*, vol. 3.
Bourgeon, J.-L. (1971) *Les Colbert avant Colbert*, Paris: PUF.

Boutruche, R. (1947) *La crise d'une société: seigneurs et paysans du Bordelais pendant la Guerre de Cent Ans*, Paris: Lettres.

—— (1966) *Bordeaux de 1453 à 1715*, Bordeaux: Fédération Historique du Sud-Ouest.

Braudel, F. (1988) *The Identity of France*, 2 vols, London: Collins.

Braudel F. and Labrousse, E. (eds) (1970–7) *Histoire économique et sociale de la France*, 3 vols, Paris: PUF.

Briggs, R. (1989) *Communities of Belief: Cultural and Social Tensions in Early Modern France*, Oxford: OUP.

—— (1991) 'The *Académie Royale des Sciences* and the pursuit of utility', *Past & Present*, no. 131.

Brockliss, L. (1992) 'Richelieu, education and the state', in L. Brockliss and J. Bergin, *Richelieu and His Age*, Oxford: Clarendon Press.

Brown, H. (1934) *Scientific Organisations in Seventeenth-Century France*, New York: Russell and Russell.

Burke, P. (1992) *The Fabrication of Louis XIV*, London and New Haven: Yale University Press.

Butel, P. (1993) *L'économie française au XVIII siècle*, Paris: SEDES.

Cabourdin, G. (1977) *Terre et hommes en Lorraine 1550–1635*, 2 vols, Nancy: Université de Nancy.

Caillard, M. *et al.* (1963) *A travers la Normandie des XVII et XVIII siècles*, Cahier des Annales de Normandie, vol. 3, Caen.

Carrier, H. (1988, 1991) *La presse de la Fronde: Les Mazarinades (1648–1653)*, vol. I: *La conquête de l'opinion*; vol. 2: *Les hommes du livre*, Geneva: Droz.

Castang, C. (1967) *La politique de la mise en culture des terres à la fin de l'Ancien Régime*, Paris: Thèse Droit.

Cavanaugh, G.J. (1974) 'Nobles, privileges and taxes in France: a revision revised', *French Historical Studies*, vol. 8.

Chagniot, J. (1979) 'Mobilité sociale et armée (vers 1660–vers 1760) ', *XVII Siècle*, no. 122.

Chaplin, S.L. (1968) 'The Academy of Sciences during the eighteenth century: an astronomical appraisal', *French Historical Studies*, vol. 5.

Charbonnier, P. (1980) *Une autre France: la seigneurie rurale en Basse-Auvergne du XIV au XVI siècles*, 2 vols, Clermont-Ferrand: Institut d'Etude du Massif Central.

Charmeil, J.-P. (1964) *Les trésoriers de France à l'époque de la Fronde*, Paris: Picard.

Chauleur, A. (1964) 'Le rôle des traitants dans l'administration financière de la France de 1643 à 1653', *XVII Siècle*, no. 65.

Chaunu, P. and Gascon, R. (1977) *Histoire économique et sociale de la France*, vol. 1, pt 1. Paris: PUF.

Chaussinand-Nogaret, G. (1991) *Histoire des élites en France du XVI au XX siècle*, Paris: Tallandier.

Chevet, J.M. (1993) 'Marchés régionaux, marché national dans la France des XVI–XIX siècles: l'exemple du blé', Paper given to European historical economics workshop, Lerici.

Church, W.F. (1969) *The Impact of Absolutism on France*, New York: John Wiley.

—— (1972) *Richelieu and Reason of State*, Princeton, NJ: Princeton University Press, 1972.

Clark, J.G. (1981) *La Rochelle and the Atlantic Economy*, Baltimore: Johns Hopkins University Press.

Clouatre, D. (1984) 'The concept of class in French culture prior to the Revolution', *Journal of the History of Ideas*, vol. 45.

Cole, C.W. (1939) *Colbert and a Century of French Mercantilism*, 2 vols, New York: Columbia University Press.

Collins, J.B. (1988) *Fiscal Limits of Absolutism: Direct Taxation in Early Seventeenth-Century France*, Berkeley: University of California Press.
—— (1989) 'The economic role of women in seventeenth-century France', *French Historical Studies*, vol. 16.
Collomp, A. (1983) *La maison du père: famille et village en Haute Provence aux XVII et XVIII siècles*, Paris: PUF.
Comminel, G.C. (1987) *Rethinking the French Revolution*, London: Verso.
Constant, J.-M. (1972) 'Gestion et revenus d'un grande domaine aux XVI et XVII siècle d'après les comptes de la baronnie d'Auneau', *Revue d'histoire économique et sociale*, vol. 30, no. 2.
—— (1974) 'L'Enquête de noblesse de 1667 et les seigneurs de Beauce', *Revue d'histoire moderne et contemporaine*, vol. 221.
—— (1979) 'La mobilité sociale dans une province de gentilshommes et paysans', *XVII Siècle*, no. 122.
Corvisier, A. (1959) 'Les généraux de Louis XIV et leur origine sociale', *XVII Siècle*, nos. 42–3.
Coste, J.-P. (1970) *La ville d'Aix en 1695. Structure urbaine et société*, Aix-en-Provence: La Pensée universitaire.
Couturier, M. (1969) *Recherches sur les structures sociales de Chateaudun*, Paris: SEVPEN.
Croix, A. (1985) *La Bretagne au XVI et XVII siècles*, 2 vols, Paris: Maloine.
Cubells, M. (1967) 'Le parlement de Paris pendant la Fronde', *XVII Siècle*, no. 35.
—— (1970) 'A propos des usurpations de noblesse en Provence sous l'ancien régime', *Provence historique*, vol. 81.
Cuttler, S.H. (1987) *The Law of Treason and Treason Trials in Later Medieval France*, Cambridge: CUP.
Davies, A. (1964) 'The origins of the French peasant revolution of 1789', *History*, vol. 49.
Davis, N.Z. (1975) *Society and Culture in Early Modern France*, London: Duckworth.
Dégarne, M. (1962) 'Études sur les soulèvements provinciaux en France avant la Fronde: la révolte de Rouergue en 1643', *XVII Siècle*, no. 56.
Delafosse, M. (1949) 'La Rochelle et les Iles', *Revue d'histoire des colonies*, vol. 26.
—— (1963) 'Origine géographique et sociale des marchands rochelais au XVII siècle', *Actes du 87 congrès national des sociétés savantes, section d'histoire moderne et contemporaine*.
Delevaud, L. (1891) 'Troubles en Poitou, Saintonge, Aunis et Angoumois en 1643–4', *Archives historiques de Saintonge et Aunis*, vol. 19.
Delumeau, J. (1966) 'Le commerce extérieur de la France au XVII siècle', *XVII Siècle*, nos. 70–1.
Dessert, D. (1975) 'Le lobby Colbert: un royaume ou une affaire de famille?', *Annales E.S.C.*, vol. 30.
—— (1984) *Argent, pouvoir et société au grand siècle*, Paris: Fayard.
—— (1987) *Fouquet*, Paris: Fayard.
Devèze, M. (1960) 'Les communautés rurales en Bourgogne en 1665 d'après les questionnaires de l'intendant Bouchu sur la Bourgogne', *Actes du 84 congrès nationale des sociétés savantes*.
Devyver, A. (1973) *Le sang épuré: les préjugés de race chez les gentilshommes français de l'ancien régime, 1560–1720*, Brussels: Université de Bruxelles.
Dewald, J. (1980) *The Formation of a Provincial Nobility*, Princeton, NJ: Princeton University Press.
—— (1987) *Pont-St-Pierre 1398–1789: Lordship, Community and Capitalism in Early Modern France*, Berkeley: University of California Press.

—— (1993) *Aristocratic Experience and the Origins of Modern Culture 1570–1715*, Berkeley: University of California Press.

Deyon, P. (1966) 'La production manufacturière en France au XVII et ses problèmes', *XVII Siècle*, nos. 70–1.

—— (1967) *Amiens, capitale provinciale: étude sur la société urbaine au dix-septième siècle*, Paris: École Pratique des Hautes Études.

—— (1975) 'Relations between the French nobility and the absolute monarchy during the first half of the seventeenth century', in R.F. Kierstead (ed.) *State and Society in Seventeenth-Century France*, New York: Franklin Watts.

Dontenwill, S. (1973) *Une seigneurie sous l'Ancien Régime: l'étoile en Brionnais du XV au XVIII siècles*, Roanne: Horvath.

Dornic, F. (1956) 'L'évolution de l'industrie textile aux XVIII et XIX siècles: l'activité de la famille Cohin', *Revue d'histoire moderne et contemporaine*, vol. 3.

Doyle, W. (1974) *The Parlement of Bordeaux and the End of the Old Regime*, London: Ernest Benn.

—— (1989) *The Oxford History of the French Revolution*, Oxford: OUP.

Duby, G. (1980) *The Three Orders: Feudal Society Imagined*, Chicago: University of Chicago Press.

—— (ed.) (1981) *Histoire de la France urbaine*, 3 vols, Paris: Seuil.

Dumont, F. (1964) *Études sur l'histoire des assemblées d'états*, Paris: PUF.

Dunckley, K.M. (1980) 'Patronage and power in seventeenth-century France: Richelieu's clients and the Estates of Brittany', *Parlement, Estates and Representation*, vol. 1.

Dupâquier, J. (1989) *Histoire de la population française*, 4 vols, Paris: PUF.

Dupont-Ferrier, G. (1923) *Les institutions de la France sous le règne de Charles V*, Paris: Journal des Savants.

Durand, G. (1979) *Vin, vigne et vignerons en Lyonnais et Beaujolais XVI-XVIII siècles*, Paris and La Haye: Mouton.

Durand, Y. (ed.) (1971) *Les fermiers généraux au XVIII siècle*, Paris: PUF.

—— (1981) *Hommage à Roland Mousnier: clientèles et fidélités en Europe à l'époque moderne*, Paris: PUF.

El Kordi, M. (1970) *Bayeux au XVII et XVIII siècles*, Paris and La Haye: Mouton.

Elliott, J.H. (1984) *Richelieu and Olivares*, Cambridge: CUP.

Ellis, H.A. (1988) *Boulainvilliers and the French Monarchy: Aristocratic Politics in Early Eighteenth-Century France*, Ithaca: Cornell University Press

Emmanuelli, F.-X. (1981) *Un mythe de l'absolutisme bourbonien: l'intendance du milieu du XVII siècle à la fin du XVIII siècle*, Aix-en-Provence: Université d'Aix-en-Provence.

Esmonin, E. (1923) 'Les intendants du Dauphiné', *Annales de l'Université de Grenoble*, vol. 34.

Etienne, R. (1990) *Histoire de Bordeaux*, Toulouse: Privat.

Fairchilds, C. (1976) *Poverty and Charity in Aix-en-Provence*, Baltimore: Johns Hopkins University Press.

Farr, J.R. (1988) *Hands of Honour*, Ithaca: Cornell University Press.

—— (1989) 'Consumers, commerce and the craftsmen of Dijon: the changing social and economic structure of a provincial capital', in P. Benedict (ed.) *Cities and Social Change in Early Modern France*, London: Unwin Hyman.

Flandrin, J.-L. (1979) *Families in Former Times: Kinship, Household and Sexuality*, Cambridge: CUP.

Foisil, M. (1970) *La révolte des nu-pieds et les révoltes normandes de 1639*, Paris: PUF.

—— (1981) 'Parentèles et fidelités autour du duc de Longueville, gouverneur de Normandie pendant la Fronde', in Y. Durand (ed.) *Hommage à Roland Mousnier: clientèles et fidelités en Europe l'époque moderne*, Paris: PUF.

Fontenay, M. (1957) *Paysans et marchands ruraux de la vallée de l'Essonne dans la seconde moitié du XVII siècle*, Paris: Fédération des sociétés historiques et et archéologiques de Paris et l'Ile de France.

Forster, R. (1960) *The Nobility of Toulouse in the Eighteenth Century*, Baltimore: Johns Hopkins Press.

—— (1963) 'The provincial noble: a reappraisal', *American Historical Review*, vol. 68.

Frêche, G. (1975) *Toulouse et la région Midi-Pyrénées au siècle des lumières vers 1670–1789*, Toulouse: Editions Cujas.

Frostin, C. (1979) 'La famille ministérielle Phélypeaux: esquisse d'un profil Pontchartrain', *Annales de Bretagne*, vol. 86.

—— (1980) 'L'Organisation ministérielle sous Louis XIV: cumul d'attributions et situations conflictuelles', *Revue historique de droit français et étranger*, vol. 58.

Gallet, J. (1975) 'Research on the popular movement at Amiens in 1635 and 1636', in R.F. Kierstead (ed.) *State and Society in Seventeenth-Century France*, New York: Franklin Watts.

—— (1983) *La seigneurie bretonne (1450–1680): l'exemple du Vannetais*, Paris: Pub. de la Sorbonne.

Garlan, Y. and Nières, C. (1975) *Les révoltes bretonnes de 1675: papier timbré et bonnets rouges*, Paris: Editions Sociales.

Garnault, E. (1899) 'Les bourgeoises rochelaises des temps passés et les causes de décadence du commerce rochelais', *Revue historique*, vol. 70.

Garnier, J. (1982) *Bourgeoisie et propriété immobilière en Forèz aux XVII et XVIII siècles*, St Etienne: Centre d'Etudes Foréziennes.

Garrisson, J. (1985) *L'Édit de Nantes et sa révocation*, Paris: Seuil.

Gascon, R. (1971) *Grand commerce et vie urbaine au XVI siècle*, 2 vols, Paris: Mouton.

Germain, A. (1839) 'Les commencements du règne de Louis XIV et la Fronde à Montpellier', *Académie des sciences et lettres de Montpellier. Mémoires de la section des lettres*, vol. 3.

Giesey, R. (1985) *Cérémonial et puissance souveraine XV-XVII siècles*, Paris: Armand Colin.

Gille, B. (1947) *Les origines de la grande industrie métallurgique en France*, Paris: Domat.

Golden, R. (1981) *The Godly Rebellion: Parisian Curés and the Religious Fronde, 1652–1662*, Chapel Hill: University of Carolina Press.

Goubert, P. (1954) 'Une fortune bourgeoise au XVII siècle: Jean Pocquelin, bisaïeul probable de Molière', *Revue d'histoire moderne et contemporaine*, vols 1–2.

—— (1956) 'The French peasantry in the seventeenth century', *Past & Present*, vol. 10.

—— (1959) *Familles marchandes sous l'ancien régime: les Danses et les Motte de Beauvais*, Paris: SEVPEN.

—— (1960) *Beauvais et Beauvaisis de 1600 à 1730: contribution à l'histoire sociale de la France du XVII siècle*, Paris: SEVPEN.

—— (1969–70) *L'Ancien Régime*, 2 vols, Paris: Armand Colin.

—— (1976) *Clio parmi les hommes*, Paris and La Haye: Mouton.

—— (1986) *The French Peasantry in the Seventeenth Century*, Cambridge: CUP.

Grassby, R.B. (1960–1) 'Social status and commercial enterprise under Louis XIV', *Economic History Review*, ser. 2, vol. 13.

Gross, J.-P. (1993) 'Progressive taxation and social justice in eighteenth century France', *Past & Present*, no. 140.

Guenée, B. (1964) 'L'histoire de l'Etat en France à la fin du moyen âge vue par les historiens français depuis cent ans', *Revue Historique*, vol. 232.

Guéry, A. (1978) 'Les finances de la monarchie française sous l'ancien régime', *Annales E.S.C.*, vol. 33.

—— (1988) 'Etat, classification sociale et compromis sous Louis XIV: la capitation de 1695', *Annales E.S.C.*, vol. 41 ii.

Guichard, P. (1966) 'D'une société repliée à une société ouverte: l'évolution de la région d'Andance de la fin du XVII siècle à la révolution', in P. Léon and B. Chorier (eds) *Structures économiques et problèmes sociaux du monde rurale dans la France du Sud-Est*, Paris: Belles Lettres.

Gutton, J.-P. (1971) *La société et les pauvres: l'exemple de la généralité de Lyon 1534–1789*, Paris: Belles Lettres.

—— (1975) 'Le cahier de doléances de la noblesse du Beaujolais aux Etats-Généraux de 1649', *Revue Historique*, vol. 253.

—— (1981) *Domestiques et serviteurs dans la France de l'ancien régime*, Paris: Aubier Montaigne.

Guyot, Ch. (1889) *Le métayage en Lorraine avant 1789*, Nancy: Berger-Levrault.

Hamon, J. (1959) 'Une exemple de morcellement du bien censif du au partage égal prescrit par la coutume du Maine', *Le Pays-bas Normand*, vol. 52.

Hamscher, A. (1976) *The Parlement of Paris after the Fronde*, Pittsburgh: University of Pittsburgh Press.

—— (1987) *The Conseil Privé and the Parlements in the Age of Louis XIV: A Study in French Absolutism*, Philadelphia: Transactions of the American Philosophical Society 77.

—— (1991) 'Parlements and litigants at the king's councils during the personal rule of Louis XIV', in M.P. Holt (ed.) *Society and Institutions in Early Modern France*, London: Humanities Press International.

Hanley, S. (1983) *The Lit de Justice of the Kings of France. Constitutional Ideology in Legend, Ritual and Discourse*, Princeton, NJ: Princeton University Press

—— (1989) 'Engendering the state: family formation and state building in early modern France', *French Historical Studies*, vol. 16.

Harding, R.R. (1978) *Anatomy of a Power Elite: The Provincial Governors of Early Modern France*, New Haven: Yale University Press.

Harris, J.R. (1988) 'The diffusion of English metallurgical methods to eighteenth-century France', *French History*, vol. 2.

Harsin, P. (1933) *Crédit public et banque d'état en France du XVI au XVIII siècle*, Paris: Droz.

Harth, E. (1985) *Ideology and Culture in Seventeenth-Century France*, Ithaca: Cornell University Press.

Hayden, J.M. (1974) *France and the Estates General of 1614*, Cambridge: CUP.

Hinckner, F. (1971) *Les Français devant l'impôt sous l'ancien régime*, Paris: Flammarion.

Hoffman, P.T. (1984) *Church and Community in the Diocese of Lyon 1500–1789*, New Haven: Yale University Press.

—— (1986) 'Taxes and agrarian life in early modern France: land sales 1550–1730', *Journal of Economic History*, vol. 46.

Holt, M.P. (ed.) (1991) *Society and Institutions in Early Modern France*, London: Humanities Press International.

Hufton, O. (1973) *The Poor of Eighteenth-Century France*, Oxford: OUP.

Huppert, G. (1977) *Les bourgeois gentilhommes. An Essay on the Definition of Elites in Renaissance France*, Chicago: University of Chicago Press.

Irvine, F.M. (1989) 'From Renaissance city to Ancien Régime capital, Montpellier *c.* 1500–1600', in P. Benedict (ed.) *Cities and Social Change in Early Modern France*, London: Unwin Hyman.

Isherwood, R.M. (1973) *Music in the Service of the King*, Ithaca: Cornell University Press.

Jackson, R.A. (1971) 'Peers of France and princes of the blood', *French Historical Studies*, vol. 7.

Jacquart, J. (1974) *La crise rurale en Ile-de-France 1550–1670*, Paris: Armand Colin.

Jones, P.M. (1988) *The Peasantry in the French Revolution*, Cambridge: CUP.

Jouanna. A. (1968) 'Recherches sur la notion d'honneur au XVI siècle', *Revue d'histoire moderne et contemporaine*, vol. 15.

—— (1977) *Ordre sociale: mythes et hiérarchies dans la France du seizième siècle*, Paris: Hachette.

—— (1989) *Le devoir de révolte: la noblesse française et la gestation de l'état moderne, 1559–1661*, Paris: Fayard.

Jouhaud, C. (1985) *Mazarinades: la Fronde des mots*, Paris: Aubier.

Julien-Labruyère, J. (1983) *Paysans charentais*, 2 vols, La Rochelle: Ed. Rupella.

Kaplan, S. (1976) *Bread, Politics and Political Economy in the Reign of Louis XV*, 2 vols, The Hague: Martin Nijhoff.

—— (1979) 'Réflexions sur la police du monde de travail 1700–1815', *Revue Historique*, vol. 529.

Keohane, N.O. (1980) *Philosophy and the State in France from the Renaissance to the Enlightenment*, Princeton, NJ: Princeton University Press.

Kettering, S. (1978) *Judicial Politics and Urban Revolt in Seventeenth-Century France: The Parlement of Aix 1629–1659*, Princeton NJ: Princeton University Press.

—— (1981) 'A provincial parlement during the Fronde', *French Historical Studies*, vol. 11.

—— (1982) 'The causes of the judicial Frondes', *Canadian Journal of History*, vol. 17.

—— (1986a) *Patrons, Brokers and Clients in Seventeenth-Century France*, Oxford: OUP.

—— (1986b) 'Patronage and politics during the Fronde', *French Historical Studies*, vol. 14.

—— (1989) 'The patronage power of early modern French noblewomen', *The Historical Journal*, vol. 32.

Kierstead, R.F. (1975) *State and Society in Seventeenth-Century France*, New York: Franklin Watts.

Klimrath, H. (1843) *Travaux sur l'histoire du droit français*, Paris: Joubert.

Krailsheimer, A.J. (1962) *Studies in self-interest from Descartes to La Bruyère*, Oxford: Clarendon Press.

Kretzer, H. (1977) 'Remarques sur le droit de résistance des calvinistes françaises au début du XVII siècle', *Bulletin de la société de l'histoire du Protestantisme français*, vol. 123.

Labatut, J.-P. (1958) 'Situation sociale du quartier du Marais pendant la Fronde parlementaire', *XVII Siècle*, no. 38.

—— (1963) 'Aspects de la fortune de Bullion', *XVII Siècle*, no. 60.

—— (1972) *Les ducs et pairs de France au dix-septième siècle: étude sociale*, Paris: PUF.

—— (1980) 'Louis XIV et les chevaliers de l'Ordre du Saint Esprit', *XVII Siècle*, no. 128.

Labrousse, E. (1990) *La crise de l'économie française à la fin de l'ancien régime*, Paris: PUF, 2nd edn.

Laissaigne, J.-D. (1962) *Les assemblées de la noblesse de France au XVII et XVIII siècles*, Paris: Cujas.

Lebigre, A. (1976) *Les grands jours d'Auvergne*, Paris: Hachette.

—— (1988) *La justice du Roi: la vie judiciaire dans l'ancienne France*, Paris: Albin Michel.

Le Goff, T.J.A. (1981) *Vannes and Its Region*, Oxford: Clarendon Press.

Lemarchand, G. (1969) 'Le féodalisme dans la France rurale des temps modernes. Essai de caractérisation', *Annales historique de la révolution française*, vol. 41.

Léon, P. (1953) *La naissance de la grande industrie en Dauphiné: fin du règne de Louis XIV*, 2 vols, Paris: PUF.

—— (1960) 'L'industrialisation en France en tant que facteur de croissance économique du début du XVII siècle à nos jours', *Première conférence internationale d'histoire économique, Stockholm*, Paris and The Hague.

—— (1967) 'La région lyonnaise dans l'histoire économique et sociale de la France', *Revue Historique*, vol. 237.

Le Roy Ladurie, E. (1966) *Les paysans de Languedoc*, Paris: SEVPEN.

—— (1974) 'Révoltes et contestations rurales en France de 1675 à 1788', *Annales E.S.C.*, vol. 29, p. i.

—— (1975) *Histoire de la France rurale: l'âge classique des paysans 1340–1789*, Paris: Seuil.

—— (1982) *Love, Death and Money in the Pays d'Oc*, London: Scolar Press.

—— (1987) *The French Peasantry 1450–1660*, Aldershot: Scolar Press.

—— (1994) *The French Royal State*, Oxford: Blackwell.

Lespagnol, A. (1991) *Messieurs de St Malo: une élite négociante au temps de Louis XIV*, Saint Malo: A. Bretagne.

Levantal, C. (1987) *La robe contre l'épée: la noblesse au XVII siècle 1600–1715*, Paris: Diffusion Université-Culture.

Levron, J. (1960) *Les Courtisans*, Paris: Seuil.

—— (1968) *Daily Life at Versailles in the Seventeenth and Eighteenth Centuries*, London: George Allen and Unwin.

Levy-Bruhl, H. (1933) 'La noblesse de France et le commerce à la fin de l'ancien régime', *Revue d'histoire moderne et contemporaine*, vol. 8.

Lewis, G. (1933) *The French Revolution*, London: Routledge.

Ligou, D. (1955) 'La bourgeoisie montalbanaise à la fin de l'ancien régime', *Revue d'histoire économique et sociale*, vol. 33.

Lloyd, H.A. (1987) 'The State and Education: University Reform in Early Modern France', Inaugural Lecture, Hull: Hull University Press.

Logie, P.M. (1951) *La Fronde en Normandie*, Amiens: published by the author.

Lougee, C.L. (1976) *Le Paradis des Femmes: Women, Salons and Social Stratification in Seventeenth-Century France*, Princeton, NJ: Princeton University Press.

Lough, J. (1957) *Paris Theatre Audiences in the Seventeenth and Eighteenth Centuries*, London: OUP.

—— (1978) *Writer and Public in France: From the Middle Ages to the Present Day*, Oxford: Clarendon Press.

Lublinskaya, A.D. (1968) *French Absolutism: The Crucial Phase 1620–29*, Cambridge: CUP.

—— (1972) 'The contemporary bourgeois conception of absolute monarchy', *Economy and Society*, vol. 1.

—— (1973) 'Popular masses and the social relations of the epoch of absolutism: methodology of research', *Economy and Society*, vol. 2.

Lux, D. (1989) *Patronage and Royal Science in Seventeenth-Century France: The Académie de Physique in Caen*, Ithaca: Cornell University Press.

Magendie, M. (1925) *La politesse mondaine et les théories de l'honnêteté en France aux XVII siècle de 1600 à 1660*, 2 vols, Paris: Alcan.

Major, J.R. (1980) *Representative Government in Early Modern France*, New Haven: Yale University Press.

Maland, D. (1970) *Culture and Society in Seventeenth-Century France*, London: Batsford.

Mandrou, R. (1965) *Classes et luttes de classes en France au début du dix-septième siècle*, Florence: Casa Editrice G. d'Anna Messina.

Markovitch, T.J. (1971) 'Le triple tricentennaire de Colbert: l'enquête, les règlements, les inspecteurs', *Revue d'histoire économique et sociale*, vol. 49.
—— (1976) *Histoire des industries françaises: les industries lainières de Colbert à la Révolution*, Geneva: Droz.
Mentzer, R.A. (1994) *Blood and Belief. Family Survival and ConfessionaL Identity among the Provincial Huguenot Nobility*, West Lafayette, IN: Purdue University Press.
Merle, L. (1958) *La métaire et l'évolution agraire de la Gâtine poitevine*, Paris: SEVPEN.
Mettam, R. (1988) *Power and Faction in Louis XIV's France*, Oxford: Blackwell.
Meyer, J. (1983) *Etudes sur les villes en Europe occidentale. Milieu du XVII siècle à la veille de la révolution française*, Paris: SEDES.
—— (1985) *La noblesse bretonne au XVIII siècle*, 2 vols, Paris: Ecole des Hautes Etudes et Sciences Sociales.
Molinier, A. (1985) *Stagnations et croissances: le Vivarais aux XVII et XVIII siècles*, Paris: Ecole des Hautes Etudes en Sciences Sociales.
Moote, A.L. (1971) *The Revolt of the Judges*, Princeton, NJ: Princeton University Press.
—— (1989) *Louis XIII, the Just*, Berkeley: University of California Press.
Moriarty, M. (1988) *Taste and Ideology in Seventeenth-Century France*, Cambridge: CUP.
Morineau, M. (1971) *Les faux-semblants d'un démarrage économique: agriculture et démographie en France au dix-huitième siècle*, Paris: Cahier des Annales.
Morrill, J.S. (1978) 'French absolutism as limited monarchy', *Historical Journal*, vol. 21, p. ii.
Motley, M. (1991) *Becoming a French Aristocrat: The Education of the Court Nobility, 1580–1715*, Princeton, NJ: Princeton University Press.
Mougel, F.-C. (1971) 'La fortune des Bourbon-Conty, revenus et gestion 1655 1791', *Revue d'histoire moderne et contemporaine*, vol. 18.
Mousnier, R. (1946–7) 'Les règlements du conseil du Roi sous Louis XIII', *Annuaire Bulletin de la Société de l'histoire de France*.
—— (1949) 'Quelques raisons de la Fronde. Les causes des journées révolutionnaires parisiennes de 1648', *XVII Siècle*, nos. 2–3.
—— (1951–2) 'Les idées politiques de Fénélon', *XVII Siècle*, nos. 12–14.
—— (1955) 'L'Opposition politique bourgeoise de la fin du XVI siècle et au début du XVII siècle', *Revue Historique*, vol. 213.
—— (1958) 'Recherches sur les soulèvements populaires en France avant la Fronde', *Revue d'histoire moderne et contemporaine*, vol. 5.
—— (1959) 'Recherches sur les syndicats d'officiers pendant la Fronde', *XVII Siècle*, nos. 42–3, in *La plume, la faucille et le marteau*, Paris: PUF, 1970.
—— (1962) 'Les mouvements populaires en France au XVII siècle', *Revue des travaux de l'académie des sciences sociales et politiques et comptes rendus de ses séances*.
—— (1963) 'L'Evolution des institutions monarchiques en France et ses relations avec l'état social', *XVII Siècle*, nos. 58–9, in *La plume, la faucille et le marteau*, Paris: PUF, 1970.
—— (1967) *Fureurs paysannes: les paysans dans les révoltes du XVII siècle*, Paris: Calmann-Levy.
—— (1969) *Les hiérarchies sociales de 1450 à nos jours*, Paris: PUF.
—— (1970) *Le Conseil du Roi de Louis XII à la Révolution*, Paris: PUF, 1970.
—— (1971a) *La vénalité des offices sous Henri IV et Louis XIII*, Paris: PUF, 2nd edn.
—— (1971b) 'D'Agusseau et le tournant des Ordres aux classes sociales', *Revue d'histoire économique et sociale*, vol. 69.

—— (1972) 'Les concepts d'"ordres", d'"états", de "fidelité" et de monarchie absolue en France de la fin du XV siècle à la fin du XVIII', *Revue historique*, vol. 247.

—— (1979 and 1984) *The Institutions of France under the Absolute Monarchy*, 2 vols, Chicago: University of Chicago Press.

Muchembled, R. (1985) *Popular Culture and Elite Culture in France 1400–1750*, trans. L. Cochrane, Baton Rouge: Louisiana State University Press.

Nadal, O. (1948) *Le sentiment de l'amour dans l'œuvre de Corneille*, Paris: Gallimard.

Neuschel, K.B. (1989) *Word of Honour: Interpreting Noble Culture in Sixteenth-Century France*, Ithaca: Cornell University Press.

Neveux, H. (1981) *Vie et déclin d'une structure économique: les grains du Cambrésis, (fin du XIV–début XVII siècle)*, Paris: Mouton.

Norberg, K. (1985) *Rich and Poor in Grenoble 1600–1814*, Berkeley and London: University of California Press.

Orlea, M. (1980) *La noblesse aux Etats-Généraux de 1576 et 1588: étude politique et sociale*, Paris: PUF.

Ourliac, P. (1952) 'Le retrait lignager dans le sud-ouest de la France', *Revue historique de droit français et étranger*, ser. 4, vol. 30, 1952.

Ourliac, P. and Malafosse, J. (1968) *Histoire du droit privé*, 3 vols, Paris: PUF.

Pagès, G. (1936) 'Le gouvernement et l'administration monarchique en France à la fin du règne de Louis XIV', *Revue des cours et conférences*.

Parker, D. (1971) 'The social foundation of French absolutism, 1610–30', *Past & Present*, no. 53.

—— (1978) 'The Huguenots in seventeenth-century France', in A.C. Hepburn (ed.) *Minorities in History*, London: Edward Arnold.

—— (1980) *La Rochelle and the French Monarchy: Conflict and Order in Seventeenth-Century France*, London: Royal Hist. Soc.

—— (1981) 'Law, society and the state in the thought of Jean Bodin', *History of Political Thought*, vol. 2.

—— (1983) *The Making of French Absolutism*, London: Edward Arnold.

—— (1989) 'Sovereignty, absolutism and the function of the law in seventeenth-century France', *Past & Present*, no. 122.

Peret, J. (1976) *Seigneurs et seigneuries en Gâtine poitevine: le duché de la Meilleraye XVII-XVIII siècles*, Poitiers: Société des Antiquaires de l'Ouest.

Perroy, E. (1962) 'Social mobility among the French *noblesse* in the later Middle Ages', *Past & Present*, vol. 21.

Petot, P. and Vandenbossche, A. (1962) 'Le statut de la femme dans les pays coutumiers français du XVII et XVIII siècle', *Recueil de la Société Jean Bodin*, vol. 12.

Pillorget, R. (1975a) *Les mouvements insurrectionels de Provence entre 1596 et 1715*, Paris: Editions A. Pedone.

—— (1975b) 'Les Cascaveoux: l'insurrection Aixoise de l'automne 1630', *XVII Siècle*, no. 64 (1964), trans. in R.F. Kierstead (ed.) *State and Society in Seventeenth-Century France*, New York: Franklin Watts.

Plaisse, A. (1961) *La baronnie de Neufberg, essais d'histoire agraire, économique et sociale*, Paris: PUF.

Poussou, J. (1983) *Bordeaux et Sud-Ouest au XVIII siècle*, Paris: L'Ecole des Hautes Etudes en Sciences Sociales.

Porshnev, B. (1963) *Les soulèvements populaires en France de 1623 à 1648*, Paris: SEVPEN.

Ramière de Fortanier, J. (1932) *La justice seigneuriale dans la sénéchaussée et comté de Lauragais 1533–1789*, Toulouse: Librairie Marqueste.

Ranum, O. (1963) *Richelieu and the Councillors of Louis XIII*, Oxford: OUP.

—— (1980a) *Artisans of Glory*, Chapel Hill: University of Carolina Press.

—— (1980b) 'Courtesy, absolutism, and the rise of the French state', *Journal of Modern History*, vol. 52.

—— (1984) *Paris in the Age of Absolutism*, New York: John Wiley.

Richard, G. (1960) 'Un aspect particulier de la politique économique et sociale de la monarchie au XVII siècle: Richelieu, Colbert, la noblesse et le commerce', *XVII Siècle*, no. 49.

—— (1974) *Noblesse d'affaires au XVIII siècle*, Paris: Armand Colin.

Richet, D. (1977) 'Elite et noblesse: la formation des grands serviteurs de l'Etat (xvi – début xvii siècle)', *Etudes sur la noblesse, Acta Poloniae Historica*, vol. 36.

Riley, J.C. (1986) *The Seven Years War and the Old Regime in France: The Economic and Financial Toll*, Princeton, NJ: Princeton University Press.

Roche, D. (1967) 'Aperçus sur la fortune et les revenus des princes de Condé à l'aube du XVII siècle', *Revue d'histoire moderne et contemporaine*, vol. 14.

Root, H.L. (1986) *Peasants and King in Burgundy: Agrarian Foundations of French Absolutism*, Berkeley and Los Angeles: University of California Press.

Roques, H. (1908) *L'Administration municipale de Toulouse de 1693 à 1699*, Toulouse.

Rothkrug, L. (1965) *Opposition to Louis XIV: The Political and Social Origins of the French Enlightenment*, Princeton, NJ: Princeton University Press.

Roupnel, G. (1955) *La ville et la campagne. Etude sur les populations dijonnaises au XVII siècle*, Paris: A. Colin.

Rule, J.C. (1976) 'Colbert de Torcy, an emergent bureaucracy, and the formulation of French foreign policy, 1698–1715', in R. Hatton (ed.) *Louis XIV and Europe*, London: Macmillan.

Sabatier, G. (1966) 'Une économie et une sociétié en crise. L'Emblavès au début du XVIII siècle (1695–1735)', in P. Léon and B. Chorier (eds) *Structures économiques et problèmes sociaux du monde rurale dans la France du Sud-Est*, Paris: Belles Lettres.

Sabean, D. (1976) 'Aspects of kinship behaviour and property in rural western Europe before 1800', in J. Goody *et al.* (eds) *Family and Inheritance: Rural Society in Western Europe 1200–1800*, Cambridge: CUP.

Saint-Jacob, P. (1960) *Les paysans de la Bourgogne du nord au dernier siècle de l'ancien régime*, Dijon: Université de Dijon.

Saive-Lever, E. (1979) 'La mobilité sociale chez les artisans parisiens dans la première moitié du XVII siècle', *XVII Siècle*, no. 122.

Salmon, J.H.M (1969) *Cardinal de Retz: The Anatomy of a Conspirator*, London: Weidenfeld and Nicolson.

—— (1975) *Society in Crisis: France in the Sixteenth Century*, London: Ernest Benn.

—— (1984) 'The Audijos revolt: provincial liberties and institutional rivalries under Louis XIV', in *Renaissance and Revolt: Essays in the Intellectual and Social History of Early Modern France*, Cambridge: CUP, 1987.

Sauzet, L. (1897) *Le métayage en Limousin*, Paris: A. Rousseau.

Schaeper, T.J. (1980) 'Colonial trade policies late in the reign of Louis XIV', *Revue française d'histoire d'outre-mer*, vol. 67.

—— (1983) *The French Council of Commerce 1700–1715: A Study of Mercantilism after Colbert*, Columbus: Ohio State University Press.

Schalk, E. (1986) *From Valor to Pedigree: Ideas of Nobility in France in the Sixteenth and Seventeenth Centuries*, Princeton, NJ: Princeton University Press.

Schneider, R.A. (1989a) *Public Life in Toulouse*, Ithaca and London: Cornell University Press.

—— (1989b) 'Crown and Capitoulat: municipal government in Toulouse 1500–1789', in P. Benedict (ed.) *Cities and Social Change in Early Modern France*, London: Unwin Hyman.

Scoville, W.C. (1950) *Capitalism and French Glassmaking 1640–1789*, Berkeley and Los Angeles: University of California Press.

—— (1960) *The Persecution of the Huguenots and French Economic Development*, Berkeley and Los Angeles: University of California Press.

Shaffer, J.W. (1982) *Family and Farm: Agrarian Change and Household Organisation in the Loire Valley 1500–1900*, Albany: State University of New York Press.

Shennan, J.H. (1968) *The Parlement of Paris*, London: Eyre and Spottiswoode.

Sicard, G. (1956) *Le métayage dans le midi Toulousain à la fin du moyen âge*, Toulouse: Offset Soubiran.

Sicard, R. (1953) *Toulouse et ses capitouls sous la régence. L'Administration capitulaire sous l'ancien régime*, Toulouse.

Skinner, Q. (1966) 'Thomas Hobbes and his disciples in France and England', *Comparative Studies in Society and History*, vol. 8.

Smith, J.M. (1993) '"Our sovereign's gaze": kings, nobles and state formation in seventeenth-century France', *French Historical Studies*, vol. 18.

Solnon, J.-F. (1987) *La Cour de France*, Paris: Fayard.

Soule, C. (1966) 'Le rôle des États-Généraux et des assemblées de notables dans le vote de l'impôt', in F. Dumont (ed.) *Études sur l'histoire des assemblées d'États*, Paris: PUF.

Spooner, F.C. (1972) *The International Economy and Monetary Movements in France 1493–1725*, Paris: 1956, Cambridge, MA: Harvard University Press.

Sturdy, D.J. (1976) 'Tax evasion, the *faux-nobles* and state fiscalism: the example of the *généralité* of Caen', *French Historical Studies*, vol. 9.

—— (1986) *The D'Aligres de la Rivière: Servants of the Bourbon State in the Seventeenth Century*, New York: St Martin's Press.

Sumner, M. (1995) *Poverty and Charity in the* Ancien Régime. *The Hospitals-General of Albi and Castres 1689–1765*, Unpublished Ph.D. thesis, University of Leeds.

Taylor, G.V. (1964) 'Types of capitalism in eighteenth-century France', *English Historical Review*, vol. 79.

Temple, N. (1966) 'The control and exploitation of French towns during the Ancien Régime', *History*, vol. 51.

Thibaut, L. (1979) 'Les voies navigables et l'industrialisation du nord de la France', *Revue du Nord*, vol. 61.

Thomson, J.K.J. (1982) *Clermont-de-Lodève 1633–1789: Fluctuations in the Prosperity of a Cloth-Making Town*, Cambridge: CUP.

Tilly, C. (1986) *The Contentious French*, Cambridge: Belknap Press

Toutain, J.C. (1961) *Le produit de l'agriculture française de 1700 à 1958*, 2 vols, Paris: Cahiers de l'Institut de Science Economique Appliquée, no. 115.

Trénard, L. (1975) *Les mémoires des Intendants pour l'instruction du duc de Bourgogne (1698). Introduction générale*, Paris: Bibliothèque Nationale CTHS.

Trocmé, E. (1950) *La Rochelle de 1560 à 1628*, Doctorat en théologie, Université de Strasbourg.

Venard, M. (1957) *Bourgeois et paysans au XVII siècle: recherches sur le rôle des bourgeois Parisiens dans la vie agricole au sud de Paris*, Paris: SEVPEN.

Villers, R. (1964) 'Le rôle financier des Etats de Normandie', in F. Dumont (ed.) *Etudes sur l'histoire des assemblées des Etats*, Paris: PUF.

Walton, G. (1986) *Louis XIV's Versailles*, Chicago: University of Chicago Press.

Westrich, S.A. (1972) *The Ormée of Bordeaux*, Baltimore: Johns Hopkins University.

Wood, J.B. (1980) *The Nobility of the Election of Bayeux 1463–1666*, Princeton, NJ: Princeton University Press.

WORKS ON ENGLAND (INCLUDING ANGLO-FRENCH COMPARISONS)

Appleby, J. (1978) *Economic Thought and Ideology in Seventeenth-Century England*, Princeton, NJ: Princeton University Press.

Ashcraft, R. (1980) 'The two treatises and the exclusion crisis: the problem of Lockean political theory as bourgeois ideology', in J.G.A. Pocock and R. Ashcraft, *John Locke*, Los Angeles: University of California Press.

Aylmer, G. (1959) 'Office-holding as a factor in English history 1625–42', *History*, vol. 44.

—— (1961) *The King's Servants: The Civil Service of the English Republic*, London: Routledge and Kegan Paul.

Beier, A.L. (1989) 'Poverty and progress in early modern England', in A.L. Beier, D. Cannadine and J.B. Rosenheim (eds) *The First Modern Society: Essays in English History in Honour of Lawrence Stone*, Cambridge: CUP.

Berg, M. and Hudson, P. (1992) 'Rehabilitating the Industrial Revolution', *Economic History Review*, ser. 2, vol. 45.

Brenner, R. (1993) *Merchants and Revolution*, Cambridge: CUP.

Brewer, J. (1989) *The Sinews of Power: War Money and the English State 1688–1783*, New York: Alfred A. Knopf.

Britnell, R.H. (1993) *The Commercialisation of English Society 1000–1500*, Cambridge: CUP.

Cannon, J. (1984) *Aristocratic Century: The Peerage of Eighteenth-Century England*, Cambridge: CUP.

Chartres, J. (1977) 'Road carrying in England in the seventeenth century: myth and reality', *Economic History Review*, ser. 2, vol. 30.

—— (1991) 'City and towns, farmers and economic change in the eighteenth century', *Bulletin of the Institute of Historical Research*, vol. 64.

Childs, J.C.R. (1988) '1688', *History*, vol. 73.

Clark, J.C.D. (1986) *Revolution and Rebellion: State and Society in the Seventeenth and Eighteenth Centuries*, Cambridge: CUP.

Clark, P. and Slack, P. (1976) *English Towns in Transition*, Oxford: OUP.

Clarkson, L.A. (1971) *The Pre-Industrial Economy in England 1500–1700*, London: Batsford.

Clay, G. (1984) *Economic Expansion and Social Change: England 1500–1700*, 2 vols, Cambridge: CUP.

Coleman, D.C. (1977) *The Economy of England 1450–1750*, Oxford: OUP.

—— (1992) *Myth, History and the Industrial Revolution*, London: Hambledon Press.

Cooper, J.B. (1985) 'In search of agrarian capitalism', in T.H. Aston and C.H.E. Philpin (eds) *The Brenner Debate*, Cambridge: CUP.

Corfield, P. (1976) 'Urban development in England and Wales in the sixteenth and seventeenth centuries', in D.C. Coleman and A.H. John (eds) *Trade, Government and Economy in Pre-Industrial England*, London: Weidenfeld and Nicolson.

—— (1982) *The Impact of English Towns*, Oxford: OUP.

Cornwall, J. (1954) 'Farming in Sussex, 1540–1640', *Sussex Archeol. Colls.*, vol. 17.

Corrigan, P.P. and Sayer, D. (1986) *The Great Arch: English State Formation as Cultural Revolution*, Oxford: Blackwell.

Croot, P. and Parker, D. (1985) 'Agrarian class structure and the development of capitalism: France and England compared', in T.H. Aston and C.H.E. Philpin (eds) *The Brenner Debate*, Cambridge: CUP.

Crouzet, F. (1966) 'Angleterre et France au XVIII siècle. Essai d'analyse comparée de deux croissances économiques', *Annales E.S.C.*, vol. 21, p. ii.

—— (1990) *Britain Ascendant: Comparative Studies in Franco-British Economic History*, Cambridge: CUP.

Cust, R. (1986) 'News and politics in early seventeenth-century England', *Past & Present*, no. 112.

Cust, R. and Hughes, A. (eds) (1984) *Conflict in Stuart England*, Harlow: Longman.

Davis, R. (1962) 'English foreign trade 1660–1700', in F.M. Carus-Wilson (ed.) *Essays in Economic History*, 2 vols, London: Edward Arnold.

Dickson, P.G.M. (1967) *The Financial Revolution*, London: Macmillan.

Dickson, P.G.M. and Spurling, J. (1970) 'War finance 1689–1714', *New Cambridge Modern History*, vol. 6, Cambridge: CUP.

Du Boulay, F.R.H. (1964–5) 'Who were farming the English desmesnes at the end of the Middle Ages?', *Economic History Review*, ser. 2, vol. 17.

Dyer, C. (1968) 'A redistribution of incomes in fifteenth-century England', *Past & Present*, no. 39.

Elliott, J.H. (1963) *The Revolt of the Catalans: A Study in the Decline of Spain*, Cambridge: CUP.

Evans, J.T. (1974) 'The decline of oligarchy in seventeenth-century Norwich', *Journal of British Studies*, vol. 14.

Farnie, D.A. (1902) 'The commercial empire of the Atlantic', *Economic History Review*, ser. 2, vol. 15.

Fisher, F.J. (1948) 'The development of London as a centre of conspicuous consumption in the sixteenth and seventeenth century', T.R.H.S., vol. 30.

—— (1950) 'London's export trade in the early seventeenth century', *Economic History Review*, ser. 2, vol. 2.

Fletcher, A. (1981) *The Outbreak of the English Civil War*, London: Edward Arnold.

Foster, A. (1989) 'Church policies of the 1630s', in R. Cust and A. Hughes (eds) *Conflict in Stuart England*, Harlow: Longman.

Havinden, M.A. (1961) 'Agricultural progress in open-field Oxfordshire', *Agric. Hist. Rev*, vol. 9.

Hill, C. (1961) *The Century of Revolution*, Edinburgh: Thomas Nelson.

—— (1964) *Puritanism and Society in Pre-Revolutionary England*, London: Martin Secker and Warburg.

—— (1965) *The Intellectual Origins of the English Revolution*, Oxford: Clarendon Press.

—— (1967) *Reformation to Industrial Revolution: A Social and Economic History of Britain 1530–1780*, London: Weidenfeld and Nicolson.

—— (1986) 'Political discourse in early seventeeenth-century England', in C. Jones *et al.* (eds) *Politics and People in Revolutionary England*, Oxford: Blackwell.

Hinton, R.W.K. (1960) 'English constitutional doctrines from the fifteenth to the seventeenth centuries', *English Historical Review*, vol. 75.

Hirst, D. (1975) *The Representative of the People?*, Cambridge: CUP.

—— (1978) 'Unanimity in the Commons, aristocratic intrigues and the origins of the English Civil War', *Journal of Modern History*, vol. 50.

—— (1991) 'The failure of godly rule in the English republic', *Past & Present*, no. 132.

Holmes, G. (1986) 'The electorate and the national will in the first age of party', in *Politics, Religion and Society in England 1679–1742*, London: Hambledon Press.

Hoskins, W.G. (1965) 'An Elizabethan provincial town', in *Provincial England*, London: Macmillan.

Houlbrooke, R. (1984) *The English Family, 1450–1700*, London: Longman.

Hoyle, R.W. (1987) 'Custom, class conflict and agrarian capitalism: the definition and development of tenant right in north-western England in the sixteenth century', *Past & Present*, no. 116.

—— (1990) 'Tenure and the land market in early modern England: or a late contribution to the Brenner debate', *Economic History Review*, ser. 2, vol. 43.
Hughes, A. (1989) 'Local history and the origins of the English Civil War', in R. Cust and A. Hughes (eds) *Conflict in Stuart England*, Harlow: Longman.
Jones, E.L. (1970) 'English and European agricultural development 1650–1750', in R.M. Hartwell (ed.) *The Industrial Revolution*, Oxford: Blackwell.
Kellet, J.R. (1958) 'The breakdown of gild and corporation control over the handicrafts and retail trade of London', *Economic History Review*, ser. 2, vol. 10.
Kerridge, E. (1967) *The Agricultural Revolution*, London: Allen and Unwin.
—— (1969) *Agrarian Problems in the Sixteenth Century*, London: Allen and Unwin.
—— (1985) *Textile Manufactures in Early Modern England*, Manchester: MUP.
—— (1992) *The Common Fields of England*, Manchester: MUP.
King, P. (1974) *The Ideology of Order: A Comparative Analysis of Jean Bodin and Thomas Hobbes*, London: Allen and Unwin.
Lake, P. (1989) 'Anti-popery: the structure of a prejudice', in R. Cust and A. Hughes (eds) *Conflict in Stuart England*, Harlow: Longman.
Lang, R.G. (1974) 'Social origins and social aspirations of Jacobean London merchants', *Economic History Review*, ser. 2, vol. 27.
Le Roy Ladurie, E. (1979) 'The chief defects of Gregory King', in *The Territory of the Historian*, Hassocks: Harvester.
Levy-Leboyer, M. (1968) 'Le processus de l'industrialisation, le cas de l'Angleterre et de la France', *Revue Historique*, vol. 239.
Macfarlane, A. (1978) *The Origins of English Individualism: The Family, Property and Social Transition*, Oxford: Blackwell.
Mcloskey, D. (1981) *The Economic History of Britain since 1700*, 2 vols, Cambridge: CUP.
MacPherson, C.B. (1962) *The Political Theory of Possessive Individualism*, Oxford: OUP.
Mate, E. (1993) 'The Sussex land market in the late Middle Ages', *Past & Present*, no. 139.
Mathias, P. and O'Brien, P. (1976) 'Taxation in Britain and France 1715–1810: comparison of the social and economic incidence of taxes collected for the central government', *Journal of European Economic History*, vol. 5.
Mendle, M. (1993) 'Parliamentary sovereignty: a very English absolutism', in N. Phillipson and Q. Skinner (eds) *Political Discourse in Early Modern Britain*, Cambridge: CUP.
Mercer, E. (1954) 'The houses of the gentry', *Past & Present*, no. 5.
O'Brien, P. (1977) 'Agriculture and the Industrial Revolution', *Economic History Review*, ser. 2, vol. 30.
—— (1988) 'The political economy of English taxation 1600–1815', *Economic History Review*, ser. 2, vol. 41.
O'Brien, P. and Keyder, C. (1978) *Economic Growth in Britain and France 1780–1914: Two Paths to the Twentieth Century*, London: Allen and Unwin.
Outhwaite, R.B.E. (1986) 'Progress and backwardness in English agriculture 1500–1650', *Economic History Review*, ser 2, vol. 39.
Parry, G. (1985) *The Golden Age Restored: The Culture of the Stuart Court 1603–1642*, Manchester: MUP.
Pawson, E. (1977) *Transport and Economy: The Turnpike Roads of Eighteenth-Century England*, London: Academic Press.
Pocock, J.G.A. (1957) *The Ancient Constitution and the Feudal Law*, Cambridge: CUP.
—— (1993) 'A discourse on sovereignty: observations on the work in progress', in N. Phillipson and Q. Skinner (eds) *Political Discourse in Early Modern Britain*, Cambridge: CUP.

Popofsky, L.S. (1990) 'The crisis over tonnage and poundage in Parliament 1629', *Past & Present*, no. 126.

Pound, J.F. (1966) 'The social and trade structure of Norwich 1525–1575', *Past & Present*, no. 34.

Richards, J. (1986) '"His Nowe Majesty" and the English monarchy: the kingship of Charles I before 1640"', *Past & Present*, no. 113.

Rosenheim, J.M. (1989) 'County governance and elite withdrawal in Norfolk 1660–1720', in A.L. Beier, D. Cannadine and J.B. Rosenheim (eds) *The First Modern Society: Essays in English History in Honour of Lawrence Stone*, Cambridge: CUP.

Russell, C. (1979) *Parliaments and English Politics*, Oxford: OUP.

Sacks, D.H. (1986) 'The corporate town and the English state: Bristol's "little businesses" 1625–41', *Past & Present*, no. 110.

Schwoerer, L.G. (1993) 'Whig resistance theory, 1688 to 1694', in N. Phillipson and Q. Skinner (eds) *Political Discourse in Early Modern Britain*, Cambridge: CUP.

Searle, C.T. (1986) 'Custom, class conflict and agrarian capitalism: the Cumbrian customary economy in the eighteenth century', *Past & Present* no. 110.

Sharpe, K. (1986) 'Crown, Parliament and locality: government and communication in early Stuart England', *English Historical Review*, vol. 391.

—— (1987) 'The image of virtue: the court and household of Charles I, 1625–1642', in D. Starkey (ed.) *The English Court from the Wars of the Roses to the Civil War*, London: Longman.

Simpson, A.W.B. (1964) *An Introduction to the History of the Land Law*, Oxford: OUP.

Smuts, R.M. (1989) 'Public ceremony and royal charisma: the English royal entry into London, 1485–1642', in A.L. Beier, D. Cannadine and J.B. Rosenheim (eds) *The First Modern Society: Essays in English History in Honour of Lawrence Stone*, Cambridge: CUP.

Sommerville, J.P. (1986) *Politics and Ideology in England 1603–40*, London: Longman.

—— (1989) 'Ideology, property and the constitution', in R. Cust and A. Hughes (eds) *Conflict in Stuart England*, Harlow: Longman.

Speck, W.A. (1989) *Reluctant Revolutionaries: Englishmen and the Revolution of 1688*, Oxford: OUP.

Spufford, M. (1974) *Contrasting Communities*, Cambridge: CUP.

—— (1981) *The Great Reclothing of Rural England: Petty Chapmen and their Wares in the Seventeenth Century*, London: Hambledon Press.

Starkey, D. (1987) 'Introduction: court history in perspective', in D. Starkey (ed.) *The English Court from the Wars of the Roses to the Civil War*, London: Longman.

Stone, L. (1965) *The Crisis of the English Aristocracy 1558–1641*, Oxford: Clarendon Press.

Thirsk, J. (ed.) (1967–) *Agrarian History of England and Wales*, London: CUP.

—— (1978) *Economic Policy and Projects: The Development of a Consumer Society in Early Modern England*, Oxford: OUP.

—— (1992) 'Agrarian problems and the English Revolution', in R.C. Richardson (ed.) *Town and Countryside in the English Revolution*, Manchester: MUP.

Thompson, E.P. (1964) *The Making of the English Working Class*, London: Victor Gollancz.

Tully, J. (1993) 'Placing the two treatises', in N. Phillipson and Q. Skinner (eds) *Political Discourse in Early Modern Britain*, Cambridge: CUP.

Tyacke, N. (1973) 'Puritanism, Arminianism and counter-revolution', in C. Russell (ed.) *The Origins of the English Civil War*, Basingstoke: Macmillan.

—— (1987) *Anti-Calvinists: The Rise of English Arminianism c. 1590–1640*, Oxford: OUP.

Underdown, D. (1985) *Revel, Riot and Rebellion: Popular Politics and Culture in England*, Oxford: OUP.

Van Caenegam, R.C. (1988) *The Birth of the English Common Law*, Cambridge: CUP.

Weir, D. (1984) 'Life under pressure: France and England, 1670–1870', *Journal of Economic History*, vol. 44.

—— (1989) 'Tontines, public finance and revolution in France and England 1688–1789', *Journal of Economic History*, vol. 49, no. 1.

Weston, C.C. (1960) 'The theory of mixed monarchy under Charles I and after', *English Historical Review*, vol. 75.

Weston, C.C. and Greenburg, J.R. (1981) *Subjects and Sovereign: The Grand Controversy over Legal Sovereignty in Stuart England*, Cambridge: CUP.

Wrightson, K. (1982) *English Society 1580–1680*, London: Hutchinson.

Wrigley, E.A. (1987) *People, Cities and Wealth: The Transformation of Traditional Society*, Oxford: Blackwell.

Wrigley, E.A. and Schofield, R.S. (1981) *The Population History of England*, Cambridge: CUP.

THEORETICAL AND MISCELLANEOUS WORKS

Abrams, P. (1982) *Historical Sociology*, Shepton Mallet: Open Books.

Anderson, P. (1974) *Lineages of the Absolute State*, London: New Left Books.

Armstrong, J. (1972a) 'Old regime administrative elites', *Revue internationale des sciences administratives*, vol. 38.

—— (1972b) 'Old regime governors: bureaucratic and patrimonial attitudes', *Comparative Studies in Social History*, vol. 14.

Ariazza, E.L. (1980) 'Mousnier and Barber: the theoretical underpinning of the "Society of Orders" in early modern Europe', *Past & Present*, no. 89.

Braudel, F. (1972–3) *The Mediterranean and the Mediterranean World in the Age of Philip II*, 2 vols, London: Collins.

—— (1981–4) *Civilisation and Capitalism*, 3 vols, London: Collins.

Brenner, R. (1977) 'The origins of capitalist development: a critique of neo-Smithian Marxism', *New Left Review*, no. 104.

—— (1985a) 'Agrarian class structure and economic development", in T.H. Aston and C.H.E. Philpin (eds) *The Brenner Debate*, Cambridge: CUP.

—— (1985b) 'The agrarian roots of European capitalism', in T.H. Aston and C.H.E. Philpin (eds) *The Brenner Debate*, Cambridge: CUP.

—— (1989) 'Bourgeois revolution and the transition to capitalism', in A.L. Beier, D. Cannadine and J.B. Rosenheim (eds) *The First Modern Society: Essays in English History in Honour of Lawrence Stone*, Cambridge: CUP.

Chaunu, P. (1971) *La civilisation de l'Europe des lumières*, Paris: Arthaud.

Cohen, G.A. (1978) *Karl Marx's View of History: A Defence*, Oxford: OUP.

Dobb, M. (1946) *Studies in the Development of Capitalism*, London: George Routledge and Sons.

Dowdall, H.C. (1923) 'The word "State"', *Law Quarterly Review*, vol. 29.

Draper, H. (1977) *Karl Marx's Theory of Revolution*, 2 vols, New York and London: Monthly Review Press.

Dyson, K.H.F. (1980) *The State Tradition in Western Europe*, Oxford: Robertson.

Eisenstadt, S.N. (1963) *The Political System of Empires*, Glencoe, IL: Free Press of Glencoe.

Elias, S. (1983) *The Court Society*, trans. E. Jephcott, Oxford: Blackwell.
Elliott, J.H. (1984) *The Revolt of the Catalans: A Study in the Decline of Spain*, Cambridge: CUP.
Engels, F. (1844) *The Origin of the Family, Private Property and the State*, in K. Marx and F. Engels, *Collected Works*, vol. 26, London: Lawrence and Wishart, 1976.
—— (1892) 'Introduction to the 1892 edition of *Socialism: Utopian and Scientific*, in K. Marx and F. Engels, *Collected Works*, vol. 27, London: Lawrence and Wishart, 1976.
Evans, R.J.W. (1979) *The Making of the Habsburg Monarchy*, Oxford: Clarendon Press.
Flinn, M.W. (1981) *The European Demographic System*, Brighton: Harvester Press.
Gellner, E. (1988) *Plough, Sword and Book*, London: Collins.
Gilmore, M.P. (1941) *Argument from Roman Law in Political Thought*, Cambridge, MA: Harvard University Press.
Goodman, J. and Honeyman, K. (1988) *Gainful Pursuits: The Making of Industrial Europe*, London: Edward Arnold.
Goody, J. (1976) 'Inheritance, property and women', in J. Goody *et al.* (eds) *Family and Inheritance: Rural Society in Western Europe 1200–1800*, Cambridge: CUP.
Guenée, B. (1985) *States and Rulers in Later Medieval Europe*, Oxford: Blackwell.
Gusfield, J.R. (1967) 'Tradition and modernity: misplaced polarities in the study of social change', *American Journal of Sociology* vol. 72, 351–62.
Hayek, F.A. (1954) *Capitalism and the Historians*, Chicago: University of Chicago Press.
Henshall, N. (1992) *The Myth of Absolutism*, London and New York: Longman.
Hobsbawm, E.J. (1956) 'The general crisis of the seventeenth century', in T. Aston (ed.) *Crisis in Europe*, London: Routledge and Kegan Paul, 1956.
—— (1971) 'Class consciousness in history', in I. Mezsaros (ed.) *Aspects of History and Class Consciousness*, London: Routledge and Kegan Paul.
Jago, C. (1981) 'Habsburg absolutism and the Cortes of Castile', *American Historical Review*, vol. 86.
Kennedy, P. (1988) *The Rise of the Great Powers*, London: Unwin Hyman.
Kiernan. V. (1980) *State and Society in Europe 1550–1650*, Oxford: Blackwell.
Lagarde, G. de (1951) 'Réflexions sur la cristallisation de la notion d'État au XVI siècle', in E. Castelli (ed.) *Umanesimo e Scienza Politica*, Milan: DoH Carlo Marzorati.
Lis, C. and Soly, H. (1979) *Poverty and Capitalism in Pre-Industrial Europe*, Hassocks: Harvester Press.
Marx, K. (1843) 'On the Jewish question', in K. Marx and F. Engels, *Collected Works*, vol. 3, London: Lawrence and Wishart, 1976.
—— (1847) 'Moralising criticism and critical morality', in K. Marx and F. Engels, *Collected Works*, vol. 6, London: Lawrence and Wishart, 1976.
—— (1852) *The Eighteenth Brumaire of Louis Napoleon*, in *Collected Works*, vol. 11, London, Lawrence and Wishart, 1976.
—— (1867) *Capital*, vol. 1, London: Everyman, 1974.
—— (1871) *The Civil War in France*, in K. Marx and F. Engels, *Collected Works*, vol. 22, London: Lawrence and Wishart, 1976.
—— (1894) *Capital*, vol. 3, London: Penguin Books, 1981.
Marx, K. and Engels, F. (1845–6) *The German Ideology*, in K. Marx and F. Engels, in *Collected Works*, vol. 5, London: Lawrence and Wishart, 1976.
Mohl, R. (1933) *The Three Estates in Medieval and Renaissance Literature*, New York: Fred Ungar.

Parker, D. (1973) 'Europe's seventeenth-century crisis – a Marxist review', *Our History*, no. 56.

—— (1990) 'French absolutism, the English state and the utility of the base–superstructure model, *Social History*, vol. 15.

Polisensky, J.V. (1971) *The Thirty Years War*, London: Batsford.

Prestwich, M. (ed.) (1971) *International Calvinism 1541–1715*, Oxford: Clarendon Press.

Romano, P. (1978) 'Between the sixteenth and seventeenth centuries: the economic crisis of 1619–1722', in G. Parker and L.M. Smith (eds) *The General Crisis of the Seventeenth Century*, London: Routledge and Kegan Paul.

Russell, C. (1982) 'Monarchies, wars and estates in England, France and Spain *c.* 1580–1640', *Legislative Studies Quarterly*, vol. 7, p. ii.

Sabean, D. (1976) 'Aspects of kinship behaviour and property in rural Western Europe before 1800', in J. Goody *et al.* (eds) *Family and Inheritance: Rural Society in Western Europe 1200–1800*, Cambridge: CUP.

Sayer, D. (1987) *The Violence of Abstraction: The Analytic Foundations of Historical Materialism*, Oxford: Blackwell.

Shennan, J.H. (1974) *The Origins of the Early Modern State 1450–1725*, London: Hutchinson.

—— (1986) *Liberty and Order in Early Modern Europe: The Subject and the State 1650–1800*, London and New York: Longman.

Skinner, Q. (1978) *The Foundations of Modern Political Thought*, 2 vols, Cambridge: CUP.

Slicher Van Bath, B.A. (1960) 'The rise of intensive husbandry in the Low Countries', in J.S. Bromley (ed.) *Britain and the Netherlands*, London: Chatto and Windus.

Thompson, I.A.A. (1976) *War and Government in Habsburg Spain*, London: Athlone Press.

—— (1982) 'Crown and Cortes in Castile, 1590–1665', *Parliaments, Estates and Representation*, vol. 2.

Tilly, C. (1975) *The Formation of National States in Western Europe*, Princeton, NJ: Princeton University Press.

—— (1981) *Where Sociology Meets History*, New York and London: Academic Press.

Tipps, D.C. (1973) 'Modernisation theory and the comparative study of societies: a critical perspective', *Comparative Studies in Society and History*, vol. 15, 1973.

Wallerstein, I. (1974 and 1980) *The Modern World System*, 2 vols, New York and London: Academic Press.

INDEX